Letter and Spirit
Evasion, Avoidance, and Workarounds in the Halakhic System

Michael Scharf Publication Trust
Yeshiva University Press

מגיד
MAGGID

Rabbi Daniel Z. Feldman

LETTER AND SPIRIT

Evasion, Avoidance, and Workarounds in the Halakhic System

The RIETS Hashkafah Series
Rabbi Daniel Z. Feldman, Series Editor

The Michael Scharf Publication Trust of Yeshiva University Press
Maggid Books

Letter and Spirit
Evasion, Avoidance, and Workarounds in the Halakhic System

First edition, 2024

Maggid Books
An imprint of Koren Publishers Jerusalem Ltd.

POB 8531, New Milford, CT 06776-8531, USA
& POB 4044, Jerusalem 9104001, Israel
www.korenpub.com

The publication of this book was made possible
through the generous support of *The Jewish Book Trust*.

ISBN 978-1-59264-650-0, *hardcover*

Printed and bound in the United States

עמודי תורה

Dedicated by Mr. and Mrs. Ralph and Judy Herzka in Memory of

Rabbi Yaakov Yitzchak and Esther Herzka

Dedicated by

Yaakov and Jennifer Gulkowitz

In loving memory of our grandparents

Moshe and Liba Gulkowitz
משה בן אהרן - ליבא בת משה אברהם

Harry and Helen Kleiner
צבי יהודה בן יעקב - הענטשא בת משה

Avram and Rozi Mann
אברהם בן ברוך הלוי - בלימא רבקה בת צבי

Zarmeleib and Baila Wieder
יקותיאל יהודה בן משה - בילא בת צבי

תהא נשמתם צרורה בצרור החיים

לזכר נשמת

משה צבי בן יהושע
יוסף שמואל שמעלקא בן יצחק

Dedicated in memory of Emily Carla Blum a"h by Leon Metzger

מחזיקי תורה

In honor and memory of our dear grandparents, whose unwavering dedication to Torah values and way of life continue to inspire us

Jerry ז״ל *and Gloria Greenman*
גרשון מרדכי בן יהושע מנחם ז״ל וגולדה חסיה בת שמואל צבי

David ז״ל *and Esther Schwartz*
דוד בן ישראל זאב ז״ל ואסתר וויכנא בת יהודה לייב

Morris ז״ל *and Marylin Stadtmauer*
משה רפאל בן יהושע ז״ל ומערא בת יואל

Asher ז״ל *and Joan* ז״ל *Cornfield*
אשר ליפמן מרדכי בן ר׳ משה ז״ל ויונינה בת מנחם ז״ל

Sammy and Julianna Schwartz

Dedicated by Warren and Esther Feldman
In honor of their parents

Sol and Minna Feldman

Irving Draznin

Genia Draznin

תומכי תורה

Dedicated in honor of

מורנו ורבנו
הרב הגאון דניאל צבי פלדמן שליט״א

Through his profound teachings, unwavering support, and genuine care, he has transformed all of his talmidim, their families, and communities into true bnei Torah and talmidei chachomim. Rebbe's wisdom and guidance have enriched our understanding of Halacha and inspired us to lead lives filled with compassion, kindness, and humility, inspiring us to strive to be true talmidei chachomim and leaders of Klal Yisroel. We are forever grateful for our Rebbe's lasting imprint on our hearts and the countless brachot he has bestowed upon us.

מִזְמוֹר לְדָוִד ה׳ מִי־יָגוּר בְּאָהֳלֶךָ מִי־יִשְׁכֹּן בְּהַר קָדְשֶׁךָ: הוֹלֵךְ תָּמִים וּפֹעֵל
צֶדֶק וְדֹבֵר אֱמֶת בִּלְבָבוֹ: לֹא־רָגַל | עַל־לְשֹׁנוֹ
לֹא־עָשָׂה לְרֵעֵהוּ רָעָה וְחֶרְפָּה לֹא־נָשָׂא עַל־קְרֹבוֹ

By Rav Feldman's Talmidim:

David Benhamu
Sam Cohen
Ezra Cooper
Eric Farbowitz
Omer Galer
Caleb Gitlitz
Yaron Kahan
Shim Koshner
Zanvy Lesnoy
Jordan Levovitz
Eli Shlomo Litwin
Moshe Nasser
Yedidya Schechter
Jordan Stebbins
Netanel Tager
Jonah Tripp
Jonathan Wenger

Dedicated in honor of our Rebbe, Rav Daniel Feldman, who infuses all of his talmidim with ahavas haTorah, yiras shamayim, and middos tovos. We had the privilege of being chavrusas and learning from our Rebbe for three-and-a-half incredible years in his shiur and are thankful to still have many opportunities to learn from him. He taught us how to plumb the depths of Shas, and how it's our responsibility as Torah Jews to treat others with love and respect. We are very blessed to have a Rebbe who teaches us his wisdom with nuance, a touch (or more) of humor, and remarkable patience. We want to thank him for all he has done to set us up for a lifetime mission of being the greatest ovdei Hashem we can be.

With profound hakaras hatov,
Jacob Saks and Jed Zaslow

עטרת זקנים בני בנים

ותפארת בנים אבותם

לזכר נשמת הורינו היקרים והאהובים

שמהם למדנו דרך חיים ואורחות יושר

ובזכותם הגענו עד הלום.

הר"ר מנחם יצחק בן הר"ר יעקב ישראל ז"ל

ומרת רחל לאה בת הר"ר חיים אשר הכהן ע"ה

הר"ר חיים אבא בן הר"ר יוסף ז"ל

ומרת מרים מערה בת ר יששכר ע"ה

יהי רצון שלא ימוש התורה מפינו

ומי זרע זרענו עד עולם

ונזכה לראות בנים ובני בנים

עוסקים בתורה ובמצוות.

חיים אשר ומעניא ארלינסקי

נודבים

In deep appreciation of Rabbi Feldman's selfless dedication to assisting Agunot

Josh and Shoshi Ross

In honor of

Rav Daniel shlita and Rebbitzen Leah Feldman

In memory of

HaRav Yaakov Moshe Hacohen Lesin zt"l
Mashgiach Ruchani RIETS 1975–1942

By Hennie and Shimon Wolf

In honor of Shlomo Greenwald, who lives Judaism without cynicism – TL

Sean Weinberg

In loving memory of
Allen and Regina Hurwitz by Dr. David Hurwitz

Dedicated in honor of my parents,

Gabriel and Aliza Sosne,

who live life with purpose and אהבת ה׳*. Their commitment*
to self-improvement and emphasis on sharing
their good with others inspire me to grow.

I am blessed to be a תלמיד *of Rabbi Daniel Feldman* עמו״ש*,*
whose erudition is surpassed only by his humility and warmth.
May ה׳ *bless him and his family for his dedication to his* תלמידים*,*
and may many others similarly benefit from his teachings.

Betzalel Sosne

לכבוד הרב דניאל צבי פלדמן,

ידיד נפשי, חכם ומאיר עיני חכמים בתורה ובתעודה, איש חסד,
המסור בלב ונפש לתורה, לומדיה, ולכל בני עמו. אוהב את
הבריות ומקרבן לתורה, אוהב ואהוב למטה ולמעלה.

הננו רוצים לסייע למפעלו העצום בחלק קטן וזעיר ולחזק ידו בחידוש
ובהבאת כלים חדשים מלאים ישן נושן לתלמידים ותיקים ומתחילים כאחד
כספר הפתוח המכבד את הלימוד והלומדים ברעיונות גדולות ונשגבות.

יה״ר שיראה נחת וברכה ממשפחתו, מתלמידיו, וכל מעשה ידיו.

באהבה, הכרה והוקרה,
יצחק ושושנה שכטר
ויוני ושרה לאה, דניאל ואילת, ידידיה, נועם ונאוה

Contents

Acknowledgments

With deep gratitude to the *Ribbono Shel Olam*, I humbly tender this work to the reading public.

This book is being published through the auspices of Yeshiva University Press and the Michael Scharf Publication Trust. Our projects are carried out under the banner of the Rabbi Isaac Elchanan Theological Seminary, which has the good fortune of being led with wisdom and creativity by Rabbi Menachem Penner, the Max and Marion Grill Dean, and by President Rabbi Dr. Ari Berman, both of whom have always made themselves available to me on a personal level with deeply appreciated guidance, and who have focused attention on the projects of the Press, which have also benefitted greatly in recent months from the efforts of Rabbi Ari Rockoff.

This book, as have been so many of our projects, is produced in partnership with Maggid/Koren, and we greatly appreciate the wonderful work of Rabbi Reuven Ziegler, Rabbi David Silverstein, Taly Hahn, Dr. Yoel Finkelman, and Marc Sherman.

I extend deep thanks to my revered rebbe, Rabbi Hershel Schachter, whose world-famous shiurim I have been privileged to hear and grow from for many years, for all of his influence and counsel, and for his warm and kind encouragement. I express my profound gratitude to my rebbe, Rabbi Menachem Mendel Blachman of Yeshivat Kerem B'Yavneh, for all of his support, as I also acknowledge the continuing influence of the founding Rosh Yeshiva of Kerem B'Yavneh, Rabbi Chaim Yaakov Goldvicht, z"l. Rabbi Dr. Norman Lamm, z"l, longtime President and Chancellor of Yeshiva University, was a source of support and advice from my earliest days on campus, as has been Rabbi Zevulun Charlop, who served for almost four decades at the helm of the Rabbi Isaac Elchanan Theological Seminary. I thank my senior *chavrusas* and mentors Rabbi Baruch Simon and Rabbi Zvi Sobolofsky for their ongoing support and guidance. A special thanks goes to Rabbi and Mrs. Hershel Reichman for all they have done for me and my family.

Rabbi Mordechai Willig, whom I have been fortunate to hear shiurim from and to draw influence from for many years in many contexts, has always made himself available to advise and assist in all ways big and small, and I am immensely grateful for that, and for so much more. Regarding this project in particular, my gratitude to him is on a whole different level. He has a unique association with much of the subject matter: he is a national teacher on the subject of *mekhirat chametz*, organizing a sale in which dozens of rabbis from the greater New York area participate on behalf of their congregations, and creating instructional materials to educate even beyond that; as the *Av Beit Din* of the Beth Din of America, he is a leading authority on issues such as the *hetter iska* and inheritance law; and he is the co-author of the BDA Halakhic Prenuptial Agreement. R. Willig kindly went over the entire manuscript and provided many valuable observations.

Similarly, my cherished mentor Rabbi Yona Reiss, who shares his erudition and insight on all of our projects, and has done so much toward all of my efforts at Yeshiva, also occupies leadership roles in both the BDA and the Beth Din of the Chicago Rabbinical Council, and I am deeply grateful that he thoroughly reviewed this work, offering a wealth of greatly helpful comments and perspectives.

I thank Mrs. Bella Wexner a"h and, *tibadel l'chaim*, Ms. Susan Wexner, for their generous sponsorship of the Bella and Harry Wexner Kollel Elyon at Yeshiva University, in which I was privileged to learn for four years at RIETS, and to hear shiurim and gain direction from Rabbi Willig and Rabbi Michael Rosensweig.

This project began as a seminar given to fellows of the Wexner Kollel, and I am grateful to Rabbi Neal Turk for his support and encouragement to develop the material into a book. I thank Rabbi Jeffrey Saks, editor of the journal *Tradition,* for his patience and support during the production of this book. I originally wrote about the *hetter mekhirah* at the request of the Rabbinical Council of America, and a version of that presentation appeared in *Tradition* in the Fall 2014 issue; the chapter here is significantly modified from what appeared at that time.

My dear friend Rabbi Moshe Schapiro was constantly available to provide assistance in locating sources and materials with great skill and enthusiasm. I thank Allen Friedman for his help in clarifying aspects of taxation law. My cherished longtime *chavrusa,* Rabbi Yaakov Werblowsky, read the entire manuscript and offered many helpful observations.

I wish to express my appreciation to the administrations of the schools that currently give me the opportunity to teach Torah under their auspices, including President Berman, Rabbi Penner, Rabbi Yosef Kalinsky, and the Rabbi Isaac Elchanan Theological Seminary; Dr. Noam Wasserman, Dr. Moses Pava and the Sy Syms School of Business; as well as to all of the synagogues, schools, and other institutions that have hosted my lectures and classes. And to my students and participants at these institutions, I offer my thanks for listening, for challenging me, and helping me to gain a clearer understanding of all I would hope to teach.

To the wonderful people of Ohr Saadya of Teaneck, and all who have joined with us in various stages throughout the years, I convey my gratitude, and my pride and my appreciation in our shared experiences and endeavors, and the blessing that the future bring only success and happiness in the fulfillment of our goals and aspirations.

I extend a very special thank you to Mr. Terry D. Novetsky, who with great patience, insight, and graciousness with his time made it possible for previous efforts to get to print. I also express deep gratitude to our friends Warren and Esther Feldman, whose generosity, care, and foresight have done so much to further our efforts and those of so many others.

My brother Rabbi Jonathan, who graciously went over the entire manuscript and offered his edits, and his wife Rachel and their family are constant and invaluable sources of love and support. My sister Rebecca, together with her husband Dr. Tal Becker and their family, extends her wise counsel and warm compassion with consistency and devotion, and I am a most fortunate beneficiary.

I extend my profound gratitude to my father-in-law Rabbi Mordechai Feuerstein, for all of his kind support and encouragement, and we will forever be inspired and guided by the memory and the life-work of my extraordinary mother-in-law, Rebbetzin Shaindel Feuerstein, a"h. We are deeply fortunate to have the love and guidance of my wife's esteemed grandmother, Mrs. Shirley Feuerstein, and of so many beloved aunts, uncles, and cousins, on both sides of the family.

It is an immense blessing that our children are guided by the life and legacy of two sets of grandparents who, following their own parents, placed the vision of *chesed* and societal responsibility at the forefront of all that they ever did, and crowned their many accomplishments with kindness, compassion, and boundless communal service.

Nothing I do would begin to be possible without my wife Leah; and still nothing can begin to be expressed, as her modesty combines with the limitations of language in preventing me from saying even a fraction of what should be said. I will only express my continued gratitude that our children, Adina, Yaakov, Miriam, Shaindel, Tehilla, Bracha Golda, and Meira, have the role model they have in all the ways of life, and that a beacon of *chesed* lights their path.

It is important to emphasize that this work is not one of advocacy, seeking to promote the devices discussed therein. (In the spirit of full disclosure, I do acknowledge that I am a student of rabbis who have crafted and recommended the BDA Halakhic Prenuptial Agreement, and am affiliated with organizations that advocate its use; although in that case also, I have endeavored to present the document in the context of alternatives as well, and alongside the objections of those who have challenged it.) If there is a cause associated with this work, it is that of sincerity in practice, of the unity of letter and spirit, and of the elimination of cynicism, which inflicts so much harm on religious expression.

Along the way, there is testament to rabbinic responsibility throughout the generations, the careful considerations of leadership in seeking to maximize religious fulfillment while maintaining awareness of the limitations present upon the people.

It is with this backdrop that I dedicate this work to my parents, to the memory of Rabbi Dr. David M. Feldman z"l, and the honor of Rebbetzin Aviva Feldman, to whom I of course owe literally everything. More specifically regarding publications, my father, with his own writings, was a pioneer in the field of writing English-language books that dealt with advanced rabbinic literature, doing so with clarity, sophistication, and deep scholarship, and thus set a model for so many after him to follow. More personally, he was always ready to give of his time to review my own writings, and would constantly go above and beyond in his attentive assistance.

Even more directly relevant to this project, my parents, over the course of many decades of joint efforts in the rabbinate, sought to uplift and inspire the population while also recognizing the need of meeting the individual "*b'asher hu sham*" (Gen. 27:17), where he or she is at the moment, and also envisioning what could be. With warmth, compassion, sensitivity, and wisdom, they sought to assist both in the realization of potential and the discovery of new potential. As my father has written about the rabbinate, it is "the rabbi's responsibility and opportunity, during critical moments, to keep our people far from the 'last temptation,' in T. S. Eliot's words, that of 'doing the right thing for the wrong reason' – and to point up a right and meaningful reason." It is this recognition of the vital significance of sincerity and continuing spiritual aspiration, and the corrosive effects of cynicism and dispassion, that is the animating force of this work.

Introduction

The subject at hand is one which, in a sense, cannot be named. To name it is to judge it, both collectively and in its parts, and therein lies the challenge that is to be addressed. Terms such as "evasions" or "workarounds" label the user as derelict in responsibility, deficient in commitment, perhaps even on some level dishonest. Similarly, or more so, "subterfuge," defined as "deceit used in order to achieve one's goal." Even worse are terms such as "loophole," which implies both an oversight by the system – a near-heretical implication when applied to the Divine Torah – and exploitation on the part of the user; or "legal fiction" which imputes insincerity to both sides. Perhaps some of these negative impressions are justified, perhaps not; either way, usage of these terms prejudges the question and undercuts the investigation before us.

Further, to name the topic of this analysis is to presume that all its components are comparable, and that again shortchanges the endeavor. A fundamental question to be explored is why it is that some of these mechanisms – for serious lack of a better term – enjoy a loftier reputation than do others that are often mentioned in the same breath. Some of these approaches have been widely accepted by the Jewish people; some are harshly opposed; and others are utilized either begrudgingly or only under certain conditions. Understanding these varying receptions is a central goal of this investigation.

In Hebrew, there is a term that is often employed in connection to our subject matter, and it itself contains ambiguity and multiple implications. The word "*ha'aramah*," in one form or another, appears many times in rabbinic literature. At times, it connotes "evasion," and imputes the dereliction mentioned above. It is evocative of the passage in the Talmud[1] that contrasts the earlier generations with the later ones regarding their attitudes about tithing their produce. The superior, earlier generations brought their produce into their houses through the main gate, clearly establishing an obligation to tithe. The latter generations would bring their produce in through the roof or the courtyard, thus technically avoiding the obligation that is described by the phrase "I have removed the consecrated from the house."[2] The Meiri deduces from this passage that the behavior of the latter generations was technically effective but still forbidden, writing that it is "*assur l'ha'arim.*"[3]

In other contexts, *ha'aramah* has more of a neutral message to it, suggesting perhaps a "sidestepping," a path that certainly does not embrace challenge, but maybe because there is a good or at least acceptable reason to avoid that challenge. At times, the Talmud uses this word as part of a recommendation presented without judgment.[4]

Indeed, early commentators suggested that the various forms of the word had sharply different meanings. The Rambam, cited by the *Tosafot Yom Tov,*[5] asserts that a permissible tactic is called "*aramah,*" while one that is prohibited is called "*mirmah.*" However, the latter word is used in the Torah regarding our forefather Jacob,[6] when he obtained

1. *Berakhot* 35b.
2. Deut. 26:13.
3. See also *Resp. Rav Poalim,* YD, 5. However, from other sources (*Pesachim* 9a, *Avodah Zarah* 41b, *Niddah* 15b), it seems that this behavior is permissible even if not especially admirable, and the *Talmud Yerushalmi* (*Ma'asrot* 3:1) attributes this practice to *tana'aim,* and it is recorded as permissible in *Mishneh Torah, Hil. Ma'asrot,* 3:6.
4. See e.g. *mishnah, Ma'aser Sheni* 4:4, although note that the *Talmud Yerushalmi* provides a justification, implying one is needed; see *Mareh Panim* and *Pnei Moshe,* and note the innovative interpretation of *Resp. Chatam Sofer,* OC 62. See also *Shabbat* 117b, where the need for a justification for a *ha'aramah* seems to be in dispute.
5. *Temurah* 5:1.
6. Gen. 27:35.

the blessings from his father; accordingly, he maintains, there must be a difference between Biblical usage and rabbinic usage.[7]

Indeed, the labeling of Jacob's actions as *mirmah,* by his own father Isaac, does draw attention to the potential meanings of that form of the word. Rashi, citing the *Midrash Rabbah,* renders it "*chokhmah*" (as does Onkeles), perhaps understood best as "cleverness." Ibn Ezra, however, takes it as an indication of falseness, prompting a strong objection from R. Ya'akov Tzvi Mecklenberg in his *HaK'tav V'HaKabbalah,* both to the criticism of Jacob and to the notion that Isaac would disparage him in that fashion. In response, he offers a lengthy discourse on the multiple meanings and forms of the word, and marshals scriptural and Targumic evidence that it can have not only neutral but positive meanings. Thus equipped, he sees Isaac's description of Jacob's behavior as an appreciation of a creative strategy that will ultimately bring about the optimal result for all involved (including Esau).

In some of the Talmudic sources, the word is used to represent outright deception, utilized to describe a possible abuse of a situation in which dishonesty will not be detected. For example, the Jerusalem Talmud[8] discussed the case of one who finds *chametz* in his home after *Pesach,* and claims to have performed "*bitul,*" properly disassociating himself from any *chametz* that may have been there, which would save him from any violation and should render this *chametz* now permissible. However, the concern is, apparently, that he did not actually do so – that his claim is a mere "*ha'aramah,*" and thus, according to one opinion, policy should dictate that the *chametz* be prohibited regardless.[9]

7. See also *Rashash* and *Yachin* to *Temurah.* See the analysis of the distinction in *Chamudei Yitzchak al HaTorah,* Gen. 27:35.

8. *Pesachim* 2:2.

9. This is the understanding of the *Rosh* (*Pesachim* 2:4) and the *Tur* and *Shulchan Arukh* (OC 448:5). See, however, *Resp. Rashba,* I, 70, and *Chavalim B'Ne'imim,* I, p. 66. Notably, further, there is some debate as to whether the concern is that this instance of *bitul* was false, or, perhaps, this one was legitimate, but a policy must be enacted regarding the possibility of falsehood in the future. While most sources indicate the former understanding, *Resp. Noda B'Yehudah, kama,* OC, 18 (and see also #19) took the latter understanding, and thus ruled that it would not make a difference even if *bitul* could be proven, such as if it was performed in front of witnesses, against the view of R. Ya'akov Reisher (*Torat HaShelamim,* 6, and *Chok Ya'akov* to OC 448).

As the great halakhic decisor R. Moshe Sofer noted in a responsum on the subject,[10] the translation of *ha'aramah* is elusive, as it clearly changes from one context to the next, and necessarily, the attitude changes with it. Moreover, we are dealing with a moving target to begin with, because whether or not the label of *ha'aramah* should even be affixed is generally an open question. This circular phenomenon appears repeatedly in the literature: debate over whether a particular approach is a *ha'aramah,* and if it is, if that is a bad thing in the first place.

Of course, language matters. Regarding this subject, it matters even more. It frames the discussion, and may thereby prejudge it. Further, as we will see, in a halakhic/philosophical version of the observer effect, the judgment may create its own evidence.

See R. Nachman Kahana, *Orchot Chaim,* OC 448:6 and 18. However, R. Avraham Zvi Hirsch, *Resp. Brit Avraham,* OC, 30, understands differently, and suggests that the *ha'aramah* concern here is not to a false *bitul,* but that one will rely only on *bitul* and neglect the full responsibility.

10. *Resp. Chatam Sofer,* OC 62.

Chapter 1

Evasion, Artifice, or Acceptable Alternative?

In contemporary Jewish life, the *eruv,* a structure by which carrying becomes permitted outdoors in a designated area on *Shabbat,* has attracted disproportionate controversy as an apparent attempt to manipulate Jewish law to serve human needs or, less charitably, conveniences. However, this is misleading; the controversies that surround contemporary *eruvin* are more about implementation. Points of contention include halakhic disputes in construction, or in the qualifications of a given area; disputes with residents unwilling to accept an *eruv* in their midst; or governmental impediments. Conceptually, the *eruv* is not in dispute from a religious perspective; it is a rabbinic enactment, actually designated specifically in parallel to rabbinic additions to the prohibition of carrying on *Shabbat,*[1] and is the subject of an entire tractate in the Talmud. Accordingly, we will not be discussing the *eruv* here.

1. See Rashi, *Eiruvin* 2a, s.v. *mavuy.*

Our focus will instead be on other devices, mostly of later origin, that have engendered controversy in their very concept, as alleged methods to evade the proper demands of Jewish law. Prominent examples are the *hetter iska* document to allow loans for business capital, the *hetter mekhirah* that arranges for sale of land in Israel for the *Shemittah* year, and the sale of *chametz* before *Pesach.* These approaches vary greatly in their degree of acceptance, creating confusion and some degree of cynicism both inside and outside of the observant Jewish community.

In attempting to clarify why these mechanisms are sometimes embraced and sometimes resisted, a few factors have been noted. One is to draw a distinction between Torah law and rabbinic law, with a "*ha'aramah*" being acceptable for the latter but not for the former. This is postulated in a number of rabbinic sources, and is invoked in practice both by some *poskim* and by custom. The view is frequently associated with the *Bekhor Shor,* R. Alexander Shor (b. 1736), who staked this position in connection with the sale of *chametz.* As his position is understood, he asserted[2] that *mekhirat chametz* is a *ha'aramah,* and accordingly should only be utilized in connection with *chametz* that is prohibited only on a rabbinic level.

The position of the *Bekhor Shor* has a significant presence in the literature on this topic, and it should be noted that statements either in support or in challenge of his view are relevant to two separate components of his statement: first, that *mekhirat chametz* specifically is considered a *ha'aramah,* a position that will be discussed further below; and second, that any mechanism deemed a *ha'aramah* should only be implemented in cases of rabbinic law.

This second premise is supported by the *Bekhor Shor* through a reference to a Talmudic passage[3] which does contain a phrase suggesting that only a "*ha'aramah b'drabanan*" is acceptable. However, that usage is arguably different, in that it refers to the performance of an actual rabbinic violation, under the pretext of a permissible act, in contrast with the mechanisms under discussion here which avoid the situation

---

2. *Chiddushim* to *Pesachim* 21a.
3. *Shabbat* 139b. A similar distinction in the *Talmud Yerushalmi* can be found in *Pesachim* 3:3.

of halakhic applicability.[4] However, this discrepancy is presumably not an oversight on the part of the *Bekhor Shor,* but rather it is a part of his overall premise; he sees *mekhirat chametz* itself as a charade, and therefore appropriately compared to the scenario discussed in the Talmudic prooftext.[5] Essentially, in his formulation, the two components are intertwined: the methods under discussion are inherently disingenuous, and are therefore unacceptable in conjunction with Torah law. There is extensive debate among later authorities as to whether the stance of the *Bekhor Shor* is accepted as normative.[6]

There were earlier authorities who also maintained the general distinction, among them R. Shimon ben Tzemach Duran (1361–1444), who wrote in his responsa[7] that *ha'aramot* are not "found" regarding Torah law, and that this is not done "*lekhatchilah,*" *ab initio.* However, he does not indicate that he is referring to an approach to *mekhirat chametz,* and the scenarios he cites and the case he is discussing are in the category of assuming a pretext to cover an otherwise problematic behavior.[8]

---

4. See *Mekor Chaim,* 448:11 and *Magen HaElef,* 448:10; *Resp. Mahari HaKohen, tinyana,* YD 24; *B'ikvei HaTzon,* p. 76, in fn, and *Resp. Minchat Asher,* II, 45:4. See also R. Yeshayahu Bassan, *Resp. Lachmei Todah,* 3.
5. In fact, his grandson, R. Ephraim Zalman Margolios, argues in his *Makneh U'Kinyan* that the *Bekhor Shor* saw *mekhirat chametz* as potentially worse than the pretexts discussed in the Talmud, because there at least the prohibited act was concealed from the public; in his assessment, the Passover sale was openly fraudulent.

   Equating *mekhirat chametz* with the *ha'aramot* discussed in this Talmudic passage opens up another problem, however, in that that passage, in addition to limiting the license to instances of rabbinic law, also restricts its availability to Torah scholars, an exclusion not found at all in *mekhirat chametz* or in any other contemporary "*ha'aramah*" under discussion here. (Indeed, *Resp. Pri Tevuah,* 8, raises this question against the *Bekhor Shor;* the default is a *ha'aramah* should not be allowed regarding Torah or rabbinic law.) A number of suggestions are offered to explain this difficulty; see *Chavalim B'Neimim,* I, *sugya* 20; *Ma'adanei Aretz;* and *Mishpat HaKinyan,* IV, pp. 124–125.
6. For a survey of views on the matter, see Appendix.
7. *Resp. Tashbetz,* I, 138.
8. Similarly, *Radbaz, Resp.,* IV, 236, makes a reference to a situation described as a *ha'aramah* being permissible especially because rabbinic law is involved. However, this also seems to be a direct reference to the Talmudic instances, and he also mentions the fact that a Torah scholar is involved, as also found in the Talmudic context. Nonetheless, *Resp. Maharsham,* IV, 66, cites this responsum as agreeing with the

A POSSIBLE EXPLANATION OF A DISTINCTION BETWEEN TORAH LAW AND RABBINIC LAW

If, though, there is a distinction made between Torah law and rabbinic law in this area, it must be considered why that should be. The initial impression is that it is simply a matter of reverence for the law. Torah law, with all of its severity and primacy, commands unqualified adherence; rabbinic is perhaps less intimidating. This explanation, however, would again seem to reflect poorly both on the user and the system, as rabbinic law is a crucial component of the halakhic framework. Perhaps there is an alternative approach that may be suggested.

One factor that greatly contributes to *ha'aramot* falling into disrepute is "the spirit of the law." If the perception is that the mechanism is a "workaround" or an "evasion" that is technically compliant but ignores the purpose of the commandment, then discomfort on the part of the user and disdain from detractors is well-earned, and such an approach would be at a minimum discouraged and perhaps even termed prohibited.

This consideration may yield an alternative approach to a possible distinction between Torah law and rabbinic law. There is a prominent opinion in the later halakhic literature, most often associated with R. Ya'akov of Lisa, author of the work *Netivot HaMishpat,* that posits a

---

Bekhor Shor that "in a matter of Torah law, it is prohibited." See also the responsum of R. Yehoshua of Krakow (1593–1648), *Responsa Pnei Yehoshua,* OC 14, which does discuss *chametz,* and is operating on the premise that the viability of a *ha'aramah* will hinge on whether rabbinic law or Torah law is at play.

The *Maharsham* also asserts (*Resp.,* IX, YD, 79) that there is an earlier source for the position of the *Bekhor Shor,* one that has escaped the notice of all of those who participated in the debate. His reference is to *Teshuvot Maimoniot,* 16, which discusses an attempt to undercut the rule of *bar metzra,* which gives right of first refusal for purchasing land to one who already owns adjacent land. There, the fact that this rule is rooted in the Biblical precept of "the right and the good" is highlighted; apparently, there is particular impropriety in utilizing a *ha'aramah* in relation to Torah law.

However, it seems difficult to extrapolate from this responsum to other areas. The reference to the "right and the good" has significance in a number of ways, possibly also to emphasize that it is a meta-value, and one that should not be subverted, all the more so through a manipulative scheme. Further, in the actual response, he refers to the rule as a rabbinic enactment, and objects that to allow it to be sidestepped this way would render it meaningless.

fundamental distinction between the two systems. In this view – which many dispute but many others endorse[9] – Torah law, authored by the Creator of the world, represents inherent spiritual realities. Rabbinic law, by contrast, is a function of the mandate to obey rabbinic leadership. Accordingly, there is no inherent spiritual principle at stake in a violation of rabbinic law, only a generalized failure to respect rabbinic authority.

Building on this principle, it might be suggested that a *ha'aramah* is frowned upon in the context of Torah law because while it may adhere to the letter of the law, it neglects the spirit of the law. However, regarding rabbinic law, it may be the case that there is no spirit of the law, other than compliance with rabbinic authority. Accordingly, one who is technically fulfilling a rabbinic law is in complete accord with all of its elements.[10]

This would be especially true of rabbinic rules that are categorized as "safeguards." By their very nature, these laws do not reflect inherent spiritual harm or benefit, but exist to distance one from violations that do. If so, there is even greater basis to assert that there is no spirit of the law beyond the maintaining of the safeguard. Alternatively, there may indeed be a spirit of the law, but it will be defined according to that consideration specifically.

An additional path to explaining a distinction between Biblical law and rabbinic law in this area is found in some later writings,[11] and reflects a completely different perspective on the issue. It asserts that fundamentally, *ha'aramot* are effective for both rabbinic and Biblical

---

9. See *Binah BaSefarim: Bnai Binah,* II, 2 for the relevant sources and positions. It might be noted that R. Ya'akov himself disputed the position of the *Bekhor Shor* (see Appendix). Nonetheless, this does not prevent his view from being useful in understanding the position.
10. One possible difference between the two explanations we have provided for the "rabbinic law standard" may be reflected in a nuanced distinction between different formulations. Some advocates of this standard assert that *ha'aramot* are ineffective in regard to Torah law, while others simply state that it is wrong to utilize them in that context, while presumably acknowledging that they may be effective. It may be that the first formulation is premised on a conceptual distinction in the mechanics of Torah law and rabbinic law, while the latter is assuming a greater severity to Torah law, and thus a moral objection to *ha'aramot* that does not assume their invalidity.
11. R. Shlomo Kluger, in a responsum printed in *Resp. Ne'ot Deshe;* see also *Resp. Chatam Sofer,* OC 62, and *Resp. Yabbia Omer,* X, YD 38.

law; the issue is their permissibility.[12] It was the Rabbis who forbade their utilization, and as such had discretion to issue this prohibition only in regard to Torah law, and not in cases of rabbinic law. While there are various ways to understand this differentiation, it is possible that it is similar to the approach suggested above, in that the Rabbis did not feel it necessary to forbid the utilization of *ha'aramot* regarding their own laws, as concern for the "spirit of the law" is less of a factor in that area.

The *Maharsham*[13] put forward a different understanding of a rabbinic prohibition in this case. While he endorses the distinction of the *Bekhor Shor,* his stated rationale is, in a significant sense, the inverse of his position. He grants that those who engage in *ha'aramot* can do so with full sincerity. However, the appearance that is created is one of neglect, or even violation of *halakhah.* This, in turn triggers suspicion (*chashad*) in observers, and thus is behavior the Rabbis prohibited.

This theory also presumes an enactment instituted only regarding Torah law and not rabbinic law, for a number of reasons. Further, it explains the position that the concern is specifically regarding an overt, recognizable *ha'aramah.* If there is no visible component subject to harsh judgment by an onlooker, there would be less reason to prohibit.

DISTINGUISHING BETWEEN PROHIBITIONS AND OBLIGATIONS

The significance of the spirit of the law in the objection to *ha'aramot* is relevant to another distinction that is invoked, which focuses on the character of the initial law. R. Hershel Schachter notes,[14] based on a comment of *Tosafot,*[15] that the sources indicate that if the law at hand is a positive commandment, it is wrong to implement a *ha'aramah.* When a negative commandment is involved, by contrast, there is no objection to avoiding its application through a *ha'aramah.* The rationale is apparent; as a positive *mitzvah* represents an active obligation, it would be

12. See the suggestion in *Resp. Neta Sorek,* OC, 33.
13. *Resp.*, III, 124, and IX, YD, 79.
14. *B'ikvei HaTzon,* 15:1.
15. *Bekhorot* 3b.

wrong to attempt to escape that responsibility. However, in the case of a prohibition, if it is simply rendered inapplicable, nothing is lost.[16]

The fervent prayers offered by Moses at the end of his life, begging for a repeal of God's decree not to allow him to enter the Land of Israel, are easily understandable on an emotional level. Nonetheless, the Talmud[17] provides an explanation that speaks to an additional element. Many of the *mitzvot* can only be performed in the Land. Moses would not have the opportunity to become obligated in these *mitzvot.* This exemption provided him with no relief; he desperately wanted, and pleaded, to become commanded by these precepts and to realize their fulfillment.

The attitude goes to a fundamental principle of religious duty, and is reflected in a Talmudic passage[18] regarding the Biblical commandment of *tzitzit,* which is mandatory only for a garment that is both four-cornered and made out of certain materials. Accordingly, one can easily choose not to wear such a garment, and thus escape any obligation of *tzitzit,* and presumably not be subject to any liability. Nonetheless, the implication of this passage is that it is wrong to maneuver oneself into an exemption through strategic ploys (*tatzdeki*), and, furthermore, at times of Divine anger, there may even be punishment in store for one who does so.[19]

---

16. R. Schachter also considers possible distinctions within the category of positive commandments, such as avoiding a commandment before it officially takes effect (per *Mishnah Achronah* to *Negaim* 14:13), or distinguishing between an action that effects permissibility through its performance (a *matir*), and an actual imperative with inherent value. See also the discussion in *Sha'arei Osher: Shiurim B'Aggadot Chazal,* #50.
17. *Sotah* 14a.
18. *Menachot* 41a.
19. Compare also *Mishneh Torah, Melakhim* 5:9. Note the commentary of *Maharsha* to *Menachot,* which suggests that the punishment "in a time of anger" is connected to the responsibility of those particularly righteous to take on extra commitments to acquire merit on behalf of the generation. This shifts the focus of the Talmudic statement, and may also be relevant to the statement in *Mishneh Torah.*

    Alternatively, it is possible that the *mitzvah* of *tzitzit* is uniquely valuable, in that it is intended to serve as a reminder for all other *mitzvot.* See *Mo'adim U'Zmannim,* III, 267, who makes this point and explains that this is why there is no encouragement to put on multiple garments in order to fulfill the *mitzvah* of *tzitzit* many times; one fulfillment is sufficient.

Rabbenu Yonah[20] explains that punishment is warranted for this individual who "did not desire in his heart the beauty of the *mitzvah* and its reward." Indeed, some sources indicate that one who is not obligated in a specific commandment should seek to place themselves in its orbit, if possible.[21] Specifically regarding *tzitzit,* the Rambam[22] writes that one should always strive to wear a garment that requires *tzitzit* in order to fulfill the *mitzvah,* and the *Rosh*[23] asserts that a Heaven-fearing individual will not wear a garment with fewer than four corners so as to escape this *mitzvah.*

It is noteworthy that, in reference to the Divine punishment in times of anger, there are some who distinguish between those who employ devices to exempt themselves from an obligation, and those who simply do not exert efforts to become obligated.[24] This may depend on the explanation for the punishment; it would seem that Rabbenu Yonah's explanation does not support such a distinction.[25] Nonetheless, the distinction is logical in light of the general principle that punishments correlate to sins of commission, and thus it is the evasive technique that earns the consequence, even if the underlying attitudes are reflected in the passive sins of omission as well.[26]

---

20. *Sha'arei Teshuvah,* 3:22.
21. See *Tosafot, Pesachim* 113b, s.v. *v'ein,* and *Mekor Chaim,* 331, s.v. *b'din.* For different views, see *Resp. Radbaz,* I, 61, and *Resp. Maharsham,* I, 209. See *Shiurei Leil Shishi,* III, pp. 456–459, and R. Daniel Rapp in the journal *Beit Yitzchak,* XXVIII, p. 408ff. *Resp. B'Tzel HaChokhmah,* VI, 127, considers at length the question of what preparatory steps are expected so that one who is obligated in a commandment does not become exempt due to lack of necessary resources.
22. *Hil. Tzitzit,* 3:11.
23. *Tosfei HaRosh, Niddah* 61b.
24. See *Tosafot, Arakhin* 2a, s.v. *hakol chayavin.*
25. Nor does that of the *Maharsha,* although it begins with a more limited application.
26. The assumption that only actions earn punishments is itself what is brought up in the original Talmudic passage; according to this distinction, the conclusion would seem to be that absolute passivity indeed would not earn a punishment.

    Regarding the parameters of activity and passivity in this area, a responsum of R. Yosef Chaim of Baghdad (*Resp. Rav Poalim,* YD 5) is instructive. He considers the situation of a Jew who owns two animals, of comparable size and worth, in partnership with a non-Jew, and has the opportunity to divide the property as he wishes. If he maintains partial ownership in both, he will be exempt from the priestly gifts; if he

What is expressed here is the premise that a technical commandment is a formality that conveys the fact that the Divine will is that the act be performed. One may escape the reach of the obligation, but that does not erase the fact of the Divine will. Any sincere servant of God will certainly be as committed to fulfill that will, despite the ability to avoid formal obligation.

R. Moshe Feinstein applies this attitude sharply in a responsum[27] regarding the *mitzvah* of eating in the *sukkah* on the festival of *Sukkot,* which does not apply to one who is traveling. R. Feinstein maintains that the trip must be a necessary one, for example a pressing business need. Otherwise, one is subject to the above condemnation regarding *tzitzit,* in choosing to avoid the fulfillment of a *mitzvah.*[28]

Notably, R. Yosef Shalom Elyashiv[29] disagreed with this ruling, observing that in the passage regarding *tzitzit,* the individual will not fulfill that commandment at all. The situation regarding *sukkah* is not comparable; that individual displays his connection to the commandment throughout the rest of the festival. It is only temporarily that he is placing himself outside that context. This position is also instructive as to the scope and the basis for the Talmud's condemnation.

It seems also to be the case that an actual prohibition to evade a positive obligation is codified in the *halakhah.* The *Talmud Yerushalmi*[30] records a prohibition to make *challah* "*kab* sized," in small portions less than the measurements that would trigger the obligation of *challah*

chooses complete ownership in one animal, he will be obligated to offer the gifts from that animal. R. Yosef Chaim is certain he is obligated to choose the second option.

27. *Resp. Iggerot Moshe,* OC, III, 93; EH IV, 32:8.
28. See also the comments of R. Feinstein in *Darash Moshe,* Deut. 4:41, which may be relevant to this position. Similarly, R. Aharon Lichtenstein, in an analysis of the permissibility of a recreational trip on *Sukkot* when accessibility to a *sukkah* is not guaranteed (*Minchat Aviv,* pp. 582–584; reprinted in *Batei Yosef: Elul Tishrei,* pp. 395–397), permits the trip on technical grounds but is harshly critical on philosophical grounds, arguing that the willingness to leave behind the *mitzvah* of *sukkah,* even more so than that of *tzitzit* which is available throughout the year, displays a lamentable spiritual deficiency.
29. *He'arot B'Massekhet Sukkah,* 26a, s.v *holkhei derakhim.*
30. *Challah* 3:1; see also the reference in the *Bavli, Pesachim* 48a–b.

separation. This is termed a *ha'aramah,* and the rule is codified as practical *halakhah.*[31]

The *Rashba*[32] characterizes this as intended to prevent "the forgetting of the Torah of *challah.*" The *Prishah* (ibid., #25) does note that this is not a blanket ban on making smaller loaves, but is only addressed to those who would do so intentionally to escape the *mitzvah.*[33]

Further, in the context of *ma'asrot* (tithes), there is also a specific rabbinic enactment to prevent the evasion of this commandment through the transfer of property to a non-Jew. By Torah law, grain that has been smoothed (*meruach*) by a non-Jewish owner is exempt from that mandate. However, the Rabbis decreed otherwise, concerned that wealthy people (*ba'alei kisin*) would temporarily sell their grain to a non-Jew so as to prevent the application of the *mitzvah.*[34]

The Talmudic discussion that surrounds this enactment is illuminating. It would have made sense, seemingly, for such an enactment to be applied also to the commandment of *challah,* in which non-Jewish ownership also theoretically exempts, and the temptation of evasion is also present. However, the decision was that a parallel enactment in that case would be ineffectual, because *challah* can be evaded more easily than that, by simply preparing in quantities that are beneath the threshold for obligation. It is then noted that there also exists a simpler evasion for *ma'asrot,* that is, bringing the produce in through a side entrance, which prevents the obligation from taking effect. The explanation is then given that there is less of a concern that such a method will be employed, as it takes place in public, and the owner would be embarrassed to be seen engaging in such a subterfuge. These arguments in this passage serve to illuminate the moral and psychological contours involved in escaping

31. See *P'nei Moshe* to *Challah; Mishneh Torah Hil. Bikkurim* 6:16; *Tur,* YD 324. However, there are some who see this rule as founded in a technical concern not applicable to broader *mitzvah* considerations; see *Ohalei Ya'akov,* III, p. 253.

32. *Piskei Challah,* cited in *Beit Yosef* to *Tur.*

33. Similarly, R. Chaim Kanievsky, *Derekh Emunah, Bikkurim,* ch. 6. #129–130, lists a number of legitimate reasons to make smaller loaves that would not run afoul of this prohibition.

34. *Menachot* 67a–b, *Mishneh Torah, Hil. Terumot,* 1:13. See also R. Naftali Hertz Landau, *Cheker Halakhah,* II, *ot chet,* 21, in explaining this concern.

an obligation, and the considerations of the Rabbis in preventing such behavior.[35]

The impression created is that while an automatic prohibition on any one evasive act may not exist, the Rabbis were concerned that such behavior not become widespread and come to define the religious observance of the populace, either regarding specific *mitzvot* or religious obligations in general. Accordingly, they enacted prohibitions on behaviors that posed a greater risk of having a broader effect, while not passing judgment on discrete instances that are less likely to impact practices in general.

However, there are additional elements that make a consistent theory more complex. Rashi[36] explains the aforementioned distinction between *ma'aser,* where an enactment was made, and *challah,* where it was not, differently than stated above. The alternative option of making smaller batches of *challah* is, in his words, not only easier, but "permitted." If the rabbinic prohibition is to prevent evasive maneuvers, it is unclear why this should be different, in Rashi's language *l'irumei b'heteira* ("to commit a permissible *ha'aramah*").

The *Chatam Sofer*[37] understood that the enactment regarding *ma'aser* was specifically because it required a transfer of ownership. The concern was that the non-Jew would have no intent to actually take possession.[38] Hearkening back to the *Bekhor Shor,* the issue was not only evasive action, it was ineffective evasive action.

While the possibility of a rabbinic enactment forbidding evasive behavior is highly significant, even more striking is a statement of Rashi that seems to locate this prohibition in the text of the Torah itself. Regarding the obligation to stand for a learned elder, the Torah[39] concludes with the words, "and you shall fear your God, I am Hashem." In explaining that phrase, the Talmud[40] teaches that the intent is to address

35. See *Derekh Emunah,* ibid., in *Biur Halakhah* to 6:16, s.v *assur l'adam.*

36. *Menachot* 67b, s.v. *efshar.*

37. *Resp.,* OC 62.

38. The *Chatam Sofer* explains the difference between this situation and the sales of *chametz* and *bekhor,* which he believes are effective.

39. Lev. 19:32.

40. *Kiddushin* 32b–33a.

one who would close his eyes so as not to see the elder approaching. Rashi interprets the admonition: "you should have feared the Creator, who knows your thoughts, that you are seeking strategies to become exempt from His commandments." A prohibition to this effect is recorded in *Shulchan Arukh.*[41]

Still, the scope of such a scriptural condemnation requires clarification. The Tosafists,[42] noting an apparently more permissive attitude to evasive tactics in other areas, suggest that standing before elders, as a component of the honor shown to the Torah, is subject to unusual reinforcement. As R. Yosef Shaul Nathanson[43] states in greater detail, this commandment is specifically centered on increasing the love one has for the Torah and its scholars, and accordingly, actively embracing the opportunity is a part of its directive.[44]

Others suggest that the avoidance involved in closing one's eyes to the approach of the elder earns particular condemnation because it is by its nature artificial. In contrast with other cases where an obligation is genuinely prevented from materializing, in the case of standing in respect the situation demanding the respect is actually in effect; the shutting of the eyes does not change that, just creates a weak justification for the individual to claim he is not fully aware. The "exemption"

---

41. YD 244:3.
42. *Moshav Zekenim,* Lev. 19:32.
43. *Resp. Sho'el U'Meishiv, telita'ah,* I, 120.
44. See the analysis of this position in R. Ya'akov Elyah Undsdorfer, *Ohalei Ya'akov,* III, pp. 240–241. He suggests that the same logic would apply to the *mitzvah* to show honor to a *kohen,* and accordingly one would not be allowed to ask a *kohen* to leave the room during the reading of the Torah in order to allow a non-*kohen* to receive the first *aliyah.* However, one could distinguish between the two and suggest that the honor to the Torah involved in standing for the learned elder is a more demanding obligation, in that it connects to the entire value system, while the honor shown to the *kohen* is of a narrower focus.

   See also *Ohalei Ya'akov* there for several other approaches from the later literature to explain the added severity associated with evading the obligation of standing for the learned elder.

   See also *Pardes Yosef,* Ex. 34:24. #138, and his citation of authorities who distinguish between positive obligations that are inherently incumbent upon Jews in general, and those that would only become applicable under specific circumstances.

is superficial and completely technical at best, and may not reflect on other more genuine exclusions from a *mitzvah* obligation.[45]

Another possible indication of a prohibition to remove oneself from an obligation in *mitzvot* can be found in a statement of the Talmud[46] forbidding one from leaving the land of Israel, except under extreme circumstances. While there are a number of explanations given for this, the Rashbam[47] understands the concern to be that one is thereby exempting himself from the agriculturally based commandments.

Further illumination on this subject may come from one instance of a "sale approach" that is addressed in the Talmud itself. One who owns an animal that is pregnant with a first-born offspring is faced with the possibility of owning an animal imbued with *kedushat bekhor.* However, in the modern era, with no functional Temple or active Priesthood, there is no viable way to properly handle the situation. Accordingly, the Talmud[48] discusses the partial sale of the mother animal to a non-Jew, which would prevent the sanctity from taking effect.[49]

It is related there that R. Mari bar Rachel attempted this, selling the ears of his cows to non-Jews. Even so, he acted stringently, treating the offspring as if they had sanctity. Nonetheless, the Talmud indicates there was something inappropriate about what he did, and it did not end well. Two explanations are offered as to what the offense was, especially given his stringent treatment of the animals, as if he had not taken any steps to escape any obligation.

The first answer addresses the spiritual impact of what he did. Even though his conduct was just as exacting as it would have been regardless, he still removed these animals from a status of sanctity. The second answer addresses a secondary practical impact. Even though he was knowledgeable and able to properly address all aspects of the

45. See *Resp. B'Tzel HaChokhmah,* ibid., and see also *Resp. L'Horot Natan,* V, 58, 12, and in general see his wider discussion on evading obligations in ibid., 56–61, and in particular the sources cited in 60:25.
46. *Bava Batra* 91a.
47. S.v. *ein yotz'in.*
48. *Bekhorot* 3a–b.
49. See *Bekhorot* 13a.

situation, a less knowledgeable individual may witness his actions, attempt to do the same, and fail to execute it properly.

While the specific parameters may be debated, a clear principle certainly emerges, establishing the value of the positive *mitzvot* of the Torah, even when escape from obligation is possible, and even when that obligation has not yet materialized. This desire to fulfill the will of God, with or without formal command, is what characterized the forefathers, who devoted themselves to God before the Torah was given, and, according to the Talmud[50] fulfilled the principles of the Torah that they had intuited through their own philosophical insight.[51] Notably, the Maharal of Prague[52] assumed this initiative was limited to what would be the positive commandments of the Torah, as it was specifically these that represented inherently valuable acts, even prior to formal command. Likewise, these actions continue to have inherent value, and to seek an escape from them is frowned upon.

R. Asher Weiss, in his responsum on the subject, ultimately concludes with a similar distinction. He asserts that a *ha'aramah* to avoid a positive obligation is not subject to an actual prohibition, but is instead a general shirking of religious commitment and against the "will of the Torah." In his formulation, avoiding a prohibition, while less objectionable, is not completely neutral; it should only be done in response to some kind of need.

EVASION VS. AVOIDANCE: THE TAXES MODEL

The distinctions invoked above can be illustrated and considered through a comparison to a matter of civil law. Much has been written about the difference between tax evasion, a jailable offense, and tax avoidance, which evokes no legal consequences.

One of the most often cited attitudes on this issue is that of a former US Appeals Court Judge, Learned Hand, who wrote in 1934: "Any one may so arrange his affairs that his taxes shall be as low as possible; he is not bound to choose that pattern which will best pay the Treasury;

50. *Yoma* 28a.
51. See *Resp. Rashba* I, 94.
52. *Gur Aryeh,* Gen.46:10.

there is not even a patriotic duty to increase one's taxes."[53] Similarly, in 1947: "Over and over again courts have said that there is nothing sinister in so arranging affairs as to keep taxes as low as possible. Everyone does it, rich and poor; and all do right, for nobody owes any public duty to pay more than the law demands."[54]

In this formulation, the only determinant as to whether a strategy is a legitimate avoidance or an illegitimate evasion is whether it is itself legal. However, this statement leaves much that needs clarification. First, the very question of legality must be established through some standard. Second, the position does require some substantiation: perhaps the demands of patriotism do indeed exceed the reach of legal enforceability?

Lastly, but most importantly for our purposes, it is certainly possible that the moral responsibilities of a committed Jew are determined wholly differently than civil legal obligations. Still, as likely as that is to be the case, exploring the considerations regarding tax evasion can be instructive toward appreciating the nuances of our topic as well.

It is perhaps more helpful to consider the formulation frequently attributed[55] by tax attorneys to former Supreme Court Justice Louis D. Brandeis, who served from 1919 to 1939:

"I lived in Alexandria, Virginia. Near the Supreme Court chambers is a toll bridge across the Potomac. When in a rush, I pay the toll and get home early. However, I usually drive outside the downtown section of the city and cross the Potomac on a free bridge. The bridge was placed outside the downtown Washington, D.C. area to serve a useful social service: getting drivers to drive an extra mile to help alleviate congestion during rush hour.

"If I went over the toll bridge and through the barrier without paying the toll, I would be committing tax evasion. However, if I drive the extra mile outside the city of Washington and take the free bridge, I

53. Gregory v Helvering, 1934.

54. Commissioner v Newman, 1947.

55. According to Peter Scott Campbell, author of *The Quotable Brandeis,* this was not actually said by Brandeis (who also did not live in Alexandria). Nonetheless, the example is instructive.

am using a legitimate, logical and suitable method of tax avoidance, and I am performing a useful social service by doing so. For my tax evasion, I should be punished. For my tax avoidance, I should be commended. The tragedy in life is that so few people know that the free bridge even exists."

Construed as such, illegitimate evasion refers to a situation in which by all merits a responsibility exists, yet is not being fulfilled. Legitimate avoidance, by contrast, involves choosing to sidestep the circumstances that trigger the responsibility in the first place. Still, more detail is necessary to distinguish between the two. In the toll bridge version, the neglected responsibility is the result of simple abandonment, while the acceptable avoidance is due to not having used the service that requires payment. What would be the status of someone who did use the service, but somehow reclassified that usage in a way to not be subject to payment? Which category would apply in that case would presumably depend on the genuineness of the classification, as well as the plausibility of such a reclassification being relevant in a meaningful way.

This question involves another aspect of tax law, namely, the "sham transaction doctrine." This rule indicates that the desired tax treatment of a transaction will be denied if the steps taken to achieve it are artificial or transitory, and serve no nontax business purpose. That being said, there has been tremendous variance in judicial interpretation as to what does or does not fall under this heading.

Judge Hand's comments and those attributed to Justice Brandeis' speak to the broader question of evading a moral responsibility, while the sham transaction doctrine addresses the more localized issue of whether a given instance is sincere (in the sense that the taxpayer's action has significant non-tax importance) or artificial. At times, the two questions become intertwined and impact on each other, and parallel many of the discussions found in the halakhic literature regarding *ha'aramot.*

Among the issues courts have considered in applying the "sham transaction doctrine" include: Was the price associated with the transaction reasonable or excessive? Was there a genuine intent by the buyer to pay the full purchase price? Was the seller receiving a real economic benefit from the sale of the property other than purely tax benefits? Notably, parallels to all of these questions are hotly debated in regards to *mekhirat chametz* and related devices.

What emerge from the above perspectives are actually a number of objections to *ha'aramot,* that come from different directions, and are not always sharing the same underlying premises about the facts at hand. Accordingly, in much of the later literature, the disputation takes place on non-intersecting tracks, as the advocates of one position or another may not be in agreement as to either the basic definitions or facts under discussion.[56]

Essentially, there are at least two major objections being put forward. One, is that the process itself is fraudulent, that it is not actually what it claims to be. The second is that regardless of the authenticity of what is happening in the moment, there is an evasion of the Divine will.[57] This itself can be occurring in two different ways. One is when the process is in technical compliance with the law, but in abandonment of its spirit. Another does not concern the process, but the very fact that an obligation is being avoided, and the assumption that that is in and of itself an abdication of religious responsibility.

The reality of differing points of concern complicates the effort to understand why some *ha'aramot* are received differently than others;

---

56. For another example of this distance, note that the *Shulchan Arukh* (OC, 335:3), in discussing a leniency in the laws of *Shabbat* that is permitted only when needed to host guests, adds "and one should not do a *ha'aramah* and invite guests who do not need to eat [in order to make use of the leniency]." The *Rama* adds there that if one does do that, it is permissible anyway. The *Magen Avraham* (ibid., #3) questions why anybody would think otherwise; in fact, it is not even a *ha'aramah,* as he is genuinely inviting the guests. However, the application of the term is found in the *mishnah (Shabbat* 117b) where there is a dispute about the permissibility of the strategy. Perhaps the difference is as to the factual reality of whether the benefit is actually directed to the guests or not.

    The Rambam's application of this is open to interpretation: he writes (*Hil. Shabbat* 22:16) "and if one did a *ha'aramah* in this, it is permitted." Apparently, he does not feel there is any prohibition to do this (as noted by *Magen Avraham*), although he does term it a *ha'aramah* (perhaps against *Magen Avraham*). The *Maggid Mishnah* explains the Rambam's view as reflective of the position that one may employ a *ha'aramah* to get a lenient result in a matter of rabbinic law. Whether or not this is a precedent for the view of the *Bekhor Shor* is dependent on the understanding of all the component parts, as noted above.

57. The *Chatam Sofer,* in his response to the *Bekhor Shor,* assumes the latter is objecting on both fronts. However, from his language, it appears his focus is on the first issue.

often those promoting or opposing are not speaking to the same concerns or answering the same objections. This is often the case even when one author is directly engaging another, and all the more so when attitudes are being discerned across centuries and subcultures. Nonetheless, there are certain components and elements within each of the strategies we will consider that can inform the status they occupy in rabbinic thought, and the beginnings of a framework can emerge.

Chapter 2

A Possible Formula for Assessment

Beyond the broader attitudes and arguments discussed thus far, it is possible to posit a general approach to the question, in the form of a sort of formula, or algorithm, to explain the degree of acceptance and/or resistance to any one of the mechanisms. The formula would consist of four parts, with some of those parts potentially themselves comprising multiple components. These parts are (A) the letter of the law; (B) the spirit of the law; (C) the sincerity, or integrity of the approach; and (D) the level of need, or urgency.

To expand on these parts, which we will identify herein with these letters:

PART A: THE LETTER OF THE LAW

Part (A), the letter of the law, is first and foremost. Every approach must be analyzed for compliance with the technical requirements of Jewish law, and if this test is failed absolutely, the approach is a non-starter. As we will see, an obstacle from *halakhah* may be that the specific approach is ineffective in its goal. Further, it may be theoretically effective, but prohibited to execute, which may create a situation acceptable after the fact but forbidden *ab initio*.

PART B: THE SPIRIT OF THE LAW

While the first part is a crucial step, it is Part (B), the spirit of the law, that is often the most relevant consideration in these matters. Thus, it must be considered whether the intent of the Torah, as it can best be understood, is being respected by the approach being utilized. While discerning the intent of the Torah is somewhat speculative, attempting to do so is nonetheless a critical responsibility of the serious Jew, mandated by many halakhic sources. Most notably, the Ramban's understanding of the Biblical verses "you shall be holy"[1] and "you shall do the right and the good"[2] is to obligate compliance with the spirit of the law.

Along these lines, the *Chazon Ish,*[3] in assessing when the Rabbis may have proactively prohibited evasive behavior, assumes that the "intent of the Torah" is a decisive factor in explaining the presence or absence of these prohibitions.

It might be the case that if it can be determined that a given alternative approach is less at odds with the spirit of the law, it may be more acceptable, or perhaps even desirable. It may be possible to prove this from a somewhat cryptic passage in the *Talmud Yerushalmi,* which in turn is commenting on a surprising statement of the *Mishnah.* As this passage plays an important role in some of the literature, it is worth a brief exploration of its somewhat complex content.

The subject is the *ma'aser sheni,* the second tithe of fruits which, by Torah commandment, must be brought to Jerusalem and consumed there in sanctity. If the owner does not wish to transport the actual fruits, he has the option of redeeming the fruits onto money, which would then be spent in Jerusalem on other food items which would instead be consumed there in place of the original fruits. If that option of redemption,

1. Lev. 19:2.
2. Deut. 6:18.
3. *Zeraim, likkutim,* 2:1.

known as *pidyon,* is utilized, the owner must add a percentage, called a "*chomesh,*"[4] to the assessed value of the fruits.

There are exceptions to this required addition; for example, one who is redeeming the fruit of another is not required to add the *chomesh.* As such, the *Mishnah*[5] mentions a possible "*ha'aramah*" (using that term explicitly): one can transfer his money to another, such as an adult child, who will be instructed to carry out the redemption; no *chomesh* will be required as it will not be done by the owner of the fruits.[6]

The *Talmud Yerushalmi*[7] comments on the unusual instance of the *mishnah* proposing a *ha'aramah,* and tersely attributes it to the fact that "*berakhah*" (blessing) is written in conjunction with the concept, presumably a reference to a word included in the verse[8] that describes the farmer who has too much produce to transport to Jerusalem.

As noted, much discussion in the later literature surrounds this passage, and its implications for the broader question of acceptance of *ha'aramot*: given that *ma'aser sheni* is Torah law, does this show that *ha'aramot* are acceptable for Torah laws,[9] or perhaps just the opposite, as the *Yerushalmi*'s need for an explanation indicates it is an exception? What is the nature of the "blessing" being referred to, and how does that affect the equation?[10]

---

4. The literal translation of *chomesh* is a fifth; however, since it refers to a fifth of the new total, in practice, it means adding 25%.
5. *Ma'aser Sheni* 4:4
6. Regarding the usage of the term *ha'aramah* in this context, see R. Aryeh Leib Tzinz, *Magen Ha-Elef,* OC 448:10, whose analysis is consistent with the above point regarding the varying concerns; he notes that it could refer to the effort to escape the *chomesh,* but also to the concern that the transfer of the funds, motivated only by this goal, is insincere.
7. *Ma'aser Sheni* 4:3.
8. Deut. 14:24.
9. It should be noted that the *Talmud Bavli, Gittin* 65a, established this *mishnah* as referring to a context of rabbinic law; however, this is in addressing a different point, and need not restrict its applicability regarding *ha'aramot* and Torah law, especially as codified by the Rambam (*Hil. Ma'aser Sheni,* 5:8–9). See *Chavalim B'Neimim,* I, ibid., and R. Aryeh Leib Houpt, *Resp. Divrei Ta'am.* 66:3. (Note, however, *Resp. Chatam Sofer,* OC 62, and his citation of *Resp. Beit Ephraim*). See also R. Eliyahu Kalatzkin, *Imrei Shefer,* 64.
10. See *Resp. B'Tzel HaChokhmah,* ibid.

It may be possible to suggest the following approach. *Ha'aramot* are most objectionable when they undermine the intent of the Torah, such as when they facilitate the avoidance of a *mitzvah* that can be understood as an inherent value. However, the addition of *chomesh* may not be an inherent value; it is circumstantially dependent, only required when fruits are being redeemed rather than brought directly to Jerusalem.[11] Further, it could be argued that in the ideal situation, the fruits will be brought to Jerusalem, and the redemption is the less preferred alternative, with the *chomesh* emerging as possibly somewhat of an economic disincentive.[12]

With that background, we can consider the relevant section in the Torah that is referenced by the *Yerushalmi*:[13] "You shall tithe all the produce of your seed, that the field brings forth year by year; and you shall eat before the Lord your God, in the place which He shall choose to place His Name there…; And if the way is too long for you, so that you are not able to carry it, or if the place is too far from you… when the Lord has blessed you; Then you shall turn it into money…."

What is described here is a situation in which one is literally "not able" to perform the ideal version of the *mitzvah*, and yet is confronted by what may be intended as a disincentive to choose what is actually his only choice, as a result of a situation the Torah describes as meant to benefit him – a "blessing." Rashi, in fact, identifies the blessing specifically as the increase in produce that precludes the farmer from bringing all of it to Jerusalem. Whether or not *chomesh* actually is meant as a disincentive – there are alternate possible theories – it may in any event be the case that it may be unaffordable to the farmer, and thus would clearly undermine what the Torah is calling a "blessing." Accordingly, it is reasonable to assume that if one were to orchestrate a situation in which he did not have to pay the *chomesh*, he would not be contradicting the

11. Regarding the distinction between the *chomesh* and the *pidyon* itself and its impact on the acceptability of a *ha'aramah*, see R. Zvi Hirsch Orenshtein's *Resp. Birkat Retzeh*, 80, in the glosses of R. Aryeh Leib Broide, *Milchamot Aryeh*, 1.

12. *Chatam Sofer, Resp.*, ibid., sees redemption as the preference, although it is unclear why that would be, and *Resp. Even Shitiyah*, 1, notes the order of the verses implies the opposite, and this is also the position of Ramban, *Sefer HaMitzvot*, 128. The notion of *chomesh* as a disincentive is speculative but flows from that point.

13. Deut. 14:22–25.

spirit of the law; in fact, he would be protecting another aspect of the expressed intent of the Torah. Notably, while "blessing" is mentioned in this passage, *chomesh* is not mentioned at all (the requirement is known from elsewhere in the Torah).

What emerges from this statement in the *Talmud Yerushalmi* is apparent support for the idea that the acceptability of a *ha'aramah* can be measured by the degree to which it aligns with the intent of the Torah, which may itself be a complex and subjective question, but a real one nonetheless.

It is true that the question of adjudicating *halakhah* in accordance with assumed intent of *mitzvot,* or "*darshinan ta'ama d'kra,*" is the subject of a debate in the Talmud, and is generally assumed to be problematic, separate and apart from the challenge of actually discerning the accurate intent. However, that is not the issue at hand: as noted by R. Kook in his writings on the *hetter mekhirah,* such a concern would apply to an assertion that a given *mitzvah* or law should not apply, due to its assumed intent. It would not extend to prohibiting the use of a "permissible *ha'aramah*" when the reasoning would have indicated leniency.[14]

It is readily understandable why this is so. If Part (A), the letter of the law, can indeed be satisfied, it is specifically the assumed intent that would create the opposition to the practice under consideration. If the intent can be understood to be satisfied as well, the opposition would disappear, or at least be mitigated in proportion to the extent it is aligned.

Of course, the assessment of the intent remains speculative and susceptible to human error and bias. This would apply equally, though, both to the concern that comes from the spirit of the law and to the resolution.

PART C: SINCERITY

Part (C), the issue of sincerity, or genuineness, has to do with the individual approach and the claims that surround it. For example, if it is claimed that there is a sale taking place, that claim must be examined for sincerity. If it were to be a sale in name but less so in fact, that would undermine the legitimacy of the approach at hand, and thus manifest, in a different way, an abdication of the spirit, even if the letter is superficially maintained (if that is still possible).

---

14. *Shabbat HaAretz,* p. 112.

It has been joked that the rabbis have prohibited smoking, but still the Orthodox Jews are not concerned; they will simply sell their lungs to a non-Jew. This joke represents a failure of both parts (B) and (C): selling one's lungs to another would do nothing to protect the seller from the harm of the cigarette smoke; and it would be no kind of a sale, as the lungs would remain in the body and under the active use of the seller.

PART D: NEED

Part (D), the level of need, is a component of the formula that is always a factor but varies in importance, in relation to the strength or weakness of the first two factors. Ideally, the rules of the Torah would be upheld in their fullest and most faithful sense. If there is any alternative mechanism that is being proposed, presumably there is at least some degree of need involved. If Part (B), for example, were to be particularly weak, a greater degree of need would have to be present to justify the implementation of the mechanism. Of course, when Part (A), the letter of the law, is lacking, it is difficult to allow the plan at all; an extraordinary level of need would have to be brought to bear (in conjunction with at least some, albeit strained, claim for compliance with the letter of the law).

This aspect can perhaps be illustrated through the aforementioned concept of selling a pregnant animal to avoid the obligations of *kedushat bekhor.* In the modern era, with no functional Temple or active Priesthood, there is no viable way to properly handle the situation. Accordingly, the Talmud discusses the partial sale of the mother animal to a non-Jew, which would prevent the sanctity from taking effect. While as noted, the Talmud seems to be critical of this practice, it seems that in that era there were alternatives. In contemporary times, however, the codifiers of Jewish law[15] have ruled that it is a "*mitzvah*" to enter into joint ownership with a non-Jew in order to avoid any mishap in this area.

This plan is on solid ground regarding Part (A), as the sale indeed brings about this result. However, it is less impressive on Part (B), as the sale completely circumvents the *mitzvah* and its responsibilities, directly comparable to the "later generations" mentioned above who avoided the obligation to tithe their produce. However, the crucial distinction is

15. *Tur* and *Shulchan Arukh,* YD 320:6.

that the animal owners have no alternative available to them, while the produce owners of the Talmudic era could simply have participated in the tithes, as the Torah intended. Accordingly, the plan of the produce owners is condemned, while that of the animal owners is advocated.[16]

This reflects only one kind of "need," in fact a nobler kind, the drive to most appropriately address a halakhic conundrum. More common, however, will be situations of human needs such as economic pressures. These are found as well in the halakhic sources. For example, the Talmud[17] discusses two people who are traveling together, one of whom has nothing to eat, and the other who does; however, that person has taken a vow forbidding the first person from benefiting from him or his property. He is thus advised to first give his available food to a third party, who would then pass it on to the needy one; if there is no one else present, he may place the food on a rock and declare it ownerless. This

16. This element is indeed particularly significant, because in truth, as a Torah commandment, the sanctity of a firstborn animal would seem to be ineligible for a sales mechanism, according to the position of the *Bekhor Shor* regarding *ha'aramot*. This was raised as an objection to the original position by *Mekor Chaim*, 448:11, as well as by R. Yitzchak Eizek Chaver in his *Resp. Binyan Olam*, OC. 21, and many others. This is also the concern raised by the questioner in *Resp. Har Zvi*, YD, 253, and thus the reason for alternative approaches considered by R. Zvi Pesach Frank in his responsum there; see also R. Meshulam Roth, *Resp. Kol Mevaser*, I, 62. See also the discussion in *Imrei Shefer*, ibid.

Presumably, the *Bekhor Shor*'s tolerance of this possibility indicates that great need justifies a *ha'aramah* even for Torah law according to his view as well, reflecting the degree of variability in the formula under discussion. See also *Resp. Chatam Sofer*, OC, 62, who understands the *Bekhor Shor*'s view to be that a prohibition to utilize *ha'aramah* regarding Torah law is itself a rabbinic enactment, and in the case of *bekhor*, given the lack of viable alternatives, the Rabbis did not impose an enactment. *Resp. Maharsham*, IV, cites this responsum and notes that *bekhor* is a unique situation in which, had *ha'aramot* not been available, there would be no choice but to outright permit, and that the *Bekhor Shor* would agree in this case; but see also his different approach in IX, YD 71.

However, the *Bekhor Shor*'s grandson, R. Ephraim Zalman Margolios, in his *Makneh U'Kinyan*, asserts at length that his grandfather would have seen this sale as distinct from *mekhirat chametz* as he would not have had the same reasons to assume the sale to be insincere. See also *Mishpat HaKinyan*, IV, p. 132.

17. *Nedarim* 43a, codified in YD 221:9.

is an evasive maneuver, but it is permitted, as the commentaries stress,[18] because otherwise the first person will go hungry.[19]

The great Polish Talmudist R. Yosef Engel[20] points to a passage in the *Talmud Yerushalmi*[21] that conveys the importance of preventing material loss to the public[22] due to halakhic prohibition. This is done by identifying an "*eela*." The Jastrow dictionary provides for this word these options: circumvention, intrigue, falsehood, pretext. Acknowledging some ambiguity in the concept, R. Engel understands it as "any minimal angle (possibility) or logic that the action can be associated with that which is permissible." He notes that this notion appears a number of other times in the *Talmud Yerushalmi,*[23] as well as the *Talmud Bavli.*[24] He proceeds to explain that there are two components here: the justification (public loss, in this passage) and the process (the identification of an "*eela*").

In between the two areas of "need" may fall situations in which the rabbinical leadership perceives a societal need of a spiritual nature. There may be circumstances in which the insistence on the law in its ideal form ultimately leads to a dereliction among the populace, perhaps because of economic pressures, and thus allowing an alternative preserves maximal spiritual potential for the largest number of people.[25]

The impact of such concerns will be considered as we explore the various mechanisms individually, each through the prism of the four-part formula.

---

18. *Rosh* to *Nedarim, Shakh,* YD 221:52.
19. Similarly, the *Talmud Yerushalmi* (*Beitzah* 3:4) implies that a *ha'aramah* is justifiable when the motivation is to protect the property of the Jewish people from loss. See also the discussion in *Chazon Ovadiah: Prozbol,* p. 229.
20. *Otzerot Yosef: Shvi'it BaZman HaZeh,* III, sec. 80.
21. *Avodah Zarah* 2:9.
22. He emphasizes that this should be the proper rendition of the phrase, "*davar shel rabbim,*" as opposed to the rendition of the commentary *Pnei Moshe* (s.v. *g'vinta*) of "*hefsed merubah,*" a "great loss." The distinction between the two is that in R. Engel's view only a loss to the public, rather than to an individual, would justify such an approach.
23. *Dmai,* 6:5; *Terumot,* 10:5. See also *Pesachim* 3:3, and *Korban HaEdah,* s.v. *v'ka'an.*
24. See *Ketubot* 20b, and Rashi s.v. *eela.*
25. The *Chatam Sofer,* ibid., and #131, understands this to be the intent of the *Talmud Yerushalmi* (*Ma'aser Sheini* 4:3). The derivation is a complicated one; see *Resp. Even Sh'tiyah,* 1, and *Likutei Hearot* to *Resp. Chatam Sofer.* Regarding application, see also the analysis of R. Eliyahu Katz. *Resp. Rosh Eliyahu,* III, 35:10.

Chapter 3

The Prohibition of Interest and the *Hetter Iska*

The Torah absolutely forbids the charging of interest on loans.[1] In order to allow the granting of loans for business capital, a method emerged known as the *hetter iska,* which restructures the business loan as an investment in the venture of the receiver of the funds, albeit in a format that guarantees a specific return to the provider.

In the contemporary era, the *hetter iska* is widely employed. Historically, however, there has been opposition, as well as those who maintained that is indeed a *ha'aramah,* and is effective only when the relevant prohibition is rabbinic, or that it is only proper in those instances, or is premised on that assumption.[2]

1. Ex. 22:24; Lev. 25:36–37; Deut. 23:20–21.
2. See, for example, R. Avraham HaLevi of Egypt, *Responsa Ginat Veradim,* YD 6:4, and note also *Terumat HaDeshen,* 302, who writes generally regarding *ribbit* that the severity is such that when a Biblical prohibition is involved, it is wrong to search for methods to enable the transaction, while it is acceptable in the instance of rabbinic prohibitions of *ribbit.*

R. Ya'akov Breisch (1895–1976, Zurich) writes emphatically[3] that the widespread acceptance of the *hetter iska,* in particular among great rabbinic authorities, is definitive proof that it should not be termed a *ha'aramah,* and is acceptable even in situations involving Biblical law.

Appreciating the acceptability, or lack of same, of the *hetter iska,* requires a multi-pronged approach; considering what is being proposed, how it interacts with the laws of *ribbit,* and how it conforms to the intent of the laws, which first requires establishing a theory or theories as to what that intent is. (It should also be noted that while the *hetter iska* is the most widely used device to address the prohibition of *ribbit,* it is not the only one, and thus much of the conceptual discussion is relevant to other approaches as well.)[4]

The Talmud[5] describes the approach of the sages of Nehardai to designing a partnership involving a funder and a laborer. The funds provided by the investor would be designated as made up of two components, a loan (*halva'ah*), and a deposit (*pikadon*) of an equal sum. The Aramaic phrasing of this is "*palga milveh u'palga pikadon.*" In this arrangement, the provider and the receiver generally shared the profits and the losses that resulted.

The essence of the contemporary *hetter iska* is reflected in the ruling of the *Shulchan Arukh,*[6] which states that it is possible to advance funds for business purposes under the understanding that until a certain threshold is reached, that profit accrues to the provider, and what is earned beyond that goes to the recipient. Until the profit threshold is reached, the recipient is working on behalf of the provider, and in fact must be compensated, nominally, for his labor. The funds at that point are a deposit, a "*pikadon*" in the trust of the recipient. After the

3. *Resp. Chelkat Ya'akov,* YD, 68.
4. R. Yisrael Rappaport, *Resp. Mahari haKohen,* I, YD, 35, notes a distinction between two possible usages of the term "*ha'aramah*" (or its variants) in the context of *ribbit.* In one case, it refers to an avoidance of the actual violation through some kind of alternative, which, in his view, is completely acceptable. In others (see, for example, *Mishneh Torah, Hil. Malveh U'Loveh* 5:15), it refers to a deceptive labeling of an act that genuinely is *ribbit,* which leaves one in full violation of Torah law.
5. *Bava Metzia* 104b; and see 68b–69a.
6. YD 167:1.

set profit has been obtained, the rest becomes an interest-free loan, a "*halva'ah*."[7] Accordingly, this arrangement is also known as "*palga iska, palga halva'ah*," a half-deposit/half-loan.

This formulation is not without controversy. The payment of the recipient is to address the concern that his labor on behalf of the provider is motivated by the fact that he is also receiving a loan from him, which itself would constitute a prohibited form of interest.[8] The Vilna Gaon, in his commentary, took issue with this, considering the nominal compensation to be inadequate to eliminate this concern.

R. Menachem Mendel (Maharam) Avigdors, a 16th century rabbi of Krakow, Poland, formalized this structure into a document that became known as the "*hetter iska* of the Maharam," and is printed in the *Nachalat Shivah* (#40), a collection of legal documents and contracts. The author of that work, R. Shmuel HaLevi (1625–1681), appended a lengthy note to explain that the Maharam's formulation is soundly based on the foundation of earlier authorities such as R. Yehoshua Falk, author of the commentaries *Sefer Meirat Einayim, Drishah,* and *Prishah.*

Conceptually, the *hetter iska* of the Maharam actually amalgamates elements of the earlier arrangements. Superficially, it resembles the model of the Talmudic Nehardean sages. In function, though, it operates on a basis more closely aligned with the format described in the *Shulchan Arukh.* While it maintains the structure of a partnership, it functions, in some senses, through the conversion of a borrower into an agent (*shaliach*) of the provider.[9]

Later versions of the *iska* differed in various ways, often functioning more as a continuous partnership.[10] Each model has its own

7. The *Rama* adds that it would also be valid if the order was flipped, i.e. if the recipient would first work on his own behalf and then on behalf of the receiver.
8. This concern, and its remedy, is expressed in the *mishnah* (*Bava Metzia* 68a) and the subsequent Talmudic discussion. The issue was relevant to the arrangement of the Nehardean sages as well; accordingly, the agreement was tilted to the financial advantage of the laborer, with him taking on a third of the losses, and the funder two thirds.
9. See the formulation of R. Yitzchak Meir Rappaport, in *Takanat Rabbim,* p. 6. Practical ramifications of this distinction will be discussed later on.
10. On the different nuances, see *Mo'adim U'Zmannim,* VI, 41, and *Resp. Chelkat Ya'akov,* YD, 64.

strengths; for example, it has been noted that the latter model may not be subject to the Vilna Gaon's objection regarding inadequate compensation. If the recipient is a full partner at all times, it is understandable that he would labor to increase the investment, even without additional motivation.[11]

R. Yona Reiss[12] notes an additional aspect that may be fundamental to the viability of the *hetter iska.* Given that the provider retains liability for the *pikadon* portion of the funds, those funds never actually leave his ownership. The premium paid by the receiver is compensation for benefiting from the funds of the provider. It is permissible for the provider, as with any investor, to profit from assets currently in his possession.

In considering the acceptability of the *hetter iska,* it would seem that Part (A) is interwoven with both Parts (B) and (C). The prohibition of interest applies to loans, and not to investments. If what is occurring is genuinely an investment – the consideration of (C) – the letter of the law would indeed exempt the arrangement from the structures of *ribbit.* The conversion of the arrangement in the first place, however, might be seen as an unwarranted evasion of the purpose of the prohibition, and thus an investigation under the heading of (B) is called for.

The injunctions against the taking of interest are complex and open to speculation. Theories as to the intent and purpose abound. The most intuitive premise is that they are there to protect the needy borrower from being exploited and becoming further financially dependent in his moment of need. While the *Sefer HaChinnukh*[13] does emphasize this factor, it is important to appreciate that the Torah does not limit its prohibition to usury or predatory interest rates, but forbids even minimal, reasonable, and conventionally acceptable rates. Further confounding the attempts at explanation are the rules that prohibit even the voluntary payment of *ribbit,* and even place equal guilt on the borrower.

Accordingly, there are additional explanations, including that completely interest-free loans are necessary as an indication of the

11. See *Mishkan Shilo,* p. 282.
12. *Kanfei Yonah,* pp. 167–168.
13. *Mitzvah* 68.

familial bond that exists within the Jewish people;[14] that payments to the lender may unduly influence his judgment regarding where to bestow his assistance,[15] which is subject to halakhic guidelines;[16] or that insistence on payment is an affront to God, who mandated acts of kindness as a religious imperative.[17] Alternatively, it may still be that the goal is indeed to protect the borrower from exploitation, but the additional rules mentioned above are there to buffer against coercion or shifting rates.

A common premise of all of these explanations is the assumption that the prohibition of *ribbit* is directed toward the providing of loans as an act of *chesed*, kindness to those in need.[18] In fact, this is essentially spelled out in the Biblical text:[19] "If your brother has become poor, and his means fail with you, then you shall relieve him … so that he may live with you. Take no interest from him, or increase, but fear your God, so that your brother may live with you."

The *Torah Temimah*[20] expands on this point: in the pre-modern, agricultural economy, one borrowing money would essentially only be doing so for basic needs of sustenance. Similarly, the one providing the funds would not be missing opportunities or bearing any loss because of the time his funds were in the hands of another. Thus, the ideal of allowing "your brother" to "live with you" would mandate that there is neither reason nor justification for any extra funds to be given to the lender. However, once the economy transitioned to a commerce-based one, there was now a reason to borrow funds that was not connected to

---

14. See Nachmanides, Commentary to the Torah, Deut. 23:21, and *Resp. Rashba,* I, 242. R. Avraham Bornstein, in his Responsa *Avnei Nezer,* entitled a section about *ribbit* "*Brit Achim*" or "Covenant of Brothers."
15. R. Alter A. M. Eiger, in the introduction to his work *Takanat Rabbim,* notes a number of comparisons between *ribbit* and the prohibition of *shochad* (bribery), but he explains the connection differently.
16. Compare the comments of R. Ya'akov Kaminetsky, *Emet L'Ya'akov,* Deut. 14:22.
17. See "The Jewish Prohibition of Interest" in *The Oxford Handbook of Judaism and Economics,* pp. 242–245.
18. See, to this effect, *Ramban,* Deut. 23:20–21, and in *Torat HaAdam,* p. 44 (cited in *Beit Yosef,* YD, 336); *Sefer HaChinnukh,* 583; *Radak,* Ps. 15:5; *Sefer Chasidim,* 532; *Shi'iltot* of R. Achai Gaon, 114; and *Chokhmat Adam,* 130:1.
19. Lev. 25:35–36.
20. Lev. 25. #192.

existential need, and there was similarly an opportunity cost imposed upon the lender. As such, the same ideal of "living with you" could, at least in spirit, accommodate a rationale for the borrower to pay the lender.

It may also be noted that *ribbit* may be a *mitzvah* which is particularly conducive to interpretation based on its reasoning. The *Beit Yosef*[21] quotes the view of a R. Eliezer[22] that maintains that a worker whose wages have been delayed may demand an increase commensurate with his lost opportunities to profit from the wages had they been paid in a timely fashion. The *Beit Yosef* challenges this opinion, noting that the very definition of *ribbit* is money paid for waiting for funds,[23] and rejects it, although he acknowledges that there is additional support in *rishonim.*

The *Chatam Sofer*[24] advances an explanation of the view of R. Eliezer, which he considers "correct and straight." In general, we are not empowered to interpret a Torah *mitzvah* based on its presumed reasoning. However, this is not the case when the text itself makes the reasoning clear,[25] as it does regarding interest: the lender is obligated to sustain the life of the borrower, who is dependent on him. In the case of a hired worker, however, the situation is reversed: the employer, who would parallel the borrower in that he must make a payment, is the one charged with sustaining the life of the "lender," the employee. Accordingly, it is acceptable for an increase to be paid to the employee.[26]

Further, even when a capital investment is motivated by compassion for a struggling business owner, the spirit of the law may

21. YD 160:21.
22. As to the precise identity of this R. Eliezer, see the *Hagahot V'Ha'arot* in the *Machon Yerushalayim* edition of the *Tur,* ibid., #99.
23. *Bava Metzia* 63b.
24. Resp., VI, 26.
25. See *Sanhedrin* 21a.
26. Similarly, the *Avnei Nezer, Resp.,* YD 159, explains a view that the funds of minor orphans may be lent out under terms that would be a Torah violation of *ribbit.* While this is not the accepted *halakhah,* the *Avnei Nezer* asserts that the logic behind it flows from the direct linking of the prohibition of collecting interest and an affirmative obligation to lend money. In that minors are not obligated in *mitzvot,* and thus are not subject to this mandate, there would be no prohibition, Biblical or rabbinic, to collect interest on their funds.

accommodate an arrangement of an *iska* nature. The verse prohibiting *ribbit,* and mandating assistance, references not only direct aid for current expenses, but preventing the individual from falling into need in the first place. The Talmud[27] teaches, in the name of R. Abba citing Resh Lakish: "One who loans money is greater than one who gives charity, and one who puts money into a [common] purse [i.e., enters into a partnership], is greater than all of them."[28] As the *Maharsha* explains, the potential profit for the provider incentivizes him to furnish a higher level of support, and the recipient is saved any accompanying embarrassment.[29]

An additional approach to the inherent acceptability of the *iska* arrangement points to the structure of the transaction as reflective of a completely different dynamic. As one contemporary author, R. Matityahu Hirschman,[30] posits, the fundamental problem with *ribbit* may be that a fee is charged for the mere providing of funds that must be themselves fully repaid, thus "biting" the recipient who must turn elsewhere to find the resources to repay. An *iska* arrangement, by contrast, anticipates that profit will come from the funds provided, and thus no additional burden will be placed on the recipient, who is only asked to share a portion of what he is gaining.

This last explanation reorients the attitude toward *ribbit* by locating its harm in the effect on the borrower, in contrast with the previous explanations which mostly focus on some deficiency in the act of the lender.[31] At the same time, it allows for *iska* to be understood as wholly outside the concerns that would normally be associated with *ribbit,* thus generating a license of a more confident nature.[32]

Before moving beyond this point of the "spirit" of *ribbit,* there is another aspect regarding the nature of *ribbit* to consider, that is conveyed

---

27. *Shabbat* 63a.
28. See *Ahavat Chesed,* II, ch. 21, in gloss.
29. See *Beit Yosef,* YD 249:6.
30. *Beit Matityahu, ribbit,* #19.
31. For an extensive discussion about the ramifications of the prohibition focusing on one element or the other, see *Resp. Mahari HaKohen,* YD, 23.
32. The essay in *Beit Mattityahu* proceeds to apply the theory at length to various details and disputes within the realm of *iska.*

in the words of the *Tur.*[33] He writes that *ribbit* is an area in which one should not seek out any permissible method, as the collection of interest is greatly tempting, and will draw individuals into deeper and deeper involvement until they are involved in actual prohibited interest. It is an open question whether this concern would be applicable even to loans that could otherwise arguably have been thought to have been outside the spirit of the prohibition.

It seems, in any event, that it may be maintained that the providing of capital for business endeavors is outside the scope of the spirit of this law. As the letter of the law nonetheless prohibits any payment for a loan, an approach is necessary to convert the loan into an investment, thus moving it technically out of the jurisdiction of *ribbit.*

If the above does satisfactorily address parts A and B, attention must still be paid to C, the issue of the accuracy of labeling the transaction as an investment. The biggest threat to this is a detail of how the *hetter iska* is most commonly conducted, namely a clause that sets the rate of return at a point basically equivalent to what the provider would have collected as interest on a loan of the same amount. In the most common formulation, the funds are provided half as a loan, which is given with no interest whatsoever. The other half is framed as an investment in the venture that the receiver plans on undertaking. Normally, an investment would mean that the specific return would not be predictable; the investor would earn more if the business is successful, or less if it is less so, or perhaps even would lose all of his contribution. In fact, this would seem to be a core difference between a loan and an investment, in that a loan essentially guarantees the lender a specific return, barring default, while an investment has the potential to provide a greater return, but by its nature involves risk.

However, in the case of the commonly used *iska,* the risk is practically eliminated. The rate is set in advance, although it is presented as an alternative to the standard expectation that the return would be proportional to the success of the business. The provider of funds asserts that he reserves the right to disbelieve the receiver's claim of poor returns, as it is in the receiver's interest to maintain that he has lost the money, and thus

33. YD 160.

exempt himself from turning over the actual full amount. Accordingly, the provider insists on a high level of proof of any loss,[34] typically involving taking an oath, which is generally an anathema to observant Jews, as well as the awkward requirement of bringing his rabbi or other prominent figures to vouch for his claim.[35] Should the receiver be unwilling to do this, as is the expectation, he has the alternative option to agree to pay the predetermined sum, and no further proof will be demanded.

R. Shilo Raphael, a prominent rabbinical court judge who died in 1994, suggested that the requirement for an oath be replaced, as it has lost its inhibiting character in the modern era. Instead, he felt, the stipulation should be that if the recipient wishes to be excused from his obligation, he must agree to allow the provider complete access to all his books and records, and full power as an active partner. Presumably, this will deter even a recipient who would be willing to take an oath.[36]

This arrangement raises questions as to the sincerity of the investment claim, in that it essentially guarantees a return, and one identical to the rate that would have been forthcoming in the case of an interest-bearing loan. Accordingly, this aspect of the formula, part (C), may be weakened.[37] There are a number of variations that exist that mitigate this impact.

One possible modification is to the rate of return itself. R. Shlomo Zalman Auerbach, in his responsa,[38] noted the problem posed by the unusual level, noting that such a high rate may in and of itself constitute *ribbit,* as the generosity exhibited by the receiver appears to be motivated by his gratitude for the accompanying loan, and would therefore be a

34. See *Resp. Mabbit,* I, 244
35. This aspect is meant to be difficult, but apparently not irrelevant; it is based on the *Terumat HaDeshen,* 302, also cited in *Taz,* YD, 167:1, where it is specified that the rabbi and the cantor should "understand business." *Mishkan Shilo,* p. 287, assumes that this is necessary to prevent a *ha'aramah.* See also *Resp. Chelkat Ya'akov,* YD, 64:2.
36. *Mishkan Shilo,* p. 288.
37. In fact, the *Maharsham, Resp.,* IX, YD, 71, considered the widespread practice of demanding an unattainably high standard of proof indefensible, rendering the *iska* an overt *ha'aramah* against Torah law.
38. *Resp. Minchat Shlomo,* I, 28:5. It is noteworthy that even as R. Auerbach invokes this difficulty, he stresses that he is not challenging the validity of the *iska,* as it is "known and accepted as permissible" (*yadua u'mekubbal l'hetter*).

form of paying interest. Attention to the rate, with a possible downward adjustment, would, to some extent, alleviate this issue.

One alternative *iska* arrangement that exists achieves such an adjustment, while also improving the arrangements from another direction. Known as the "*kulo pikadon*" *iska,* this arrangement does not contain any component of a loan, and all of the funds are designated as the investment. Spreading the return over the entire sum cuts the rate in half, thus reducing the appearance of *quid pro quo* special treatment for a benefactor. More fundamentally, it may actually eliminate the possibility of a *ribbit* violation, which can only occur in relation to a loan. If it can be sincerely maintained that there is no loan at all, then indeed the transgression is successfully avoided in a more absolute fashion.[39] However, this also hinges on the premise that the profit generating component, whether it be partial or total, indeed be recognized as an investment and not a loan.

That classification is challenged by the risk factor, seemingly crucial to the definition of an investment and yet lacking in this arrangement.[40] Some nuances may soften this concern. For one, there is some degree of risk, albeit greatly diminished from that of a conventional investment.[41] For example, the receiver may "call the bluff" of the provider, and comply with all of the requirements necessary to establish his credibility in claiming underperformance. In that event, he would only be obligated to pay the return proportional to actual profits, if there are any at all, and the provider would indeed not receive funds that would have securely come his way in the case of an interest-bearing loan.

Further, there may be circumstances in which the receiver's venture has failed so completely and publicly that it is not plausible to

---

39. This is the premise of *Resp. Chelkat Ya'akov*, YD, 64. However, it may be that this is still considered a form of a loan on a rabbinic level, which will still significantly reduce the issue; see *Chelkat Binyamin,* p. 730, sec. 24, who also suggests (p. 732 n221) that for this reason the nominal wage should still be paid in this version as well.
40. Some *rishonim* maintain that it is specifically the risk factor that differentiates an investment from a loan, and that removes the prohibition of *ribbit;* see *Ritva, Bava Metzia* 70b, s.v. *ein mekabblim.* See, at length, Jeffrey L. Callen, "Risk and Incentives in the *Iska* Contract" in *The Oxford Handbook of Judaism and Economics,* ch. 4.
41. Regarding the significance of this element, see *Resp. Maharshag,* YD, 4.

maintain that the provider does not believe the claim, in which case it would presumably be wrong for the provider to accept the original rate under the premise that he questions the reliability of the self-reporting of the receiver.

Similarly, many authorities maintained that in the event that the provider has firsthand knowledge of the failure of the business venture (or other lack of profitability), it would be improper to demand an oath of the recipient.[42] One exception is R. Shimon Greenfield,[43] who asserted that given that the oath was a stipulation of the agreement, its demand is not frivolous. Further, R. Shilo Raphael[44] argued that in the event of a corporate bankruptcy, all should agree to the legitimacy of demanding an oath, as those could result from any number of related factors and are not necessarily proof of the failure of any one specific venture.

Relevant to the question of "plausible denial" is the degree of awareness the provider had as to the receiver's plans. Accordingly, there are varying approaches as to how much of the business plan should ideally be disclosed. In some formulations, the documents call for specifications as to the usage of the capital. The assumption is presumably that such knowledge legitimates the premise that the provider is an actual investor acting rationally. Alternatively, R. Moshe Feinstein[45] recommended as little disclosure as possible, to preserve the provider's credible refusal to accept the receiver's report.

Whether or not it is identified in detail, the reality that the funds are going to a profit-generating endeavor is crucial to both the spirit and the letter of the law. To attempt to utilize a *hetter iska* in the context of a loan provided to a person in need would certainly violate the spirit of the law of *ribbit*. The *Chafetz Chaim*, in his work *Ahavat Chesed*,[46]

42. See *Resp. Panim Meirot*, II, 30; and *Resp. Teshurat Shai*, I, 23. See also the discussion in *Resp. Divrei Chaim*, II, *hashmatot*, 16.
43. *Resp. Maharshag*, ibid.
44. *Mishkan Shilo*, p. 284.
45. *Resp. Iggerot Moshe*, II, YD 62. R. Feinstein's position is that if the provider does have personal knowledge of the failure of the business venture, it would be forbidden for him to demand an oath from the receiver, which would be considered "in vain." This is a topic of dispute among authorities.
46. Section II, ch. 15.

bemoaned the reduction of *chesed* that results from widespread use of the *hetter iska,* and recommended that all who are involved in funding for profit set aside in advance money to lend interest free, so that they may fulfill the vital *mitzvah* of lending to those in need.[47] Further, as R. Moshe Feinstein noted, assistance loans using a *hetter iska* would fail as well by the standard of the letter of the law, as it would not make sense to apply the rationale of *iska* to an endeavor that has no potential of generating profits.[48]

---

47. The words of the *Chafetz Chaim* are somewhat ambiguous, as he implies that there is no *mitzvah* fulfillment if the *iska* is utilized. However, he may be referring to a distinction between loans to the poor, which are certainly characterized as *chesed,* and loans for capital, which may be understood as morally neutral. Accordingly, his lament may be that the availability of the *hetter iska* incentivizes one with available funds to direct all of them to the profitable endeavor of subsidizing business initiatives, and leaves little remaining to assist the poor. This is the more direct implication of his words earlier in that work (I, 2:3).

    Later on (Part II, Ch. 21, in a gloss) he states that the general obligation of *chesed* is fulfilled only when the benefactor does not profit at all. However, regarding the lending of money, there is a specific mandate in the Torah to save one from falling into financial collapse, and it is understood, as noted above, that this could include supporting another's business in a mutually beneficial fashion. In that context, the benefit to the provider encourages increased assistance. However, the *Chafetz Chaim* draws a distinction, in that in a standard partnership, if the business fails, the impact will be felt equally by both partners, as will be the case regarding profits if it succeeds. In an *iska* arrangement, it is possible that the needy laborer may profit only minimally, with a larger amount owed to the provider. The *Arukh HaShulchan,* YD 249:14, assumes that the *mitzvah* fulfillment of the investor in a business is completely dependent on whether the motivation is to help the recipient or for personal profit.

    In any event, it seems that a loan not connected to any business venture, but purely to assist in current expenses, would be an inappropriate candidate for a *hetter iska,* and in the *Chafetz Chaim*'s assessment, would not constitute an act of *chesed.*

48. This point is also strongly stressed in *Resp. Ginat Veradim,* ibid. See also *Kovetz Teshuvot,* I, 80, and R. Chanoch Padwa, *Resp. Cheshev HaEphod,* I, 96.

    That being said, it must still be determined what is and is not included in the acceptable category. For example, it is widely accepted that an *iska* may be used with a house mortgage, in that a house that is purchased is expected to appreciate in value, even if that was not the goal of the purchase. See *Chelkat Binyamin,* p. 725, n163. (However, R. Padwa does not accept this, unless some part of the house is intended to be rented out.) Further, many allow an *iska* to be used with a student loan, as the funds are considered an investment in the future earning potential of the student.

Earlier authorities had been more permissive on this point, but largely because they felt the rationale of the *iska* could be applied more expansively. One example is the renowned and prolific *posek* R. Yosef Shaul Nathanson, who wrote a number of responsa[49] essentially arguing that, seeing as personal debts can force one to abandon their current livelihood to seek something more lucrative, or to sell real estate they currently own, enabling the repayment of these debts can be considered a sort of investment.[50]

R. Shilo Raphael[51] advanced a technical argument to cover situations that are not inherently profit-bearing. Given that the payment to the provider is framed as a remission to escape an oath, rather than a direct representation of the profits from the endeavor, it would not necessarily matter if that venture did not itself yield a profit.[52]

Nonetheless, many subsequent authorities, in line with the position of R. Feinstein, insisted on the funds being directly applied to a profit-bearing enterprise.[53] A number of contemporary authorities do maintain that if the recipient is involved at all in a business, even if the loan does not directly go to that endeavor, a *hetter iska* can be considered legitimate, in that all of his personal finances are interconnected, and stability in any one area may lead to profitability in another.[54] Extending this notion, R. Moshe Shternbuch[55] asserted that in the modern era,

49. See *Resp. Shoel u'Meishiv, kamma,* III, 160, and *telita'ah,* I, 133. See also *Resp. Maharsham,* II, 216, and R. Chaim Berlin, *Resp. Nishmat Chaim,* 100, who also takes a more lenient stand, with some nuances. R. Meir Arik, *Resp. Imrei Yosher,* I, 108, questions the approach and offers alternative suggestions.

50. See also similarly in *Resp. Chatam Sofer,* YD, 134.

51. *Mishkan Shilo,* p. 284.

52. A similar approach, among others, is advanced in a lenient responsum on the topic by *Resp. Chelkat Ya'akov,* YD 74. See also the discussion in *Resp. Chavatzelet HaSharon,* YD, 64, and see the comments of *Chelkat Ya'akov,* 75.

53. See *Resp. Imrei Yosher,* I, 108, and *Resp. Erekh Shai,* 177:7. Rabbi J. David Bleich surveys the views on this issue as part of wide-ranging analysis of all aspects of the *hetter iska* in *The Oxford Handbook on Judaism and Economics,* ch. 10, "Hetter Iska: The Permissible Venture." On this point, see pp. 206–208. See also the survey of opinions in *Chelkat Binyamin* to *Hilkhot Ribbit,* p. 723.

54. See *Brit Yehudah,* ch. 40 n29, and *Chelkat Binyamin,* pp. 724–725.

55. *Mo'adim U'Zmannim,* VI, 41, p. 70.

widespread investment in the stock market bestows this status to all stockholders.

Another aspect relevant to this component of the formula is the sincerity of the two parties involved in perceiving the arrangement as an investment rather than a sale. Pursuant to this question, the third Lubavitcher Rebbe, the *Tzemach Tzedek,*[56] considered the issue of whether a *hetter iska* had to be in writing, or could be expressed orally. In addressing the issue, he references a statement in the Talmud that implies that if a woman waives the rights to part of her marital contract, it is valid only if done in writing. The *Ritva* explains the reasoning: if the waiving was only verbal, it was likely only a "*ha'aramah,*" and does not represent an adequate fulfillment of the marital obligation. If this distinction is true in general, argues the *Tzemach Tzedek,* then a written *hetter iska* is necessary (at least *ab initio*), as here as well, we cannot tolerate a *ha'aramah.*[57] Nonetheless, many authorities do assume that a verbal declaration is effective in establishing a *hetter iska.*[58]

Alongside the question of sincerity is that of knowledge. R. Moshe Feinstein,[59] among others, stressed the importance of the parties understanding the content, and that it not be perceived as some kind of a magical formula that makes the prohibition of *ribbit* disappear, regardless of how the parties relate to it.[60]

---

56. *Resp.*, YD 88.
57. See also *Resp. Sha'arei Deah,* I, 5, who cites this in reference to the sale of *chametz,* and explains accordingly the multiple methods used to ensure that the sale is valid. This attitude is expressed in regard to the *Shemittah* sale of land as well, in the insistence on a written contract; see *Resp. Yabbia Omer,* X, YD, 38.
58. See *Resp. Tuv Ta'am V'Da'at,* III, Part 2, 43, and, emphatically, R. Isser Zalman Meltzer, in *Osef Chiddushei Torah MiMaran HaGra Kotler,* #46. See *Orchot Chesed* to *Ahavat Chesed,* II, 15, n2, who assumes this to be the view of most authorities. See also *Resp. Yashiv Yitzchak,* XLIV, 39.
59. *Iggerot Moshe,* ibid.
60. See similarly *Resp. Nishmat Chaim,* ibid., and *Mo'adim UZ'mannim,* VI, 41. It should be noted that the *Tzemach Tzedek,* in the aforementioned responsum, considered this element even more important than sincerity, as he considered understanding necessary even after the fact, and assumed that it can be taken for granted that understanding was present if the *hetter iska* was written, but would need to be determined if it were verbal.

The *Shelah*, in his writings,[61] emphasized the importance of both understanding – without which the *iska* would be *"k'chukha v'itlula,"* like a mockery – and of sincerity, without which it would be a "*aramah.*" In the latter case, he asserts, the prohibition of *ribbit* would remain in full force, noting that it is for this reason that the Torah accompanies the teaching with the warning "and you shall fear your God,"[62] a statement often interpreted to indicate that God can discern the true motives of man, invoked in instances where inner motivations are definitive.

Nonetheless, others felt these concerns could be overcome. R. Breisch[63] advances a novel argument, although he notes with gratification a similar approach is found in the writings of R. Eliyahu Kalatzkin (1852–1932). In other areas of *halakhah,* such as when a *get* may be legitimately coerced, the Rambam assumed that the inherent authority of *mitzvot,* and the innate desire of any Jew to comply with their mandates, supplants the expressed desire of the individual and thus establishes intent in line with the *halakhah.*[64] Similarly, in the case of *hetter iska,* it can reliably be assumed that the provider and the receiver of funds both sincerely wish to behave in accordance with Torah law, and thus fully commit to the permissible categorization of their transaction.[65]

The *Chatam Sofer, Resp.* CM, 48, relates that in his managing of the funds of orphans as loans, he was careful to explain the nature of the *iska* to borrowers, and the *Chakhmat Adam,* 143:3, quoting the *Sma,* requires a document that makes clear to both parties the nature of the arrangement (although *Resp. Levushei Mordechai,* I, YD, 95, assumes this knowledge to be required initially, but its absence not disqualifying after the fact; see also R Shlomo Kluger, *Resp. Tuv Ta'am V'Da'at,* III, Part 2, 43, although his conclusion seems specific to the facts of the case involved).

The *Chafetz Chaim,* in *Ahavat Chesed,* II, 15, laments the lack of understanding in the utilization of an *iska,* but it is unclear if he feels that to be disqualifying (see *Brit Yehudah,* 35:13), or merely less than ideal. *Divrei Soferim (Hil. Ribbit,* 177, in *Birur Halakhah* s.v. *l'shanot),* assumes that awareness of the *hetter iska* is enough; see *Orchot Chesed* to *Ahavat Chesed,* for an explanation of this position.

61. *Shnei Luchot HaBrit,* Lev. 25:36. See *Chulin, Ner Mitzvah* ch. 56.
62. See also Rashi there.
63. *Chelkat Ya'akov* ibid. 68–69.
64. See *Mishneh Torah, Hil. Gerushin* 2:20. For further discussion of this position of the Rambam, see Appendix.
65. He addresses there the fact that one could theoretically say the same of *mekhirat chametz,* and nonetheless the *Bekhor Shor* had termed that a *ha'aramah* that is only

This comparison could be challenged by noting that in cases such as the granting of the *get,* for example, when there is a religious obligation, that becomes the dominant motivation. However, in the case of the loan, there is no mandate to provide funds that are expected to increase in any form, such that there is a Torah obligation that defines the intent. Presumably, to solidify the comparison, one would need to incorporate some of the other elements that have been mentioned. R. Breisch asserts, in that vein, that an *iska* is therefore effective even if one or both parties is irreligious or unknowledgeable and is not participating in *iska* with full consent or awareness; just as with the recalcitrant husband, the Torah obligation overrides the declared intent.[66]

An alternative lenient approach is recorded in the rulings of R. Shlomo Kluger,[67] who ruled that a lack of understanding on the part of the recipient is acceptable, as long as in the event a court was asked to enforce the arrangement, it would not be collecting based on interest, but rather on the *iska* arrangement. Overall, while there is certainly a preference among the halakhic authorities that both parties are sincere and knowledgeable about the nature of the terms of the *iska,* many do find grounds for leniency at least after the fact.[68]

However, there may be a level worse than ignorance. R. Ya'akov Yeshaya Bloi, in his work *Brit Yehudah,*[69] asserts that if one party or the other asks what the *hetter iska* is, and the other party responds with a dismissive statement that it doesn't matter, it is just something that must

---

appropriate for rabbinic law (as discussed below). He notes the distinction that *mekhirat chametz* involves a non-Jewish purchaser, who would not be subject to the same assumptions regarding commitment to Torah law, and is also often not financially capable of making the purchase in a genuine way. Ultimately, however, while he writes his response in an effort to satisfy the standard of the *Bekhor Shor,* he indicates as well his independence from his opinion, and the rejection of that view by other great rabbinic authorities.

66. See also the comments of R. Zalman Nechemiah Goldberg, in the journal *HaYashar V'HaTov,* III, Tishrei 5767, pp. 7–8, regarding the assumption that every Jew should be assumed to desire the most permissible characterization of his actions, and the concomitant need to identify permissible approaches in the area of *ribbit.*

67. *Resp. Tuv Ta'am V'Da'at, telita'ah,* II, 43.

68. See *Brit Yehudah,* ch. 40, n. 14.

69. ibid.

be done to permit the transaction, then indeed the *hetter* is ineffective. As R. Binyamin Cohen[70] explains, the response is essentially a claim that the *iska* is meaningless, and that the transaction is being conducted as an actual interest-bearing loan.[71]

THE *HETTER ISKA KLALI*

The practice in Jewish banks has been to publicize their utilization of a "*hetter iska klali,*" a general *hetter,* in the form of a commitment that all of their dealings are understood to be within the framework of the *hetter iska.* This is a protocol that is first mentioned by the Maharsham,[72] who understood that this was effective in establishing the status of all their transactions, and also advocated that this be announced in all the synagogues and study halls, so that both sides of the transactions should be fully aware.[73] In this context, there also has been a lenient attitude regarding understanding, in that it is assumed that customers understand that there are complex rules in place.[74] Notably, R. Shmuel Engel[75] not only supported this model, but argued that it was the responsibility of rabbinic leadership to promote it, and failing to do so was a dereliction of the obligation to minimize the transgressions of others whenever possible.[76]

There were those who proposed expanding the use of this model. In an essay published in a Polish rabbinical journal[77] in 5684 (1924), R. Alter Azriel Meir Eiger of Lublin, a grandson of R. Leible Eiger, and a great-great grandson of R. Akiva Eiger, bemoaned the

70. *Chelkat Binyamin, Hil. Ribbit, Kuntres Hetter Iska,* 5, n62.
71. See also R. Moshe Shternbuch, *Dat V'Halakhah,* p. 96–97.
72. *Resp.,* 1, 20. See also *Resp. Har Tzvi* YD, 126 and 137, and *Pesakim V'Hanhagot,* p. 183, with n. 163.
73. See *Brit Yehudah,* ch. 40, n. 21, for an extensive discussion of this system, and its strengths and weaknesses, as well as the text to be used. See also the concerns and recommendations in *Resp. Imrei Yosher,* I, 189. R. Moshe Feinstein outlined the details he considered appropriate for a *hetter iska* for a bank in *Resp. Iggerot Moshe,* YD, III, 41.
74. See *Resp. Mechkarei Aretz,* pp. 100–101.
75. *Resp. Maharash,* VII, 133.
76. From the sources he brings it is clear he means that halakhically, and not merely homiletically.
77. *Drushim,* I, part 2, 38:1 (published by the *Agudath HaRabbanim* of Poland).

widespread neglect of the laws of prohibited interest among Jews conducting business, while also sympathizing with the many causes of this neglect, including lack of education, distraction, and economic pressure. Wishing to remove a stumbling block from the masses, as well as to preserve at least the awareness of the severe prohibition of interest, he proposed that a personal "*hetter iska klali*" be executed by every Jew once in their lifetimes, at the onset of their business careers, declaring that all relevant transactions be understood as functioning under this arrangement. He made it clear that this would surely not be an ideal situation, and any knowledgeable and aware Jew should certainly utilize a specific *hetter iska* for every transaction; nonetheless, this general version could serve as a remedy for all who forget, are unaware, or otherwise would fail to make one.

R. Eiger notes that the technical validity of his proposal hinges on a fundamental question as to the mechanics of the *hetter iska*. If the process is an actual commitment of the nature of a *kinyan* (formal acquisition), it is difficult to say it can be applied to a transaction that is not currently in existence. By contrast, if the *iska* represents a condition that characterizes an interaction, such a condition should be valid when stipulated in advance. In fact, the *halakhah* contains many such conditions specifically aimed at addressing subsequent incidents of forgetfulness or distraction at the relevant moment. Drawing on the aforementioned position of the Rambam regarding a coerced *get,* he asserts further that the inner desire of a Jew to comply with *halakhah* combines with the advance stipulation and is thus effective.

In an endorsement published later, R. Yitzchak Rappaport posited that the validity of the proposal hinged on another factor. The original *iska* model, as described by the Talmud, is premised on a partnership, involving shared ownership of a business venture. Such an arrangement would require a genuine, bilateral method of acquisition.[78] However, the later model of the Maharam Avigdors, which is premised on the recipient initially laboring on behalf of the funder, is accomplished through agency (*shlichut*), and that indeed

78. See *Rama,* CM 176:3.

can be arranged in advance, even unilaterally through an as-yet not designated agent.[79]

The proposal was accompanied by supportive responses from two prominent rabbinic voices.[80] R. Eliyahu Kalatzkin further buttressed the technical validity with additional textual proofs, while R. Meir Arik modified the suggestion, proposing that the formula be executed once a year rather than once a lifetime,[81] and noting that the ten days of repentance between Rosh HaShanah and Yom Kippur would be a conducive time for this.

The editors of the journal concluded this section by noting the urgency of the matter toward the spiritual salvation of the masses, and with a call for further endorsements or objections. The next issue indeed brought a number of responses, some of them supportive, including by prominent rabbinic scholars such as R. Shmuel Engel.[82] R. Chaim Yehudah Ginzberg agreed on the condition that the individual also took an oath not to reverse the commitment. R. Avraham Ya'akov Horowitz considered the proposal sound, but worried that it would lead to a laxity in the usage of specific *iska* arrangements, and beseeched the rabbinic leadership to issue clear instructions and exhortations to the public.

Others expressed their concerns more strongly. R. Ya'akov Meisels, in addition to raising technical objections, feared that the entire concept of prohibited interest would become forgotten. In this assertion, and in the exchange surrounding it, some of the themes of the broader *ha'aramah* debate can be detected. It is clear that R. Meisels' position was that in contrast to this newer proposal, a specific *iska* document would not constitute a threat to the integrity of the *ribbit* prohibition. Further, the editor's response there displays some of the familiar arguments invoked in support of alternative approaches. He asserted that *ribbit* has already been forgotten by the populace, with no mitigating

79. See, however, *Mo'adim U'Zmannim,* VI, 41, p. 48, who argues that the plan would not work according to the text of the Maharam.

80. Ibid 38:2 and 3.

81. R. Eiger had supported the notion of an advance stipulation with a comparison to the advance nullification of vows represented by *Kol Nidrei.* In that case, R. Arik notes, the declaration is made annually.

82. His support is also recorded in *Resp. Maharash,* ibid.

justification; this proposal, if valid, would at least alleviate the transgression, and, further, a yearly renewal of the document will serve to preserve the awareness of *ribbit*.

R. Meir Abawitz worried about its enforceability, and thought the only viable plan would require local communal enactments that would address and instruct all the inhabitants. This, he noted, would also serve to protect the consciousness of *ribbit*. Similarly, R. Yehudah Leib Fein offered his own alternatives, both drawing on communal leadership: either have every individual who comes to sell *chametz* before *Pesach* sign the declaration,[83] or, even better, every year at *Kol Nidrei* services on the night of *Yom Kippur* there should be an announcement that all transactions are with this understanding, and any who protest should express their disapproval. With that step, the arrangement, having been endorsed both by the rabbinic leadership and by the acquiescence of the populace, would take on the power of a binding enactment. This, he asserted, would be even more effective than an actual *hetter iska,* which individuals perform as a "*ha'aramah*"; this would transform the loan into a bona fide *iska*.

Perhaps the strongest opposition came from two preeminent scholars, R. Aharon Kotler, later to found the yeshiva in Lakewood, NJ, and his father-in-law, R. Isser Zalman Meltzer.[84] R. Kotler, in addition to arguing with the relevance of the proofs brought in support, asserted that for both conceptual and technical reasons, the *iska* understanding must be mutually agreed upon, and no unilateral declaration could suffice.[85]

Similar objections were leveled by R. David Menachem Manish Babad, in a responsum[86] written at R. Eiger's request. He articulated additional functional issues with a unilaterally executed *iska,* and worried

83. *Otzar Machmadim,* VII, p. 108, reports that R. Meir Schapiro, the Rosh Yeshiva of Chachmei Lublin and founder of the Daf Yomi, also agreed to the proposal and made this same suggestion.

84. These two responses were also reprinted in the volume *Osef Chiddushei Torah M'Maran HaGra Kotler,* #45 and 46, respectively.

85. The viability of a unilateral *hetter iska* had been debated earlier; see *Resp. Maharam Shik,* YD, 164; *Resp. Maharshag,* YD. 5 and 22; *Resp. Cheshev HaEphod,* I, 96; *Resp. Shraga HaMeir,* VI, 91:2; and *Resp. Yashiv Yitzchak,* XVI, 23.

86. *Resp. Chavatzelet HaSharon,* YD, 63.

that an enactment of this sort would do more harm than good, in that it would lead to all memory of an individual *iska* being erased.

R. Meltzer, following his son-in-law's objection, questioned the value of the proposal, when (in his view) a simple verbal declaration of *iska* would suffice to bestow that status. Accordingly, he maintains, the motivation for this approach must be that the borrower is hesitant to even remind the lender of the concept, fearing that the loan may not be granted under these terms. The journal editor disputed that contention, remarking that the proposal is meant for God-fearing Jews, and no claim was ever made that it should be effective against the will of a lender who would decline the terms of a *hetter iska.*

The issue of the need for bilateralism in the arrangement was addressed by some of the supporters, who maintained that if this proposal was widely accepted, it would be executed by both borrowers and lenders and thus all transactions would have both parties covered by its terms.[87] R. Kotler was not satisfied by this, noting the challenge in assuming that enough of the populace would adopt the suggestion, or remember to carry it out. One proponent, R. Moshe Berman, observed that this is an additional reason to recommend the renewal of the declaration on an annual basis.

Five years after his initial proposal, R. Eiger published a volume dedicated to the suggestion, with additional modifications and endorsements, entitled *Takanat Rabbim.* R. Ya'akov Yeshaya Bloi, in his work *Brit Yehudah* on the laws of *ribbit,*[88] estimates that the majority of rabbis who took up the suggestion at the time agreed with the premise, although he is unaware if the practice indeed was adopted at all in Poland at that time. More recently, the matter was taken up by two authorities of the British rabbinate, R. Yitzchak Ya'akov Weiss[89] and R. Chanoch Padwa,[90] both who expressed their hesitations about the validity of the approach. R. Padwa does offer that two individuals who consistently do business with each other may create a standing *iska* relationship so that it is

87. This is also advocated by R. Moshe Shternbuch in his *Ta'am Ribbit,* p. 11.

88. Ch. 40, n. 19–20.

89. *Resp. Minchat Yitzchak,* I, 20–21.

90. *Resp. Cheshev HaEphod,* I, 96.

unnecessary to execute a new agreement each time. R. Shilo Raphael,[91] for his part, lamented the fact that the proposal had not gained acceptance, and recommended it be revisited, asserting that executing such a document in front of a rabbinic court would solve many problems.

In current practice, it does not seem that R. Eiger's proposal has been utilized, presumably due to any number of the above objections and concerns.[92] Nonetheless, there has been more acceptance of the usage of the *hetter iska klali* in businesses where a declaration is hung publicly,[93] and it especially remains in use for banks, where detailed conditions are understood to be involved, and the arrangement is fixed and publicized, and many feel that the hesitations directed at the personal version are generally not applicable.[94]

THE ELEMENT OF NEED

Regarding part (D) of the formula, the element of "need" is considered a significant factor in the acceptance of the *hetter iska.* One example is another presentation of R. Breisch, who introduces the relevant section of his *Resp. Chelkat Ya'akov* with an additional essay emphasizing the complete dependency of the economic functioning of the Jewish community on the ability to provide business capital. He goes so far as to assert that the attitude of leniency that is associated with freeing *agunot* should be extended to this area as well, as this affects the entire population.

In sum, it would appear that the acceptability of the *hetter iska,* as assessed by our formula, is predicated on the following four premises: (A) As an investment, it is not subject to the regulations of a loan, and

---

91. *Mishkan Shilo* p. 288.
92. See *Otzar Machmadim,* ibid.
93. See *Resp. Yashiv Yitzchak,* ibid.
94. See *Chelkat Binyamin,* p. 733. However, see the questions raised there is *biurim,* p. 732, as well as the objections in *Mo'adim U'Zmannim,* ibid., p. 70. See also the objections of R. Yitzchak Mandel, *Resp. Cheker Halakhah,* III, 6, who also notes that this would certainly not satisfy the standard of the *Tzemach Tzedek,* mentioned above, that the *hetter iska* be in writing. In this case, the passivity of the parties is even less genuine than the oral *iska* he deemed insufficient, and the concern of *ha'aramah* would remain.

the returns are not categorized as interest; (B) The spirit of the Torah's prohibition against taking interest is directed at doing so in the context of loans of assistance to the needy; (C) The transaction involved is genuinely executed as an investment, rather than as a loan; and (D) the need for the utilization of this mechanism is vital to the economic survival of the Jewish community.

As we have seen, the strength of each of these four premises varies from one to the other, as does the rabbinic assessment of each one in and of itself. Accordingly, while the *hetter iska* is widely in use today, there are a range of attitudes towards it nonetheless, reflecting different evaluations of these components. Notably, R. Samson Raphael Hirsch apparently takes issue with the assumption taken above that the spirit of this law is inapplicable to business endeavors, and in a complex analysis, explicitly applies the theory to business capital.[95]

More sweepingly, R. Asher Weiss has characterized the *hetter iska* as essentially a device to permit what is actually *ribbit,* tolerated only by the recognition that without it, loans would simply be unavailable to those who need them, due to the lack of willingness among potential lenders.[96] In this formulation, the acceptance of the *iska* is more begrudging, and the key factor in it being accepted at all moves to the last column, the factor of need, emphasizing an additional component, the need for a different directive of the Torah, the providing of loans, to be realized in practice. Further, this could draw upon part (B) as well, in that it could be cogently argued that the purpose of the prohibition of *ribbit* is to support the imperative of loaning money, and accordingly the spirit of the law would endorse, albeit with regret, the prioritizing of that imperative over the prohibition that exists to strengthen it.

95. See Commentary of R. Samson Raphael Hirsch, Ex. 22:24 and Lev. 25:36.
96. Indications of this attitude can also be found in the above cited introduction of the *Chelkat Ya'akov.*

Chapter 4

Sales Mechanisms

In considering the level of acceptance of the sale of *chametz* before *Pesach,* as well as the sale of land in Israel prior to the *Shemittah* year, it is helpful to broadly compare them to each other before considering their individual aspects. On the surface, the two seem comparable, both involving a sale to a non-Jew, and thus creating an exclusion from Torah regulations, in line with the aforementioned sale of an animal about to bear a first born. Indeed, one of the great endorsers of the *Shemittah* sale, R. Yehoshua of Kutno, expressed his approval by asserting that it should be considered akin to the sale of *chametz,* and thus benefit from equivalent acceptance.[1]

Nonetheless, in practice, while some controversy has attached to the sale of *chametz,* the controversy that surrounds the *Shemittah* sale is far more vehement. As will be demonstrated, application of the formula should help greatly in explaining that disparity. It can be displayed that the two sales, despite their external similarity, vary in practically all parts of the formula: in the issues surrounding (A) compliance with Torah

1. This is also expressed by R. Ovadiah Yosef, *Resp. Yabbia Omer,* X, YD, 38.

law; perhaps most significantly, in (B) compatibility with the spirit of the law; in (C) the sincerity and genuineness of the sale; and also in (D) the need for the innovation.

It should be noted as well that there are many other examples of sales mechanisms in *halakhah* beyond these two, each with its own details, strengths, and weaknesses, and levels of acceptance. There is also at least one instance in the Talmud in which a transfer seemingly of this type is disparaged and declared invalid. This situation, known as *matnat Beit Choron,* is described in a *mishnah*[2] and entailed an event in which a man wanted to invite his father to his own son's wedding, despite the fact that the father had taken an oath not to benefit from the son. In an attempt to work around this problem, he gifted the wedding hall and the meal to another, who promptly declared his intent to consecrate this property. When the original owner objected and said this was not his intent in the gift, the recipient asserted that he correctly perceived the intent, to violate the oath at his expense. The *mishnah* concludes the story by asserting that no sale is valid unless the recipient can successfully consecrate the property involved. The *Talmud Yerushalmi*[3] adds the phrase, "[no sale] that is a *ha'aramah* [is valid under these circumstances]."

However, this scenario is extreme and need not cast aspersion on all sales approaches. As commentaries observe, there are several elements present that in particular may be disqualifying. Among these are the explicit statement of the actual goal of the transfer (the presence of the father at the meal); the visible indications of the original owner's interests being served (the wedding meal); and the complete lack of any benefit to the recipient from his "ownership."[4]

2. *Nedarim* 48a.
3. *Nedarim* 5:6.
4. The *Ran* (s.v. *kol matanah*) and other *rishonim* note that the ability to consecrate would actually not be crucial if some other benefit were present. As *Tosafot (Bava Batra* 134a, s.v. *kol; Sukkah* 41b, s.v. *heilakh*) conclude, the decisive factor is that the transaction here is an evident "*aramah,*" clearly being used here in the sense of "falsehood" (the Ran uses similar language). See also *Pnei Moshe* to the *Yerushalmi,* ibid., who indicates that the inability to consecrate would not matter were it not for the explicit verbal indications that the sale was a subterfuge.

Resp. Minchat Asher, II, 42:5, surveys the interpretations of this passage and notes the important differences relevant to *mekhirat chametz.* An extensive analysis

Factors such as these serve to undermine the effectiveness of the sale in a way that is self-evident and thus negate them in the eyes of all participants. Nonetheless, this need not be the default assumption. In fact, some maintain that as a general rule, a sales mechanism is more legitimate than the pretextual *ha'aramot* described in the Talmud, because a transaction that is between two parties should be defined by the spoken terms of that transaction, regardless of whether one party or the other is harboring unspoken intentions that are insincere.[5]

---

of the viability of *mekhirat chametz* in light of this and related passages appears in R. Ovadiah Yosef Toledano, *Mishpat HaKinyan, sha'ar* 1, 4:10. R. Ben Tziyon Shternfeld, *Resp. Sha'arei Tziyon,* I, 14, notes per the Ran's language in the following comments (s.v. *v'im hochiach,* s.v. *lo shanu,* and s.v *lishna acharina*) that the main issue is that the language used in the transaction makes it clear it is an artifice, as distinct from *mekhirat chametz.*

In fact, as he notes, the Ran's comments actually amount to an endorsement of *mekhirat chametz,* in that apparently, in the absence of a verbal indication, the transfer would be valid, despite the blatantly visible ulterior motive, and the undeniable truism that no one would make the effort to prepare a wedding feast that is not actually his own.

This is also evident from the Ran's comments regarding an earlier *mishnah* (43a) which conveys a debate as to whether one who wants to provide food for another, who has vowed not to benefit from him, may declare his food ownerless so the other individual can then take it. R. Yose prohibits this, and the Talmud (43b) explains that is a preventative policy due to the concern of "*Matnat Beit Choron.*" The Ran identifies the concern, that maybe one may assume this can be done even if "he states explicitly" his evasive intent. Apparently, even when this intent is obvious to all (*anan sahdi*), it only becomes invalidated when stated overtly.

The Ran (48a, s.v *lishna achrina*) does cite a dispute in the matter, associating the above opinion with *Rashba,* while noting the view of the Rambam (*Hil. Nedarim* 7:15; accepted by *Shulchan Arukh,* YD 221:9) that the disqualifying verbalization could be at a later point. Nonetheless, *Sha'arei Tziyon* notes the comment of the *Kessef Mishneh* that the Rambam is referring to a statement in some proximity to the transfer. By contrast, regarding *chametz,* no verbal indication will be conveyed for the duration of *Pesach.*

Still, this does not mean that there is no need for concern; *Sha'arei Tziyon* stresses that if one, in the course of selling their *chametz,* would make statements indicating insincerity, that would indeed jeopardize the validity of the sale, and care must to be taken to avoid that. For that reason, he is inclined to oppose the selling of the animals for *Pesach,* as in that more complicated arrangement it is difficult to avoid such declarations.

5. See, for example, R. Moshe Rotenburg, *Resp. Maharam M'Rotenberg HaAcharonim,* 12.

The limits of this category have been tested through numerous rabbinic debates. For example, sometimes a transaction is made with the understanding, implicit or explicit, that the item will be transferred back to the original owner after a given period of time. The fact that the receiver is circumscribed in his ability to either retain ownership or to choose who his buyer will be indicated to some authorities that the sale was never genuine in the first place; others did not consider this to be an inherent disqualification, while to still others, other factors were determinative.[6]

A similar objection to insincere sales found in Talmudic texts addresses the motivation of the transfer itself. In general, Talmudic law seems to invalidate a transfer of property that is done for evasive purposes, as indicated by a passage discussing a woman who gifted her property to her daughter prior to her own remarriage in order to conceal it from her new husband; she was later permitted to retake the property.[7] As the commentaries explain, in this case, it is the circumstances surrounding the event that establish the lack of intent, even without verbalization.[8]

To briefly examine one detail that has been debated within the context of sales mechanisms, some authorities objected to the suggestion of the *Resp. Beit Shlomo* (YD I, 191) that the prohibition against cutting

6. The *Shulchan Arukh* (OC 246:3) requires one who has rented out an animal to a non-Jew to receive it back before *Shabbat* so as not to violate the prohibition of allowing one's animals to work on *Shabbat*. If the renter has delayed in returning it, so it remains in his possession as *Shabbat* begins, the Jewish owner, in order to avoid the prohibition, may declare the animal ownerless, only for the duration of *Shabbat*. This is true, despite the fact that there will be no opportunity for any outside party to actually take possession, in that it is currently being rented, and that after the term of the rental the period of ownerlessness will end.

   Building on this, some authorities (see R. Menachem Mendel Krochmal, *Resp. Tzemach Tzedek*, 20) allowed the prohibition of *ribbit* to be circumvented by selling an item to a lender, and then buying it back at a profit. Others, however, objected to this (see *Taz*. OC 246:5), arguing that this was an unacceptable "*ha'aramah*" in that the purchaser, in actuality a lender, had no discretion to sell the item to anyone else. See the discussion in R. Yosef Shaul Nathanson, *Chelek L'Shivah*, 254, to *Nachalat Shivah*, 40, and R. Baruch Frankel Teomim, *Resp. Ateret Chakhamim*, YD 14.

7. *Ketubot* 78b–79a.

8. *Tosafot*, ibid., s.v. *katvinhu; Ran, Kiddushin* 49b; *Resp. Rosh*, 78:3.

down fruit bearing trees could be addressed through the sale of the trees to a non-Jew, asserting that such a sale would constitute a *ha'aramah*.[9] One response to this objection is to assert that sales are only *ha'aramot* when the item reverts to the original owner later; however, if there is no such return (such as the case with the trees, which are cut down), the sale poses no questions.[10]

This last approach is adopted by R. Shimon Greenfield, known as *Maharshag*,[11] who, accordingly, does term the sale of *chametz* and of the firstborn animal a *ha'aramah*. He does, however, posit another unresolved objection to the sale of the trees: in that the nature of the prohibition is the destruction of the trees, selling them to a non-Jew for the purpose of destruction may itself be considered the forbidden act of destruction. Perhaps ironically, in the context of arguing that this sale is not a *ha'aramah*, but rather problematic for other reasons, *Maharshag* is actually identifying one of the indications of an unacceptable *ha'aramah*: a ploy that results in the intent of the Torah's rule being thwarted.

In fact, in a different responsum addressing another issue regarding a sale, *Maharshag* draws a distinction between appropriate and inappropriate utilizations. Asked about one who wishes to sell his business to a non-Jew to allow it to function on *Shabbat*, *Maharshag*[12] notes that there are two possible scenarios. In one, the Jew wishes to profit from commerce on *Shabbat*, and is selling his business in order to enable that. This would be a thwarting of the intent of the *halakhah*. However, in other situations, the Jew would be happy to forgo the earnings from *Shabbat*; however, regulations force him to keep his business operational seven days a week. In that case, he is driven by the basic need to make a living at all. Accordingly, it is understandable that he is seeking to sell his business for the duration of *Shabbat*, and he should do so genuinely

9. See *Resp. Arugat HaBosem*, YD 121, working with the premise of the *Bekhor Shor*, that a *ha'aramah* is unacceptable for a Torah prohibition. *Resp. Neta Sorek*, YD 42, agrees that a *ha'aramah* is involved, but does not accept the rule of the *Bekhor Shor*.
10. See also *Resp. L'Horot Natan*, XIII, 64. Compare also the situation discussed in *Resp. Shvut Ya'akov*, II, OC, 39.
11. *Resp. Maharshag*, II, 46.
12. *Resp. Maharshag*, II, 18.

and with sincerity, turning over the profits from that day to the non-Jewish purchaser.[13]

A related issue is the sale of utensils to avoid the obligation to immerse them, as this *mitzvah, tevilat kelim,* is incumbent upon Jews who acquire ownership of certain kinds of utensils previously owned by non-Jews. On *Shabbat,* when it is forbidden to perform the immersion and the utensils would thus be unusable, the *Shulchan Arukh* records a recommendation to transfer ownership to a non-Jew.[14] Such an approach certainly raises the issue of *ha'aramah,* and resultant limitations on its implementation.[15] Nonetheless, there were those who maintain that this practice does not involve a *ha'aramah.*[16]

---

13. For another application of this distinction, see *Resp. Meishiv B'Halakhah,* II, 323, n. 134.

    It is noteworthy that *Maharshag,* after noting another halakhic issue in the specific inquiry and suggesting how it might be navigated, laments that the livelihood of a Jew is no small matter, and at times great efforts and compromises must be undertaken to find leniency.

14. OC 323:7, YD 120:16.

15. See *Resp. Rashbash,* 468. The *Taz* (YD 120:18) emphasizes that this approach should only be utilized over the course of *Shabbat,* and the *Pri Chadash* (sec 42) stresses this even more strongly.

16. Somewhat subject to interpretation is the view of those who applied this advice to situations that were permanent, but still had a component of difficulty involved, e.g. large utensils that could not be immersed or even moved. See, for example, *Chiddushei R. Akiva Eiger* to YD, ibid., 1, and *Darkei Teshuvah,* 112. These authorities may still see the measure as *ha'aramah* but still tolerable due to the lack of better alternatives, thus affected by the last part of the formula, the component of "need." For a discussion of various approaches of this nature to avoid the obligation of *tevilat keilim,* see *Choshen L'Ma'aseh,* #22.

    There are some authorities who explicitly assert that the sale of utensils in this case is not a *ha'aramah.* Among these were R. Shlomo Kluger, who discussed this in various places in his writings, including as part of an essay printed a number of times, first as an introduction to his work *Nidrei Zeruzin,* Vol. II (5615), and with additions in *Korban Pesach* (*Makhon Chokhmat Shlomo,* 5764, sec. 448). Among his arguments were the claim that in contrast to the *Beit Choron* story, there is nothing to indicate that the gift is not genuine, especially as, in the situation described in *Shulchan Arukh,* it only needs to last over the course of *Shabbat;* at least for that day, the utensil would be happily gifted to the non-Jew. Interestingly, one could have pointed to the usage by the Jew as an undermining of the seriousness of the sale; R. Kluger does note that *tevilat keilim* is required only for utensils that are owned by

It seems that the difference between these two positions is the focus of the *ha'aramah* concern. Those who feel that the very existence of a sale invokes the issue of *ha'aramah* appear to be objecting to the escape from the situation of halakhic regulation. In other words, once there is a *mitzvah* in place, even a negative prohibition, the spirit of the law requires that the prohibited act not occur, even if it were possible to technically remove the applicability of the prohibition.

The responses that accept the sales, by contrast, are placing focus on the nature of the sale itself, apparently taking the position that if the sale is indeed genuine, there is no impediment. However, if the sale itself is questionable, as the property transfer itself appears not to be genuine, that would constitute a *ha'aramah.*

In an interesting twist, for many of the authorities who were concerned with the commitment of the parties to the sale, the presence of a religious imperative, and the desire to avoid that imperative, is actually the solution to the problem. Even in situations where the facts of the transaction would otherwise indicate the sale to be null and void, if there is a religious motivation that the sales should be valid, a number of halakhic decisors considered this sufficient basis to validate a transaction that otherwise would have been ineffective.[17] Some of

---

Jews, not by those that are used by them, although that addresses a different aspect of the issue. R. Asher Weiss, in a number of places in his writings (see *Resp. Minchat Asher* III, 57:4), maintains that this approach is indeed a *ha'aramah;* his student R. Ovadiah Yosef Toledano, in his *Resp. Meishiv Mishpat,* II, 16, records an exchange with R. Weiss on the subject along with the view that it is not a *ha'aramah* (however, compare his presentation in III, 13:1).

It should also be noted that there is a dispute as to whether the obligation of *tevilat kelim* is mandated by Torah or rabbinic law, which, as we have seen, impacts the *ha'aramah* discussion as applied to that *mitzvah.* See *Yeshuot Ya'akov,* OC 13:4.

It is also noteworthy that the situation that is discussed in *Meishiv Mishpat* actually describes an ownership structure of a different nature, in which a requirement of *tevilah* is avoided because even though the utensil was manufactured by non-Jewish workers, the materials were owned by Jews. Even if this is termed a *ha'aramah,* it may be arguable that it is not as vulnerable as the "evident *ha'aramah*" of the Jewish owner of a utensil who transfers it to a non-Jew, and yet continues to use it.

17. A source for this may be *Tosafot, Avodah Zarah* 71a, s.v. *Rav Ashi,* where it is asserted that a sale of part of a pregnant animal to avoid *bekhor* status is valid even if the price is not proportional, because the seller will be motivated to commit to the sale

these authorities extended this premise even to two parties who were unaware of or unconcerned by the religious elements, while for others such overriding of individual intent was a bridge too far.

It should be noted as well that not only sales have been conducted for the ulterior motive of addressing halakhic challenges, but even marriages have been, as well, and this is recorded in early rabbinic literature. The *Tosefta*[18] relates that in a time of famine, R. Tarfon enabled hundreds of women to partake of the *terumah* reserved for *kohanim* by marrying them, thus providing the benefit allowed to the wife of a *kohen*. The *Talmud Yerushalmi*[19] refers to this action as a *ha'aramah*. Apparently, these marriages were valid, despite the motivation; otherwise, the endeavor would have been pointless.[20]

It may be productive to compare this to "green card marriages," in which a citizen (for example, of the US) marries a non-citizen in order to extend the benefits of citizenship to the spouse. This is a felony, and can lead to prosecution of both parties. With the exception of situations where the citizen is deceived by the immigrant, in which case the latter is in violation of "marriage fraud," the allegation is that the two parties have entered into a "sham marriage." Various indications may be considered confirmation of that charge, such as if the non-citizen paid money to the citizen to go through with the marriage, or if the "spouses" are discovered not to live together or share other aspects associated with genuine marriage.

Thus, if the parties are pursuing the marriage with no purpose or result other than obtaining citizenship status, it is deemed a sham marriage. If, by contrast, an American chooses to marry a non-citizen because of a loving relationship, and enters into a marriage in all senses of the word, the union is completely legal (even if they are forced to disprove the suspicions of government officials). What lies in between is a situation where a citizen marries a foreigner in order to provide

regardless, due to religious factors. See *Chiddushei R. Akiva Eiger*, YD 294:15; *Resp. Har Tzvi*, OC, II, 44; R. Shlomo Zalman Auerbach, *Ma'adanei Aretz, Shvi'it*, 1 and 18.

18. *Ketubot* 5:1.

19. *Yevamot* 4:12

20. See *Resp. Yabbia Omer*, X, YD, 38:3.

citizen benefits, but having done so, proceeds to live a married life that is genuine in all respects.

In the realm of *halakhah,* according to many authorities, that last scenario would be completely valid. Motivation, in this view, is irrelevant; all that matters is authenticity within the facts of the situation. Given that halakhic reality is determined by God's approval, and not a government official susceptible to being deceived, the only reason to pursue either a sale or a marriage for halakhic purposes is to fully commit to its standards. At that point, the impetus for initiating the arrangement no longer matters.[21]

In any event, the two kinds of ulteriorly motivated marriages (civil and halakhic) may be related. A number of authorities ruled, based on the R. Tarfon case, that one who marries solely for the purpose of addressing some legal requirement, without any kind of genuine relationship, is nonetheless fully married in the eyes of Jewish law.[22]

However, R. Zvi Pesach Frank argued that the two should not be connected. One who marries for a purely halakhic purpose must be considered married, because there would not be any reason to go through with it without full conviction, in order to effect the desired halakhic status. By contrast, one who marries to satisfy civil authorities would have no reason to express the intentionality needed to effect a halakhic marriage.[23] He continues to assert that this logic is the reason that sales such as that of land for the *Shemittah* year are valid; any situation that requires halakhic effectiveness to accomplish its purpose can be assumed to possess that intent.

Beyond the broader concepts debated above, the details of each situation impact the assessment, and halakhic authorities worked in

---

21. There are, in actuality, three relevant categories: halakhic marriages carried out to accomplish an ulterior halachic purpose; sham halakhic marriages (at least structurally) to accomplish a civil legal purpose; and sham civil marriages. For a survey of additional halakhic positions taken by authorities regarding the latter two categories, see R. Zvi Ryzman, *Ratz K'Zvi,* on Fertility and related topics, pp. 623–638.
22. See *Resp. Maharsham,* II, 8 and *Resp. Tzofnat Pa'aneach,* 5. The Maharsham did note, however, that if one "spouse" would die, the other would be exempt from mourning obligations, due to the lack of any emotional connection.
23. *Resp. Har Tzvi* EH 29.

each case to evaluate and refine the aspects of each iteration to confirm compliance with both the letter and the spirit of the law.

For example, regarding the practice of selling an animal to address the *bekhor* issue, there were authorities who felt that the appearance of *ha'aramah* was too strong and led to an attitude of insincerity in the populace. Accordingly, various suggestions were advanced in order to enhance the process. For example, it was advocated that the owner sell only one limb of the animal (as even joint ownership with a non-Jew exempts from the obligations of *bekhor*). Then, after the animal was eventually slaughtered, that limb would actually be given to the non-Jew, making the sale genuine in all senses of the word.[24] Further, as others noted, selling a small part of the animal, even without physically transferring it, allows for the setting of a realistic price, which can be paid upfront.[25]

It is clear that in all cases, the details certainly matter. Many of the variables are in the hands (and minds) of the parties to adjust and enhance, and continuous attention to them is reflected in the rabbinic treatment of the various iterations throughout the development of halakhic practice.

As *chametz* and land in Israel during *Shemittah* are two of the most well-known subjects of sales, a comparison of their elements and their varied receptions can be instructive.[26]

---

24. R. Moshe Ze'ev Margolios, *Resp. Agudat Ezov,* 14, and, at great length, *Resp. Chut HaMeshulash,* II, 4.
25. See *Shulchan Arukh HaRav, Hil. Mekhirat Beḥemah HaMevakeret,* s.v *m'inyan.*
26. Regarding the possible differences between various "sales mechanisms" that exist in *halakhah,* and the significance of these differences, see *Resp. HaBari V'HaShema,* III, pp. 362–363, and in particular the detailed footnote (#40).

Chapter 5

The Sale of *Chametz*

The sale of *chametz* is widely utilized in Jewish communities around the world, and has become a standardized part of the annual preparation for *Pesach*. Jews purchase *chametz* knowing in advance it will be sold, and some *poskim* even consider the question of whether it should be an obligation to sell one's *chametz* as part of the appropriate safeguards for Pesach.[1]

However, there is a history of controversy surrounding the practice, and in contemporary times as well, there are some who do not participate, while there are many who will only sell *chametz* that is prohibited on a rabbinic level, but not that which is Biblically prohibited, reflecting the distinction mentioned above that is sometimes applied to *ha'aramot*, as well as other possible concerns.[2] Notably, the

1. See *Resp. L'Horot Natan* VI, 25, and *Halikhot Shlomo,* 6:3 in *Dvar Halakhah* 5. For an argument against utilizing *mekhirat chametz* in this fashion, see R. Aharon Miasnik, *Minchat Aharon, Pesach,* 11:8; and R. Boruch Simon, *Imrei Boruch: Tokef HaMinhag B'Halakhah,* 22.
2. See *Elyah Rabbah,* 448:7; *Chayei Adam, klal* 124; R. Aharon Miasnik, *Minchat Aharon, Pesach,* pp. 149–151; R. Asher Weiss, *Haggadat Minchat Asher* p. 280.

Vilna Gaon expressed his opposition to the sale of any *chametz* that was not sold permanently.[3]

Some have complained that the sale seems like a game: the *chametz* does not leave the original owner's residence (something some *poskim* insisted should happen);[4] the purchaser does not appear interested in actually taking possession of the *chametz*;[5] rarely if ever does the seller have to open his doors and cabinets to the new owner of his food; and the *chametz* invariably reverts to its original ownership immediately after *Pesach*.

The divergence of views manifests itself repeatedly in the language of the literature, and to address what will seem like an inconsistency in the presentation, it should be noted at the outset that some of the participants in the ongoing debate refer to the sale as a *ha'aramah* that should be minimized, limited, or even avoided entirely; some as a *ha'aramah* that is entirely acceptable, for various reasons; and some as not a *ha'aramah* at all. Many feel that it is a *ha'aramah* when conducted in one fashion, and not in another, and all points in between.

This can be found already in the earliest rabbinic literature. The *Tosefta*[6] speaks of a situation in which a Jew, finding himself stuck at sea

3. *Ma'aseh Rav*, #176–177, #178–179, or #180–181 (depending on the edition). It is not spelled out there what was his precise objection; *Minchat Aharon*, pp. 151–152, surveys a number of possibilities, and concludes with the suggestion that the Gaon was primarily concerned with sales conducted by individuals that were likely to be flawed and possibly ineffective, and would not be similarly opposed to the contemporary method of a sale conducted by a rabbinic court. This interpretation assumes that the objection was focused on process, which is consistent with the second comment, which refers to the sale as "*mekhirah garua*", an inferior sale. See also the analysis of possibilities in *Mo'adim L'Simchah*, pp. 165–166, n10; he assumes the Gaon would have been more accepting of the contemporary sales that are carried out by rabbinic agents (although he would not have kept *chametz* in his house over *Pesach* in either case).

   However, it may also be that he objected to an evasion of the responsibility, which could be supported by noting that a similar objection was expressed to the utilization of methods to avoid the prohibition of *ribbit*.
4. See *Terumat HaDeshen* 119 and *Bach*, OC 448, s.v. *katav*.
5. See *Machatzit HaShekel*, OC 448:4; *Resp. Chatam Sofer*, YD 310; *Resp. L'Horot Natan*, II, 27
6. *Pesachim* 2:6–7. A version of this appears as well in *Yerushalmi Pesachim* 2:2.

as *Pesach* approaches, transfers ownership of his *chametz* to a non-Jewish fellow traveler, and reclaims it after the holiday. However, the impression is one of an unplanned, non-ideal, and isolated incident; the current reality, where entire communities plan in advance to preserve their stocks of *chametz* through annually scheduled arrangements with their local rabbi, appears to be a significant expansion of the depicted scenario. The *Machatzit HaShekel*[7] bemoans this development, and assumes that much has deteriorated over the generations in terms of the sincerity of the sale, while trying to find justification for its continued acceptance.[8]

A number of *rishonim,* in relating the *Tosefta*'s ruling, include the assertion that one who utilizes this option is justified "as long as he does not engage in *ha'aramah.*"[9] The *Beit Yosef,*[10] citing Rabbenu Yerucham, expresses astonishment: the entire plan appears to be a *ha'aramah,* and yet, it is permitted!

Various interpretations can be found as to the *ha'aramah* that is being referenced here. Together with them, the question must be asked as to the nature of the condition: is it a prohibition, that is to say, one must not undertake actions that display the behavior as insincere? Or is it actually disqualifying, rendering the sale invalid and the *chametz* prohibited?[11]

According to a number of *rishonim,*[12] the intent is that this should not become a regular practice. To some of the commentaries, this interpretation is suggested by the picture painted by the *Tosefta,* in which the scenario depicted is of an individual traveling on a boat when *Pesach* approaches; the impression that is created is that it is an unanticipated,

---

7. OC 448:4.
8. In response to the *Machatzit HaShekel,* see *Resp. Chatam Sofer,* YD, 310. *Resp. Maharshag,* II, 80:4, asserts that the custom has shown that the concerns of the *Machatzit HaShekel* need not be attended to at all.
9. The *Beit Yosef* cites this addition from the *Behag,* (as does Rabbenu Yerucham, *Netiv* V, part V, 46a), but a number of sources indicate that this represents a textual variant of the *Tosefta* itself; see *Resp. Rashba,* I, 70; *Chiddushei HaRitva, Pesachim* 21a, s.v. *ha-mokher; Meiri; Ohr Zarua,* 256; and *Bach.*
10. OC 448:3–4
11. See *Resp. Machzeh Avraham,* OC, 86.
12. *Ritva* ibid., citing R. Amram Gaon; *Meiri, Pesachim* 6a; *Maharam Chalavah, Pesachim* 30b.

unusual situation, and also probably necessary to preserve the livelihood of the Jewish traveler. Such an understanding would indeed look askance at the contemporary implementation of *mekhirat chametz*[13] (it is noteworthy that the "boat scenario" is included in the codification of the Rambam,[14] but not that of the *Shulchan Arukh*).

The notion that the necessities of livelihood were a crucial factor in justifying the sale is certainly one that has been evident in the history of the literature, and informs some of the discomfort with the widespread contemporary sales. For example, R. Eliyahu Schapira (1660–1712), in his *Elyah Rabbah,*[15] opined that *mekhirat chametz* should be limited to those who manufacture their own *chametz* products (he was referring to alcoholic products) for sale to others, as they must do so in large quantities and are unable to dispense with all of it before *Pesach.* By contrast, those who purchase products from non-Jews for resale, should buy in smaller quantities with *Pesach* in mind, or should return unsold inventory to their distributors.[16] Still, even to those predicating the sale on significant financial need, a restriction of the sale to only occasional, unplanned situations is a step beyond.

It is instructive to consider why this factor would be significant. One possibility is that the sale itself is only tolerated begrudgingly and is premised on the assumption that it is necessary and unusual.

---

13. See the discussion of this in *Resp. Shem Olam,* OC 2:2.
14. Nonetheless, there is no other indication that the Rambam forbids repeated usage of this mechanism. Accordingly, it requires explanation as to why he does include this fact in his description. Interestingly, R. Aharon Miasnik, *Minchat Aharon,* p. 169, suggests that it is to indicate that the Rambam is even less concerned about a *ha'aramah* in the transfer of *chametz,* and the "boat scenario" it is included to show even greater openness. Presumably, the Jew was traveling on the boat together with his *chametz* in order to sell it at his destination; this would make it even less likely that he is sincerely interested in selling it to anyone who was already traveling with him. Even so, the transfer is considered valid. The *Arukh HaShulchan,* OC 448:15–17, already made a similar point in the language of the *Tosefta* and the *Yerushalmi,* seeing the usage of the boat scenario as an endorsement of a number of the aspects of the sale that have been subject to challenge.

    For an alternate explanation as to the formulation of the Rambam, see *Resp. Divrei Nechemiah,* 35.
15. OC 448:7.
16. Note the description of the license to transfer *chametz* in *Resp. Ori V'Yishi,* 121.

Once it becomes planned and regular, this indulgence is strained.[17] Alternatively, the objection may be more fundamental: once a pattern is established that the *chametz* always reverts to the original owner, the sale itself may be revealed as insincere. Even more fundamentally, it could be argued that the purchaser feels a responsibility to protect the *chametz,* and thus the Jew maintains an interest in the *chametz* over the course of *Pesach.* Indeed, the *Ritva* goes so far as to prohibit after the fact *chametz* that was sold under such circumstances.[18]

However, other interpretations of the *ha'aramah* exhortation are less problematic to contemporary practice. Another understanding of the concern is that the *chametz* should not remain in the house of the Jew, but should instead be brought to the physical property of the gentile. At first blush, this does seem to be a serious issue for contemporary practice, as the *chametz* generally does stay in the Jew's house. Despite the appearances, this requirement is not actually being ignored. In response to societal and economic developments that made actual relocation of the *chametz* impractical, adjustments have been made so that the circumstances are considered equivalent to the standard of actual removal.

This process began with the *Bach,*[19] who asserted that it was sufficient to sell the room of the house where the *chametz* is, and to provide the purchaser with the key to the area where the *chametz* is located. The *Bach* considered the providing of the key to be crucial to prevent the sale from being artificial,[20] and also required that no seal indicating Jewish ownership be left in place that may dissuade the purchaser from entering

17. An interesting indication of this understanding can be found in *Resp. L'Horot Natan,* VI, 97:21, who cites the *Ritva*'s view as a basis to undermine the appropriateness of a *ha'aramah* that is used in an ongoing fashion, apparently despite the fact that in regards to *mekhirat chametz,* this view has not been accepted. Further, the *Ritva* states, as noted above, that the *chametz* becomes prohibited after Pesach, suggesting a more fundamental objection, that would not be transferable to other areas.
18. This ruling is based on a passage in the *Talmud Yerushalmi (Pesachim* 2:2); however, other *rishonim* interpret this passage differently (see *Rosh, Pesachim* 2:4, and *Ohr Zarua* II, 246).
19. OC 448; also in *Magen Avraham,* OC, 448:4, and *Chok Ya'akov,* #12.
20. Some asserted that failing to turn over the key was a particularly blatant *ha'aramah (ha'aramah nikeret)* that would be unacceptable even regarding rabbinic law, and the *chametz* would be prohibited after *Pesach;* see *Taz,* OC 448:4.

and taking his purchased *chametz.*[21] To that end, R. Malkiel Tennenbaum[22] asserted that the contract must also make it clear that the purchaser has the right to enter the property of the seller as needed to access the *chametz,* and was surprised not to find this in earlier contracts.[23]

Still, the *Mishnah Berurah* took the leniency further, stating that it was self-evident ("*pashut*") that identifying the location of the key is sufficient. What emerges from the discussions regarding the key is at least two distinct concerns: one, that the purchaser must functionally have access to the *chametz,* and two, that the retaining of the key transmitted a message to the purchaser that the sale was not serious, thus solidifying the *ha'aramah* issue.[24] Relevant to both points, a number of

---

The first Lubavitcher Rebbe, R. Schneur Zalman of Liady, *Shulchan Arukh HaRav,* OC 448:13–14, wrote that for the Jew to place his seal on the *chametz* after the sale would be prohibited, but would not disqualify the sale, as this does not actually reduce the rights of the purchaser in any way. However, to fail to provide the key, or to forcibly take back the key after it was given during the transaction, would invalidate the sale, as the purchaser would have no access to the *chametz* and could not be said to bear any responsibility for it. (His grandson, the *Tzemach Tzedek,* OC 44–45, suggests several scenarios in which there would be room for leniency, generally situations in which the failure to provide the key can be explained in a way that does not convey intentional denial of access.)

However, the *Magen Avraham,* 448:4, cites the *Resp. Mas'at Binyamin, #59,* as ruling leniently after the fact. The *Noda B'Yehudah, kama,* OC 18, strongly disputed the idea that the failure to hand over the key could invalidate the sale, asserting that the seller's insincerity cannot negate his explicit obligations to the purchaser, and the latter's rights would be upheld in any court should the seller wish to retake his property.

This does not mean, nonetheless, that the *ha'aramah* should be permitted; indeed, in the *Noda B'Yehudah*'s sales contract, printed in his son's responsa, *Shivat Tziyon,* 11, it states in strong terms that the key must be given to the purchaser, together with full, unrestricted access to the property, and no mark of the Jewish owner may remain.

21. R. Dov Eliezerov, *Resp. She'ali Tziyon, kama,* II, 14–16, addresses at great length the question of one who is imprisoned, together with his *chametz,* which may not legally be separated from him. Among other arguments, he asserted that in that the obstacle was not the fault of the seller, the sale is valid. He notes there that R. Zvi Pesach Frank agreed (see also *Har Tzvi, Pesakim V'Hanhagot, Pesach,* 5).
22. *Resp. Divrei Malkiel,* IV, 22:13.
23. Regarding the question of the seller entering the sold areas during *Pesach,* see *Resp. Yashiv Yitzchak,* XLVI, 11,
24. Accordingly, R. Shlomo Kluger (responsum published in *Neot Deshe*) asserted it was only necessary because refusing to turn over the key would strengthen the appearance

contemporary authorities maintained that providing the key was necessary only when the *chametz* was sold directly by the original owner, but with the contemporary method of a mass sale carried out by an agent, it is sufficient to write in the contracts that the keys will be made available to the purchaser on request.[25]

Regarding the selling of the room, there is some dispute. Many have the policy to not actually sell the rooms, but to rent them to the purchaser of the *chametz*. The *Avnei Nezer*[26] explained this distinction in a manner that is connected to the core concern regarding *ha'aramot*. It is plausible, he maintained, that the Jew is genuinely and sincerely selling his *chametz* over the course of *Pesach*. It is less believable, however, that he is actually selling any part of his house for this time period, regardless of what the purchase price is. Invoking the concern of the *Bekhor Shor*,[27] he asserts that in order to avoid a *ha'aramah*, the real estate transfer must be a rental rather than a sale.[28] Still, a number of major authorities, most

---

of a *ha'aramah*. However, if it was not practical to turn over a key, for example if it were lost, it was not necessary to do so.

Addressing the latter point, *Shvilei David*, YD, *kuntres hakinyanim*, asserts that if the Jew stores other, permissible property in that area, his retention of the key does not convey any discouraging message regarding the *chametz*.

25. See *Resp. Maharash Engel*, I, 34, and *Resp. B'Tzel HaChokhmah* VI, 34.
Not all acknowledged the key requirement in the first place. The *Pri Chadash*, in a comment responding to the *Bach*, denied a requirement to turn over the key. See also *Resp. Yeshuot Malko*, OC, 39, who considers the providing of the key a mere stringency. See also *Resp. Meishiv Mishpat*, III, 3:11.

26. *Resp.*, OC 346:3.

27. Interestingly, he describes the limitation as one excluding *ha'aramot* "on *Pesach*" rather than mentioning a distinction between Torah law and rabbinic law.

28. The same position is taken by *Resp. Avnei Tzedek*, OC, 21, who explains in this fashion why there is no possibility of a Jew selling his house or his field every *Shabbat* to allow a non-Jew to work there. The sale would be an open *ha'aramah*, as there is no plausibility to the claim that he is genuinely selling his real estate for that time period. (See also the creative approach to this problem in R. Meir Horowitz of Zikiv, *Resp. Imrei Noam*, I, 2.)

This is also expressed by R. Avraham Teomim, *Resp. Chesed L'Avraham*, YD 112, who applies this logic as well to one who anticipates the death of a relative and wants to sell his store to another for the mourning period, during which he is prohibited from engaging in business. With this step, he plans to continue benefiting from the business conducted in the store during this time. *Chesed L'Avraham* prohibits this,

notably R. Ya'akov of Lisa in his *Mekor Chaim,* differed on this point and required the room to be sold rather than rented.[29]

---

asserting that it is completely implausible that anyone would genuinely sell his business, the source of his income, to another, just to avoid the loss of a week's profits. He contrasts this with the sale of *chametz;* in that case, given that the *chametz* would become halakhically worthless if he maintains it in his possession, it can be assumed that the owner commits to genuinely selling it, as that is the only financially feasible option. (This is the same logic used by the *Bekhor Shor,* in his closing comments, to distinguish between the sale of the *chametz* itself, and that of the animals, which he had considered insincere.) However, it is credible that the mourner may desire to rent out his store for a week rather than sell it, especially in that he would not be able to occupy it himself during that time. Accordingly, he does allow the rental. Nonetheless, he does refer to even the rental as a *ha'aramah;* apparently it is one of lesser offense and would not invalidate the transaction, in contrast with the sale, which is so egregiously and transparently false that it is indeed invalidated in his opinion. (He also states there that *ha'aramot* are effective in regards to both Torah and rabbinic law.) (On this issue, see also *Resp. Ramatz,* YD 86.)

See also *Resp. Beit Shlomo,* OC, 91, who asserts in a responsum regarding *Pesach* that the sale of the rooms is even less plausible than the sale of the animals that the *Bekhor Shor* critiqued; however, his proposed resolution is more complicated. See *Resp. Ori V'Yish'i,* 121, and *Resp. Shivat Tziyon,* 10, for other reasons to use a rental rather than a sale (and see similarly, *Resp. Divrei Malkiel,* IV, 22, 9), as well as *Resp. Tzvi V'Chamid,* OC 41, who notes that legal standards for real estate sales also contribute to the *ha'aramah* perception. See also R. Yehudah Leib Orbach, *Mechokek Yehudah,* OC 448, and *Mo'adim U'Zmannim,* III, 269:3. Note also *Iggerot Moshe,* OC VI, 150, as well as in CM, II, 62, where he notes, in the course of a discussion of a different topic, that it is "obvious" (*pashut*) that for *chametz* purposes real estate should be rented, not sold, due to the obstacle of civil legal requirements.

R. Moshe Shternbuch, *Resp. Teshuvot V'Hanhagot,* VII, 50, raises an additional concern of this nature that impacts a related area. There are some people who, whether or not they sell their *chametz,* do rent out parts of their house prior to Pesach so that they will be exempt from the obligation of *bedikat chametz.* He addresses the question of whether it is acceptable to rent out isolated areas within rooms in a house, and asserts that this should be disqualified as a *ha'aramah,* because no genuine rental would happen in this fashion. It is true, he concedes, that *mekhirat chametz* is itself a *ha'aramah* that is nonetheless accepted, but in that case the *ha'aramah* is in the later reversal of the sale, while the sale itself is credible. If, however, the very terms of the sale, or the rental, are implausible, then a *ha'aramah* that is unacceptable is being employed.

29. This was the original position of the *Bach;* see *Mekor Chaim,* 440:3, in *kuntres acharon,* #1. The *Mekor Chaim* was addressing an additional *ha'aramah* factor he considered severely problematic: the fact that purchaser paid only a nominal down payment to

While these modifications appear to be significant leniencies applied to the requirement to remove the *chametz* from the Jew's home, they can be more easily appreciated with the background context that it is unclear why this condition exists to begin with. *Chametz* that is owned by a non-Jew and is stored in the house of a Jew does not trigger a violation of the prohibition of ownership.[30] As such, technically speaking, there should be no need to remove the *chametz* from the house. Apparently, this is a stringency connected to the particular circumstances of the

---

the value of the *chametz,* and if the *chametz* were to become damaged, the purchaser would certainly not agree to cover the loss, nor would a court compel him to. He felt the only remedy to this issue was to have the purchaser assume ownership of the room. Among those who questioned this position were *Resp. Divrei Chaim,* II, OC, 40, and *Resp. Chayei Aryeh,* 15; among those defending it were *Resp. Minchat Shai,* I, 68. See *Orchot Chaim,* 448:9, for an extensive survey of literature addressing aspects of the *Mekor Chaim*'s position.

R. Ovadiah Yosef, *Resp. Yabbia Omer* X, YD, 38, considers this latter position – in particular, that a temporary sale of real estate was feasible and not an automatic *ha'aramah* – to be the dominant one, and notes that that is of vital importance to the viability of the *hetter mekhirah* for *Shemittah,* observing that it would not be effective if a temporary sale of fields would be considered automatically implausible and thus invalid.

R. Shmuel Engel, *Resp,* ibid., relates this question to the above issue of turning over the key. In his assessment, a sale would obviate the key concern, because a sale would have its own validity due to its spoken terms that cannot be overridden by an implicit message of denying the keys. However, in the case of a rental, which is limited to providing access rather than ownership, denial of that access may indeed negate the arrangement.

The initial issue raised by *Mekor Chaim,* the lack of financial liability on the part of the purchaser, was flagged because the alternative seems to be that the Jew bears financial liability, which would seem to put him in a category that violates the *Pesach* prohibition. A number of the responders dismissed this concern, noting that the Jew would not actually incur any obligation to pay for any destroyed *chametz,* which would have made him interested in the *chametz*'s preservation; he simply will not be compensated by the non-Jew in the event of loss.

However, a related issue of the modern era has troubled some halakhic analysts, namely the question of *chametz* that is insured. If the policy pays out to the Jewish owner, this seems to create a dual issue: this very fact contradicts the premise of non-Jewish ownership, and also, if the Jew does file a claim, this may constitute an act of deception, or perhaps even fraud, against the insurance company. For a discussion of the various aspects of this issue, see *Ratz KaTzvi: B'Ma'agalei HaShanah,* II, 11.

30. *Pesachim* 6a; *Shulchan Arukh,* OC, 440:2.

non-permanent transfer, which expresses itself in a number of concerns.[31] Among the most straightforward of these is the simple realization that given the history and the anticipated future return of this *chametz,* the fear of inadvertent consumption by the original Jewish owner is real.[32]

A highly significant component of this requirement is one that is mentioned by the *Bach* in his original formulation. Were the Jewish owner to maintain both the *chametz* in his house and the keys to enter the storage location, the purchaser would doubt the genuineness of his acquisition, given that his access is so inferior to that of the original owner.[33] Whether or not current arrangements fully satisfy the *Bach*'s intent, a vital principle emerges: the validity of the sale requires active endorsement from both sides, the seller and the buyer.

It should also be noted that transferring ownership of the rooms in which the *chametz* is located has an additional purpose, according to some authorities. These authorities accept the first two premises of the *Bekhor Shor,* that the sale is a *ha'aramah* and is not effective regarding Torah law. However, they do not necessarily accept the other premise of his position, that *bitul* renders the prohibition of *chametz* ownership rabbinic. Transferring the rooms creates another avenue to this status. According to some views,[34] *chametz* owned by a Jew but not stored on his property does not constitute a Torah prohibition. Thus, the real estate transfer converts the issue to a rabbinic one, allowing a *ha'aramah* to be effective according to all opinions.[35]

A third understanding of the disallowed "*ha'aramah*" is that the intent is that the sale should be absolute, and not conditioned on a mandated reversal of the sale after *Pesach.*[36] This requirement

31. See *Chazon Ish,* OC 124; *Minchat Aharon,* pp. 135–137; *Birkat Yechezkel,* Lev., pp. 91–92.
32. See *Pri Chadash,* 448:3.
33. See *Avnei Shoham,* 40:13–14, regarding different gradations of this concern.
34. Such as the *Ran, Ramban,* and Vilna Gaon.
35. See *Resp. Teshuvot V'Hanhagot,* I, 290; V, 107, and 112, and elsewhere. See also *Resp. Chatam Sofer,* OC 119.
36. Indeed, in the *Talmud Yerushalmi,* and in the Lieberman edition of the *Tosefta,* the phrase is included as requiring a "*matanah gemurah,*" with the *Korban HaEdah* explains as excluding a gift conditioned on return.

prompted some discussion, as the general rule is that a gift conditioned on eventual return, a "*matanah al menat le-hachazir*," does constitute, for the duration of its term, a gift. Accordingly, strictly speaking, the transaction should be valid, despite its limited term, and should successfully remove the Jew from ownership of the *chametz* during that time. Here, again, explanations that are offered reflect the two basic concerns about *ha'aramot* in general. To some, the issue is that a transaction of this type does indeed undermine the sincerity of the process in a fundamental way. For example, the *Radbaz*[37] understood that the condition of return transformed the transaction into one in which the non-Jew is expected to safeguard the *chametz*, and that a sale contingent on any future detail cannot be considered absolute until that condition has been clearly fulfilled.[38]

To others, however, the issue was not the validity of the transfer, but rather the attitude which a condition of reversibility displayed towards the issue at hand. Thus, some felt the objection was not fundamental, but rather an expression of the stringency that should appropriately be shown to the prohibition of *chametz*.[39]

There are significant implications as to which of these understandings is correct. If a conditional sale somehow calls into question the validity of the sale itself, the stakes are high: the owner may remain in violation of the Torah prohibition of retaining his *chametz*, which would be permanently forbidden after *Pesach*. By contrast, if the issue was a stringency due to the severity of *chametz*, and perhaps even a function of rabbinic law alone, the conditional sale would violate the spirit of the

---

37. *Resp.* V, 1416.
38. See also *Resp. K'tav Sofer*, OC 90. See *Chazon Yechezkel* to the *Tosefta*, ch. 2, #6, who asserts that in the case of a sale conditioned on return the *chametz* remains the property of the Jew. However, note the objection of *Mechokek Yehudah*, OC 448:7, to the original claim of the *Radbaz*.
39. See, for example, *Hagahot Maimoni, Hil. Shabbat*, 6:1:2, and *Magen Avraham*, OC 448:5. In fact, the *Radbaz* himself takes this position in a different responsum (I, 240). R. Yisrael Yehoshua of Kutno considers the positions in *Resp. Yeshuot Malko*, OC, 39. See also *Resp. Avnei Nezer*, YD, 182:2, who asserts that the sale is saved from disqualifying *ha'aramah* status by the fact that the seller is willing to allow the purchaser to keep the *chametz*, should he be ready to pay full value.

law, and perhaps the spirit of *mitzvah* observance overall, but would not carry the consequences of an invalid sale.[40]

The *Terumat HaDeshen,* in a responsum[41] that requires a non-reversible transfer, makes it clear that it would still be acceptable if the non-Jewish recipient was a friend of the Jew who understood that the *chametz* should be preserved for return to him after *Pesach,* and fully intended to do so, so long as no explicit condition of transaction required him to;[42] he even adds "and such is appropriate to instruct in practice" (*v'khein rauy l'horot*).[43] This is indeed consistent with how the sale is conducted generally. The *Beit Yosef* concludes with this understanding and it is this that is recorded in *Shulchan Arukh.*[44]

---

40. See the analysis on this point of *Machaneh Ephraim, Hil. Ma'akhalot Asurot,* 8:16, and *Birkat Yechezkel al HaTorah,* Lev., pp. 83–87. Regarding the practical implications of *chametz* sold under this condition, see the sources quoted in R. Nachman Kahana, *Orchot Chaim,* 448:14. See also the extensive discussion of temporary sales of *chametz* in R. Yitzchak Mandel, *Resp. Cheker Halakhah,* II, 91–96.

    There is an in-between possibility as well. Some assert that the issue with the conditional sale is the possibility that the purchaser will renege on the agreement, thus retroactively invalidating the sale. However, others object to that as a consideration, noting that as long as the purchaser does not renege, the sale remains valid, and therefore this should not be a reason to disqualify all conditional sales regardless. This exchange yields another formulation: the problem with the conditional sale is simply the fact that it is tenuous, and subject to abrogation by the purchaser, despite the full commitment of the seller. Accordingly, the reason to prohibit the conditional sale is that it is an inadequate method of disposing of one's *chametz,* in that the finality of the sale is uncertain and out of the hands of the seller to guarantee.

    Another distinction between the various explanations would be whether the issue is specifically a condition to return the *chametz,* or any condition at all put on the sale. See *Chazon Yechezkel,* ibid.

41. #120.

42. See also R. Ya'akov Di Boton, *Resp. Edut L'Ya'akov,* 116, who defends this manner of sale through textual proof. However, since there cannot be a stipulation guaranteeing the return, if the purchaser should decide to instead sell the *chametz* to a third party, that sale must be recognized as valid.

43. See the extensive analysis and support of the *Terumat HaDeshen's* position in R. Moshe Ze'ev Margolios, *Resp. Agudat Ezov,* YD, 15.

44. OC 448:3.

While the sale could not be made contingent on a future return, it is nonetheless clear from the *Shulchan Arukh* and other major sources that the sale is valid when the return is an unspoken understanding, and in fact, even if there is some verbal reference to that return at the time of the initial transfer.[45] A number of sources make reference to such a comment (sourced in the *Tosefta,* in the continuation of the boat scenario)[46] expressed by the Jew at that point, that essentially conveys the message that the original Jewish owner would be willing to pay more than another potential buyer would for that *chametz.*[47]

The inability to lock down the repurchase was the subject of a fascinating responsum by the *Mas'at Binyamin,*[48] R. Binyamin Aharon Solnick (1530–1620). The question involved unscrupulous Jews who would rush after *Pesach* to buy the *chametz* of different Jews that had been sold to a non-Jew. Knowing that the non-Jew had paid only a nominal amount, there was an opportunity here to acquire for one's self a significant amount at a very low markup. The original owner would then find that the *chametz* that they believed they could rely on reacquiring was no longer available.

---

45. There is some discussion as to a situation where the particular *chametz* has some sentimental value, and the original owner wishes for it to be preserved in its original state and returned to him, such as food received by *Chasidim* from a revered rebbe; see R. Moshe Greenwald, *Resp. Arugat HaBosem,* OC, 112, and R. Menachem Mendel Schneerson, *Shulchan Menachem,* OC, II, 226. Both authors recommend against including this item in the sale, but for different reasons and with different alternative suggestions.
46. *Pesachim* 2:7, and in *Yerushalmi Pesachim* 2:2.
47. This is the understanding of the *Bach,* commenting on the version that appears in the *Tur,* OC 448, and citing the *Agudah,* implying that even an explicit pledge to repurchase is acceptable; see there also for variant readings and interpretations. See, in particular, the formulation in the *Rosh, Pesachim,* 2:1.

    According to R. Yechezkel Abramsky, *Chazon Yechezkel,* #7, this statement renders the transaction a *ha'aramah,* but it is permitted because of *bitul,* an apparent reference to the position of the *Bekhor Shor.* Presumably, the statement does not invalidate the sale on any level, especially as it is not even a conditional sale; accordingly, this understanding seems to convey that were Torah law to be involved, anything that undermines the spirit of the process would be inappropriate.
48. *Resp.* 43.

The *Mas'at Binyamin* wrote poignantly about the anguish this behavior caused him. Many of the Jews selling the *chametz,* he noted, were merchants who were completely dependent on that *chametz* for their livelihood. If the sale arrangement were to become untenable due to the actions of unprincipled opportunists, these merchants would be financially ruined. And yet, the free market was a reality, and guaranteeing the resale to the original owner was unacceptable. There seems to be no solution, but the *Mas'at Binyamin* wrote that he would be unable to rest until he found one.

Indeed, he did come up with a creative solution. He drew on a number of Talmudic sources, mostly dealing with the regulations of marketplace competition, in which there is some degree of protectionism legislated by the Rabbis. Among these rules is the notion that a businessman who has extended efforts within a certain market is given priority in accessing that market. Given that the original owner of the *chametz* is far more invested in this *chametz* than the devious interloper, his rights would be recognized here to the point of enforcement.[49]

In authoring this responsum, the *Mas'at Binyamin* deftly walked a tightrope. From the perspective of the non-Jewish purchaser, the sale is absolute and without any preconditions limiting his autonomy regarding the resale of the *chametz.* Regarding, however, a scheming outsider who would undermine the process, a clear moral line is drawn.[50]

---

49. A similar conclusion was also reached independently by *Resp. Chatam Sofer,* OC, 115. The *Mas'at Binyamin* also made use of the mishnaic discussion of "the law of Sicarii" (*Gittin* 5:6). This addressed a situation in which violent individuals would extort fields from their original owners with threats. Under these circumstances, the original owner is given priority in reacquiring the land, as he can maintain that he never meant to sell it away in the first place. The *mishnah* then proceeds to apply this concept even to less dramatic circumstances that also involve property sales that may have been carried out without full intent, again giving those original owners priority in reacquisition. *Mas'at Binyamin* advances a number of arguments to assert that the *chametz* situation is an even more compelling fit for such policies.
50. *Resp. Beit Shlomo,* OC 83, mentions the ruling of *Mas'at Binyamin* as a given in a responsum mainly directed against a Jewish seller who would prohibit the non-Jewish purchaser from selling to anyone else, considering that a *ha'aramah* that

This narrow balance is also significant when taken in conjunction with the creative analysis of a later author, R. Shmuel ben Yosef HaLevi, in his *Resp. Bigdei Yesha.*[51] R. Shmuel was greatly concerned with the general practice of the sale, in which the non-Jewish purchaser paid a very small amount as a down payment. Often, the purchaser is destitute, with no conceivable possibility that he would be able to come up with the rest of the payment necessary to enable him to keep the *chametz* in the long term. It would seem that the only reason to go through such a process is to create a temporary holding pattern until the original owner can buy it back after *Pesach.* As such, it should be an unacceptable *ha'aramah.*

To further explain the problem, the non-Jew does understand that the Jew must sell the *chametz* or otherwise forfeit it all. However, why not sell it for as much as he can? Certainly, with minimal effort, he will find higher bidders. The only reason he is selling for so little must be to lock in his ability to reacquire. In fact, suggests *Bigdei Yesha,* this must be why the original scenario in the *tosefta* involves travel on a boat. In these confined circumstances, the Jew can find no other buyers before the onset of *Pesach* prohibitions, so it is understandable that he will sell to the only available non-Jewish passenger, for whatever price he can pay. But, absent such extreme circumstances, it could not be explained other than as an effort to preserve his access following *Pesach,* and is thus a *ha'aramah.*

Bigdei Yesha asserted that all could be explained neatly through the following foundation. It is true that the non-Jewish purchaser, at the moment, has no possibility of paying the full price of the *chametz.* However, the Jew is providing him with a business opportunity that may prove beneficial to them both.

The original owner will set a price close to the full value of the *chametz,* but with some significant reduction. The purpose of that

---

he would be inclined to prohibit after the fact. R. Moshe Feinstein, *Resp. Iggerot Moshe,* OC, I, 48, questions the position of *Mas'at Binyamin* and takes a different perspective, while the *Mishnah Berurah,* 448:13, cites a similar position in the name of "*acharonim.*"

51. *Resp.,* 2, first published in 1844.

reduction is to allow the purchaser the potential for a profit, if he is able to find a second purchaser who can pay the actual value of the *chametz.* To enable this possibility, the seller is willing to allow the first purchaser to put down a minimal down payment, and convert the rest to a debt. If, after *Pesach,* that plan has not been realized, the original owner will buy the *chametz* back with a slight increase for his efforts.

Bigdei Yesha maintained that this framework addresses all the issues, most importantly, establishing that this sale of *chametz* is not a *ha'aramah* at all. The seller fully commits his property to be sold, and the buyer genuinely has a potential value in purchasing the *chametz,* and will have his losses covered with a modest profit if that potential does not materialize. Further, all parties understand that the most likely eventuality is that it will not materialize, while they can also accept the small possibility that it may.

Of course, *Bigdei Yesha*'s elaborate model does not necessarily represent, in all of its aspects, the working understanding of every participant or advocate of *mekhirat chametz* throughout the long history of its practice. Nonetheless, as a model that is mutually beneficial, transparent, and unwilling to tolerate any degree of *ha'aramah,* it is illuminating.[52]

UNIQUE FACTORS AFFECTING THE RELATIONSHIP BETWEEN *CHAMETZ* AND *HA'ARAMOT*

What emerges is the fact that the question of *mekhirat chametz* as a *ha'aramah,* intensely controversial in recent generations, was explicitly addressed in the writings of the *rishonim,* and the common element in their approach is that the issue is determined by how it is done (or, in

52. *Bigdei Yesha* also makes use of his approach to address a number of other debated points within *mekhirat chametz,* among them the issue of rental versus sale of a location; rental is vastly preferable, as a part of a house has no resale value to any third-party. He also maintained that his model allowed for the sale of animals, challenging the initial position of the *Bekhor Shor,* that such was not permissible. Of course, his entire thesis is completely at odds with the *Bekhor Shor,* who was assuming the sale to be at least some degree of a *ha'aramah,* while *Bigdei Yesha* is insisting it cannot be a *ha'aramah* at all.

one interpretation, by how regularly it is done), rather than the assumption being that *mekhirat chametz* is automatically a *ha'aramah.* (A possible exception to this may be the Rabbenu Yerucham in the *Beit Yosef,* in his initial reaction that *mekhirat chametz* is a *ha'aramah* that the *tosefta* nonetheless legitimates; however, his conclusion, that the *ha'aramah* reference is to an automatically reversed sale, may constitute a retraction of that statement.)

The idea of a *ha'aramah* status arising more from execution than from concept is evident in that in the writings of some *rishonim* the concern is expressed also regarding *bitul,* which is mentioned in the Talmud and is in fact considered an obligation. Through *bitul,* one declares the *chametz* that may remain in his possession over *Pesach,* following all attempts to eliminate it, to be worthless and of no interest to the original owner. However, this is presumably only effective if done with full sincerity; as such, the clause of "as long as he does not engage in *ha'aramah*" is applied by some commentaries[53] to *bitul* as well.[54]

As referenced above, the *Bekhor Shor*[55] asserts (at least initially) that *mekhirat chametz* is indeed a *ha'aramah,* emphasizing that in this case, neither the seller nor the buyer are actually in the business of these transactions, and the buyer is often financially incapable of actually following through with the purchase. For this reason he maintains it is ineffective against a Biblical prohibition of owning *chametz.* He assumes, however, that the *chametz* at hand is only subject to a rabbinical prohibition, because, as the Talmud[56] states in the context of *bedikat chametz,* the *bitul* of *chametz* is effective to negate the Torah prohibition.[57] However,

---

53. See, for example. *Chiddushei Rabbenu David, Pesachim* 6b, s.v. *mihu.* See, at length, *Resp. Pnei Yehoshua,* OC, 14.
54. As to why the *Bekhor Shor* did not raise his objection to *bitul,* see *Minchat Aharon,* pp. 152–154.
55. *Pesachim* 21a
56. *Pesachim* 10a.
57. Others who accepted this premise include *Ketzot HaChoshen,* 194:4; R. Meshulam Igra, *Resp.* 39:1; R. Aharon Walkin, *Resp. Zekan Aharon,* II, 23; and R. Natan Note Kahane, *Resp. Divrei Rinanah,* 30 (and see the references in the footnotes, #11, by

many *acharonim*[58] challenged that premise, noting that the *chametz* that is negated is not the same *chametz* as that which is sold, and thus a Biblical

R. Yitzchak Hershkowitz). The *Ridbaz*, in his introduction to *Beit Ridbaz*, begins from this assumption and maintains that the selling of *chametz* is actually a stringency mandated by the Rabbis to enhance the nullification (this is a part of his argument against the *Hetter Mekhirah* for *Shemittah*, in maintaining that the selling of *chametz* should not be seen as a precedent). See also R. Yitzchak Shmuel Shechter, *Resp. Yashiv Yitzchak* X, OC 9.

R. Yosef Shaul Nathanson, in many of his responsa, overtly accepts the premise, writing repeatedly that *mekhirat chametz* is only necessary on a rabbinic level because of *bitul* and is thus effective despite being a *ha'aramah*; see *Resp. Shoel U'Meishiv, kama*, I, 84, 93; *tinyana*, II, 63 (in *telita'ah*, I, 219, he accepts the premise regarding *ha'aramot* without reference to *chametz*). However, it is interesting to compare that in at least three other responsa (*kama*, I, 95 and II, 42, and *tinyana*, IV, 80) he considers specific incidents of *mekhirat chametz* where sales were called into question, and he addresses the circumstances to explain why in those cases "there is no concern of *ha'aramah*" without invoking the general attitude. More strikingly, in another responsum (*kama*, III, 220), he expresses the objection (mentioned below) of the detractors to the *Bekhor Shor*'s position in strong terms, and leaves it as an unanswered question. He does, however, offer a resolution in a later responsum (*tinyana*, II, 77).

There perhaps is some irony in that for some of these authorities, acceptance of the argument of the *Bekhor Shor* leads to a lenient position; essentially that *mekhirat chametz* is only necessary to address a rabbinic prohibition and thus can itself rely on various leniencies. Accordingly, for example, the language of the *Pri Megadim* (*Eishel Avraham* 448:10), in expressing his disagreement, is "the implication of all the decisors is that an absolute sale is required, with no *ha'aramah*, and [the sold *chametz*] is not included in the *bitul* at all." Significantly, many of these authorities are acknowledging the *Bekhor Shor*'s position only in the direction of leniency, in that they believe that the sale is only necessary by dint of rabbinic law; but they do not necessarily acknowledge the stringency of his position, i.e. that the sale of *chametz* is fundamentally flawed, and would only work for purposes of rabbinic law. See *Resp. Shevivei Eish*, OC, 31:4.

58. See for example *Pri Megadim*, ibid.; *Mekor Chaim* 448:9; *Shulchan Arukh HaRav*, *Hil. Mekhirat Chametz; Nishmat Adam, Hil. Pesach*, #3; *Resp. Beit Shearim*, OC, 197; *Resp. Maharsham*, IV, 66; R. Aryeh Leib Tzinz, *Haggadah Birkat Shir, dinim l'Pesach*, #5, and (at greater length regarding the details of the *Bekhor Shor*'s position) *Magen Ha-Elef*, OC 448:10; *Resp. Chatam Sofer*, OC, 63; *Resp. Uri V'Yishi*, 121; *Resp. Mahari HaKohen*, OC, 17; *Resp. Ateret Chakhamim*, YD, 14; *Resp. Yabbia Omer*, X, YD, 38. See also *Resp. Sha'arei Deah*, I, 5; R. Yechezkel Paneth, *Resp. Mareh Yechezkel*, 21; and see the lengthy analysis of *Resp. Minchat Yitzchak*, VIII:41. See also the discussion of R. Asher Weiss in *Haggadah Minchat Asher, sha'arei hateshuvot*, 16. R. Tuviah Goldstein, *Resp. Emek Halakhah*, II, 36:2, asserts that it is the view of the majority

prohibition would still attach; as such, one who would utilize *mekhirat chametz* must be comfortable that it is effective on a Torah level.[59]

One alternative path to understanding a lesser standard for sale quality regarding *chametz* is to focus on the mechanism of *bitul* and what it says about the nature of *chametz* ownership on *Pesach.* The nature of *bitul*'s functionality was questioned by the *rishonim,* with some noting that it does not satisfy the requirements for "*hefker,*" a formal declaration deeming property ownerless. Accordingly, the *Ran* asserts that *bitul* is

---

of decisors that the sale is an absolute sale, separate from the *bitul,* and that is the logical position; this is also the conclusion maintained in *Resp. Shevet HaLevi,* IV, 49.

Many assert that even according to this position, it is proper to conduct the *bitul* after the sale, as the reverse order calls into question the integrity of the *bitul,* even regarding the chametz that is not sold; see *Chatam Sofer,* ibid.; and R. Aharon Miasnik, *Minchat Aharon, Pesach,* 11:9. This relates as well to the question of whether a *bitul* after the sale can impact *chametz* that was designated for sale, but the sale was for some reason invalid. See *S'dei Chemed, Asufat Dinim, ma'arekhet chametz u-matzah,* 5:45, who cites R. Yozpe of Vaklava that the phrase found in the text of the *bitul,* "*d'biarti v'dlo biarti,*" refers to the possibility of invalid sales (the literal translation, "that I have destroyed or have not destroyed," is difficult, as *chametz* that was destroyed would not need *bitul;* however, the same could be maintained about *chametz* that is sold). As a practical matter, the *S'dei Chemed* distinguishes between *chametz* that was sold in an ineffective manner and that which was not sold at all (for example, the sale was delayed and neglected).

However, some authorities maintain the inverse position, that specifically a *bitul* prior to a sale can potentially include that which was ineffectively sold, but a subsequent *bitul* would by nature exclude that which was intended for sale; see *Resp. Beit Shlomo,* OC 72, and *Resp. Ramatz,* 29:3, both discussed in *S'dei Chemed.* See *Avnei Shoham,* 44. See also the discussion in *Mikraei Kodesh, Pesach,* I, 66–67.

59. The Kogzalglover Rav offers a creative explanation of the *Bekhor Shor*'s view in his *Resp. Eretz Tzvi,* I, 84. See similar approaches in *Resp. Noda BeYehudah, kamma,* OC, 19 and *Resp. Pnei Meivin,* OC, 97; however, see the objection of *Resp. Achiezer,* III, 1:3.

R. Moshe Shternbuch, *Resp. Teshuvot V'Hanhagot* I, 90; II, 217; and V. 107:1, and 13, utilizes a different approach to downgrade the prohibition to rabbinic, with various ramifications (and note, however, V, 12, where he raises questions on his approach and adopts a particularly stringent stance).

It is noteworthy that R. Meshulam Igra, *Resp.* 39:1, who as noted above fully endorses the position of *Bekhor Shor,* requires that the sale happen before the *bitul,* because a sale afterwards would invalidate the *bitul,* and only the sale would remain, which he emphasizes is an ineffective *ha'aramah.* His view is also recorded in *Igra Ramah, dinim mi-hilkhot Pesach,* #6–8.

only effective because *chametz,* in that it is by Torah law prohibited in all benefit to Jews, is essentially not subject to actual ownership. Instead, there is, as the Talmud[60] teaches, a quasi-ownership that is imposed by the Torah representing the prohibition. It is this lower level of ownership that can be neutralized by a declaration of divestment.

As such, it is possible that the understanding is that after this quasi-ownership has been addressed through *bitul,* there remains a rabbinic obligation to take further steps, which is what the sale is accomplishing. Even if the sale is inferior or insincere, it is adequate for this purpose, as it need only address a rabbinic obligation that is itself tailored towards a degree of ownership that is itself inferior, and has already been diminished through *bitul.*[61]

A version of this formulation appeared in the writings of an earlier author, the aforementioned *Mas'at Binyamin.*[62] He understands the *Ran*'s explanation of *bitul* to reflect more broadly a weaker notion of ownership regarding *chametz* on *Pesach,* and suggests that this explains the tolerance that is found for otherwise flawed processes of sale.[63]

---

60. *Pesachim* 6b.

61. See also R. Asher Weiss, *Haggadat Minchat Asher, Sha'arei HaTeshuvah,* 1, who is inclined to agree that the sold *chametz* and that which is subject to *bitul* are two different groups, but suggests as an explanation for the *Bekhor Shor*'s position that the *bitul* is done on all *chametz* conditionally, in case the sale is ineffective. See also *Shevilei David,* CM, 194:3, and OC 448:2.

62. Resp., 59.

63. Notably, the *Mas'at Binyamin* takes pains to distinguish between the different rabbinic uses of the word *ha'aramah* in this context. It may be the case that this logic allows us to make use of the sale that, for example, we know will be reversed; it should not be taken to mean that we are unconcerned about overt dishonesty. In other words, he would not use this approach to permit *chametz* after *Pesach* in a situation when there is reason to believe that the owner did not even make any effort to sell it.

This is particularly relevant because there is a discussion in the later literature as to whether or not to accept the view of *Mas'at Binyamin,* and if so, how far could it be extended: would it be applicable in a situation where the sale was definitely invalid? What if there was no sale at all, but the owner regrets that fact; would that regret suffice to satisfy the lower standard of disassociating oneself from his *chametz?* Later authorities found it difficult to accept these conclusions (see *Resp. Chemdat Shlomo,* OC, 1, and *Haggadat Minchat Asher, Sha'arei haTeshuvah,* 1.) Presumably, the *Mas'at Binyamin* would also not accept them either; his application was only to extend the *Ran*'s understanding of quasi-ownership to explain why a transaction that assumes

However, this explanation is open to a number of challenges, and is not what is articulated by the *Bekhor Shor*.[64]

R. Chaim Chizkiyah Medini, in his extensive halakhic compendium *S'dei Chemed*,[65] challenges the premise that *mekhirat chametz* is a *ha'aramah*, supporting his point both with arguments and with the opinions of other authors. In addition to citing many objections regarding the relationship of *bitul* and the sale, he questions the widespread assumption that even the *Bekhor Shor* actually considered *mekhirat chametz* a *ha'aramah*. He notes that he seems to conclude differently: his main subject is the sale of animals over *Pesach*, which he believes is done insincerely and is both ineffective and unnecessary. Regarding the sale of *chametz* itself, however, he seems to concede that the owners, seeing no better option available, will sell the *chametz* with complete commitment, and thus it will be a genuine transfer.[66] This is also the position recorded by his descendant R. Chaim Mordechai Margolios in his commentary to the *Shulchan Arukh*,[67] citing his uncle, who was the son of the *Bekhor Shor*. If this is correct, then even the *Bekhor Shor*

later reversal, or is subject to a dispute among *rishonim* as to its validity, is acceptable, in the latter case after the fact. This is presumably also relevant to addressing the objection of *Resp. Avnei Tzedek*, OC 52. Regarding one who mistakenly believes his *chametz* to have been sold, see also *Mikra'ei Kodesh, Pesach*, I, 68.

64. Another resolution is asserted by R. Yitzchak Shmelkes in his *Resp. Beit Yitzchak*, CM, 70:4. See also *Mikra'ei Kodesh, Pesach*, I, 66:1, and, more extensively, #67. Note also *Resp. Sha'arei Tzedek*, OC, 69, and see the approach in *Resp. Har HaKarmel*, OC, 13.
65. Vol. VIII, *ma'arekhet chametz u'matzah* 9:15.
66. R. Shlomo Kluger, *Resp. HaElef Likha Shlomo*, 229, argues that the same logic should apply to the sale of the animals too; he proves that the motivation to commit to the sale comes not from the financial loss, but from the fear of transgression, which applies also in the case of the animals. Notably, it is clear from his responsum that he is focusing on a different *ha'aramah* concern than the *Bekhor Shor* is; as we have noted, this is a common pattern. After asserting that the sale of the animals will be executed sincerely, he writes that there is still the problem of "*ha'aramah*"; presumably, he is referring to the desire to escape the *halakah*'s applicability. To address that, he recommends selling the animals and the feed to two separate non-Jews, so that the *ha'aramah* will not be as blatant. See also his suggestion in ibid., 230, as well as the distinction he draws in ibid., 247, where he suggests the *ha'aramah* concern would be mitigated if the purchaser is wealthy and could pay for the animals.
67. *Sha'arei Teshuvah*, OC 448:8. Similarly, R. Ephraim Zalman Margolios assumes in his *Makneh U'Kinyan* that his grandfather distinguished between the validity

did not oppose *mekhirat chametz* in and of itself, and thus it becomes unnecessary to establish the sale as applying only to circumstances of rabbinic law to satisfy his opinion.

It must be noted, however, that as a matter of practice, there are many who restrict the sale of *chametz* to that which is prohibited on a rabbinic level, essentially accepting the limitation initially mentioned by the *Bekhor Shor,* but without relying on *bitul* to shift the status, and thus applying the standard more stringently.[68] There are a number of reasons for this policy, including concerns over the adherence to standards demanded for the sale (such as removal from the premises,[69] or other conditions).[70] Nonetheless, there are many who did not accept this limitation; R. Eliezer Waldenberg, in his *Resp. Tzitz Eliezer,*[71] declares that many scholars and Torah giants, already in earlier generations, sold absolute *chametz,* and immediately following *Pesach* served that *chametz* to pious guests.[72]

THE CONTROVERSY OVER THE COLLECTIVE SALE

In the nineteenth century, a major escalation developed in the controversy surrounding *mekhirat chametz* that emerged, ironically, from efforts to enhance its effectiveness.[73] In the earlier iterations of the sale, individual Jews sold their *chametz* to non-Jews of their acquaintance. As the laws surrounding these transactions are quite complex, mistakes would often be made, sometimes serious enough to invalidate the sale and thus to defeat the entire purpose. Examples of the most egregious mistakes included conditioning the sale on full payment after the holiday (which would retroactively nullify the sale completely) or conducting the sale

---

of the sale of *chametz* itself and that of the sales of the animals over *Pesach,* which he rejected.

68. See the discussion and the suggestion in *Resp. Hosif Moshe,* 39.
69. See *Elyah Rabbah,* OC 448:7.
70. See, for example, *Resp. Shevivei Eish,* OC, III, 12.
71. XX, 51:2. See *Haggadat Minchat Asher,* p. 284, and *Avnei Shoham,* 47.
72. See also *Avnei Shoham,* 47.
73. A detailed history of this episode, by Dan Rabinowitz, can be found at Kitniyot and Mechirat Chametz: Paradoxical Approaches to the Chametz Prohibition – The Seforim Blog. https://seforimblog.com/2022/04/kitniyot-and-mechirat-chametz-paradoxical-approaches-to-the-chametz-prohibition/.

after the time when *chametz* becomes prohibited in benefit (which would make the sale impossible). To avoid these errors, a process developed in various communities across Russia and Poland to concentrate the sale into one transaction, in that all of the Jews in a given region would sell their *chametz* to a single Jew, who would in turn sell all of it to the gentile purchaser.[74]

This single, collective sale attracted objections, with a flashpoint of the controversy erupting in the Romanian city of Yos (Jassy), between the two rabbis of the city, R. Yosef Landau, who had instituted this system, and R. Aharon Moshe Tauber (Toibesh), who objected.[75] Among other complaints, the general thrust is that the innovation brought the *ha'aramah* allegation to a whole new level. It is one thing to claim that an individual Jew is sincerely selling his own *chametz* to an individual non-Jewish purchaser. It is a much greater strain on credulity to maintain that a single Jew, who does not engage in this business the entire year, suddenly and immediately before *Pesach*, would decide to become the purchaser of the *chametz* of hundreds or thousands of other people, prior to selling all of that to a single non-Jew. While there were many details to the objection, the repeated emphasis was that it pushed the "*ha'aramah*" element beyond any tolerable limits.

Further, he argued, this process added a *ha'aramah* to what was already a *ha'aramah,* itself an unacceptable innovation, adding a quantitative offense to the qualitative offense. This in turn besmirches the original *mekhirat chametz,* as it implies that this degree of implausibility was always an accepted element of the sale.

The eminent authority R. Shlomo Kluger was asked to weigh in on the matter, and in a responsum[76] he supported the innovation, suggesting it had Talmudic precedent.[77] R. Kluger's responsum is reflective

---

74. The first Lubavitcher Rebbe, R. Schneur Zalman, records this process in the responsa printed in his *Shulchan Arukh HaRav,* #4.
75. His objections were published a number of times and are republished in the responsa of his grandson, R. Uri Shraga Toibesh, *Resp. Ori V'Yishi.* 121.
76. Printed in the back of R. David Shlomo Eibshutz's *Ne'ot Deshe,* in a special section, #2.
77. *Pesachim* 13a, with Rashi's commentary. *Resp. Shem Olam,* OC 2 and 3, argues with this interpretation and provides an alternative explanation of the text. Note also *Resp. Be'er Yitzchak,* 1.

of some of the balance of considerations sometimes found regarding these subjects: he notes that the detractors of the collective sales have not served as rabbis of large Jewish populations, and thus may not appreciate the degree of error that can enter into the practice of the masses. The collective sale, with all of its weaknesses, might still be considered by the rabbinate to be a preferable alternative. His language repeatedly bespeaks the practicality he associates with rabbinic responsibility. He critiques the objector's failure to perform a spiritual cost-benefit analysis, exhorts him to focus on the big picture and to choose the "lesser evil," one that he acknowledges involves some compromises and convolutions.

Still, despite his fundamental defense of the concept, R. Kluger acknowledged various practical concerns and pitfalls, and advised God-fearing Jews to continue conducting their own personal sales, enlisting rabbinic help when necessary.

THE TRANSITION TO THE RABBINIC AGENT

Whatever position is taken regarding this historical debate, the issue is mostly academic today because an alternative practice developed, and this is the more common approach currently.[78] In this version, the single Jew at the center of the sale does not himself purchase the *chametz*. Rather, this individual, usually a rabbi, is empowered by the others as an agent to effect the transfer. In this formation, there is no longer the extraordinary claim of an implausible purchase involved, but the significant advantage of having one knowledgeable individual conduct the complicated sale is preserved.[79]

---

78. The *Arukh HaShulchan* (OC 448:27), first published in 1884, writes that this has been the practice for many generations.

79. Notably, the eminent authority R. Yosef Shaul Nathanson, *Resp. Shoel U'Meishiv*, II, 2:77, raised technical objections to this innovation, citing elements that he felt either exacerbated the *ha'aramah* issue, or were subject to higher standards already because of the *ha'aramah* status, and actually preferred the previous method. See *S'dei Chemed*, VIII, 9:6, pp. 380–381, and *Minchat Aharon*, pp. 133–134 for responses to his objections. It should also be noted that contemporary methods of sale often address some or all of his concerns.

See also R. Tuviah Freund, *Mo'adim L'Simchah, Nisan* I, #7, n8, who expresses a number of other complications in the "agent" model, and accordingly recommends that the sale of the firstborn animal should be done through selling to the

The involvement of a rabbinic intermediary did bring its own questions. One issue that requires clarification, with significant ramifications, is the status of the rabbi; i.e., is he purchasing the *chametz* from his congregants, and then reselling all of it to a non-Jewish purchaser? This would be only marginally different than the model that had triggered such controversy, albeit with a more trustworthy and knowledgeable individual at the center. In addition to the plausibility concerns, there is still the fear that even a learned single purchaser may commit an error in the complicated resale to the non-Jew, thus accomplishing nothing other than concentrating all the transgressions of *chametz* ownership within himself.

Rather, the far more common model has become the appointing of the rabbi as an agent, who never himself takes ownership of the *chametz* but is empowered to sell it on behalf of the actual owners.[80] The authorization is usually effected by the owner putting into writing the specific information regarding the type of *chametz*, the value, and the location, and then signing to his agreement that the *chametz* be sold through the efforts of the rabbinic agent.

Generally, some kind of symbolic transaction is performed to concretize the appointment. Technically, this action is not necessary in order to validate the appointment of an agency for sale; many understand that it is performed per the recommendation of the Rambam[81] to ensure that the arrangement is taken seriously, a particular advantage when it comes to the sale of *chametz*.[82] Others recommend a more formal process in order to satisfy civil legal requirements for the appointment

---

intermediary, rather than appointing him as an agent. See also ibid., n. 7, regarding at what point in history the rabbinic agent model came into use.

The question of whether it is crucial that the owners realize that they are appointing the rabbi as an agent, rather than selling to him (especially in light of the imprecise language often used in making the appointments) is addressed in *Resp. Shevivei Eish*, OC III, 19.

80. On this distinction, see also R. Ya'akov Ariel, *Resp. B'Ohalah Shel Torah*, II, 59.

81. *Hil. Mekhirah* 5:12–13.

82. See the extensive discussion about this in R. Moshe Ze'ev Zorger, *Resp. VaYeshev Moshe*, I, 118, where this practice is specifically related to the *ha'aramah* concerns in the sale of *chametz*.

of agency.[83] These factors are also relevant to the practice of having the seller signing the forms, which many authorities did not consider actually necessary.[84] (This is distinct from the signature on an actual contract of sale, the frequent omission of which being the subject of many earlier responsa and one of the motivations to shift the sale away from the individual owners toward the rabbinic agent.) The rabbi later carries out the actual sale to the non-Jewish purchaser, who takes possession of the written forms with the relevant information.

This information is considered important for the integrity of the sale, but just how important is a matter of dispute. The view of the Rambam[85] was that a sale involving an undefined object was invalid, while the *Tur*[86] was of a different view. The Rambam's position led a number of authorities to maintain that *chametz* that was not identified could not be legitimately sold,[87] while others disagreed, for a number of reasons.[88] R. Moshe Feinstein[89] argued that concern for lack of detail would apply to an individual sale, where smaller numbers are involved and there may indeed be mistaken impressions in the sale. However, for the mass sales done in contemporary times, the numbers are so large that missing details would not impact the buyer's commitment.

Accordingly, one question that sometimes arises is whether the sale can still be effected if the rabbi does not have the forms (e.g., if they have been lost). The importance of the forms lies not only in the proof of authorization, but also in the description of the purchased items to the

83. See *Haggadat Shel Pesach Mo'adim U'Zmannim.*

84. See *Avnei Shoham,* 49:4–5. *Mekor Chaim,* OC 448:8, did consider the signature crucial; see the analysis of his position in *VaYeshev Moshe,* ibid.

85. *Hil. Mekhirah* 21:1–3.

86. CM 241.

87. See *Mekor Chaim,* 448:9, and see also *Resp. HaElef Likha Shlomo,* 253, who takes an absolutely stringent position, even after the fact (however, in #223, he is willing to be lenient under certain circumstances).

88. *Resp. R. Akiva Eiger, tinyana,* 7; *Resp. Be'er Yitzchak,* OC, 6; *Resp. Beit Shlomo,* OC, 70. See also *Resp. Chayei Aryeh,* 15. See also *Resp. Meishiv Mishpat,* III, 6, who, for this and other reasons, validates the sale of absolute *chametz* that belonged to someone who generally does not sell such *chametz,* but whose wife included some in his sale without his knowledge.

89. *Resp. Iggerot Moshe,* OC, I, 150.

buyer, thus calling into question the genuineness of a sale that does not convey this information, essentially a "grab bag" sale. R. Asher Weiss[90] has maintained that an effective sale can nonetheless be conducted, making a number of points on different levels: the information can be recovered later from the original owners; while less than ideal, this deficiency is not more damaging than others than are tolerated for *mekhirat chametz;* and, perhaps most significantly, the sale is technically valid, with the main purpose of the providing of information an enhancement of the seriousness of the seller, which has been accomplished.[91]

The approach of the "rabbinic agent" has a number of advantages to it, among them, as the *S'dei Chemed* asserted, a significant reduction of the "*ha'aramah*" appearance. No longer does one need wonder why a single individual, with no previous involvement in this business, and no credible capitalization, is purchasing and selling, in the course of one day, the *chametz* of an entire locality. By contrast, an agent to carry out a transaction needs no financial capacity or independent motivation, and such agents are commonly appointed.[92] Still, some details remain to be clarified.[93]

---

90. *Haggadat Minchat Asher,* ibid., 2.

91. Others have raised objections (see *Resp. Shevivei Eish,* OC III, 15 and 26). By contrast, R. Moshe Shternbuch, *Mo'adim U'Zmannim,* III, 269:7, insists that specificity in the contracts is highly important, particularly in reference to the location of the *chametz.* If one wishes to include *chametz* in unspecified locations, he recommends listing it as a gift, arguing it is more credible than assuming one would purchase such items. However, in light of other positions of his noted below, it cannot be that he felt this issue to be disqualifying.

92. *Resp. Maharsham,* III, 124, creatively suggests an additional advantage to the collective sale, in that its public nature eliminates concerns of suspicion, which, as noted earlier, he felt is the reason *ha'aramot* are prohibited regarding Torah law. Accordingly, he reasoned, even according to the *Bekhor Shor,* a *ha'aramah* could be utilized for *mekhirat chametz,* even without recourse to *bitul.*

93. One major distinction that would emerge would be in the event that the original Jewish owner dies in between meeting with the rabbi and the sale on *erev Pesach.* If the meeting constituted a sale, the rabbi would still be empowered to resell the *chametz* to the non-Jew, and the heirs would acquire it after *Pesach.* However, if, as is commonly done today, the meeting was an appointment of agency, the rabbi would lose his authority to conduct a sale with the death of the owner, and a new

One issue that emerged from this arrangement stemmed from the fact that the appointing of the rabbi as an agent could be seen as an honor, including the possibility of compensation for his service.[94] As such, there were those who desired to bring such benefits to more than one rabbi, and wanted to appoint multiple agents. This would seem, at first glance, to be problematic, as it would call into question the seriousness of all the sales. Nonetheless, there were authorities who allowed this, reasoning that in any event the original owner is committed to selling, and the inclusion of additional agents comes from benevolence;

---

arrangement would have to be pursued by the heirs prior to *Pesach.* See *Shevivei Eish,* OC, III, 25.

94. Some authorities considered it appropriate to give some remuneration to the intermediary, as a function of a halakhic standard that allows reliance on an agent specifically when he is paid; see, for example, R. Moshe Shternbuch, *Resp. Teshuvot V'Hanhagot,* I, 291 and II, 218 (in the latter responsum he advances another, technical benefit to the sale when the agent is compensated). It is noteworthy, however, that the higher standard of reliability is generally applied to matters of Torah law (see *Eiruvin* 32a); according to R. Shternbuch and others, *mekhirat chametz* itself is only acceptable in regard to rabbinic law. (R. Shternbuch alludes to this point in the latter responsum but does not reconcile the apparent contradiction.)

The above may be true because compensating the intermediary may convert him from an agent of the owner to an employee who serves as his extension. As noted by *Divrei Malkiel,* IV, 22:17, this may bring additional advantages, among them related to an issue of practical importance that was debated by authorities, i.e. the status of *chametz* purchased after the intermediary is appointed. If the intermediary was himself an interim purchaser, it is clear that only *chametz* that was in ownership before that transaction is included. If he is an agent, there is room to debate as to whether such agency can include property not yet in ownership. If he is an employee, it is more plausible that he may continue to act on behalf of his employer, even regarding *chametz* that is acquired later. See also *Resp. Tzemach Tzedek,* OC, 46, who uses different logic to permit. See *S'dei Chemed,* 9:7, and *Ma'adanei Yom Tov, mo'adim,* IV, 96.

For a survey of other explanations of the practice of compensation, see *Mo'adim L'Simchah,* pp. 221–222. It seems reasonable as well to suggest that this practice developed to some degree to counter the *ha'aramah* aspects of *mekhirat chametz;* both so that the seller should take the process more seriously, and also so that while the main monetary value of the *chametz* is being preserved, some expenditure should nonetheless be extended toward this *mitzvah.*

As to potential financial liability for the rabbi, should he fail to execute the sale (thus resulting in the *chametz* becoming worthless), see *Resp. Shevivei Eish,* OC III, 25.

accordingly, at least one sale should be valid and the others harmless.[95] However, it seems difficult to avoid the ambiguity this can create regarding the buyer, and other authorities discouraged this practice.[96]

An additional issue connected to the rabbinic agent involves the reacquisition of the *chametz* by the original owners after *Pesach*. It is considered vital that this be done through a genuine acquisition, to avoid the appearance of a *ha'aramah*.[97] In the case of a direct sale, the original owner could simply purchase the *chametz* back from the buyer. When an intermediary is involved, some clarification may be needed to establish the functionality of his acquiring *chametz* on behalf of another who is not present, and, more commonly in the contemporary context, multiple parties. In addition to technical issues with the effectiveness of agency in these circumstances,[98] there is the question of whether this ability is actually included in the original authorization to sell. Theoretically, this issue is severable from the effectiveness of the initial sale; nonetheless, ambiguity in this area may cast aspersions on the sincerity of the entire process. In practice, there are a number of solid premises to understand the justification for the rabbi to conduct this transaction.[99]

95. See *Resp. Pri HaSadeh*, III, 92:4; *Orkhot Rabbenu, inyanei mekhirat chametz*, 2; and, less absolutely, *Resp. Minchat Yitzchak*, VI, 38.
96. See *Resp. Teshuvot V'Hanhagot*, I, ibid., and *Avnei Shoham*, 44:7.
97. See *S'dei Chemed, ma'arekhet chametz u'matzah*, 9:23, and *Biur Halakhah*, OC 448, s.v. *mekhirah*.
98. See R. Moshe Williger, *Badei Moshe*, I, 14.
99. Among these is the ability of one to acquire on behalf of another without their knowledge when it is purely for their benefit (*zakhin lo l'adam sh'lo b'fanav*). This is in conjunction with the impropriety, noted above, of any Jew purchasing, for his own use, the *chametz* sold for *Pesach* by another Jew; see *Ma'adanei Yom Tov*, IV, pp. 717–718. Alternatively, one might assume that discretionary action in the interest of the appointer is implied; compare *Resp. Avnei Nezer*, OC 347, who argues that it should be acceptable, in the instance an appointed rabbinic agent takes ill, for a new one to replace him; since the owner has expressed his willingness to sell, it stands to reason it is not of consequence who is actually carrying out the intent. (He subsequently raises technical issues.)

    For the sake of clarity, Leon M. Metzger has advised the emendation of forms commonly used to read "to transact" in the *chametz* rather than "to sell," and to make the appointment of agency irrevocable for the relevant time period. This last condition is to protect against a situation in which the original Jewish seller decides

THE SALE OF CHAMETZ AND THE *HA'ARAMAH* FORMULA

In applying the formula to *mekhirat chametz,* a number of points can be considered. Regarding Part (A), the *mishnah*[100] does teach that selling one's *chametz* to a non-Jew is permissible up until *chametz* becomes prohibited in benefit, and presumably does fulfill the requirement of removal. Accordingly, the letter of the law should be satisfied, assuming the factors mentioned, particularly the anticipated reversal of the possession, are not considered an actual negation of the original transfer.

The objections are mostly related to parts (B) and (C). To first consider part (C), the genuineness of the sale itself, many argued that the eventual return of the *chametz* after *Pesach* does not in any way detract from the sale, either because the parties are presumed to be sincere,[101] or because the inner attitudes are irrelevant if the actual communications are consistent with a genuine sale,[102] especially in that the religious goal is only accomplished if the sale is actually valid.[103]

---

mid-*Pesach,* for whatever reason, not to reacquire his *chametz* after *Pesach.* In addition, he recommends the *chametz* be valued at cost basis, to avoid any implications regarding taxes or other legal regulations.

100. *Pesachim* 21a.

101. See *Resp. P'nei Yehoshua,* 14, and *Shulchan Arukh HaRav, Hilkhot Mekhirat Chametz.*

102. See *Resp. Noda BeYehudah, kamma,* OC, 18; *Resp. Chatam Sofer,* OC 113 and YD 310; *Resp. Ramatz,* YD 86; R. Ovadiah Yosef, *Resp. Yabbia Omer,* X, YD 38; and see *Resp. Keren L'David,* 123. See also *Minchat Aharon,* pp. 145–146, as well as p. 149, where he notes that this approach presumably also explains the prevailing attitude to approve the sale of even those who have no religious commitment and cooperate only in order to obtain rabbinic certification, in contrast with the view of R. Yosef Shalom Elyashiv, who invalidated such sales.

103. See *Resp. Hitorerut Teshuvah,* I-II, 221–223. In #222, he rules that the sale is valid even when the government has strictly rationed the wheat that citizens can have, and there may be reason to think the Jew is unwilling to actually part with *chametz* when he may be unable to replace it after *Pesach;* despite that factor, it remains true that there is no point to sell the *chametz* without committing to it sincerely. In #223, he suggests that the premise that the seller will certainly commit to the sale to avoid the prohibition may only be valid when a Torah prohibition is involved, while he may not be as concerned if there is only a rabbinic prohibition. This leads to the ironic conclusion that if, due to *bitul,* there is only a rabbinic prohibition remaining (the premise of the *Bekhor Shor*), then the sale would not work. He then offers a creative resolution to that problem.

In response to the specific question of the seriousness of the purchaser, the *Chatam Sofer*[104] deemphasizes the role of the purchaser in general, asserting that the situation with *chametz* is distinguished from other areas involving sales. In this case, the focus is not so much on non-Jewish ownership, but rather on the removal of the *chametz* from the orbit of the Jew. Accordingly, it is only, or primarily, the Jew's intent and commitment that is significant for this purpose.[105] Even without this argument,[106] though, the *Chatam Sofer* believed the sale to be genuine and complete.[107] Others[108] added that the fact that the purchaser knows that the motivation of the seller is only to address the *chametz* issue does not interfere; he also knows that this is only accomplished through an actual sale, and conducts it as such.[109]

Other steps are ideally taken to enhance the genuine character of the sale, relating to intent, process, deed and attitude over the course of *Pesach* itself. These include ensuring that the purchaser has reasonable access to the *chametz*, and as much knowledge as possible of its nature, value,[110] and location;[111] that the *chametz* is in a location not likely to

104. *Resp., Yoreh Deah* 310.

105. Contrast with *Resp. R. Yehudah Assad,* YD, 341; see also the objections of R. Ben Tzion Shternfeld, *Resp. Sha'arei Tziyon,* I, 14; and see also *Resp. L'Horot Natan,* II, 27:3. R. Yissachar Dov Goldstein, *Likutei He'arot* to *Responsa Chatam Sofer,* VI, pp. 99–100, surveys the objections of a number of respondents to the *Chatam Sofer's* suggestion, and considers whether he is referencing here the concept of "*hefker*," or something similar, or an unrelated concept. See, however, a similar suggestion in *Resp. Eretz Tzvi,* 84, who accordingly permits utensils sold to a non-Jew for *Pesach* purposes to be reacquired without requiring *tevilah.*

106. The *Chatam Sofer's* student, *Maharam Shik, Resp.,* OC, 204, points out that the *Chatam Sofer* was not actually relying on this argument for his position (but see that responsum for possible implications).

107. See *Resp.,* OC. 113.

108. *Resp. Shem Aryeh,* CM 22.

109. See also *Resp. Chut HaMeshulash,* II, 5, for another approach addressing concerns of insufficient intent on the part of the purchaser.

110. According to some (*Mekor Chaim,* 448:8; *Chayei Adam,* 124:3) this information is crucial to the validity of the sale, while others do not consider it as integral (*Resp. R. Akiva Eiger, tinyana,* 7; *Resp. Be'er Yitzchak,* 6; *Resp. Iggerot Moshe,* OC, I, 103). See also *Minchat Aharon,* pp. 139–141.

111. Regarding the level of detail necessary about the location, and its impact on the validity of the sale, see *Resp. Minchat Chen,* I, 31, in notes, sec. 3, and the sources cited therein.

be encountered or viewed by the original owner; and that the original owner fully and sincerely empowers his rabbinic agent to carry out a fully legal sale, which he then proceeds to do in a serious fashion consistent with all applicable methods and requirements of both Jewish[112] and secular law.[113]

One of the objections raised by the *Bekhor Shor* was the financial incapacity of the purchaser to actually follow through with the conditions of the sale. Indeed, this often is an issue, although it is questionable to what extent that endangers the validity of the sale. Nonetheless, some rabbinic authorities[114] do insist on selling to an individual who is both capable of putting together sufficient capital, and knowledgeable of the business fundamentals to a degree that he is able to both fully understand the sale and commit to it in a genuine fashion.

Regarding the broader question of whether the intent of the Torah is being subverted by the sale itself, R. Hershel Schachter notes that his aforementioned distinction between positive commandments and negative ones is highly relevant here. The Torah both affirmatively commands the divestment from *chametz* as well as negatively prohibits its ownership. While the positive commandment, "*tashbitu,*" should not be circumvented, most observant Jews do actively destroy at least some

---

112. Regarding the involvement of qualified experts of Jewish law, see *Resp. Bigdei Yesha,* ibid., and R. Shalom Toibesh, *Resp. She'alat Shalom, tinyana,* 91. Regarding a sale that is valid in civil law but not in Jewish law, see *S'dei Chemed, ma'arekhet chametz u'matzah,* 9:39.

113. As to the efficacy of a sale not recognized by secular law, see *Resp. Chatam Sofer,* OC 113; *Resp. Shoel U'Meishiv, tinyana,* II, 63; *Resp. Divrei Chaim,* OC, II, 37; *Resp. Avnei Nezer,* CM 55; *Resp. Yashiv Yitzchak,* XXVII, 9; *Ashrei HaIsh, Pesach* #12, p. 333; and *Resp. HaBari V'haShema,* III, 3:4. R. Zvi Pesach Frank believed it was only important that the sale be valid according to *halakhah;* see *Mikra'ei Kodesh, Pesach,* 95:4; *Resp. Har Tzvi, Zeraim,* II, 49:1; and *Har Tzvi, Pesakim V'Hanhagot, Pesach,* #4. Regarding the commitment of the seller to the legal validity, see, in particular, *Resp. Teshuvot V'Hanhagot,* V, 108.

One major question regards the inclusion in the sale of stock shares in companies that possess *chametz,* a transfer that involves challenges from the perspective of secular law and from the implications on the plausibility of the sale; see *Resp. Teshuvot V'Hanhagot,* IV, 95–96; *Resp. Minchat Yitzchak,* III, 1; *Resp. Shevivei Eish,* OC, III, 24; *Ma'adanei Yom Tov, mo'adim,* IV, p. 544.

114. See R. Mordechai Willig, *Am Mordechai, Moed* 35:1.

small quantity of *chametz,* and thus the sales should not be perceived as evading that obligation.[115] What the sale does accomplish is preventing a transgression regarding the remainder of the *chametz,* which, according to this approach, is a valid utilization of a *ha'aramah.*

More specifically, it may be possible to assert that the selling of *chametz* is actually not a *ha'aramah,* or perhaps even if it is, it is one that is qualitatively different and less objectionable than other comparable devices. To contrast and compare, the sale of land in Israel during the *Shemittah* year effectively reverses the intent of the Torah, allowing the land to be worked despite the commandments specifically that it should not be worked.[116] In the case of *chametz,* perhaps an explanation can be advanced that would either eliminate or significantly reduce the deviation from the Torah's intent.

It would begin by considering the prohibitions of *bal yeraeh* and *bal yematze* that the sale is meant to address. The *Ran*[117] asserts that these prohibitions serve as a kind of "*syag min HaTorah,*" a Biblically mandated safeguard for other commandments of the Torah.[118] In essence, the Torah is really primarily concerned that we should not eat *chametz.* However, if *chametz* is kept in one's possession, there is a great risk that in a distracted moment, or in the search of a semi-awake midnight snack, one might prepare himself a meal of the normally-permitted *chametz.* To avoid this eventuality, all *chametz* must be removed from one's possession.

By embracing *mekhirat chametz, Klal Yisrael* is declaring that there are two things that can prevent them from eating *chametz*: not having any, and the transgression of *gezel* (theft). If the *chametz* is in one's house,

---

115. R. Asher Weiss, *Resp. Minchat Asher,* ibid., addresses this detail differently, suggesting that the positive commandment is only present to reinforce the prohibition, and thus should not be perceived as imposing an independent responsibility. Alternatively, it is also possible that sale to a non-Jew is itself a fulfillment of *tashbitu;* see R. Shlomo Wahrman, *She'erit Yosef,* III, 18.

Tashbitu, and the question of its fulfillment as opposed to its circumvention, also plays a role in the ideal that the *chametz* be not only sold but removed from the home of the Jew; see *Minchat Aharon,* pp. 149–151.

116. See R. Ze'ev Weitman, *L'krat Shemittah Mamlakhtit B"Medinat Yisrael,* p. 20.

117. *Pesachim* 1a, s.v. *u-mah.* See *Peri Megadim, Petichah* to *Pesach* 1:9.

118. See R. Yosef Engel, *Lekach Tov,* 8:1

but is off-limits because of the prohibition of stealing, that is enough to keep the Jews away from its consumption. Accordingly, it is immaterial whether or not the *chametz* will ever be picked up by its purchaser, or whether or not the sale will be reversed after *Pesach*. All that does matter is that during *Pesach*, the *chametz* legally belongs to another; that is enough to make sure it will be untouched.

As such, the "*ha'aramah*" component of *mekhirat chametz* is significantly reduced in comparison to other mechanisms perceived as *ha'aramot*. While those are devices to avoid halakhic regulation, in some cases essentially reversing the spirit of the law, *mekhirat chametz* is an alternative path to fulfill the Torah's commandment. There is significant debate as to whether or not it is an adequate method, accounting for a degree of controversy, but it can be coherently argued that the selling of *chametz* is largely compatible with the spirit of the law and its intent.[119]

It should be emphasized that in order to maintain the integrity of this approach, it is necessary to relate to the *chametz* that has been sold as completely off limits.[120] This may affect a number of halakhic issues that arise over the course of *Pesach*, in which one may find the need to access, destroy, or transfer *chametz* that has already been sold.[121]

---

119. In a similar vein, the *Imrei Emet* of Ger is cited (see *Avnei Shoham*, 43:8) as drawing a distinction between the sale of *chametz* before *Pesach* and the sale of land in Israel before *Shemittah*, in favor of the former, by noting the relevant formulations in the Torah. Regarding *chametz*, the intent of the Torah is that one should not possess *chametz*, and any method of dispossession is included. In reference to *Shemittah*, there is no focus on ownership of the land, rather on the individual not to work the land.

120. See *Shulchan Arukh*, OC 440:2; *Resp. Kinyan Torah*, I, 140; and *Avnei Shoham*, 48. Strikingly, R. Chaim Aryeh Horowitz, *Resp. Chayei Aryeh*, 15, last paragraph, considered an argument along these lines to permit, after the fact, *chametz* that was actually discovered not to have been sold.

121. Examples include destroying *chametz* that has been found over the course of *Pesach*, (thereby risking unjust appropriation/destruction of the property of the non-Jew, as noted by *Resp. Chelkat Yoav*, OC, 15); see *Resp. Shevevei Eish*, OC, III, 12:7; *Resp. Shevet HaLevi*, VI, 53; *Resp. V'Shav V'Rapha*, I, 19; *Teshuvot V'Hanhagot* V, 114; *Haggadat Minchat Asher*, ibid., 16:1, and 17; *Resp. Meishiv Mishpat*, III, 6:2; and *Resp. Tzvi V'Chamid*, OC 42) (and note R. Zvi Pesach Frank, *Mikraei Kodesh, Pesach*, I, 72, who included even *chametz* that became leavened during the festival in the sale; and see also a different path to leniency in ibid., 102, and *Har Tzvi, P'sakim*

The extent to which this is the case is reflected in a fascinating responsum of R. Shlomo Kluger.[122] He describes a scenario in which one has sold his *chametz* to a non-Jew. Over the course of *Pesach,* the non-Jewish purchaser was arrested, and is now locked up, unavailable to sell the *chametz* back to the Jew after *Pesach* has concluded.

One might think that, given that the *chametz* is physically stored in the home of the Jew, he can simply just take it back. This could especially be justified in light of the fact that the non-Jew has not yet paid the full purchase price; the *chametz* is both physically accessible and subject to repossession because it is collateral for an unpaid debt, which surely will not be repaid now.

Nonetheless, declared R. Kluger, the Jew must absolutely not avail himself of this self-justice. To do so would be to retroactively label the entire sale an overt *ha'aramah.* One who is owed property by another is not entitled to simply confiscate that property, even if it is physically possible to do so and he has a legitimate claim. Rather, he must pursue justice through the proper channels.

So too, maintained R. Kluger, that must be the process here. The Jew may turn to a rabbinical court and explain his position. They will assess the situation and the monetary commitments, and, if they accept the claim, will authorize repossession on his behalf. All of this effort is necessary so as not to render the sale a *ha'aramah.*[123] It is necessary as

---

V'Hanhagot, Pesach, 33); or assuming, without confirming, permission from the purchaser to take from the *chametz* to feed pets, or for use for *erev Pesach* that falls on *Shabbat.* In each of these situations, there are various halakhic positions, but it should be appreciated that an attitude premised on the belief that the purchaser waives his rights will undermine the effectiveness of the sale as a tool to distance the Jew from the *chametz.*

Note also R. Dov Berish Weidenfeld, *Resp. Dovev Meisharim,* II, 4, who discusses a bakery that wishes to sell its entire operation to non-Jews for *Pesach* who will produce bread for soldiers. He considers the plan workable, with the crucial exception of a situation in which the Jewish owners insist on being physically present. In that case, he rules, in addition to other problems, there is now a glaring *ha'aramah,* and the sale is invalidated.

122. *Resp. HaElef Likha Shlomo,* 221.

123. Compare also the sources cited in R. Nachman Kahana, *Orchot Chaim,* 448:12, in particular the *Eishel Avraham* of Butzchach. See also *Resp. Pnei Meivin,* OC, 97.

well, we can note, so as to preserve the respect for monetary boundaries so crucial to the effectiveness of *mekhirat chametz.*

Similarly, attention is paid to other details of Jewish or secular law that would be addressed in a fashion that casts doubt on the sincerity of the sale of *chametz.*[124] Generally, multiple methods of

---

124. Examples would include the question of *tevilat keilim,* immersion, for utensils that were sold and reacquired afterward. R. Shlomo Kluger wrote seemingly conflicting responsa on this issue; see *Resp. HaElef Likha Shlomo,* YD, 193, in which he assumes that the sale is a *ha'aramah,* necessary only for rabbinic law, that does not trigger an obligation of *tevilah;* but compare his ruling in *Resp. Tuv Ta'am V'Da'at, telita'ah,* II, 22, in which he writes that a sale without a subsequent immersion would be an unacceptable logical contradiction. The latter position is taken by *Resp. Yechave Da'at,* III, 24, who quotes many sources to that effect. Others who were stringent on this issue included *Chokhmat Adam* (73:3); the Gaon of Vilna (*Ma'aseh Rav, Hil. Pesach,* 47); *Pitchei Teshuvah,* YD 120:13; and R. Meshulam Igra (*Igra Ramah, Hil. Pesach* #4). R. Eliezer Deutsch, *Resp. Pri HaSadeh,* II, 26, distinguished between the Torah-mandated immersion of metal utensils, which he advocated in this case without a *berakhah,* and the rabbinic obligation regarding glass utensils, for which he allowed the lenient approach that was considered by the *S'dei Chemed (ma'arekhet chametz,* 9:27). See also *Resp. Divrei Malkiel,* IV, 22:7. See, in contrast, *Resp. Eretz Tzvi,* 84, who advances creative suggestions to bifurcate the impact of the sale regarding *chametz* and *tevilah,* while the Lubavitcher Rebbe, *Resp. Shulchan Menachem,* OC II, 227, authored an innovative understanding of the obligation of *tevilah* to justify an exemption in this case. Others considered the sale of the utensils an added stringency that does not carry the same weight as the sale of the *chametz* itself; see *Arukh HaShulchan,* YD 120:52; Even a well-grounded position that allows the reacquiring of the utensils without immersion causes complications, in that it weakens the perception the seller should have of actually having transferred ownership of the *chametz.* For this and other reasons, many authorities advocated against the sale of the utensils in the first place; see *Resp. Chatam Sofer,* OC 109; and *Resp. Shivat Tziyon,* 11. R. Shmuel Eliezer Stern, *Resp. Shevevei Eish,* OC, III, 12:7 asserts that a contract that mentions the utensils can be treated as in error and not reflective of what was actually sold. Others suggested selling the *chametz* absorbed within the utensils without the utensils themselves, which raises its own plausibility issues; see *Chashukei Chemed, Pesachim* 6a (and see also *Resp. Shevevei Eish,* ibid., 35). Regarding the general question of selling the utensils, see *Resp. Sho'alin U'Dorshin,* VIII, 58; and *Avnei Shoham,* 45.

One additional issue to consider arose in particular as *Pesach* of 5780 approached, at the very beginning of the period of the COVID-19 pandemic. At that time, there were many who unexpectedly found themselves canceling plans to be away for *Pesach* and had to suddenly prepare to spend the festival at home,

legal transfer are employed in order to ascertain that the transfer is effective according to all opinions, and the process is continuously re-evaluated to eliminate weaknesses in these areas, and to enhance the confidence and appreciation of both sides of the transaction in its genuineness.[125]

It is further worth mentioning that in a major sense, the controversy over *mekhirat chametz* is one that represents the broader debate over all "*ha'aramot*." To a large degree, the controversy has become what is known in the language of halakhic debate as a "*machloket* in *metziut*" – a debate that centers more on the reality of the situation than on conceptual halakhic analysis. Those in the "*Bekhor Shor* camp" of stringency may agree that the sale is not a *ha'aramah* when it is conducted in a serious fashion, with full commitment;[126] and those in the "*Chatam Sofer* camp" of "*mekhirat chametz* advocacy" may be less supportive when the sale is superficial

possibly for the first time. Many of these individuals had to purchase new utensils for the occasion, and circumstances were such that it was extremely difficult or impossible to bring these utensils to the *mikveh*. To address this quandary, *poskim* offered various suggestions, included among them reliance on the ruling of the *Shulchan Arukh*, YD 120:16, that under exigent circumstances, it is permissible to gift one's utensils to a non-Jew, and then borrow them back, thus allowing usage of the utensils without immersing them, as they are technically not the property of the Jew at that time. However, such an approach could create a dissonant mindset, in that at the same time, the Jew involved will have sold his *chametz*, and would need to understand that fact as prohibiting absolutely the usage of that *chametz*, while simultaneously using utensils that have also been sold. The conflicted attitude that would result is worthy of careful consideration. See also *Resp. Yashiv Yitzchak*, XLVII, 45.

Other related issues that affect the full commitment to the sale as a genuine transaction include aspects of the sale that raise questions of compliance with civil regulations, such as the sale of liquor and medications (see *Resp. Naharei Afarsimon*, EH, 32; *Resp. Minchat David*, II, 13, and compare *Resp. Teshuvot VeHanhagot*, I, 95, 295, and 764.) See also a related question in *Resp. Sho'alin U'Dorshin*, VIII, 59.

125. One recent enhancement, advocated by R. Shmuel Eliezer Stern, *Resp. Shevevei Eish*, OC, III, 13, is that the purchaser should provide a blank check as a security toward the payment of the full value of the *chametz*.

126. Indeed, as noted, the original comment of the *Bekhor Shor* appears to explicitly concede this point.

and lacking in genuineness.[127] As such, this debate may be one that is resolved not in the study hall but in the hearts and minds of the people and their leaders.

The importance of the last factor, that of necessity, is presumably connected to the assessment of the other factors. The initial scenario of the *tosefta* can be interpreted as referring to a situation in which the original Jewish owner is dependent on the relevant *chametz* for his livelihood, and implementations of the sale early in the modern era often invoked similar considerations. The legitimacy and appropriateness of the utilization of a sale for reasons of convenience, or to avoid minor loss to a consumer, would hinge on the degree of confidence that one has in all of the other factors discussed above.

TESTING THE LIMITS: SELLING THE *CHAMETZ* OF STORES THAT CONTINUE TO SELL ON PESACH

A far more complicated scenario, from the perspective of the letter of the law and certainly the spirit of the law, is the sale of the stock of stores that continue to operate over the course of *Pesach,* including the selling of *chametz* to customers of all kinds.

Immediately, a number of objections arise to such a sale. Aside from the serious issue of the owners providing *chametz* to customers, presumably including Jewish ones, over *Pesach,* there are several impediments simply to the validity of the sale of the store's inventory. First, the ongoing business transactions with the *chametz* that had been purportedly sold certainly casts aspersions on the sincerity of the store owner.

Alternatively, if the initial sale *is* considered valid, the store owner, in continuing to do business with the *chametz,* is violating theft against the original purchaser of the *chametz.* Certainly, the affirmative rationale given above for the individual who sells his *chametz* – i.e., the benefit that emerges from the seller being completely separated from his *chametz* – is wholly inapplicable in this situation.

---

127. See, for example, *Resp. Shevivei Eish,* OC, 31, who asserts that the *Chatam Sofer* would not defend the modern executions of the sale, and thus it should be utilized only for rabbinically prohibited *chametz.* See also ibid., 34:7.

Accordingly, there are objections to such arrangements that correlate to the two major fields of *ha'aramah* disputation: first, that the behavior is completely outside the spirit of the law, evading its intent in all ways; and second, that the process is itself a sham, invalid on its face due to the internal contradictions it contains.[128]

Unsurprisingly, there were a number of authorities, including R. Joseph B. Soloveitchik, who completely disapproved of such sales, with a number of them ruling the initial sale not only inappropriate but null and void, and the *chametz* accordingly prohibited.[129]

---

128. It should be noted that it is not only overt *chametz* dealers who have been subject to this judgment; some authorities disqualified the *mekhirat chametz* of any individual whose behavior indicates he does not personally respect the relevant religious principles; see *Mo'adim L'Simchah*, p. 176. Nonetheless, the situation of the merchant is certainly more extreme, both in the public nature of the nonobservance, and also in the fact of the commerce specifically undermining the claim of having sold the *chametz* to another. On the latter point, see also *Resp. Maharsham*, II, 117, regarding sale of a *bekhor.*

129. Among those who take this position are *S'dei Chemed, ma'arekhet chametz u'matzah*, 9:35; *Resp. Maharam Shik*, OC 205; R. Tuvia Goldstein, *Resp. Emek Halakhah*, II, 36:3, *Resp. Uri V'Yishi* 121, *Resp. Shevevei Eish*, OC, III, 12:5; and R. Yosef Shalom Elyashiv, quoted in R. Eliyahu Shlesinger, *Mo'adei Kodshekha*, p. 216. (See overall his discussion there, #47).

    For this position, the counterargument to the point argued below – that unspoken conditions are normally invalid – is that in this case the insincerity of the seller is blatant and evident to the world by the fact of his store remaining publicly open (now and in past years). This would equate this situation with the case of *Beit Choron* see p. 51).

    Some have argued that this situation is even less valid than that, inverting the logic of the *Chatam Sofer*, noted above, that the main consideration is the removal of the Jew from engagement with the *chametz*. In this case, the Jew is openly conducting business with the *chametz*, thus eliminating the main basis to validate the sale; see *Resp. Pri HaSadeh*, II, 124. R. Moshe Shternbuch, *Resp. Teshuvot V'Hanhagot*, I, 288, invalidates the sale because of the continuing commerce and also notes that there is no valid *bitul*, thus the sale falls short of the standard of the *Bekhor Shor*, to which he subscribes. Similarly, R. Yissachar Shlomo Teichtal, in a responsum printed in the journal *Ohalei Shem*, I:1, pp. 15–20, asserts that the weaknesses associated with *mekhirat chametz* render it more vulnerable and it is thus disqualified under these circumstances. See, similarly, *Resp. Machzeh Avraham*, OC 87.

    See also R. Eliyahu Bakshi-Doron, *Resp. Binyan Av*, IV, 20, who is in general stringent on this issue but does endeavor to find a leniency for situations of

Nonetheless, there were significant authorities who found at least some validity for these sales as well. In many respects, this question is not fundamentally different from that of allowing the participation in the sale of any non-religious Jew, who may not take the sale seriously and may in fact continue to consume his own *chametz* over the course of the festival, and many of the same arguments in both directions are applied in that case. One widely quoted responsum on this matter was authored by the prominent Chasidic rebbe and halakhic authority, R. Chaim Halberstam of Sanz (1793–1876).[130] He described a scenario in which a completely nonobservant Jew, who regularly sold his *chametz* before Pesach, one year was traveling at that time, and sent a message to his non-Jewish wife that she should arrange for the sale "superficially" (*lifnim*) so that he not be given problems later.[131]

R. Chaim was asked if, given the explicitness of his insincerity, such a sale was still valid. He answered briefly but definitively: perhaps this seller is under the impression that the sale is only superficial, due to the fact that the *chametz* returns to him after *Pesach*. However, if he were to be made aware that the requirement is to sell it absolutely before then, presumably he would agree to the nature of the sale. Accordingly, it should be considered valid and his *chametz* is permissible after *Pesach*.

While R. Chaim did not address the aspect of the seller partaking of his *chametz* over the course of *Pesach*, it must be assumed that given his non-observance and his non-Jewish spouse, this is taken as a given.[132] The core premise of his response, that the owner would agree to a genuine sale if he fully appreciated that indispensable aspect of the process, has been endorsed by many subsequent authorities.

---

significant loss. Regarding the above-noted stringent position of the *Sdei Chemed*, it is noteworthy that he does not fully follow the consequences of his position, i.e. declaring the *chametz* fully prohibited in all benefit after *Pesach*. Rather, he limits the prohibition to sale to other Jews. He explains there that while the more stringent position would be more logical, it is less likely to be observed, and consequently he is opting for the lesser evil *(ha-ra b'miuto)*. See also the various points made on this subject by R. Yisrael Belsky, *Shulchan HaLevi, Chametz U'Matzah*, 18 and 19.

130. *Resp. Divrei Chaim*, II, OC, 46.

131. See also the analysis of aspects of this situation in *Resp. Avnei Nezer*, OC, 337. See also *Resp. Yashiv Yitzchak*, XXVII, 11–14.

132. As noted expressly in *Resp. Chelkat Ya'akov* OC 194.

Later authors assumed this premise to be connected to the notion found in the Talmud[133] and expanded upon significantly by the Rambam,[134] that a bill of divorce can under the proper circumstances be coerced from a recalcitrant husband, despite the requirement of his consent, due to the assumption that his inner will is to comply with the divine law, no matter how much this is contradicted by his statements and actions. In this case, the overwhelming benefit, both to the store owner and to his customers, points to a clear desirable conclusion, and thus this can be considered his true desire.[135]

Even within the relatively lenient positions, one can note many variations, which themselves reflect various nuances of the *ha'aramah* debate:

a. The sale is completely valid, effective *ab initio* for *Pesach* purposes; and, from the perspective of business ethics, moral as well.

   This formulation rests on several premises: a) A transaction between two parties is subject only to terms that are explicit; the insincerity of a seller, even when established clearly by his later

133. *Bava Batra* 48a.

134. *Hil. Gerushin* 2:20. For further discussion of this position of the Rambam, see Appendix.

135. See *Chelkat Ya'akov,* ibid., in detail; *Mo'adim L'Simchah,* IV, pp. 176–178; and R. Yitzchak Zilberstein, *Chashukei Chemed, Pesachim* 10a.

In his comments to 13a, he considers another approach, based on a comment of *Rashba, Shabbat* 18b, s.v *gigit,* that invokes the possibility of *Beit Din* communally declaring property ownerless when doing so will prevent the populace from sinning. Accordingly, it may be possible that such a presumption is in effect regarding *chametz,* to at least validate the sale of one who participates without understanding. Even though there is no rabbinic enactment requiring the sale of *chametz,* once the practice has developed to utilize this approach to avoid transgression, perhaps the communal authorities expand on it for the spiritual salvation of the population.

The application of this position of *Rashba* was first alluded to by R. Yehoshua of Kutno, *Resp. Yeshuot Malko,* OC 36. In that context at least, R. Yehoshua rejected this logic as a validation of a questionable sale of *chametz.* The situation was itself an interesting test case: a nonobservant individual had superficially "sold" liquor in his possession to a non-Jew to avoid the regulation of the civic authorities, with no awareness of *Pesach;* would this also be effective to permit as *chametz* that he had sold? His decision was that the artifice here was too great. His implication, though, is that this approach could be applicable to one who was at least attempting to sell his *chametz* with knowledge of *Pesach,* and was pursuing a process to that effect.

actions, cannot cancel the rights of ownership acquired by a buyer.[136] b) the seller may in fact be sincere, because even if he is not personally devout, he would still prefer the more acceptable classification for his behavior.[137] c) The seller should not be considered as stealing from the one who had previously purchased his *chametz,* either because that purchaser consents to the ongoing commerce, or, more justifiably, will subtract the amount of all sales from the assessed value that he is ultimately purchasing. All of these points are endorsed by R. Moshe Feinstein, in multiple responsa.[138]

b. The sale is completely valid, unideal but effective after the fact for *Pesach* purposes; and, from the perspective of business ethics, moral as well.

---

136. R. Binyamin Aryeh Weiss, *Resp. Even Yikarah, telita'ah,* 127, goes farther and stresses that even if both the seller and the buyer agree to the cancellation of a sale that was carried out effectively, the sale would still be in effect until they actually went through the process of transferring back the acquired property. (It should be noted, though, that he was discussing a different scenario: the technical issue of *erev Pesach* that fell on *Shabbat,* and if one who sold his *chametz* in the morning of the 13th of *Nissan,* but continues to do business the rest of the day (as benefit from *chametz* continues to be permissible the whole day, as it is not actually *erev Pesach*) is nullifying the sale. (See, similarly, R. Aharon Levine, *Resp. Avnei Chefetz,* 32). There is ample room to distinguish between this and the case of one who is selling *chametz* throughout *Pesach* to customers, as the latter could be seen as more of a public declaration of noncommitment to the sale in its totality. See *Emek Halakhah,* ibid.
137. This is expressed by the Talmud (*Chulin* 4a) as a general principle, that even one who is willing to sin does not abandon the permitted when it is available and indulge in the prohibited. Or, even more than that: even if the owner explicitly states his lack of interest in compliance with Jewish law, it can still be maintained that his inner, concealed desire is to accord with God's will; see *Resp. Yashiv Yitzchak,* XVII, 12. Compare, however, R. Moshe Hirsch Fuchs, *Resp. Yad Ramah,* OC 23.
138. *Resp. Iggerot Moshe,* OC, I, 149;3; II, 91; and IV, 95. R. Yitzchak Leibes, *Resp. Beit Avi,* I, 3, initially challenges this position based on Talmudic passages (such as the case of *Matnat Beit Choron*) that rule that an individual's subsequent actions can be taken to determine his earlier intent; in this case subsequent transactions with the *chametz* should establish retroactively the falsity of the sale. He suggests that this principle is not invoked if doing so requires labeling the individual a sinner retroactively. This seems to be another version of the presumption of righteousness, or at least minimal possible transgression, seen above.

This formulation accepts much of the above, but acknowledges that while the sale may indeed be technically valid, and also, from a business perspective, allow the store owner to continue selling to the public, this arrangement fails to meet the spirit of the prohibition of owning *chametz* by any reasonable standard.

c. The sale is valid, technically effective for *Pesach* purposes, although completely outside the spirit of the law; and immoral from a business perspective, as the store owner is selling property that does not belong to him and thus engaged in theft.[139]

This formulation acknowledges only the technical point that the sale is not invalidated by the later actions of the seller; however, the assumption is that these actions are a violation of the ownership rights of the purchaser, and thus constitute theft of his property.

What emerges is a broad range of conceptual possibilities, all of which essentially agree that the position of the store owner is not ideal or even acceptable for a conscientious, observant Jew. However, a communal rabbi, assessing the impact of the alternatives, may decide, if he agrees on any level with lenient views, that the net gain in religious observance exceeds the cost, and justifies participation in such a sale.

A passionate advocate of this stance was R. Ya'akov Breisch of Zurich, Switzerland, who argued that not only were the sales of such stores permissible, they were an obligation of the rabbinate, in order to minimize sin whenever possible.[140] Dismissing implications in the Talmud and elsewhere that there is no responsibility to save intentional sinners from their actions, he advances a number of arguments to maintain that this presented a distinct opportunity that the leadership is required to pursue.

139. The question of whether the sale is a net spiritual detriment to the store owner, in that it renders him a thief, or if there are instead alternative understandings or methods that prevent this, is the subject of a detailed exchange between the author of *Resp. Chelkat Ya'akov*, ibid., and his sons, who wrote glosses appended to the responsum.

140. *Resp. Chelkat Ya'akov*, ibid.

This view was also shared by R. Menachem Mendel Schneerson, the Lubavitcher Rebbe,[141] who offered a multi-leveled argument that there is a value in such sales, even as the message was stressed that these businesses should not be operating on *Pesach*. In fact, he maintained that one of the accomplishments of these sales was to raise the consciousness of the concept of *Pesach* and the prohibitions regarding *chametz*.

Yet, there are also many who were stringent on this matter, and many variables as well that impact whether these sales are overall advantageous or disadvantageous from the perspective of communal responsibility.[142] R. Moshe Feinstein, despite his full confidence in the validity of the sale, does acknowledge that a local rabbinic authority may decide that such sales are not advisable, and that he should act according to his conscience.

This is separate and apart from the decision then left to the observant consumer, after *Pesach*, who must be guided in the decision of whether purchasing such *chametz* at that point is permissible.[143] For

141. *Sha'arei Halakhah U'Minhag*, II, 195, and *Shulchan Menachem*, OC, II, 228.

142. R. Breisch's responsum was written to R. Shlomo Schneider of Monticello, NY. In a volume published of the latter's writings, *Resp. Divrei Shlomo*, II, 123, the entire exchange can be found, including R. Schneider's original inquiry citing numerous authorities who ruled stringently, and a follow-up in which he adds later literature and concludes that it is impossible to set an absolute rule in this matter, and the time, place, and rabbinic judgment must determine whether such sales are advisable, or if instead "a passive approach is preferable." See also *Resp. Beit She'arim*, OC, 197, who acknowledges that God-fearing Jews may wish to be stringent on these issues, but there is also sufficient basis for leniency and it may be wise not to object.

143. R. Feinstein, for his part, maintained that there is no reason whatsoever for the customer to refrain from purchasing. R. Ovadiah Yosef appears to endorse this statement in *Chazon Ovadiah: Prozbol*, p. 237, and this is also the position of R. Shlomo Zalman Auerbach, *Halikhot Shlomo, Pesach*, 7:9. At the other extreme, the Vilna Gaon, in line with his opposition to all temporary sales, forbade the purchase of any *chametz* that had been sold.

R. Shternbuch, *Resp. Teshuvot v'Hanhagot*, ibid., advances an additional argument to prohibit purchase from these stores after *Pesach*. The ban on *chametz* owned by a Jew over *Pesach* is a rabbinic penalty to discourage such ownership. To allow this *chametz* to be used would, in his view, do the opposite by encouraging sinful behavior. Further, he cites a Talmudic passage (*Beitzah* 17b) that a *ha'aramah* is treated more severely than intentional sin.

them, the considerations, both in terms of the letter of the law and the spirit of the law, are shifted.

Further, this situation can still be expanded, in both directions. It should be noted that there is a scenario in which a store with Jewish owners might sell *chametz* over the course of the *Pesach* that is significantly more acceptable, perhaps even completely unobjectionable. If the Jewish owner would completely sell his interest, including all profits over the course of *Pesach,* to a non-Jewish partner, this should satisfy all concerns. Arguably, it is as or more justified than the sale of the individual consumer's personal *chametz,* as this presumably comes from a more pressing livelihood consideration.[144]

As with many of the other Talmudic passages, in this usage, *ha'aramah* refers to behavior conducted under false pretenses, rather than circumventing an obligation. However, from R. Shternbuch's perspective, the reference is certainly applicable, as this is his assessment of the nature of the sale of these stores' merchandise, similar to the *Bekhor Shor*'s assessment of the sale of animals.

Further, it is instructive to note the interpretation of Rashi to that Talmudic passage, which is relevant to broader aspects of the overall debate. He explains that a *ha'aramah* is worse than intentional sinful behavior because the intentional sinner recognizes his misdeed and there is hope he will change course. By contrast, one who is engaged in *ha'aramah* believes he is acting in a permissible fashion; accordingly, he is unlikely to change his behavior and more likely to mislead the masses.

144. See *Shulchan HaLevi,* ibid.

Some contemporary authorities consider the question of one who owns *chametz* that is being sold on his behalf through a website such as Amazon.com, and the Jew has no way of pausing this over the course of Pesach. R. Moshe Shternbuch, *Resp. Teshuvot V'Hanhagot,* VII, 51, recommends that the Jew should sell this *chametz* to a non-Jew as he would all of his personal *chametz,* and adjust the price to reflect any items that had been sold on the website over the course of Pesach. He notes that this is not comparable to the situation of the physical store that remains open over *Pesach,* which he had harshly condemned. In that case, the Jew's activity in continuing to sell the *chametz* displays his lack of seriousness in the original sale. In this case, however, he is not himself doing anything, and he is unable to stop the website from continuing to offer the items, and thus there is no action that casts aspersions on the seriousness of his sale. He does require that the Jew provide his access codes to the non-Jew, so that he would be able to retrieve the *chametz* over the course of Pesach, should he wish to do so.

R. Ovadiah Yosef Toledano, *Resp. Meishiv Mishpat,* III, 3, also addresses this issue in a responsum written to R. Shlomo HaLevi Apel. The latter had asserted that the sale of a company would raise additional issues of *ha'aramah,* in that in contrast to

Going in the opposite direction, the leniencies applied to the sale of a store, if they are accepted, could theoretically be stretched even further. Some authorities, motivated by the desire to minimize Torah violations to the greatest degree possible, have suggested the *chametz* can be sold through an agent even without the store owner's knowledge. Going even beyond that, some have maintained this can happen even with the owner's explicit disapproval. These positions are premised on an extreme formulation of the postulation that at the core, every Jew is amenable to the path that is spiritually proper, whether they are aware of it or not. As such, in that the store owners' violations will be minimized if the *chametz* is considered sold,[145] it can be presumed that they in essence agreed to the sale and its stipulations.

The question of a sale without the knowledge or consent of the actual seller comes up as well in another circumstance that is more understandable, but similarly complex, if in different ways. The unfortunate situation of an individual who is in a coma, or similarly incapacitated and unaware, as *Pesach* approaches, presents the question of what can be done to prevent his *chametz* from becoming permanently forbidden to him due to his technical ownership over the course of *Pesach*. A number of authorities felt that in such a situation an agent may sell the *chametz* of this individual. The argument in this case is significantly stronger than that of a store owner continuing to do a business with the *chametz,* but requires an assumption that there is valid agency to effect this transaction without the awareness of the actual owner. The fact that the sale is the only option, presumably, to save the *chametz* from worthlessness is a strong foundation to assume consent; the position is strengthened if the individual had a clear religious

the *chametz* itself, for which the owner would be happy to accept full payment and relinquish the *chametz* permanently if that were the decision of the purchaser, the same could not be said for one's livelihood. His suggestion was that the business and the *chametz* should be sold separately, thus allowing the company to be sold for a delimited time period. R. Toledano did not agree with the concern, but did note that one potential difficulty comes from the legal obstacles in the selling of a company, a question he leaves unanswered.

145. However, even this premise is highly questionable, as they may be trading the violation of ownership and commerce in *chametz* on *Pesach* for the sin of theft.

position on the matter and a history of selling his *chametz* in past years when he was able to.[146]

Related questions involved the inclusion, within the existing *chametz* sales, of individuals who did not make arrangements to sell but are being listed nonetheless. This is done on a mass level, such as is the practice of the Israeli chief rabbinate, or in individual cases on behalf of one who is prevented by circumstances from reaching the agent.

The latter situation is the starting point, raising the question of whether it is possible to assume the authority to sell the property of another without their expressed consent. Normally, the ability exists to acquire an item on behalf of another without their knowledge, under the presumption that this constitutes a "*zekhut,*" a benefit, for that individual. However, it is generally assumed that this cannot be extended to *selling* the property of another, as this cannot be assumed to be beneficial, or desirable, for the owner.

Nonetheless, many argue that *chametz* is unique, in that the onset of *Pesach* will deem the *chametz* completely worthless, while selling the *chametz* will preserve the value. Accordingly, a benefit in this case can be objectively established.[147]

Still, the question remains, how far can that logic be taken? It is one matter to include someone who was trying to arrange a sale but was prevented by circumstances. Could it also be extended to those who, due to lack of observance or knowledge, would never have thought to sell their *chametz*?

Such an extension would require a significant shift, both conceptually and practically. To an observant Jew, *chametz* on and after *Pesach* is

146. See *Resp. Chatam Sofer,* EH, I, 11; *Pitchei Teshuvah,* YD 320:6; *Resp. Binyan Av,* IV, 21; *Mo'adei Kodshekha,* 46; *Resp. Yashiv Yitzchak,* XXXIX, 33; *Resp. Shevet HaKehati,* IV, 127; *Choshen L'Ma'aseh,* 36.

147. While this point was questioned by some later authorities (see *Resp. Teshurat Shai,* 443, and *Resp. Avnei Nezer,* OC, 336 and 347, who limits its scope), *Resp. Imrei Yosher,* II, 23, notes that it was already ruled affirmatively by *Magen Avraham,* OC 436:11. The point is further asserted at length in *Sdei Chemed,* ibid., 9:2.

R. Shlomo Zalman Auerbach, *Ma'adanei Aretz, Shvi'it,* 1:20, asserts (in the context of the *hetter mekhirah*) that *zakhin* cannot be utilized in the context of a *ha'aramah.* However, the applicability of that term is tied to the details of the situation, for example, if the owner is acting in a way that undermines the sale.

literally worthless; there is nothing he can do with it. To one who would be willing to use the *chametz,* despite the prohibition, declaring that sale a "benefit" requires focusing exclusively on the spiritual aspect, which the actual owner does not acknowledge or appreciate.[148]

Practically, the challenges are formidable: how would the *chametz* be assessed? How could any information, at all, be provided to the purchaser?[149] What if multiple rabbis attempted to sell the same *chametz?* Would this be the prerogative only of the official rabbi of the locale, or of its rabbinical court?

To some authorities, these obstacles were indeed insurmountable. To others, however, the lack of any preferable alternatives indicated that these sales, however compromised and questionable they may be, were worth pursuing.[150] Some took the approach even further, arguing that even one who is loudly proclaiming his disinterest in the sale can nevertheless be included.[151]

As perhaps the best known of our subjects, the sale of *chametz* has often symbolized the broader debate over *ha'aramot.* The collective effort to balance the integrity of the law, religious sincerity, and concern for the spiritual and practical challenges of the Jewish people continues to play out in the exchanges of the ongoing debate.

148. See the analysis of this distinction in *Resp. Dovev Meisharim,* I, 30. For a related discussion regarding *prozbol,* see *Chazon Ovadiah: Prozbol,* pp. 75–77.

149. *Resp. Divrei Malkiel,* IV, 18, considered these problems disqualifying, while acknowledging that great authorities permitted.

150. See *Resp. Be'er Yitzchak,* OC, 1 and 2 and compare *Resp. Panim Me'irot,* II, 52. R. Moshe Shternbuch, *Mo'adim U'Zmannim,* III, 269 rules that the rabbi should include the above categories in the sale. See also *Resp. Meishiv Mishpat,* III, 5.

151. See also the discussions in *Ratz K'Tzvi: B'Ma'agalei HaShanah,* 13; *Resp. Be'er Halakhah,* OC 19; *Resp. Even Pinah,* 30 and *Resp. Shavei Tziyon,* 11; and *Avnei Shoham,* 55.

Chapter 6

Shemittah and the *Hetter Mekhirah*

To turn attention to the *hetter mekhirah* regarding *Shemittah,* and to contrast with the (relatively) less controversial *mekhirat chametz,* application of the formula may prove instructive in explaining the variance in levels of acceptance between the two. It must be emphasized that the intent here is not to disparage the *hetter mekhirah,* which has been endorsed throughout the decades by great rabbinic figures, but to attempt to explain the differing reception between the two sales mechanisms. Further, it is hoped that examination of the components of the formula will also contribute to greater understanding of both sides of this debate.

In anticipation of the *Shemittah* year of 1889 (5649), following an inquiry from R. Naftali Hertz of Yaffo, three prominent rabbinic leaders, R. Yehoshua of Kutno, R. Shmuel Mohilever, and R. Shmuel Zanvil Klapfish of Warsaw, endorsed an arrangement that would become known as the *hetter mekhirah,* and which involved the sale of Jewish-owned lands in Israel to non-Jews, under the assumption that this transfer removed the prohibitions of *Shemittah*. The arrangement was approved by R. Yitzchak Elchanan Spector of Kovno, but the *hetter* was controversial from the outset, for reasons that will be outlined below.[1] The arrangement called for the agreement and the implementation of the rabbis of Jerusalem, and, instead of unanimous agreement, an intense debate ensued.

While R. Avraham Yitzchak ha-Kohen Kook is often associated with the *hetter*, as noted, R. Kook was not the author of the *hetter*. In fact, while living in Europe, he opposed the *hetter*, together with his father-in-law, the *Aderet*. However, both of them changed their minds upon arriving in *Eretz Yisrael* and taking note of the dire circumstances there. In 1910, R. Kook wrote *Shabbat Ha-Aretz*, in which he defends the *hetter*, as he does in several responsa in his *Mishpat Kohen*.

Nonetheless, R. Kook wrote in his letters that he intentionally did not disclose all of his reasons for supporting the *hetter*, out of fear that the *hetter* would become entrenched as permanent public policy. This conflicted attitude is perhaps representative of the general controversy relating to the *hetter*. R. Kook's expressed feeling was that the *hetter* was

1. Beyond the debate itself, there was even controversy as to the nature of the endorsements. Some claimed that R. Yehoshua of Kutno had been pressured into signing the endorsement, pointing to his printed statements (*Resp. Yeshuot Malko*, YD 55). However, as R. Shlomo Yosef Zevin, *L'Ohr HaHalakhah*, 143, displays, the fuller context of his words makes it clear that his endorsement was genuine, but that he wanted the support of other prominent rabbis signing with him. Indeed, the nature of his comments, some of which are referenced below, make it hard to argue the point. Even the venerable R. Spector was not exempt from personal criticism and speculation in this matter. R. Eliezer Gordon of Telz authored a letter (printed in *Resp. R. Eliezer V'Chiddushav*, II, 76–80; for background to the letter, see pp. 73–76) in which he objected to R. Spector's endorsing the plan without gathering all the great rabbis of that time, maintaining that the issue was one affecting the entire Jewish people and thus deserving of such treatment. He assumes that R. Spector had been misled and sharply criticizes all involved (as does the *Ridbaz*, in the introduction to his *Beit Ridbaz*). R. Moshe Shternbuch, *Shemittah K'Hilkhatah*, 120, quotes a similar allegation from R. Ya'akov Orenstein's *Emek Halakha* (#22). For his part, R. Yitzchak Elchanan stated that he had not anticipated that such a fierce debate would ensue and that he was saddened by it (as quoted by R. Ezra Batzri, in his introduction to R. Yosef Yedid ha-Levi's *Resp. She'erit Yosef: Kuntres HaShemittah*, pp. 7–8). See also the introduction to R. Shlomo Zalman Auerbach's *Ma'adanei Aretz*, and R. Yechiel Michel Tukachinsky's *Sefer HaShemittah*, II, ch. 1.

far from ideal; our desire is to observe *Shemittah* fully, in following the spirit and the letter of the law.[2] However, the redemption is not yet complete, and it might be necessary to serve the goal of the ultimate settlement of the land, and the return of the entire Jewish people, for steps to be taken to ensure the continuation of the settlements in the interim.

Notably for our broader subject, R. Kook ends one of his responsa[3] surveying his defenses of the *hetter* with the words, "Although one can question this *ha'aramah* permission, because it is clear that it is a *ha'aramah*." He then proceeds to briefly reiterate some of his arguments, apparently underscoring our general thesis, that the acceptability of any given *ha'aramah,* or alleged *ha'aramah,* is the sum total of the varied factors surrounding it.[4]

Regarding Part (A), the letter of the law, there are a number of elements to consider. First is the core question of the effectiveness of the plan in and of itself, which is contingent on the understanding that selling the land to a non-Jew removes the obligations and prohibition of *Shemittah.*

A crucial component of the discussion is the premise that *Shemittah* in contemporary times is only binding on a rabbinic level,[5] an assumption that is subject to debate[6] but is shared by all of those who advocate the *hetter mekhirah.*

There are at least two versions of this position:

1. *Shemittah* in particular is rabbinic, as it is connected to the *mitzvah* of *yovel,* which is only a Torah obligation when the majority of the Jewish population is living in Israel;[7]

---

2. See, for example, *Resp. Mishpat Kohen,* 3 and 61.
3. *Resp. Mishpat Kohen,* 58.
4. R. Yosef Zvi Rimon offers a perspective on this, regarding *hetter mekhirah* specifically as well as the concept in general, in his *Shemittah,* pp. 343–344.
5. See Tur, *Yoreh Deah* 331; *Beit Yosef, Choshen Mishpat* 67, s.v. *ve-heshbon,* citing *Ralbach,* #142; *Resp. Maharshdam,* YD 192.
6. See, for example, *Sha'agat Aryeh ha-Chadashot,* 15, and R. Akiva Yosef Shlesinger, *Shenat Shabbaton,* 1:2. R. Moshe Shternbuch, *Shemittah K'Hilkhatah,* 126–128, considers the matter to be unresolved and thus requiring stringency.
7. There are two paths to the conclusion that *Shemittah* as a Torah obligation requires the Jewish population residing in Israel. One is to assume a connection to *yovel;* see *Arakhin*

2. The entire sanctity of the land is rabbinic: some maintain that the sanctity of the Land of Israel is as a whole only on a rabbinic level, as the sanctification of Ezra was temporary.[8]

This element is significant for a number of reasons: it impacts the technicalities of the effectiveness of the device; it allows for a general approach of leniency and reliance on minority opinions;[9] and as noted above, it finds a more receptive attitude regarding status as a *ha'aramah.*[10]

In addition, some objections to the *hetter* noted the fact that the Torah already acknowledged the challenges inherent in *Shemittah,* and expressed a blessing that the land will yield a crop in the sixth year sufficient for a three-year-period.[11] To this, the response was offered that the blessing applied to an observance of *Shemittah* that is Biblical in nature; when it is rabbinic, there is no such assurance, and alternative approaches may be necessary.[12]

32b, where it also emerges that the Jews must be living completely in the land, in their assigned tribal portions; and see also Rambam, *Hil. Shemittah V'Yovel,* 10:8. The other is to assume a connection to the obligation of *ma'asrot,* which in the Rambam's view is contingent on Jewish settlement of the land; see *Arakhin,* ibid., and *Hil. Shemittah V'Yovel,* 12:15–16. The difference between the two concepts, known respectively as "*rov yosheveha aleha*" and "*bi'at kulkhem,*" is analyzed at length by R. Chaim (Brisker) Soloveitchik, *Chiddushei Rabbenu Chaim ha-Levi, Hil. Shemittah V'Yovel,* 12:16.

8. See Rambam, *Hil. Terumot* 1:26.
9. See also R. Yisrael Ze'ev Gustman, *Kuntresei Shiurim, Gittin,* pp. 449–450. He discusses extensively the issues in assessing the contemporary status of *Shemittah* throughout *kuntres* 13 of that volume.
10. R. Ovadiah Yosef, *Resp. Yabbia Omer,* X, YD 38, notes that the *Talmud Yerushalmi* (*Shvi'it* 9:4) already recommends a *ha'aramah* related to *Shemittah,* establishing its acceptability in this area. This is also relevant for those who question the sincerity of the sale itself, and to whom the position of the *Bekhor Shor* regarding rabbinic law and *ha'aramot* may be relevant; see *Mishpat HaKinyan,* IV, p. 125. See also *Otzerot Yosef,* 3:67.
11. Lev. 25:21.
12. See *Sma,* CM 67:2; *Chiddushei Chatam Sofer, Gittin* 36a; *Nehor Sheraga, Yevamot* 16a; R. Yosef Zvi HaLevi, *Hora'at Sha'ah,* introduction; and *Yeshuot Malko,* YD, 53. R. Yosef Engel, *Otzerot Yosef: Shvi'it Ba'Zman HaZeh,* 3, sec. 84, asserts that the blessing, coming from the Creator of the world, amounts to a natural development emerging from the fulfillment of His commandment. Were the commandment not to be in effect, and only a rabbinic directive to be applicable, to trust in this blessing would constitute an unwarranted "reliance on a miracle."

This point would appear to be crucial to the entire endeavor: if the blessing is indeed in effect, any approach premised on the extreme difficulty of *Shemittah* observance would imply a major lack of faith in God's commitment. If rabbinic *Shemittah* does not carry this assurance, the assessment is vastly impacted.

There is an additional component to the question of the nature of the contemporary *Shemittah* obligation. A minority opinion[13] exists that in contemporary times, with the absence of *Yovel,* the *Shemittah* is not even a rabbinical obligation, and its observance is only voluntary (*middat hasidut*).[14]

It is generally assumed that in a *she'at ha-dehak* (exigent situation), a non-accepted minority opinion of an individual authority (*da'at yachid*) can be relied upon.[15] It should be noted that the perception of this view as a *da'at yachid* is disputed, in both directions. There are those who consider this opinion to be completely rejected, and not even

---

The *Chiddushei HaRim, Gittin* 36a, asserts that the blessing is applicable even when *Shemittah* is rabbinic; see the objection of *Pardes Yosef* to Lev. For other responses of opponents of the *hetter* to this position, see *Sefer HaShemittah,* p. 71.

The implication of *Chazon Ish, Shvi'it,* 18:4, is that the blessing is relevant even when there is no obligation; see also R. Moshe Scheinerman, *Ohel Moshe,* Lev. pp. 710–711. It seems that in his understanding, the reward is for spiritual effort and commitment, rather than for fulfillment of a *mitzvah.* R. Shimon Sofer, *Resp. Hitorerut Teshuvah,* CM, 11, finds it logical to maintain that a blessing should be applicable even when the commandment is only rabbinic, in that the Torah itself commands adherence to rabbinic law, and certainly nothing would impede God from bestowing His blessing to one who fulfills a rabbinic version of His commandment. Nonetheless, he accepts the view of the *Sma* that the blessing does not apply, and leaves the matter as a conceptual question. (See there the glosses *Ikvei Sofer,* by his grandson R. Akiva Menachem Sofer, who connects the question to a larger issue as to the nature of rabbinic law). R. Mordechai Eliyahu, *Ma'amar Mordechai,* p. 157, asserts that the blessing is in effect in modern times, not based on textual sources, but on empirical observation of the quantitative and qualitative success that has met those who observe *Shemittah.*

13. R. Zerachiah ha-Levi, *Gittin* 18a *be-dappei ha-Rif.*
14. R. Yosef Engel (*Otzerot Yosef,* 3:23) advocates this position. R. Moshe Shternbuch, *Shemittah ke-Hilkhatah,* 122, asserts that he does not actually embrace this view, but only uses it in conjunction with his belief that the situation was life-threatening. The *Beit HaLevi* (III, 1), among other objections on this point, maintains that R. Zerachiah was only referring to *shemittat kesafim,* the cancellation of loans.
15. See *Taz,* YD 293:4.

eligible for consideration;[16] and, on the other hand, there are those who argue that there are actually numerous authorities who hold this opinion and thus add to its weight.[17]

Another element that is entered into the discussion by some advocates is the fact that there is a dispute as to which year is actually *Shemittah*.[18] Accordingly, one might say that there is license to be lenient with the "*safek de-rabbanan*."[19] The *Beit HaLevi*[20] vigorously opposed the notion that *safek* could eliminate assigning any one year as *Shemittah*, and asserted that to the contrary: if one wanted to account for the uncertainty, one would have to treat every candidate year as *Shemittah*.[21]

The central issue for the effectiveness of the *hetter* is the assumption that non-Jewish ownership of land in Israel removes that land from the obligations of *mitzvot ha-teluyyot ba-aretz* (*yesh kinyan le-nokhri be-Eretz Yisrael lehafkia*, etc). This is an issue that is brought up numerous times in the Talmud[22] and may have different rulings for different aspects of ownership in the land of Israel.

The primary passage in the Talmud discusses whether the purchase of the land by a non-Jew would remove the obligation of *ma'aser*. There is a debate on this matter, but it emerges that all agree that there is a different rule regarding the area of "Suriya," which has the status of a private "*kibbush*," and thus would lose its sanctity with such a purchase. Rashi connects this to the idea that the obligation of *ma'aser* in Suriya is rabbinic. Accordingly, Rambam[23] rules that non-Jewish purchase is ineffective in canceling sanctity, except in Suriya.

---

16. See, for example, R. David of Karlin, *She'eilat David, Kuntras HaShevi'it*.
17. See, for example, *Resp. ha-Gryi Herzog, Mitzvot HaTeluyyot BaAretz*, 48.
18. See Rambam and Ra'avad, *Hil. Shemittah V'Yovel* 10:6.
19. R. Ya'akov Shaul Elyashar (1817–1906), who was the *Rishon L'Tziyon* (Sefardi Chief Rabbi) from 1893–1906 and was one of the prominent Sefardi proponents of the *hetter*, advocates the incorporation of this factor, along with other uncertainties, to assert the principle of *safek d'rabbanan l'kulah*, in his *Resp. Simchah L'Ish* (YD, 26). See also *Otzerot Yosef*, 3:40–42.
20. *Resp*. III, 1.
21. See also *Resp. Chelkat Ya'akov*, YD 185:10.
22. *Gittin* 47a, *Bava Metzia* 101a, *Menachot* 31a, *Bekhorot* 11b, *Yerushalmi Demai* 5:5.
23. *Hil. Terumot* 1:10.

While the majority view among *rishonim* is that the sanctity remains (*ein kinyan*), there are those authorities, such as the *Sefer ha-Terumah* and the Vilna Gaon,[24] who maintain that if the sanctity is rabbinic, then it is removed by non-Jewish ownership. Thus, it would presumably follow that since *Shemittah* is rabbinic, the transfer of ownership is effective in removing the rules of *Shemittah*.[25]

The essential question of whether produce from land owned by non-Jews is exempt from the rules of *Shemittah* was the topic of debate between the *Beit Yosef* on one side and the *Mabbit* and his son *Maharit* on the other. It is important to note that the discussion, at this point, is not about the sale of land for this purpose, but simply the status of land that happened to be owned by a non-Jew.

While many authorities ruled that non-Jews do not acquire the land to remove it from its sanctity, the *Beit Yosef* interpreted this, based on a reading of the Rambam,[26] to mean that if a Jew purchased the land from a non-Jew, the sanctity would return. However, when in the possession of the non-Jew, the product of the land would indeed be bereft of sanctity.[27] The *Mabbit*[28] and the *Maharit*[29] disagreed, and marshaled

24. *Bi'ur* to *Yoreh Deah* 331:6 and 28.

25. The *Beit HaLevi* (III, 1) maintained that this would only be true according to the view that the entire sanctity of the land is rabbinic; according to the view that the sanctity is Biblical but *Shemittah* is rabbinic, this logic should not apply. R. Soloveitchik analyzed this issue at length, as related by R. Menachem Genack, *Gan Shoshanim*, 57.

R. Moshe Shternbuch, *Shemittah K'Hilkhatah*, 128–129, denies that the Vilna Gaon actually maintains the above position, and, among other modifications, suggests that the Vilna Gaon only compared the land of Israel to the Talmudic "Suriya," where sanctity is rabbinic, in a time when most of the settlement is not in Jewish hands. However, when the land is mostly in Jewish hands, even the Vilna Gaon would agree that the sanctity is Biblical.

26. *Hilkhot Terumot* 1:10.

27. See the *Beit Yosef*'s words in his *Resp. Avkat Rokhel*, 24; and *Kesef Mishneh*, *Hil. Shemittah* 4:29; *Hil. Terumot* 1:11; and *Hil. Bikkurim* 2:15. R. Yechiel Michel Tukachinsky, *Sefer HaShemittah* pp. 84–88, argues that a distinction of this nature is necessary in order to differentiate this dispute from that of whether the sanctity enacted by Ezra was temporary or enduring; see his lengthy analysis there.

28. Vol. I, 11, 21, 217, 336; vol. III, 45.

29. Vol. I, 43.

proofs that the sanctity of the land, and particularly the laws of *Shemittah*, remains in effect when the land is in non-Jewish hands.

In support of his position, the *Beit Yosef* adds another reason specific to *Shemittah*, an interpretation found in the *Torat Kohanim*, which understands the phrase in the verse "the Sabbath produce of the land shall be *yours*"[30] as an exclusion of land that is not "yours."

While it continues to be somewhat of a debate,[31] there is a strong and prominent body of literature that asserts that the *halakhah* is in accordance with the *Beit Yosef*'s view, and that the practice in the land of Israel for generations has been to treat the produce of non-Jewish owned land as devoid of *Shemittah* sanctity. The *Pe'at HaShulchan* wrote that it is "clear" that the *halakhah* is like the *Beit Yosef*,[32] and the *Chida* in his *Birkei Yosef* wrote to disprove the allegation that the *Beit Yosef* changed his mind on this matter at the end of his life.

However, it should be re-emphasized that acceptance of the *Beit Yosef*s position does not necessarily result in embracing the *hetter mekhirah*.[33] Some of the reasons for this will be outlined below. One reason that emerges from an analysis of the *Beit Yosef* is the interpretation that his position denied the sanctity of the produce of non-Jewish lands, but did not allow the performance of labor.[34]

---

30. Lev. 25:6.
31. For an extremely detailed survey of positions on the matter, see R. Zvi Cohen, *Peirot Shevi'it*, 4:2 n. 1. See also *Chazon Ovadiah: Prozbol*, pp. 278–298.
32. See, however, R. Binyamin Yehoshua Zilber, *Resp. Az Nidberu*, 44, in note, who questions the assertions of the *Pe'at HaShulchan*.
33. An example of this is the anonymous work *Minchat HaAretz*, an entire volume which was published in 1994 to defend the position of the *Beit Yosef* (against the work *Minchat Emet*, which argued that the *Beit Yosef*s position is rejected). *Minchat HaAretz* has the enthusiastic endorsement of many prominent rabbinic authorities who oppose the *hetter*, including R. Moshe Aryeh Freund, who wrote in his approbation that "the study of this topic should be a merit so that there need to be no recourse, God forbid, to the *hetter mekhirah*, which was prohibited by the great rabbinic authorities."

    For further extensive analysis of the debate between the *Beit Yosef* and the *Mabbit*, see, for example, *Minchat Yerushalayim*, pp. 233–361, and R. Shaul Yisraeli, *Eretz Chemdah*, pp. 215–235.
34. See, for example, *Chazon Ish*, *Shevi'it* 20:7, and R. Shlomo Zalman Auerbach, *Ma'adanei Aretz*, 117. For an analysis of this distinction, and a suggestion as to its interpretation, see R. Shlomo Goren, *Torat HaMo'adim*, pp. 634–638.

Nonetheless, as R. Shlomo Yosef Zevin[35] maintains, acceptance of modern *Shemittah* as a rabbinical obligation seems to create a two-tiered support for the *hetter:* a) the position of the *Sefer HaTerumah* and the Vilna Gaon, that all would agree with "*yesh kinyan*" when the sanctity is rabbinic; and b) it should clearly be acceptable to rely on the *Beit Yosef* and those who agree with him in a matter of rabbinic law.

Former Ashkenazic Chief Rabbi of Israel R. Shlomo Goren[36] argued that the question of "*yesh kinyan*" is fundamentally affected by the reality of a Jewish government in the land of Israel. As he understands,[37] the land is owned on two levels: by the individual who holds title, and by the authority that rules the territory.[38] Thus, even if the individual sells his land, it remains under Jewish possession.[39]

Similarly, R. Shlomo Wahrman[40] argues that the support of R. Kook was contingent on factors that were no longer relevant after the establishment of the state. Citing his *Shabbat HaAretz,*[41] he notes the assertion that the sale was effective because there was not a majority of Jewish ownership of the land. However, were the land to be mostly in Jewish hands, *Shemittah* would be applicable to all of it. For this reason, he maintained, the land was not sold for this purpose in the mishnaic era.[42] He notes further a number of other indications that early support for the *hetter* was premised on a reality of non-Jewish majorities or ownership of the land, including the payment of taxes to non-Jewish authorities.[43]

---

35. R. Shlomo Yosef Zevin, *L'Or HaHalakhah,* 141.
36. R. Shlomo Goren, *Torat HaMo'adim,* 627.
37. His analysis is based on the comments of *Tosafot, Kiddushin* 36b, s.v. *kol.*
38. R. Ya'akov Ariel addresses this concern in his *Resp. B'Ohalah Shel Torah,* III, 10, p. 116
39. A similar point is argued by R. Moshe Shternbuch, *Shemittah K'Hilkhatah,* p. 121 and 130, who cites a suggestion from the Satmar Rebbe, Rabbi Yoel Teitelbaum, *Kuntres Shalosh Shavuot,* 84, that as a consequence of Jewish rulership over the land, even genuinely non-Jewish land is obligated by *Shemittah.*

    See also R. Herschel Schachter, *Nefesh HaRav,* p. 82, as well as his *Eretz HaTzvi* 30:2, pp. 210–212, who cites an innovative idea from R. Joseph B. Soloveitchik that would pose another challenge to the possibility of *hetter mekhirah.*
40. *She'erit Yosef,* II, 27.
41. P. 127; see also *Iggerot Ra'ayah,* 177.
42. See the discussion of this point in *Sefer HaShemittah,* p. 82.
43. See *Resp. Maharam Galanti;* 57, and *Shemen HaMor.*

THE LETTER OF THE LAW: PERMISSIBILITY

Crucially significant to the issue is the prohibition of "*lo techanem*,"[44] which according to Talmudic interpretation forbids the selling of land in Israel into non-Jewish hands.[45] As a Biblical prohibition specifically relevant to a sale of this type, this plays a huge role in the opposition to the *hetter mekhirah,* and could by itself explain the greater controversy in comparison to *mekhirat chametz.*

One of the primary opponents of the *hetter,* the *Netziv,*[46] maintained that because of this prohibition, the plan was manifestly counterproductive ("running away from a lion to encounter a wolf"): in order to avoid a rabbinical prohibition[47] of *Shemittah,* it promoted a Biblical prohibition of *lo techanem.* (However, another opponent of the *hetter,* R. Akiva Yosef Shlesinger, suggested that violating *lo techanem* with the sale would be the lesser of two evils; the greater being the dissemination of produce from farmers who completely ignore *Shemittah,* which would present a stumbling block for the masses.)[48]

Several defenses have been advanced by supporters of the *hetter* to refute the accusation of violating *lo techanem.*

Many of the supporters of the *hetter* felt that the issue of *lo techanem* was inapplicable to a temporary sale,[49] a position based on Ramban.[50] This is supported, as some understand, by Rambam's explanation[51] that the sale would grant permanence to non-Jewish possession of the land.

---

44. Deut. 7:2.
45. *Avodah Zarah* 20a; Rambam, *Hil. Avodah Zarah* 10:3.
46. *Resp. Meshiv Davar* II, 56.
47. The *Netziv* is here referring to the supporters' own premise; he himself subscribed to the view that *Shemittah* remains a Torah commandment in modern times.
48. *Shenat Shabbaton,* 1:6.
49. See *Resp. Shemen HaMor,* YD 4 (by R. Mordechai Robbio, the Rav of Chevron in the eighteenth century; his responsum was a crucial earlier source influential on the support of R. Yitzchak Elchanan, as attested to by the Aderet); *Resp. Mishpat Kohen,* 60. and *Resp. Yeshuot Malko,* YD 55 and 56, and 59; as well as #58, where he dismisses concerns that the non-Jew will refuse to sell back the land. See also the responsum of R. Yehoshua Long printed in *Chikrei Halakhah V'Shut* of R. Shmuel Mohilever, p. 46. Regarding the reaction of R. Yehoshua Leib Diskin to this suggestion and his subsequent recommendations, and their impact, see *Sefer HaShemittah,* p. 61.
50. Cited by the *Sefer HaChinnukh,* #339.
51. *Hil. Avodah Zarah* 10:4.

R. Shaul Yisraeli[52] goes so far as to suggest that it is ironic that opponents of the sale cite *lo techanem*, when the sale is temporary, but instead promote the purchasing of produce of non-Jewish famers, thus strengthening their economic hold in the land of Israel, and actually impinging on the intent of *lo techanem*.

Some, such as R. Yehoshua Leib Diskin, have argued against this defense by noting that there is a prohibition of renting the land to non-Jews as well.[53] It would seem that rental would be no worse than a temporary sale. R. Kook responded to this concern by asserting that in the case of a rabbinic decree, only the actual subject of the decree is forbidden; it is not necessary to assume that something that seems "worse" would be included.

Some maintained that the Arab purchasers, as Moslems, are not considered idolaters, and that the prohibition only applies when dealing with idolaters.[54] R. Kook[55] suggested that in the time of the Talmud, this mechanism of sale was not utilized precisely because of the difficulty of finding non-Jews who were not idolatrous.

There is somewhat of a distance between the two halves of this equation, as it is very possible that to avoid *lo techanem*, one would need to transact with not only a non-idolater, but an actual *ger toshav* (if even that much would be permissible). The *Netziv*, among others, argued that we do not have the structure to accept a *ger toshav* in contemporary times.[56] Others maintain that even in a modern context, a non-Jew who follows the Noahide laws is considered a *ger toshav*.

For his part, R. Zevin[57] assumes the "non-idolater" argument to be a weak argument that was only meant to be combined with other

52. In a letter to R. Eliyahu Shlesinger, printed in the latter's *Resp. Shoalin V'Dorshin*, III, 417.
53. *Avodah Zarah* 20b.
54. R. Ovadiah Yosef, *Resp. Yabbia Omer*, X, YD 38, considers this position to be correct. (See also his longer discussion of all issues of *lo techanem*, in *Chazon Ovadiah: Prozbol*, pp. 258–278.) The original endorsement of R. Yitzchak Elchanan Spector specified that the sale must be to an "Ishmaelite."
55. *Resp. Mishpat Kohen*, 58.
56. R. Kook addresses the *Netziv*'s argument in *Mishpat Kohen*, 61.
57. *L'Ohr HaHalakhah*, p. 150.

points in favor as an additional support.[58] An additional point mentioned by R. Kook[59] is a view that there is no prohibition to sell land to a non-Jew who already owns land in Israel. This is based on the impression given from some *rishonim* that the prohibition is about providing an established and permanent "resting place,"[60] and thus perhaps one who already has a resting place is excluded from this issue. Later authorities argued this point, maintaining that all additional land contributes to the permanence of the "resting place," and that all quantitative increase is significant.[61]

It should be noted that the temporary nature of the sale creates somewhat of a paradox, if the plan is to succeed. On the one hand, the demands of "*lo techanem*" call for a sale that is temporary in nature. On the other hand, the sale must have some permanence to be considered genuine and to remove the prohibitions of *Shemittah*. It would be unhelpful if the sale were to be understood as a rental, as that would not remove the sanctity of the land.[62] As the proponents observe, the arrangement is not classified as a rental, because the purchasers are able to do with the land as they please,[63] and these authorities are confident that the sale is on the appropriate side of both issues.[64]

However, this ability to "do as they please" simultaneously creates a similar complexity. On the one hand, it makes the sale more genuine

58. See also R. Yitzchak Weiss, *Resp. Minchat Yitzchak*, VI, 128, pp. 259–263, who opposes this and other defenses on the *lo techanem* issue.
59. Introduction to *Shabbat HaAretz*, 12.
60. See Rambam, *Hilkhot Avodah Zarah*, 10:4, and *Sefer HaChinnukh*, 94.
61. See R. Yechiel Michel Tukachinsky, *Sefer HaShemittah*, II, 10:2–3; *Chazon Ish*, 24:1; R. Yosef Lieberman, *Resp. Mishnat Yosef*, I, 48.
62. *Resp. Simchah L'Ish*, YD, 26, asserts that the solution is actually found in a detail that could have, ironically, cast aspersions on the sale. Since the practice is, in his understanding, to sell to a trusted non-Jew, who, due to his friendship with the seller, will understand that he may not in any way make any changes to the land, this will neutralize the concern represented by *lo techanem*.
63. See Rambam, *Hilkhot Mekhirah* 23:5.
64. *Resp. Yeshuot Malko*, 56, and *Resp. Mishpat Kohen*, 61. Concern for this issue is also part of the suggestion that the land be sold for a period of two years, which alleviates the appearance of the sale deriving profit from *Shemittah*, and also makes the sale more genuine; see R. Shlomo Yosef Zevin, *L'Ohr HaHalakhah*, 150. See also *Shevivei Esh al ha-Torah*, I, *Parshat V'Etchanan*, pp. 327–328.

when it is expressly stated that the purchaser owns the property completely during the time of the purchase, and thus may dig pits and holes at will. However, including that aspect will likely reduce the *gemirut da'at* of the seller. Accordingly, R. Ze'ev Weitman,[65] the chairman of the sabbatical committee in the office of the Chief Rabbinate, advocates eliminating this clause, and selling the land simply on the condition that it be returned (*al menat l'hachzir*), which implies it must be returned in the condition it was purchased.[66]

THE IMPACT OF PERMISSIBILITY ON EFFECTIVENESS

The above two objections are combined into a third objection: since the sale is forbidden, it is therefore ineffective. The major spokesman for this position is the *Chazon Ish*[67] who invokes the principle of "*ein shaliach l'devar aveirah*," which appears to eliminate the mechanism of agency (*shlichut*) in the commission of a prohibition. For the most part, the sale of the lands takes place through the Rabbinate, or through others who act as agents on behalf of the landholders. If the sale is in itself a transgression, it would follow that it is impossible to conduct this sale through the usage of *shlichut*. Paradoxically, the *Chazon Ish* considered this to be a good thing, as the ineffectiveness of the sale at least prevents the violation of *lo techanem.*[68]

Many responses are offered to this issue. One deals with the premise itself. The *Chazon Ish* works with the understanding of those *rishonim* who interpreted *ein shaliach l'devar aveirah* to mean the agency is ineffective. Others, though, understand the principle to mean that agency cannot transfer the sin back to the sender, regardless of the effectiveness of the act.[69]

---

65. R. Ze'ev Weitman, "The Validity of Hetter Mekhira" [in Hebrew], *Techumin* XXVII, (2006), pp. 18–19.
66. Additional suggestions regarding the *lo techanem* question, including an extensive survey and an analysis of all sides of the issue, can be found in *Sefer HaShemittah,* vol. II.
67. *Shevi'it* 24:4, and elsewhere.
68. He does acknowledge that if the farmer sold his land directly, the sale, while forbidden, would be effective; see *Chazon Ish, Hil. Shevi'it,* 10:6, and *Resp. Yabbia Omer,* X, YD 38.
69. Both opinions are cited in *Tosafot, Bava Metzia* 10b s.v. *de-Amar le-Yisrael.* The *Netivot HaMishpat* (CM 182:1) asserts that the majority opinion is that the action takes effect despite the transgression.

Others note that the agent is appointed generally, without any focus on the prohibited act.[70] Further, there are views among the authorities that the agency is effective if the agent is either unaware of the prohibition,[71] or clearly established as one who is willing to perform the transgression.[72] Both points are clearly applicable to the Rabbinate, as they are of the opinion that there is no transgression, and are established as carrying out this transaction over generations.[73]

A related concern, unconnected to agency, is the Talmudic principle of "*kol milta de-amar rachamana lo ta'avid, i avid lo mehani*"[74] which seems to invalidate any prohibited action. R. Zvi Pesach Frank[75] addresses this by citing *Resp. Torat Chesed,* that this concept is inapplicable to *lo techanem,* as the prohibition can be violated without the technical status taking effect.

In addition to the above specific issues, there were some rabbinic commentators who felt that the Torah specifically anticipated and warned against any attempt to circumvent the application of *Shemittah.* Among these were R. Meir Simchah of Dvinsk, who understood this to be message of the Torah following an iteration of the mandate of leaving the land unworked in the seventh year[76] with an exhortation to "protect" the commandment[77] (*u'v'khol asher amarti aleikhem tishameru*).[78] Similarly,

70. See *Mishpat Kohen,* 60.

71. *Tosafot, Kiddushin* 42b, and *Mordekhai, Kiddushin* 508.

72. See *Choshen Mishpat* 388:15.

73. See *Resp. Har Tzvi,* Y.D, 123, and R. Yehoshua Menachem Ehrenberg, *Resp. D'var Yehoshua,* IV, *inyanim shonim* 14. (There is some question how to reconcile R. Frank's comments in his *Resp. Har Tzvi* with his glosses to the Tur; see *Resp. Tzitz Eliezer,* VI, 32). See also R. Ya'akov Ariel, *Resp. B'Ohalah Shel Torah,* I, 60, who addresses the *Chazon Ish*'s concern from another perspective.

In recent years, the Rabbinate has switched to direct sales rather than the utilization of agency, and thus to obviate the objection of the *Chazon Ish;* see R. Mordechai Eliyahu, *Ma'amar Mordechai,* p. 111, n. 16.

74. *Temurah* 4b.

75. *Resp. Har Tzvi,* ibid.

76. Ex. 23:11.

77. Ex. 23:13.

78. *Meshekh Chokhmah,* Ex. 23:11. The verse in between discusses *Shabbat,* and accordingly R. Meir Simcha maintains that both *Shemittah* and *Shabbat* ("all of the things

the *Netziv*[79] understands the verse "*V'ha'Aretz lo timakher l'tzmitut*" as "the land shall not be sold absolutely," and coming to teach that one should not sell his fields to a non-Jew for *Shemittah* and *Yovel* and thus exempt oneself. The following verse continues "*geulah tittenu la'aretz,*" and he understands this to mean that if the land has been sold to a non-Jew, it should be redeemed to allow observance of *Shemittah* (although the reference is to a time when the land is fully in Jewish hands).[80]

THE LEGITIMACY OF THE SALE

Regarding Part (C) of the formula, to consider the legitimacy of the sale, a number of objections were raised, many of them not present, or significantly less so, in the context of *mekhirat chametz.*[81] Among these is the observation that in the case of *chametz,* the seller presumably would accept an offer of cash instead, while in the case of the land, the seller has no intent of permanently relinquishing the land under any circumstances.[82] There is also a difference in plausibility: it is one thing to believe that a limited amount of *chametz* is being genuinely purchased; it is yet another to believe that a single non-Jew is acquiring all the land in Israel (assuming an arrangement of that extreme nature).[83]

---

that I have said to you") should not be circumvented through ownership arrangements with non-Jews.

79. *Ha'Amek Davar,* Lev. 25:23.
80. Compare also *Resp. Avnei Nezer,* YD, 458 (and see his whole discussion relevant to many of the issues of the *hetter*), and see *Mishnat Avraham* to *Sma"g,* IV, p. 5.
81. It is noteworthy, though, that R. Ovadiah Yosef, *Resp. Yabbia Omer,* X, YD 38, who advocates the *hetter* as the best way to prevent transgression among the broader population, assumes there is no reason to be more stringent in this area than in *mekhirat chametz.*
82. See R. Ya'akov Breisch, *Resp. Chelkat Ya'akov,* YD 184, (who does not dismiss the *hetter* outright). A similar point is made by R. Moshe Shternbuch, *Shemittah K'Hilkhatah,* p. 120 (who does dismiss the *hetter* outright).
R. Yosef Zvi Rimon challenges this distinction with a number of arguments; see his *Shemittah,* p. 335, n. 76.
83. See *Resp. HaGryi Herzog, Mitzvot HaTeluyot BaAretz,* 48, and *Resp. Tzitz Eliezer,* VI, 32.

Further, the seller continues to maintain an interest and involvement in the cultivation of the land, in contrast with the attitude of the seller of *chametz*.[84] One innovative understanding to this problem was advanced by R. Chaim Yehudah Leib Auerbach, the father of R. Shlomo Zalman Auerbach, in an addendum entitled "*Milei D'Abba*" to the latter's work *Ma'adanei Aretz*. He notes that ownership contains two components: physical access to and control of a property; and the monetary right to transfer that property. Usually, both sets of rights inhere within the same person. However, he notes, adducing Talmudic proof, it is possible to bifurcate them, and when that is the case, it seems that the ability to transfer is the more significant indication of ownership. Accordingly, it should be that element that determines the status of the property vis-à-vis any halakhic obligations that are based on ownership. If so, the aspect of *ha'aramah* would be correspondingly reduced through the *mekhirah*, even as the Jew continues his physical involvement with the land.[85]

Additional objections have been raised based on the doubt as to whether each seller fully understands the sale or is properly committed to it, particularly in light of it being temporary, and also motivated by religious concerns rather than business concerns.[86]

Indeed, the *halakhah* does require that a transaction conform to the expectations of the environment in which it takes place in order to be valid.[87] This is despite the fact that the *halakhah* contains its own extensive repertoire of transactional methods (*kinyanim*); the concern is that the parties will not fully commit to a transaction that falls short of conventional practice. In Israel, the transfer of land legally requires registration in the Land Registry, known as the "Tabu." Failure to conform to that standard would seem to not only be unsatisfactory to the

84. See *Resp. Yabbia Omer*, YD, 38:4; and *Shevivei Eish al haTorah*, I, *Parshat VaEtchanan*, p. 326.
85. See also R. Moshe David Sharf, *Sha'arei Shvi'it*, pp. 208–214, and note his general treatment of *ha'aramot*.
86. See *Chazon Ish, Shvi'it*, 27:7.
87. See *Kiddushin* 26a and Rashi, and *Choshen Mishpat* 190:7.

law (see below) but would likely result in the seller not believing in the genuine legitimacy of the sale.[88]

To this concern, R. Kook[89] responded that it is actually the religious nature of the sale that protects its validity. Had the transaction been one of a business nature, the attendant risks would lead the parties to hold back if convention were not adhered to. However, as the arrangement is meant to accomplish a ritual purpose, the parties are presumably comfortable fully committing to that understanding. Indeed, the Talmud[90] allows for an explicit exclusion from conventional standards, and thus an easily obtainable solution exists.

R. Moshe Sternbuch[91] notes that the sellers are often philosophically uncomfortable with the sale, either for nationalistic reasons or for religious reasons, and he considers these and the above factors to conclusively interfere with the effectiveness of the sale.

R. Ze'ev Weitman, the chairman of the sabbatical committee in the office of the Chief Rabbinate, authored an article in the journal *Techumin*[92] in which he addresses a number of areas in the contracts where improvements can or should be made, primarily to enhance the confidence and the commitment of the sellers. At one point he notes an ironic development: the original authors of the *hetter* had promulgated a temporary arrangement, subject to continual review. In practice, the arrangement has become so entrenched that the contracts of a hundred years prior are still in use, leading to a situation where the sellers are unfamiliar with the purpose and the scope of much of what is contained in them. It is thus appropriate for the Rabbinate to update the contracts and the process, as he does.

---

88. R. Shlomo Eliezer Alipandri, *Resp. HaSaba Kadisha,* I, 22, asserts that for this and related reasons the sale is in the category addressed by the Talmud as invalid due to circumstances that display its unseriousness, regardless of what is stated explicitly.

    R. Ovadiah Yosef, *Chazon Ovadiah: Prozbol,* p. 253, quotes a dispute among earlier sources as to whether the two concerns are distinct, or are interrelated; see also his fuller discussion, pp. 253–257.

89. Introduction to *Shabbat HaAretz,* p. 13.
90. *Kiddushin* 26a.
91. R. Moshe Shternbuch, *Shemittah K'Hilkhatah,* 124
92. R. Ze'ev Weitman, "The Validity of *Hetter Mekhirah*" [in Hebrew], *Techumin* XXVII, (2006), pp. 13–28.

In addressing this issue, R. Shlomo Zalman Auerbach[93] suggests an approach in line with that mentioned earlier regarding *chametz,* i.e., that the need to conform with *halakhah,* so that the plan accomplish its goals, supplants any other motivation. Together with the explicit terms of the contract, this creates a valid sale. However, he notes, this would only be effective if the farmer at least is aware the sale took place, and not in a situation where the land is sold by administrators without the farmer's knowledge.

Along the lines of the above, some[94] raised the concern that the sale, as inconsistent with the legal method, was thus in violation of *dina d'malkhuta dina,* which acknowledges governmental authority in legal matters.[95]

According to R. Zevin, the major defense against the concern of '*dina d'malkhuta dina*' comes from one of the great opponents of the *hetter,* the *Chazon Ish.* In his understanding, the principle would only interfere with the sale if the government prohibited the transaction. In the case of transferring land in Israel without the register of the Tabu, the issue is that the government would not recognize the sale, not that it would be forbidden. In such a case, the sale should be considered effective.[96] However, others dispute that this is actually the *Chazon Ish*'s view, and indeed the *Chazon Ish* himself seems to write otherwise.[97]

One of the Chief Rabbis of Israel, R. Yitzchak Isaac Herzog, wrote that *dina d'malkhuta dina* was a very significant concern, particularly after the formation of the state.[98] Before that point, one could argue that the Land of Israel was excluded from non-Jewish authority.[99] While there

93. *Ma'adanei Aretz,* sec. 1:20.

94. See R. Yosef Yedid, *She'erit Yosef,* p. 103.

95. See *Bava Batra* 54b, and *Choshen Mishpat* 194.

96. An interesting inverse situation is considered by R. Yosef Lieberman in his *Resp. Mishnat Yosef.* An observant family purchased land, but the sale was not yet entered in the Tabu. The question was then if they would be culpable for *Shemittah* violations that took place on their land, which was not recognized as theirs by the offices of the government.

97. *Shevi'it* 27:7.

98. *Resp. ha-Gryi Herzog, Mitzvot HaTeluyyot BaAretz,* 48.

99. See *Ran, Nedarim* 28a, s.v. *be-mokhes.*

are views that the concept of *dina d'malkhuta dina* does not apply to any government in the land of Israel,[100] R. Herzog maintained that the delineation of property ownership would nonetheless continue to be a government function.

In 1979, the Israeli government passed a law, "*Chok Iskaot be-Mekarka'in – Kiyyum Mitzvot Shemittah*" that officially recognizes the Rabbinate's ability to sell land for the purpose of *Shemittah,* despite the facts that the sale is temporary and not registered in the Tabu. Presumably, this development would go a long way toward addressing concerns of *dina d'malkhuta dina*. R. Weitman,[101] however, maintains that while it may be effective in addressing that issue, the lack of Tabu registration continues to weaken the *gemirut da'at,* as the seller continues to base his perception of reality on the conventional practice of the society.

SPIRIT OF THE LAW

Regarding the broader issue of compliance with the intent of the Torah, this issue is unusually complex. It would seem, on initial impression, that there is a great distance between the *hetter mekhirah* and the spirit of the law. As noted above, the purpose of the sale is to allow the working of the land, exactly the activity that the Torah expressly forbids.

However, this does not at all indicate that the advocates of *hetter* were insensitive to the spirit of the law. Quite the contrary, the issue was debated on the level of the long view. The advocates, notably among them R. Avraham Yitzchak HaKohen Kook,[102] acknowledged clearly that the goal was to reach a state where *Shemittah* would be observed fully in spirit and in letter. However, at a point where that reality was both unattainable and not then Biblically mandated, a temporary approach to serve as a bridge to bring the Jewish people to the point

100. See *Ran* ibid., *Tosafot Nedarim* 28a, s.v. *be-mokhes,* and *Rosh, Nedarim* 3: 11.
101. R. Ze'ev Weitman, *Li'krat Shemittah Mamlakhtit be-Medinat Yisrael,* p. 41, n. 18.
102. See, for example, *Resp. Mishpat Kohen,* 3 and 61.

where that *was* possible, should be considered itself a realization of the spirit of the law.[103]

Also, perhaps somewhat counterintuitively, in that utilization of the *hetter mekhirah* seems to create a complete exemption from *Shemittah,* for many non-observant farmers it actually represented their only connection to *Shemittah* practice. This element factors heavily in the advocacy of R. Kook[104] as well as that of contemporary supporters.[105]

However, this concern is also complex. Opponents of the *hetter* argue that the plan's implementation at worst causes widespread sin and deception, and at best advocates a watered-down observance of a *halakhah* that could be more fully adhered to. A more directed concern is discussed by R. Weitman.[106] In an effort to include as many farmers in the sale as possible, and thus to prevent them from knowingly or unknowingly abandoning *Shemittah* entirely, the contracts and the sale are done in a manner that is vague and overly broad. As an unintended consequence, the genuine nature of the sale, and the required *gemirut da'at,* are compromised. He instead recommends (and has personally implemented) narrowing the scope of the sale, and thus enhancing its effectiveness and its acceptability when utilized. Thus, on a macro- and micro-level, the goal of maximizing "bringing merit to the masses" is clearly a complex equation.[107]

Some rabbis oppose the *hetter,* or consider it to be necessary but extremely unfortunate, because when used it can create an environment where *Shemittah* need not be thought about at all. This is

---

103. *Resp. Yeshuot Malko*, YD 53. Similarly, R. Aharon Lichtenstein, in a *sichah,* asserted that no approach to *Shemittah* observance at that time perfectly captured its spirit. (*Leaves of Faith Vol. II,* 179, 181–183; originally published as a Hebrew article in 1973, translated and updated in 1994.)

104. *Iggerot Ra'ayah,* 291.

105. See the extensive treatment of this point by R. Yehudah HaLevi Amichai, *HaTorah V'Ha'aretz* pp. 439–443.

106. R. Ze'ev Weitman, *Techumin* XXVII (2006), p. 22.

107. See also *Sefer HaShemittah,* pp. 82–83, who considers different aspects of this question, and asserts that when a greater percentage of the population would ignore the mandates of *Shemittah,* there is a greater need to arrange for permissible methods.

perhaps true to a greater degree than with other mechanisms (for example, *Otzar Beit Din*,[108] among others[109]) suggested to address *Shemittah* in a modern context.[110] R. Zevin, in the end of his essay on

108. *Otzar Beit Din* is is a method of collectively distributing fruits of the *Shemittah* year, based on a description found in the *Tosefta* (*Shevi'it* 8:1 and *Torat Kohanim, Behar* 1:6) and cited by the Ramban in his commentary to the Torah (Lev. 25:7), in which he explains that this undertaking was to address the fear that farmers would otherwise hold back or sell their produce. *Resp. Rashbash*, 258, suggests it serves the purpose of keeping the produce available for the Jewish community. By contrast, some *rishonim* seem to have not accepted the concept, either interpreting the *tosefta* differently (see *Maharash Cirilio, Shvi'it* (9:4 and 6) or not codifying it (such as the Rambam; see *Radbaz, Hil. Shemittah* 7:3).

    Accordingly, efforts in the modern era to institute an *Otzar Beit Din* structure (see R. A.Y. Kook, *Resp. Mishpat Kohen*, 76; *Iggerot Ra'ayah*, I:313; and see *Mishnat Yosef*, III, 51, regarding the *Chazon Ish*) have met with some controversy, either because of the debated validity of the model, or because of objections to the degree of compliance with the historical model (See R. Y. I. Herzog, *Pesakim U'Ketavim*, III, 72; R. Mordechai Eliyahu, *Ma'amar Mordechai*, p. 113, and *ma'amarim*, 11). Some have maintained that *Otzar Beit Din* should only be implemented in conjunction with the *hetter mekhirah* (as was the case in R. Kook's model), and thus have asserted that it is not an alternative to the *hetter* but actually an additional reason to employ it.

    However, there are those who have argued that *Oztar Beit Din* is indeed an alternative, and in fact a far superior one (R. Y.Z. Rimon, *Shemittah*, pp. 305–306, claims this will be the model in effect in Messianic times). Among other factors, this is for reasons surrounding the spirit of the law, and that are central to the *ha'aramah* question. While the *hetter mekhirah*, as noted, can lead to a complete disassociation from the awareness of *Shemittah, Otzar Beit Din* preserves the connection. Further, as R. Dr. Ari Bergmann has noted, it can be stated that *Otzar Beit Din* is actually the purest expression of the spirit of *Shemittah*.

    This premise emerges from an understanding that the "*hefker*" status of produce during *Shemittah* should not be taken in its usual sense as "ownerless." Rather, the term in this instance is meant to shift individual ownership to communal ownership. R. Yehoshua Leib Diskin (*Resp. Maharil Diskin, kuntres acharon*, 259) observes that the language of the Torah *evyonei amekha* ("the poor of your people," Ex. 23:11) indicates that the produce is not actually ownerless, but the property of the Jewish people. (A similar point is made in *Avi Ezri, Hil. Shemittah V'Yovel*, 4:24, and compare also *Sha'arei Yosher*, 5:23, s.v. *v'nireh*). Accordingly, an appropriately run *Otzar Beit Din* model, which allows the population to share in all the produce of *Shemittah*, may be seen as an affirmation of the spirit of the *mitzvah*.

109. See *Sefer HaShemittah*, p. 66.

110. See, for example, R. Yitzchak Isaac Halevi Herzog, *Pesakim U'Ketavim*, III, 48, 203–210; the articles of Rabbis Weitman, Amichai, and Weissman, *Techumin* XXVII

the *hetter mekhirah*, provides numerous recommendations for how to maintain the spirit and the consciousness of *Shemittah* while still utilizing the *hetter*.

Similarly, R. Yosef Zvi HaLevi, the son-in law and successor to R. Naftali Hertz and the rabbi of Jaffa in the late nineteenth century, writing in his work pointedly entitled *Hora'at Sha'ah* (an exigent, temporary ruling) records that he advocated to those who were utilizing the *hetter* to reserve a small portion of their land to be excluded from the sale and with that portion to fulfill all of the details of the laws of *Shemittah*, with the hope that this should be a source of merit for the speedy restoration of the full status of the obligations.[111]

An aspirational component particular to *Shemittah* informs this consideration as well. The *Beit HaLevi*,[112] as part of his objection to the *hetter mekhirah*, posits that even a rabbinic version of the *Shemittah* mandate is different in its nature than other rabbinic commandments within the pantheon of agricultural law, in which the question of non-Jewish ownership and its impact had been considered. In those contexts, for example in the geographical regions where the entire sanctity of the land is completely rabbinic, the *Shemittah* mandate is similarly devoid of Biblical character. By contrast, in the actual land of Israel proper, even if the contemporary obligation of *Shemittah* is rabbinic, it is rooted in the original Biblical obligation.[113] Accordingly, there is a value to the voluntary observance of *Shemittah* in this case as a fulfillment of the Divine will, in other words, the spirit of the law, that the sale of the land will not remove.

The major issue of *lo techanem* was also addressed on a "letter and spirit" level. While advocates of the *hetter* advanced a number of arguments to defend against accusations of violating this prohibition, a

---

(2006); R Yoel Friedman, "The Solution To 'The Shemittah Problem' on Plantations" [in Hebrew], *HaTorah V'HaAretz: Shevi'it* 6 (2000), 376.

111. See also *Sefer HaShemittah*, p. 73.

112. Resp. III, 1:7:1.

113. He draws a distinction on this point between the view that maintains that the sanctity of the land is itself rabbinic in modern times, and that which maintains that the sanctity of the land is Biblical, but *Shemittah*, linked to the practice of *Yovel*, is rabbinic.

significant track of the debate was to address the "spirit" of *lo techanem.* Among the arguments was that to avoid a temporary sale, and instead promote the purchasing of produce from non-Jewish vendors, thus strengthening their economic hold on the land, was itself a greater offense against the spirit of *lo techanem.*[114] A number of authorities asserted that *lo techanem* did not apply when the sale was for the benefit of the Jews.[115] As R. Shlomo Yosef Zevin explained, the point was not technical but conceptual: The sale is not made to facilitate "a resting place" for the non-Jews, but to ensure one for the Jews.[116]

Even more broadly, debate surrounded the wider goals of not just *Shemittah,* but the religious imperative of settling the land. The *Ridbaz* challenged the *hetter mekhirah* by stating that it defeats the point of settling the land by avoiding the fulfillment of the land-dependent *mitzvot.* R. Kook countered by asserting that living in Israel is a value in and of itself, and even toward the land-dependent *mitzvot,* it performs a preparatory role, just as Torah study is valuable even when the subject matter is not practical. Accordingly, he argued, it is the responsibility of halakhic authorities to ensure that no single *mitzvah* impedes the fulfillment of the broader imperative of settling the land, as long as there is an acceptable halakhic approach available.[117]

R. Zevulun Leib Barit, a rabbinic correspondent of R. Tzvi Hirsch Kalisher and other figures of early religious Zionism, noted in one of his letters[118] an apparent irony connected to criticism of the members of those settlements that relied on the *hetter mekhirah* or similar mechanisms. It is true, he acknowledged, that the Talmud teaches that observance of *Shemittah* is crucial for the Jewish people maintaining their presence in the land. Further, it is presumably correct that even an approach that technically succeeds in avoiding the obligation of

---

114. See R. Shaul Yisraeli, in a letter to R. Eliyahu Shlesinger, printed in the latter's *Resp. Sho'alin V'Dorshin,* III, p. 417.
115. *Resp. Yeshuot Malko,* 55 and 69; *Resp. Mishpat Kohen,* 58.
116. *L'Ohr HaHalakhah.* See also R. Yehudah ha-Levi Amichai, "Hetter Mekhirah in Shemittah – To Whom and For Whom" [in Hebrew], *Techumin* XXVII (2006), pp. 29–35.
117. *Shabbat HaAretz,* pp. 170–174; see also *Iggerot Ra'ayah,* II, p. 195.
118. Printed in *Shivat Tziyon,* I, p. 52, and dated 7th Kislev, 5751 (Nov. 19, 1890).

Shemittah may not escape this concern. However, to level this criticism is to acknowledge that settling the land is a paramount value, and the beginning of the process of redemption; accordingly, the detractors should properly credit those who are pursuing this mission, and appreciate the difficulties involved, and recognize as well that the *hetter,* controversial as it may be, developed with the support of towering Torah scholars.[119]

THE FACTOR OF NEED

The final element of the formula, the factor of need, is actually one of the greatest battleground areas in the *hetter mekhirah* debate. Even in Talmudic times, this factor was a halakhic consideration. The Talmud[120] discusses a tax known as "*arnona,*" the needs of which justified working the land during *Shemittah.* There are numerous opinions as to what it was about this circumstance that allowed such activity; some suggest that the conclusion is that a *she'at ha-dechak* could justify work during the *Shemittah* (perhaps because of the non-Biblical status). Others dispute the relevance, arguing that only life-threatening situations qualify, or that *arnona* represented actual loss rather than unrealized profit.[121]

This issue fuels the debate anew every seven years, because the assessment of just how necessary it is or is not to utilize the *hetter* is

---

119. "*Geonim Adirim asher mi-pihem anu chayim.*"

120. *Sanhedrin* 26a.

121. *Tosafot* to *Sanhedrin,* s.v. *mi-she-rabu,* offers two approaches, the second one being that the situation was deemed life or death. However, it is clear from *Tosafot*'s opening question that that is addressing the assumption that *Shemittah* is applicable on a Torah level. The first answer implies that when *Shemittah* is rabbinic, the standard is lower.

Aside from extrapolating categorically, R. Yosef Engel, *Otzerot Yosef,* 3:1–23, maintained that the specific license of *arnona* was still relevant in his day, as then as well there was a tax on the land that would not be able to be paid unless income could be derived from the land.

Tosafot, in mentioning the threat of death, cites from the *Talmud Yerushalmi* a reference to *chayei nefesh,* and understands that to mean that the Jews would be arrested for failing to pay the tax and could die in prison. R. Engel asserted that the *Yerushalmi* was actually saying something else: a number of rabbinic prohibitions have built-in exceptions for that which is necessary for basic sustenance. That is presumably what is being stated here, regarding rabbinic *Shemittah;* and since so many were completely dependent on the land for their livelihood, this exception should continue to apply (at that time).

affected by myriad factors that change over time and that are subjectively interpreted. One such example is the establishment of the State in 1948, which impacted the question in many different ways, but also affected the evaluation of need. Here, too, the nature of that impact is subject to debate. Some argue that the dependency of a national economy makes some allowance for work of the land even more urgent. Others will argue just the opposite; the *hetter mekhirah* was needed in the circumstances under which it was originally endorsed, i.e., a few scattered settlements barely subsiding with no safety net. A national infrastructure, by contrast, is able to provide much more broadly, and should not rely on the *hetter.*[122] Either way, the question is crucial. R. Ahron Soloveichik, a descendant of many of the strong opponents of the *hetter,* when asked his opinion, responded that it all came down to one issue. If it is needed, it should be used; if it is not, it should not be.

As was the case in the earlier generations, the question of need continues to be examined from both economic and spiritual perspectives. An instructive window into the considerations is a responsum published by the then-Sefardi Chief Rabbi of Israel, R. Eliyahu Bakshi Doron, regarding the usage of the *hetter* for the *Shemittah* year of 5761 (2000–2001). After acknowledging the many concerns and counterarguments relevant to applying the original leniency at that stage of modern Israel's development, he concludes,[123]

"in light of the factors, when faced with the question of the sustenance of many farmers, and the removal of a stumbling block of many regarding working during *Shemittah,* and removing the stumbling block from the many regarding the forbidden consumption of the fruits of *Shemittah,* and in particular when a result could be the faltering of the system of *kashrut,* and the broad population will stumble in the prohibition of *orlah* and of non-kosher meat on a Torah level, we have decided to rely on the permissive opinions regarding the *hetter mekhirah* this year as well, within an effort to constrict the leniency and to act as much as possible with a narrow approach rather than in a sweeping fashion."

---

122. See *She'erit Yosef,* ibid., citing several references to R. Kook's writings. See also the considerations on both sides discussed in *Sefer HaShemittah,* II, 1:5.

123. *Resp. Binyan Av,* IV, 62 (free translation).

Following this conclusion, R. Bakshi-Doron makes a bolder assertion, that this policy is a sound one not only according to those who grudgingly acknowledge the basic effectiveness of the *hetter,* but even according to those who maintain that the sale is completely invalid or functionally defective. This is based on an admittedly expansive reading of the Talmudic principle, "*mutav sheyiyhu shogegim v'al yehiyu mezidim*":[124] it is preferable for those who would be sinning in any event, to do so out of ignorance rather than informed contempt. Given that many farmers will work the land regardless, it would be an accomplishment if they would do so under the umbrella of even a mistaken, invalid dispensation rather than simply disregarding *Shemittah* entirely.[125]

As the debate indeed continues to rage, driven by these and other considerations, the intensity of the views can mask both the sincerity and the superior scholarship of those who staked positions on both sides of this contentious issue. Regardless of one's conclusions on the matter, objectivity and the honor due to great *talmidei chakhamim* demand that these qualities not be ignored.[126] All involved in this debate agree that we eagerly await the time when *Shemittah* will be completely applicable on a Torah level, to a Jewish nation fully restored to its homeland. Perhaps, the manner in which the subject is discussed will play a role in hastening that moment.

---

124. *Beitzah* 30a.

125. R. Bakshi-Doron's predecessor in his position, R. Mordechai Eliyahu, also published an essay (*Ma'amar Mordechai, ma'amarim,* 21) arguing that it is important to accept the *hetter mekhirah* at least after the fact, in that rejecting its legitimacy completely would incur a number of halakhic complexities that would be spiritually deleterious for the nation.

126. It is highly instructive on this point to read the carefully worded and painstakingly balanced statements of one of the preeminent halakhic authorities of the twentieth century, R. Shlomo Zalman Auerbach, in his introduction to *Ma'adanei Aretz* (written when he was thirty-four years old).

Chapter 7

The *Prozbol* and the Remission of Loans

One of the most widely referenced tools in the category at hand is also related to *Shemittah* observance, namely, the *Prozbol.* It is also, perhaps, the most oversimplified and misunderstood. In brief, the *Prozbol* is a document that forestalls the cancellation of loans at the end of the *Shemittah* year, and allows the lender to collect after they would otherwise have been released. This mechanism is often invoked to make the case that the rabbis are empowered to evade the Torah whenever they have sufficient motivation, in this instance, it is claimed, to benefit the lenders who would otherwise go unpaid. Given the implications of such an assertion, it is of particular importance to clarify the basis for the acceptance and utilization of the *Prozbol.*

It should be noted at the outset that the pedigree of the *Prozbol* is of a significantly different stature than the other devices we have discussed. An institution of the great leader Hillel the Elder, the *Prozbol* is already mentioned in the *Mishnah*[1] and is codified in the *Tur* and *Shulchan Arukh.*[2] The acceptance of *Prozbol* is not subject to debate;[3] accordingly, the issue left for analysis in this case is why that is so.

It similarly must be noted that contrary to common presentation, *Prozbol* most likely does not represent the abrogation of Torah law. The Talmud[4] explicitly (at least according to one opinion) relates the implementation of the *Prozbol* to the premise that in the contemporary era, the cancellation of loans, "*Shemitat Kesafim,*" is mandated only by rabbinic law. Significantly, the purpose of this enactment is identified as "a remembrance of *Shemittah,*" as Rashi frames it, "so that the Torah of *Shemittah* is not forgotten." The actual status of *Shemitat Kesafim* in modern times was debated by the *rishonim,*[5] with the *Shulchan Arukh* ruling that it is rabbinic, and the *Rama* citing views that it is actually not binding at all, but rather observed as a matter of custom.

However, *rishonim* argued as to the significance of this factor. According to the Rambam,[6] the *Prozbol* is only effective because of the rabbinic nature of *Shemittah* at present.[7] The *Ra'avad,* however, disagrees, associating that understanding with only one view in the Talmud (Abaye). However, according to the other view, Rava, *Prozbol* is a function of the rabbinic power to reassign property (*hefker beit din hefker*). Given that such authority is effective even on a Torah level, the *Prozbol* is as well.[8]

---

1. *Shvi'it* 10:3–7.
2. CM 67:18–38.
3. Meaning, not in the modern era; in the Talmud, there is objection recorded to its institution and discussion surrounding it. See *Gittin* 36b.
4. *Gittin* 36a–b.
5. Some maintain it is binding by Torah law (the *Ba'al Ha'Ittur,* and others), some that it is rabbinic (*Ramban, Makkot* 3b [although some quote him as being in the first camp]; Rambam, *Hilkhot Shemittah V'Yovel,* 9:3; *Ran* to *Gittin,* s.v. *v'yesh*), and some that it is not binding at all, but a voluntary expression of piety, a *midat chassidut* (*Ra'avad* to *Rif, Gittin,* and a number of others). See, also *Shabbat HaAretz,* and, at length, R. Shalom Pollak, *Resp. Mishnat Shalom,* I, 21.
6. *Hilkhot Shemittah V'Yovel,* 9:16.
7. See also *Bartenura, Shvi'it* 10:3.
8. The commentaries discuss why the Rambam apparently does not accept this premise; see *Melekhet Shlomo* to *Shvi'it,* 10:3; *Radbaz, Hil. Shemittah V'Yovel.* 9:16; *Minchat Asher, Gittin,* #60.

If that is the case, the significance of the rabbinic status of *Shemittah* would seem to be that while *Prozbol* could be effective in either case, its use is only advocated due to the rabbinic nature of *Shemittah*. This sentiment is expressed by *Tosafot*,[9] that there are various effective ways to avoid the cancellation of loans during *Shemittah*, but Hillel would not have recommended their utilization, had it involved the subversion of Torah law.[10]

This comment is perhaps reflective of one understanding we have seen in the avoidance of *ha'aramot* in relation to Torah law, the concern that the intent of the Torah is being undermined. When rabbinic law is involved, this factor appears to be less significant, as discussed earlier, possibly reflective of structural and conceptual differences in the two systems.

Further, there may be more local factors at play. One is that the goals of two versions of the commandment may be different. The Torah *mitzvah* of *shemittat kesafim* is presumably to provide amnesty for the needy borrowers. The rabbinic version, which as noted is to serve as a tool to preserve the memory of *Shemittah*, may be focused more on that specific purpose than on achieving the identical economic result.

Additionally, the nature of *Shemittah* without the full package of the Torah mandate, and its associated blessings, may significantly affect the dynamic, as will be explored below.

---

9. *Gittin* 36a, s.v. *mi*.
10. See *Tosafot R. Akiva Eiger, Shvi'it* 10:3; *Otzerot Yosef Shvi'it* 1, #27; and *Resp. Tirosh V'Yitzhar*, 89:1.

    Some understand the intent of this *Tosafot* to be specifically relevant to the utilization of *Hefker Beit Din Hefker*, which even when effective, would be inappropriate if it contradicted the intent of the Torah. (See *Korban Netanel* to *Rosh, Gittin*, 4:13:4, and *Maharam Shif* to *Tosafot*.) This then becomes a subtopic of the general *ha'aramah* issue, and a weighing of the letter of the law against the spirit of the law. R. Yitzchak HaLevi Herzog, in his *Techukah L'Yisrael Al Pi HaTorah*, devoted an entire section to establishing that *Hefker Beit Din Hefker* would not be utilized in a fashion that gives the impression of undermining the intention of the Torah, drawing applications to *Prozbol* as well as other areas, such as the laws of inheritance (see Chapter 8). R. Avraham Kahana Schapiro, who would himself later occupy R. Herzog's position as Ashkenazic Chief Rabbi of Israel, disputed this view in a letter later published in his *Resp. Minchat Avraham*, IV, 30.

THE OPERATING MECHANISM OF *PROZBOL*

Regarding the letter of the law, as the validity of the *Prozbol* is not in dispute, the question is more to the nature of its effectiveness. To this point, there are a number of possibilities, with some understanding that the *Prozbol* makes use of an existing mechanism, such as the aforementioned *hefker beit din hefker,*[11] or "*moser shtarotav l'beit din*" in which debtor notes are submitted to the *Beit Din,* which has the authority to collect even after *Shemittah.*[12] If so, Hillel's contribution was to advocate the usage of these preexisting mechanisms. Others understand that the *Prozbol* is its own institution, not a perfect match for the above tools.[13]

The *Prozbol* does contain the language, addressed to the *Beit Din,* of "*mosrani lakhem,*" "I turn over to you," which would seem to support the theory that it is a form of "*moser shtarotav l'beit din.*" However, R. Asher Weiss[14] advances a theory (within the view of the Rambam) that the mechanism is actually a declaration before the *Beit Din* of an intent to collect the debt at the later date.[15] Accordingly, the language is referring to the "submission" of a notification (*mesirat moda'ah*).

---

11. As per the *Ra'avad,* ibid; Rashi, *Gittin* 36b. s.v. *Rava; Rashba. Gittin* 36b, s.v. *u-mi.*
12. *Shvi'it.* 10:2. That this is the mechanism for *Prozbol* is the view of Rashi (*Makkot* 3b, s.v. *moser; Gittin* 32b, s.v *mosrani; Ketubot* 89a, s.v *prozbol*). However, *Tosafot. Makkot* 3b s.v. *ha-moser,* notes that the *mishnah* lists *moser shtarotav* and *Prozbol* as two separate things. *Ritva, Makkot,* suggests that Rashi's understanding is that Hillel established the *Prozbol* as an extension of this concept, to eliminate the need for the individual to do so himself. See also *Ran, Gittin* 36a; *Gilyonei HaShas, Gittin* 36a; and also *Mishnah Rishonah, Shvi'it* 10:2. For a possible practical ramification of the distinction between these views, see R. Elchanan Peretz, *Chukkat Mishpat,* 30. See also R. Ovadiah Yosef, *Chazon Ovadiah, Prozbol,* p. 47.

    R. Yosef Engel, *Otzerot Yosef,* 1, 29, understands that the involvement of *Beit Din* in the execution of the *Prozbol* guarantees their continuing participation in the collection of the loan at a later date, and thus grants the loan a status of collected in advance (*k'gavuy*), thus negating the *Shemittah* cancellation.
13. See R. Shlomo Wahrman, *She'erit Yosef,* I, 29, and R. Michael Rosensweig, *Beit Yitzchak,* XXXIII (5761), who both analyze the possibilities and note the distinction that if *hefker beit din* is the operative mechanism, the loan actually was canceled, but an identical sum was transferred back to the lender; while if *Prozbol* is a new rabbinic innovation, it functions by blocking the rabbinically mandated cancellation. See also *Torat Zeraim, Shvi'it,* 10:3, and *Mikra HaEdah,* XIX, 76.
14. *Minchat Asher, Gittin,* #58.
15. See also R. Betzalel Blidstein, *Chelkat Betzalel al haTorah,* 91.

THE SPIRIT OF THE LAW

It is in the area of the spirit of the law that the *Prozbol* makes its case most clearly. While it is often portrayed as a method to enable the lenders to collect, it is clearly stated in the Talmud that the concern is the borrowers, who may not find willing lenders if cancellation of the debt is threatened.

It is true that the Talmud[16] offers two understandings of the word "*Prozbol*," with the first being *pros buli*, an "ordinance for the wealthy" to be repaid, and secondarily *pros buti*, an "ordinance for the poor" to receive loans.[17] However, later commentators make clear the benefit to the wealthy is saving them from the sin of declining to loan for fear of default.[18]

---

16. *Gittin* 36b–37a.
17. Regarding the relationship between this interpretation and the actual translation of the Greek word *prozbol*, see *Chiddushei Anshei Shem, Shvi'it* 10:3, who maintains that the Talmudic statement is not intended as actual etymology but is rather a homiletic interpretation, a practice the Rabbis extended to words in foreign languages as well.
18. While some commentaries do cite this passage in reference to preventing financial loss to the wealthy (see Rashi, 37a, s.v *buli u'buti*; Rashbam, *Bava Batra* 65b, s.v. *harei*; *Rash MiSanz* to *Shvi'it* 10:3; the *Kessef Mishneh, Hil. Mamrim* 2:2, takes this position for technical reasons; see the analysis of his view in R. Yosef David Zinsheim, *Minchat Ani, erekh Prozbol*, and also the comments of R. Herzog, ibid., p. 18), others are quick to assert that the accomplishment on behalf of the wealthy was saving them from transgression (see *Bartenura, Shvi'it*, 10:3, and *Moed Katan* 3:3, and *Shenot Eliyahu* of the Gaon of Vilna to *Shvi'it*; the *Yakhin* commentary mentions both). As the *Hon Ashir (Shevi'it)* emphasizes, Hillel was concerned for spiritual protection rather than material protection. See also *Bekhor Shor, Makkot* 3b, who brings additional reasoning to show that the emphasis in terms of the wealthy is spiritual benefit. Further, R. Shalom Dov Ber Grinzon, *Resp. Hekhalei Shein*, II, 84, posits a theory of the functionality of *Prozbol* that is completely contingent on the premise that it is addressing sinful behavior.

    The assumption that a purpose of *Prozbol* is to save the lenders from transgression is also crucial to the position that one can write a *Prozbol* on behalf of another, without their knowledge, so that their collection of loans will not technically be sinful; see *Chazon Ovadiah: Prozbol*, pp. 75–77.

    The *Rama* (OC 545:5) mentions both the advantage to the rich of not losing the money and to the poor that the loans will be available, consistent with the commentary of Rashi to the Talmud. It is possible to read this as one connected idea, in that the needy will find loans available due to the rich having confidence in repayment.

Given that premise, the utilization of the *Prozbol* is a clear protection of the spirit of the law. The commandment to provide loans to the needy is one of the primary examples in the Torah[19] and the Talmud[20]

Additionally, the *Bach* (CM 67:20) describes a sort of negative synergy that is feared: many of the rich will refuse to lend. The righteous among them, fearful of the Torah prohibition, will continue to lend; however, the reduction in loan opportunities will leave the poor continuously in need, thus requiring the righteous wealthy to extend themselves further. The poor, still not adequately addressed, will be unable to pay back before *Shemittah,* and thus further impact their righteous benefactors. Thus, *Prozbol* it is necessary to prevent this cycle of harm that impacts the poor (who are unable to find sufficient financial support), the righteous wealthy (who are impacted financially more than they would otherwise be able to absorb), and the less righteous wealthy (who will be in violation of a transgression).

The *Maharik* (*shoresh* 1, s.v. *v'od yesh*) observes that the Talmud was specifically noting in this context the benefit to the poor and the wealthy, because the statement immediately followed an objection of Shmuel that *Prozbol* was an inappropriate use of rabbinic authority, apparently because it favors one party at the expense of another party. To that the response is offered that it benefits both. See *Gilyonei HaShas* to *Gittin.*

Chiddushei Anshei Shem, Shvi'it, puts forward a fascinating suggestion that while the main focus of the enactment is indeed the poor, the word highlights the benefit to the wealthy in order to show them that their financial stability is also being protected by the Rabbis, which in turn will reassure them and encourage them to lend more generously. Accordingly, even the very name used is itself a measure to aid the needy. (Compare the inverse suggestion in *Ma'amar Mordechai,* #27, pp. 405–406).

This last explanation serves also to address why the name *Prozbol* would prevail over "*Prozbot,*" thus including only the benefit to the rich in the description. Alternatively, the *Bekhor Shor* suggests this is because the poor have an alternative, in that they can agree to a stipulation not to cancel the loan, and then receive the assistance that is needed. However, if they would refuse such an arrangement, the potential lender would be in violation were he to refuse (see below). See also R. Baruch Kelai, *Resp. Mekor Baruch,* 58, who (while also considering that the focus is the preventing of the prohibition) suggests that the wording is not significant, either because it is chosen for ease of pronunciation, or because it is actually a contraction of "Prusbulibuti" and implies both aspects. However, these answers are only necessary if the assumption is that the Talmud is conveying the actual etymology of the word; if, as noted above, they are merely conveying a homiletic interpretation, no further explanation is needed.

19. Ex. 22:24 (and see *Mekhilta*); and Lev. 25:35–36.

20. See *Sukkah* 49b, and Rashi s.v. *u-v-mamono.*

of the attribute of *chesed,* itself one of the primary identifying attributes of the Jewish people.

The centrality of the *mitzvah* of financial loans is evident as well in the fact that it is the focus of a cluster of supporting *mitzvot* that surround it. Beyond the imperative of the loan itself, there is the strict prohibition against taking interest; a prohibition against pressuring the borrower for repayment;[21] and, a mandate of loan amnesty every seven years.

The Torah already strongly expressed the concern that the supporting *mitzvah* of loan cancellation does not undermine the main *mitzvah* of providing loans in the first place. "Beware that there be not a lawless thought (*bliya'al*) in your heart, saying: 'the seventh year, the year of release, is at hand;' and your eye be evil against your needy brother, and you refuse to give him; and he will cry unto the Lord against you, and it will be sin upon you."[22]

The conflict within the values of the law is highlighted by a comment of the Ramban[23] who challenges a position maintained by a number of the *rishonim*[24] that in the contemporary era, *shemittat kesafim* is not obligatory on any level, but is voluntarily practiced as an element of piety, a *midat chassidut.* The Ramban objected: given that this policy will reduce the likelihood of the needy receiving loans, what piety is there in that?

Certainly, with loan cancellation currently a rabbinic enactment, and thus a supportive measure now two steps away from the core imperative, it would be profoundly counterproductive to allow that measure to interfere with the ability of the needy to receive assistance.[25]

This background, together with a further consideration, may provide a foundation for a theory as to the operating mechanism of *Prozbol.* The Talmud teaches that it is possible for a lender and borrower

21. Ex. 22:24.
22. Deut. 15:9.
23. *Sefer HaZekhut, Gittin* 18a in pages of the *Rif.*
24. R. Zerachiah ha-Levi, *Gittin* 18a *be-dappei ha-Rif.* Meiri, *Gittin* 36a, s.v. *gorsim.*
25. R. Herzog, ibid p. 15, even suggests that the initial promulgation of the rabbinic *Shemittah,* and its acceptance by the public, was contingent on the assumption that the needy would not be deprived of financial assistance.

to stipulate that *Shemittah* not cancel a loan.[26] As such, the *rishonim* pose the question as to why *Prozbol* was a necessary enactment at all, given that the situation can be dealt with on an individual level. In fact, some understand that such a stipulation is assumed to be in effect, and that this is the justification for neglect of *shemitat kesafim* in later generations, which was justified by the explanation that the practice is not binding in the modern era.[27]

Among the suggestions offered among the *rishonim* as to why *Prozbol* was necessary when this stipulation was available were: avoiding the concern that the lender would forget to make the stipulation (and would instead decline to lend);[28] to prevent the appearance that the lender was giving up hope of collecting before the end of *Shemittah;* not to convey disrespect to *Shemittah;*[29] and, perhaps most significantly, that the *Prozbol,* in contrast to the stipulation, preserves the memory of *Shemittah,* an affirmative value.[30] Were all lenders to utilize the stipulation, all awareness of *Shemittah* would erode, in contrast to *Prozbol,* which achieves the result of the stipulation in the context of *Shemittah* observance. Further, the stipulation is a private matter, while *Prozbol* involves the *beit din,* and thus brings appropriate attention to the memory of *Shemittah.*[31]

---

26. *Makkot* 3b. As the Rambam (*Hilkhot Shemittah* 9:10) explains, this is due to the general ability to make stipulations in monetary matters.
27. *Ketzot HaChoshen.* CM 67, citing *Resp. Ha Rosh,* 77:2, 4. See *Resp. B'Dvar Melekh,* 48:2.
28. See *Ramban* and *Ritva* to *Gittin; Kaftor VaFerach* #49.
29. *Resp. Tirosh V'Yitzhar,* I, 89, understands this answer as reflective of the attitude noted earlier, that regarding the commandments of the Torah, there is an aversion to seeking methods of evasion.
30. All these suggestions are mentioned by the *Ritva* in his commentaries to *Makkot* and *Gittin.* See also *Ma'aseh Rokeach* to *Hil. Shemittah* and *Mishnah Rishonah, Shvi'it* 10:3. The *Sefer HaChinnukh,* 480, notes the question in a different fashion, formulated as why the Torah would issue a prohibition when the situation is so easily avoided, and dismisses the question, asserting the possibility of alternative approaches does not impede the Torah's general exhortation. See, also, a different approach in *Siach Yitzhak, Makkot* 3b, s.v. *u-vazeh,* and also *Geresh Yerachim, Gittin* 36a, #161.
31. See *Ramban, Gittin* 36a.

In later generations, more halakhically consequential explanations were advanced. The *Bekhor Shor* asserts that the stipulation possibility would be insufficient to assure that loans would be available to the needy, because it would only be an option if the borrower agreed to it. If he refused, and the lender consequently declined to provide the loan, the lender would be in violation of "Beware…." Only *Prozbol* allows the lender to collect on his loan, and avoid violating a prohibition, without the borrower's consent.[32] The *Chatam Sofer,* in his responsa,[33] goes even further than this.[34] In his understanding, even a lender who does make a loan, if he does so with the stipulation, would still violate the Torah's prohibition. Only through the usage of *Prozbol* would there be no violation when the lender collects his repayment.[35]

---

32. R. Yerucham Fishel Perlow, in his commentary to the *Sefer HaMitzvot* of R. Saadiah Gaon (Positive Commandment 25, Vol. I, pp. 168–169), analyzes this claim and concludes that it is against the opinions of all of the *rishonim,* with the exception of the *Ba'al HaIttur* (I, *ot peh, prozbol*) who agreed (and explains accordingly the need for the institution of *Prozbol* rather than a mandated stipulation, which would be advocating a transgression.) (An outlier in the other direction would be the *Meiri,* who preferred the stipulation to *Prozbol,* due to difficulties in meeting the standards for *Prozbol.*) See also R. Yitzchak Ralbag's footnotes to the Mossad HaRav Kook edition of *Chiddushei HaRitva, Makkot* 3b, n 211). An understanding similar to that of the *Bekhor Shor* is quoted in *Chiddushei Anshei Shem, Shvi'it* 10:3 (who also quotes the *Bekhor Shor* separately). A similar position is articulated by the *Chiddushei HaRim* at much greater length as part of his discussion in his comments to *Gittin.*

    Regarding the rationale of the majority view, the *Einayim L'Mishpat, Makkot* 3b, suggests these *rishonim* may believe a stipulation can be made against the will of the borrower. However, it may also be that since a loan is in any event being offered, there is no violation; see *Peninim MiBei Midrasha,* Deut. p. 125.

    R. Shmuel Rozovsky, *Shiurim* to *Makkot* 3b, understands the position of the *Bekhor Shor* to reflect an understanding that stipulation does not actually prevent the cancellation of the loan, but simply creates a new debt to the lender, which remains subject to the prohibition, as this cannot be imposed against the will of the borrower.
33. CM 113
34. The *Chatam Sofer* references the *Bekhor Shor,* but does not acknowledge the difference in formulation. See *Pitchei Teshuvah,* CM 67:2.
35. A similar position was taken by an earlier author, R. Baruch Kelai, *Resp. Mekor Baruch,* 58. He explains why this should be: one who will only loan with a stipulation must state as much before agreeing to the loan, thus displaying the "evil heart" (*ro'a lev*) condemned in the verse (actually the following verse, Deut. 15:10). *Prozbol,* by

R. Zvi Yechezkel Michaelson (1863–1942), in his responsa,[36] suggests this position reflects an aspect of the attitude noted earlier: it would be wrong to orchestrate an evasion of the Torah's intent, even when it is technically possible to do so. Accordingly, one who uses a stipulation to avoid the loan cancellation is removing himself from the purpose of *Shemittah;* as such, he is in violation of the Torah's directive.[37]

Whether or not these later positions are accepted, they direct a spotlight towards a crucial issue within the philosophy of *shemittat kesafim.* There is a fundamental dispute as to the focus of the prohibition of "Beware." One understanding is that it is addressed to any capable individual who declines to assist the needy with a loan. The context of *Shemittah* is utilized as a point of emphasis; even when there is a plausible basis to be concerned that the loan may be canceled, the lender still

---

contrast, is executed after the loan is already given, and thus does not cast any shadow on the lending process.

36. *Resp. Tirosh V'Yitzhar,* ibid.

37. A different version of the above question was posed in the literature as well. Given that *Shemittah* does not cancel a loan that has not yet come due, there would seem to be another option open to a lender who fears the impending *Shemittah* will cause him a loss: unilaterally extend the period of the loan so that it is due after the year is over, this preventing its cancellation. This question is premised on a view in *rishonim* that a lender may waive a debt without the consent of the borrower, and that extension is included in that right.

This question was included in R. Yoav Weingarten's list of vexing, unanswered questions, *Kava D'Kashyata* (#46, originally published in his *Resp. Chelkat Yoav*). In the edition published by R. Dovid Mandelbaum, Vol. II, pp. 105–119, he notes that the question had been raised by a number of others, and subsequently addressed at length. See, in particular, *Resp. Divrei Chaim,* 42. A number of authorities questioned components of the premise; to some, the question was the answer; the fact that *Prozbol* was considered a necessary enactment is proof that this strategy would not be effective. See also *Resp. Torat Michael,* 64, and the sources cited in the last paragraph, and *Gilyonei HaShas, Gittin* 36a, s.v. *she-ra'ah,* citing *Resp. Mishpatim Yesharim,* I, 127, and see also *Chiddushei HaRim,* CM 67:7.

R. Mordechai Eliyahu, *Ma'amar Mordechai, ma'amarim,* 26, asserts that the very concern that "the Torah of *Shevi'it* not be forgotten" that has played such a prominent role thus far is sufficient reason to disallow a lender from extending the period of his loan for this purpose.

must not refuse. All the more so, it need not be said, to decline without such justification is certainly wrong.[38]

According to others, however, "Beware" is not directed at anyone who declines to loan under normal circumstances. It is specifically the lender who is fearful of *Shemittah* who is termed *"bliya'al."* In this view, the critique is a particular condemnation, apparently, of an attempt to avoid participation in the Divine mandate of *Shemittah,* perhaps a display of lack of faith.[39]

The Maharam Shick[40] combines the two ideas in an innovative fashion. It is true, he acknowledges, that one is not obligated to lend to an individual who is not trusted to repay, at least not without collateral. Apparently, he is not required to place his funds at risk of default. However, if his fear is due to the impending *Shemittah* cancellation, he is condemned for that, even if the risk is comparable. It seems that the mandate of *Shemittah* imposes an expanded mentality of generosity and forbearance, and specifically in that context, one is sanctioned for refusal to absorb a risk that at other times would be an understandable instinct.

Similarly, Rabbenu Bachya[41] and the *Minchat Chinukh*[42] assert that the prohibition applies even in regards to a charitable donation.[43] Given that the loan cancellation would have no bearing on such a

---

38. *Sha'arei Teshuvah,* 3:67. Note also *Sotah* 47b, where the verse is apparently applied to all refusal to lend. See also R. Ya'akov Kaminetsky, *Emet L'Ya'akov,* to Deut., and the footnotes there.
39. *Mishneh Torah, Hil. Shemittah VeYovel* 9:30 and *Sefer HaMitzvot,* prohibition 231; *Sefer HaChinnukh,* 480; *Sefer Mitzvot Gadol,* prohibitions, 271; and *Lechem Mishneh, Hil. Malveh U'Loveh,* 1:1. This is also the implication of the *Chafetz Chaim* in his *Ahavat Chesed,* II, 8, in fn; although see also his formulation in *Petichah, lavin #1, Netiv HaChesed* #1. See also the analysis of *Resp. Shevivei Eish,* CM I, 38 (also published in *Shemitat Kesafim K'Hilkhatah: Shevivei Eish,* 1).
40. *Sefer HaMitzvot,* #67.
41. Commentary to Deut.
42. *Mitzvah* 480.
43. This interpretation actually is more consistent with the text, in that the exhortation of "Beware" does not appear in the context of the loan cancellation, but actually several verses later in the context of charity. Nonetheless, most commentaries do assume it is an exhortation against withholding loans for fear of cancellation.

donation, it appears that the expanded mandate of generosity in the *Shemittah* year impacts the responsibility to donate charitably as well.

R. Shimon Sofer, in his *Resp. Hitorerut Teshuvah*[44] understands that the blessing promised to those who observe the *Shemittah* mandate to leave the land fallow, that they will not be deprived of produce, is applicable to the *Shemittah* of loan cancellation as well. In other words, one who declines to loan as *Shemittah* approaches, afraid he will be left poorer, is guilty of denying the Divine guarantee that there is nothing to fear and that his finances will be secure.[45]

Notably, this approach then forces the question asked regarding the *Shemittah* of the fields, that was a crucial philosophical issue in the *hetter mekhirah* debate: if the assumption is that *Shemittah* today is a rabbinic obligation rather than a Torah mandate, does the blessing still apply?[46] The question is vital in addressing one of the major spirit of the law concerns; is one displaying a lack of faith in God's commitment if one seeks to avoid either aspect of *Shemittah*? Regarding the cancellation of loans, if the blessing does not apply, and the prohibition of declining loans is connected to that blessing, the issue is recast significantly.[47]

If, by contrast, the prohibition of "Beware" is directed at any hesitancy to loan for an inadequate reason, and *Shemittah* is simply an example, then even a rabbinically mandated *Shemittah* would certainly be sufficient to trigger the prohibition. This does seem to be the simple

44. CM 11 and 12.

45. See his later responsum (#15), in which he considers the question of whether the Torah obligates loaning to one who is intentionally timing his borrowing to benefit from the cancellation of *Shemittah.*

46. see page 111-112.

47. The *Chatam Sofer* (*Chiddushim* to *Gittin* 36a) takes this position, assuming that the prohibition is only in effect when *shemittat kesafim* is a Biblical obligation, with the attendant blessing of "because for this thing the Lord your God will bless you in all your works and all that you put your hand to" (Deut. 15:10). R. Yehoshua Leib Diskin is cited in a note in R. Yechiel Michel Tukachinsky's *Sefer HaShemittah,* p. 57, as asserting there should be no reason for the prohibition to apply in an era when the cancellation is only rabbinic in nature. See also his comments in *Sefer Ohalim, Gittin,* 36a, regarding the possibility of a rabbinic prohibition at that point. See R. Shaul Alter, *Yalkut Shiurim,* 18:2.

reading of the passage in the Talmud, and is the explicit view of authorities such as the *Sefer HaChinnukh.*[48]

If indeed *Prozbol* serves to neutralize the prohibition of "Beware…," it may then be serving one or more of two possible purposes: to assure that loans will be granted, at once saving the borrower from the pangs of poverty and the lender from the ignominy of sin; and preserving a connection to the mission of *Shemittah.*

A FRAMEWORK FOR *PROZBOL*

In the medieval era, a number of the rabbinic leaders noticed that *shemittat kesafim* was not being observed, and yet the *Prozbol* was not being utilized either.[49] In an effort to justify the practice, some posited that the dominant opinion of the time was the view, noted above, that *Shemittah* does not apply in the modern era, neither by Torah nor rabbinic law, and is only observed as a voluntary expression of piety. This view is sufficiently prominent that it is recorded in the *Rama* in the opening statement of the laws of *Prozbol.*[50]

Some argued for a more broadly based justification. The *Rosh,*[51] for example, suggested that the widespread disregard of the *Shemittah* mandate amounted to consent of the borrower to the noncancellation of the loan, and thus an implicit stipulation.[52]

---

48. *Mitzvah* 480. See also *Chiddushei HaRim* to *Gittin.* This position is also expressed by R. Shlomo Zalman Auerbach, *Resp, Minchat Shlomo,* I, 47:1, where it is connected to his understanding that the circumstances involve a loan due prior to *Shemittah.* Accordingly, the fear that repayment will be delayed until after the cancellation can be considered unreasonable. He also posits that this is indicated by the Torah's harsh characterization ("*bliya'al*"), which implies an attitude that is intuitively understood to be condemnable. See, at length, R. Yosef Lieberman, *Resp. Mishnat Yosef,* III, *petichah.* See also R. Ya'akov Yosef, *B'Itah Achishenah,* p. 3, n. 4, who brings additional sources to this effect.
49. For an extensive discussion of this phenomenon, see R. Shlomo Brody, "The Curious Case of Prozbol's Disappearance and Resurgence" in *Tradition,* Summer 2022, issue 54:3.
50. CM 67:1.
51. *Resp.,* 77:2, 3. In 77:4, however, he articulates the reasoning differently.
52. Note the objection of *Ketzot HaChoshen,* 67:1. *Rashba, Resp.* IV, 127, maintains that an implicit stipulation can only be assumed in a locale in which the populace was aware of the *Shemittah* mandate in the first place, and that they would be unable to

R. Yonatan Eibshutz[53] objected to this mentality, at least as an attitude going forward. To allow *Shemittah* to have no expression at all in Jewish behavior, he asserted, is unacceptable. This would be true, he stresses, even granted the position that *Shemittah* is not active on any level (which he ultimately does not grant). Quoting the prophet Jeremiah,[54] he notes the directive of *hatzivi lakh tziyunim,* "set up for yourself road-marks" to the path back to Zion. This is especially so, considering how fundamental the observance of *Shemittah* is to the continuing presence of the Jews in the land of Israel, and how this *mitzvah* – which through the miraculous fulfillment of God's blessings, displayed His control over all of nature – manifests the faith of the Jewish people as represented by their adherence to both the agricultural and financial directives.[55] Were any philosopher to recommend incorporating these values into our practices, he asserts, the public would see the wisdom and comply; how much more so when most of the *rishonim* maintain that the practice of *Shemittah* directives does continue to be obligatory on some level. Accordingly, he concludes, the *Prozbol* should certainly be utilized, so at least a memorial to the glorious *mitzvah* of *Shemittah* should endure.[56]

---

collect in the absence of a stipulation. See *Sma,* CM 67:4, and *Mishneh L'Melekh, Hil. Shemittah V'Yovel,* 9:10; and see at length, *B'Itah Achishenah,* p. 9ff, n. 21. See also *Gilyonei HaShas, Gittin* 37b, s.v. *tzarikh.*

The ambiguity of the situation places a moral responsibility on prospective borrowers, who may be tempted to borrow from lenders unaware of *shemittat kesafim,* and then wait until *Shemittah* and assume the loan is canceled. Such behavior likely constitutes fraud in the eyes of the *halakhah,* in addition to the likelihood that the loan is actually not canceled under those circumstances. See R. Elchanan Peretz, *Chukkat Mishpat,* 28; R. Shlomo Zalman Auerbach, *Resp. Minchat Shlomo,* III, 132:19:2, advances the argument that given that the lender would have insisted on a stipulation had he known of the situation, the stipulation can be considered implicit.

53. *Urim V'Tumim, Tumim,* 67:1.

54. Jer. 31:20.

55. See also *Resp. Heikhalei Shen,* ibid., who asserts in his responsum regarding the functional premises of *Prozbol* that the Rabbis instituted a remembrance of *Shemittah* specifically because of the role the neglect of this *mitzvah* played in causing the exile, and for this reason specifically ordained an extension of *shemittat kesafim,* which is operative in the diaspora.

56. See also *Pitchei Teshuvah,* 67:1. R. Betzalel HaCohen, *Resp. Reishit Bikkurim,* II, 1, invokes this in asserting that everyone should utilize a *Prozbol.*

In light of all of the above, perhaps the rabbinic institution of *Prozbol* was crafted in order to accomplish a number of goals at once. Fundamentally, it blocked the cancellation of loans, and removed an obstacle to the needy receiving assistance. However, if that were the only goal, individuals could have made stipulations, or, for greater reliability, the Rabbis could have created an automatic universal stipulation, "*lev Beit Din matneh aleihem.*"

Instead, a mechanism was created that required some participation from the lender, an "opt-in" approach. This is fully in accord with the goal of the rabbinically ordained *Shemittah,* which is not to bring about the same results as the Biblical *Shemittah,* but rather so that "the Torah of *Shemittah* not be forgotten."[57]

Of course, it would still seem possible to preserve the memory of *Shemittah* even more directly, and indeed some raise the question of whether it is a laudable approach to eschew *Prozbol* and instead cancel loans, as the Torah commanded. The *Hitorerut Teshuvah* assumed that in light of the nature of contemporary *Shemittah* as a memorial, it is logical that *Prozbol* accomplishes this goal, and need not be avoided.

Still, there are some who suggest that perhaps it is worthwhile, together with the execution of the *Prozbol,* to exclude at least one debt from its purview (for example, by making a loan after the *Prozbol* has been written), and to actively cancel that debt. Indeed, such a practice of pious people is recorded and commended by the *Ben Ish Chai,*[58] who did so himself. However, this has not been generally advocated by contemporary authorities.[59]

---

57. See also a similar approach in R. Yehudah Cohen, *Shiurei Leil Shishi,* III, pp. 424–427.
58. *Parashat Ki Tavo,* #26.
59. This is the assessment of R. Yitzchak Shmuel Schechter, *Resp. Yashiv Yitzchak,* V, 38, who compares this suggestion to one who lives outside of Israel acquiring ownership of land in Israel specifically to allow it to go unworked during *Shemittah,* or to one who generally sells his *chametz* before Pesach, but leaves over a small amount to burn. One could, however, challenge the comparison (and of these two actions to each other, as the latter has significantly more basis than the first). In the case of loan cancellation, there is presumably a genuine benefit to actually proceeding, as the original intent of the Torah that the needy should not have to repay could still be realized. The other two situations, each for their own reasons, are significantly different. Nonetheless, if the proposal at hand is to specifically lend money even to

PROZBOL AND THE GOALS OF *SHEMITTAH*

Much of the above has been premised on the assumption that the Torah's intent in mandating *shemittat kesafim* is to provide relief to the poor, an extension of the original benefit of financial assistance in

---

one who is not in need just so that one can technically proceed to cancel the loan, the comparison is more apt.

It is further noteworthy that the *Ben Ish Chai* specifically refers to a loan of a minimal amount, of a few coins. R. Mordechai Eliyahu, *Ma'amar Mordechai, Shvi'it, ma'amarim,* 25, suggests this reflects an inherent tension in the recommendation, in that the *mishnah* (*Shv'it* 10:9) states that one who returns a loan after the time of cancellation is acting in a praiseworthy fashion; if so, this practice encourages the borrower to act against the behavior approved of by the Rabbis. Accordingly, only a small sum should be involved. If this interpretation is accurate, it narrows the fulfillment of *shemitat kesafim* to a technical one that does not impact the finances of either party.

Nit'ei Gavriel, Shemitat Kesafim U'Prozbol, 22:2, n 3–4, does quote some supporting arguments and positions for the stringency of the *Ben Ish Chai.* However, he also records the view of R. Shlomo Zalman Auerbach not to accept this, as well as that of R. Shmuel Wosner that one who does should be careful to note that is only a stringency and not required. Further, notably, one of the sources that he references does advocate intentionally making a loan to enable the fulfillment of the *mitzvah,* but the *mitzvah* referenced is not the cancellation of the loan, but the rabbinic enactment of *Prozbol.*

R. Ovadia Yosef, *Resp. Yabbia Omer,* IX, 3:2 praises the instinct behind the suggestion without overtly recommending it, invoking the phrase "*ohev mitzvot lo yisba mitzvot,*" "a lover of *mitzvot* will never have his fill of *mitzvot,*" an adaptation of Ecc. 5:9, "*ohev kessef lo yisba kessef.*" Following this, R. Yosef's son R. Ya'akov Yosef, *B'Itah Achishenah,* pp. 12–13, n. 25–27, asserted that his father's view is that the *Ben Ish Chai*'s practice is more than a "mere stringency" and is to be supported. However, it is not clear if this can be derived from the written record; the phrasing "*ohev mitzvot…*" is often used in affectionate disagreement, to indicate that a proposal reflects the spiritual enthusiasm of the proponent but is nonetheless not accepted (see *Resp. Noda B'Yehudah, tinyana,* YD, 123, referring to the *Shlah*; although the Talmud, *Makkot* 10a, does apply the original, unaltered verse to the religious commitment of Moses).

The position of the *Ben Ish Chai* is invoked in R. Ovadiah Yosef's writings in the context of addressing a technical issue, that of whether a loan offered in the month of Elul would even be subject to cancellation, in light of the premise that by default loans do not become due before thirty days (per *Makkot* 3b, a point of disagreement between *Ohr Zarua, Avodah Zarah,* #123, and *Bach,* CM 67). See also *Resp. Yechave Da'at,* IV, 62, and *Chazon Ovadiah, Hil. Shemitat Kesafim,* 12, n15, and *gilyonot v'tziyunim,* 18. R. Eliyahu, *Ma'amar Mordechai,* ibid., suggests that the practice of the *Ben Ish Chai,* in that its entire purpose is to enable the cancellation of a loan, contains an implicit stipulation that *Shemittah* should cancel in this case, regardless of the dispute surrounding a loan of this term.

the form of loans. This is the rationale articulated by the Rambam.[60] *Sefer HaChinnukh,*[61] after noting the importance of loans as the basis of the commandment, expands on its broader messages, including an abhorrence of theft, underscored by a commandment that requires an individual to relinquish even that which is rightfully his property. Such an attitude is further conducive to a greater faith in God's providence. A similar sentiment is expressed by R. Eibshutz in his previously cited comments, where he sees the purpose of *Shemittah* as a reorienting of the focus of Jews away from the pursuit of profit and wealth as the central purpose of existence, together with a deepening appreciation of God's control over the world and all it has to offer. A parallel but differently developed perspective is found in the writings of R. Kook,[62] who painted a picture of a deliberate break from the economic environment of the nation, a year of quiet and contentment, with no individual able to pressure or control his fellow; a year of focus on the just and compassionate sustenance of God to His holy nation. Elsewhere in his writings,[63] he describes how the lender-borrower relationship uniquely places one individual, regardless of other aspects of his life story, at the mercy of another, possibly morally inferior individual, and the beauty of the power of *Shemittah* to negate that reality. As R. Y. Z. Rimon notes,[64] the dynamic that *Shemittah* disrupts is one that not only degrades humanity, but undermines the recognition of the true ruler over men, God Himself.[65]

As such, there is always room to question the extent to which *Prozbol* addresses the messages of *Shemittah.*[66] R. Aharon Lichtenstein, in a talk about the inadequacies of contemporary *Shemittah* practice,

---

60. *Moreh Nevukhim,* III, 39.
61. *Mitzvah* 477.
62. Introduction to *Shabbat HaAretz.*
63. *Ayn Ayeh, Berakhot* II, *Shvi'it* #12.
64. *Shemittah,* p. 373.
65. He observes further that it is thus understandable that *Shemittah* cancels only debts that come from loans, not those that come from unpaid business obligations. As he emphasizes, the Torah is not against capitalism and private property, but rather mitigating the control one individual has over another.
66. Regarding the position of the *Tumim* specifically, see *Otzar Machmadim,* V, 71, p. 357.

casts a critical light on the emergence of the *Prozbol*: "Anyone who considers the *Prozbol* a victory worthy of celebration does not begin to understand Hillel's thinking. Do you think he was happy to circumvent a *mitzvah*... did he not approach his task with a broken, despairing heart? Hillel unfortunately found himself and his generation in a serious predicament... If Hillel's generation had been worthy, both... goals would have been achieved. Those who needed it would have found the necessary resources, and the lenders would have learned, at least once in seven years, to relax – at least for a moment – the tight embrace in which they caress every penny as if it were the apple of their eye. But Hillel's generation was not worthy, and the possessors of wealth, who tend, like most of us, to be selective in their obedience to the warnings of the Torah, began to slam their doors in the faces of the poor. In these urgent circumstances, faced with an ultimatum on the part of the lenders, Hillel decided... that one value must be preferred over the other... but any sensitive student of the *halakhah* can perceive how much it must have hurt him to do this. What price would Hillel not have been willing to pay in order to avoid being confronted by this cruel dilemma?... when he observed the reality of the situation, he could have responded in only one way: 'You have defeated me. Here I am, the representative of the *halakhah* and of tradition. I have succeeded in escaping the dilemma, but on another level I have been broken. Instead of preserving the *mitzvah* and helping to enforce its observance, I have established a means of circumventing it."[67]

The notion of a failure of leadership necessitating the creation of the *Prozbol* is a sobering one, and it redirects attention once again to the prohibition of "Beware." It is relevant to pose the question of whether this transgression was taking place consciously and explicitly, or perhaps, subconsciously. R. Lichtenstein refers to an ultimatum; this would certainly seem to be applicable to one who refuses to lend without a stipulation to ignore *Shemittah*. *Prozbol*, however, may have been instituted to address a less blatant stance.

---

67. Most recently published in *Leaves of Faith: The World of Jewish Living*, Vol. II, pp. 183–184. See also his formulation of the issue in *Values in Halakhah: Six Case Studies*, pp. 143–144.

Those in need of financial assistance would be declined not only by potential benefactors who overtly point to the impending *Shemittah* as the basis for their refusal. Perhaps more common would be the situation in which the wealthier individual attributes his decision to a number of other considerations, such as his own liquidity, the general trustworthiness of the borrower, or other such factors.[68] Meanwhile, lurking in the back of his mind, perhaps hidden even to himself, is the *Shemittah* mandate. Eliminating the impact this would have on a multifaceted decision would require more than rabbinic exhortation.

Fully addressing this problem and its impact would require addressing the factors that affect decisions on a subconscious level as well. Indeed, there are numerous instances in *halakhah* in which we find a mandate to remove factors that can sway a decision in ways perhaps completely unacknowledged.[69] This is especially true in light of opinions,

---

68. See commentary of *Chatam Sofer* to Deut. for a creative interpretation that yields another possible rationalization. Additionally, *HaKetav V'HaKaballah* suggests the wealthy party may indeed be holding back because of *Shemittah,* but not out of fear that he will lose the funds; rather, he is asserting that in this year, all the produce is declared ownerless and free for the taking. If so, what need is there for me to provide additional assistance? To further add to the subtlety, the *Shlah, Vavei HaAmudim,* 14, interprets the verse to condemn one who, because of his stinginess, misinterprets the Torah to exaggerate the concern, and assumes that the loan will be canceled already at the beginning of the seventh year, rather than at the end. Perhaps most directly relevant to the above, the *Ben Ish Chai, derashot, Re'eh,* 14, describes a thought process that is discouraged by the burdens of *Shemittah* and ultimately declines assistance as a result.
69. Some examples of this include: the prohibition against bribery, even to a judge who would maintain he is unaffected and will render a just decision regardless, which extends even to subtle, non-monetary forms of ingratiation; the position of the *Chafetz Chaim* that even one who is making a negative report against another that is necessary for protection, do so with a lack of prior animus against the subject (*Chafetz Chaim, Hil. Rekhilut, klal* 9, *Be'er Mayim Chayim*); the position of R. Moshe Feinstein, *Resp. Iggerot Moshe,* IV, 80, disputed by R. Shlomo Zalman Auerbach, *Resp. Minchat Shlomo,* I, 7 and 8, and II, 29:6, that a doctor be allowed to return from a life-saving mission on *Shabbat,* out of fear that he will otherwise not undertake the mission in the first place. In these cases, it is understood that the judge respects his mandate to rule honestly, the reporter his obligation to avoid unwarranted *lashon hara* (malicious gossip), and the doctor his obligation to save lives regardless of any potential inconvenience. Nonetheless, the fear exists that subconscious factors will

cited above, that see the admonishment of "Beware" as uniquely subtle and complex. To these views, one who declines to loan for reasons that would have pertained had it not been the *Shemittah* year is not in violation, while a refusal predicated on *Shemittah* earns condemnation. Separating out exactly which factors are genuinely present and which are not, which are primary and which are secondary, is a near impossible task, both for the individual himself and for those who would judge him.

R. Yehoshua Leib Diskin[70] lays out the scope of the prohibition in a fashion that displays its subtlety. It emerges from the *Shulchan Arukh*[71] that one who recognizes a potential borrower as untrustworthy is not required to lend to him. If his concern is that the borrower will not repay on time, the lender can set the time of repayment prior to *Shemittah*. If the borrower insists on setting the repayment time after *Shemittah*, the lender has the right to decline such a situation.[72] If he is worried that nonetheless the borrower will allow the time to pass, he has the option of either declining the loan or securing it in another fashion, such as taking collateral (which would also not be canceled by *Shemittah*). Accordingly, the only situation which would constitute a violation of the prohibition would be one involving a borrower who has been verified as trustworthy, and nonetheless the lender is still concerned, unreasonably, that the debt will continue until *Shemittah*, and he will lose his ability to collect.[73]

The prohibition of "Beware" may be particularly conducive to a distinctive approach, because of its nature as well as its language. That verse specifically describes a "thought" (*im levavkha*, in your heart)

---

exert their influence in ways imperceptible to the otherwise pious individual, and therefore these factors must be accounted for.

70. *Resp., Kuntres Acharon*, #234.

71. CM 97:4.

72. He attributes this assumption to the Rambam, presumably a reference to his language (*Hil. Shemittah V'Yovel* 9:30) assigning guilt to one who declines to lend before *Shemittah* "lest [repayment of the] debt be delayed"; apparently it is taken as a given that the payment was due before *Shemittah*. See also *Resp. Minchat Shlomo*, I, 47:1.

73. It may be noteworthy that R. Shlomo Zalman Auerbach, *Resp. Minchat Shlomo*, ibid., maintains a similar approach; however, while he assumes that the prohibition is relevant both to Torah-mandated and rabbinic *Shemittah*, R. Diskin is cited elsewhere (see note 47) as maintaining that it does not apply to rabbinic *Shemittah* (and R. Auerbach is in fact responding to his position).

that results in a refusal to lend. This is consistent with the formulation of the Rambam,[74] who describes the verse as containing in its various parts both an imperative to lend and a prohibited thought process.[75] R. Yosef Engel, in his writings on *Shemittah*,[76] poses the question of why this transgression warrants rabbinic intervention, when sinners in other areas are not protected from their own weaknesses.[77] One suggestion he offers is that this sin is unique in that it is committed "in the heart." While he does not expand on his meaning, it is certainly possible this

---

74. *Hil. Shemittah V'Yovel*, 9:30

75. The assigning of transgressive guilt to mere thought is unusual, leading some commentators to assume this is a function of the linking of this prohibition to that of idolatry (*Ketubot* 68a, *Bava Batra* 10a), in which thought is also considered to be a violation (see *Pe'at HaShulchan*, 29:116, and *Chikrei Lev*, cited in *Sdei Chemed, ma'arekhet ha-kaf*, 75, and *ma'arekhet ha-mem* 20; see also *Ma'amar Mordechai, ma'amarim*, 24). However, it would seem there is a distinction between the two; in the case of idolatry, thought is a violation because idol worship can exist within the mental realm as well. In this instance, it seems there is a new category being referenced: a thought process which skews one's attitudes and results in a failure to perform a positive commandment (a suggestion along these lines is brought by the *S'dei Chemed* in the second reference). This category would have unique properties, in that it would have the lack of direct control associated with thought processes combined with the real-world impact of actions, and thus may merit unique attitudes.

76. *Otzerot Yosef*, 1:28.

77. *Chiddushei Anshei Shem, Shvi'it* 10:3, addresses this question differently by advancing a more complex history of *Prozbol* and the factors involved. The reluctance of the wealthy to lend was not in defiance of the Torah mandate, but rather stemmed from the fact that at that point the institution was rabbinic in nature. Accordingly, the wealthy argued that compelling them to waive their monetary rights under those circumstances was a decree that overburdened the population (*gezerah she'ein ha-tzibur yachol l'a'amod bah*) which in general is considered invalid. Thus, they refused to lend as a protest, insisting that the enactment be rescinded, and basic Torah law be restored. In response to this development, Hillel established the *Prozbol* as a countermeasure.

   A similar theory was expressed by R. Yerucham Fishel Perlow, *Sefer HaMitzvot L'Rasag*, I, p. 188. He connects two previously mentioned positions of the Rambam: that "Beware" is an injunction specifically regarding withholding a loan due to *Shemittah*, and that *Prozbol* would not be effective if *Shemittah* were in effect on a Torah level. He posits that the institution would not have been promulgated to assist sinners of that type. However, when *Shemittah* is rabbinic, and the above rationalizations were in effect, a more forgiving attitude led to the institution of *Prozbol*.

is a reference to the subconscious nature of the violation, one that may be beyond the reach of the sinner to directly control, thus justifying external assistance that would otherwise not be offered.

Further, there is another factor as well that calls for special treatment of this transgression, as well as a broader consideration of rabbinic responsibility in this case. A lapse in this instance is not merely a spiritual demerit for the transgressor; it represents a material loss to another, in this case individuals who may be desperately in need. As such, the possibility of even a slightly reduced compliance on the part of the lenders may result in a grave crisis for the needy. In light of this, the responsibility of a rabbinic leadership in this case, together with the assessment of its success, incorporates the complex balancing of the spiritual character of one group with the material needs of another.[78]

This reality can perhaps be seen as well in the objection the Ramban raised against the view that *Shemittat Kesafim* in the contemporary era is not obligatory on any level, but is rather a voluntary expression of piety (*middat chasidut*). What piety is there, he asked, in slamming the door in the face of the needy? On the surface, the objection is hard to understand; if the cancellation is voluntary, those who would decline to lend if their debts would be canceled could merely refuse to participate in the initiative. Presumably, any social pressure to even voluntarily cancel the loans would create an environment where perhaps even a small number of potential lenders may hesitate to get involved to begin with, rather than suffer negative judgment for the more visible act of collecting on their loans.

Further, the issue of whether *Prozbol* represents a failure of leadership and education is perhaps implicit in a question posed by the Talmud.[79] The issue of whether Hillel enacted *Prozbol* specifically for his own generation, or, rather, for future generations as well, is presented, and a number of practical ramifications are attached. It would seem that if, indeed, the enactment was made for future generations as well, the implication is that it did not simply reflect a spiritual weakness of the population at that time, but rather an inherent challenge with

78. See the lengthy comment of the *Alshich* to Deut., which touches upon both points.
79. *Gittin* 36b.

the arrangement and human nature (at least as long as *Shemittah* is not mandatory on a Torah level).[80]

Yet another aspect to consider in this instance can be illustrated by noting a difference between two of the commandments that address the loaners of money: the mandate to cancel outstanding loans with *Shemittah,* and the prohibition of charging and collecting interest. On the surface, these two commandments seem similar in nature and in purpose, and indeed there is much to connect them. However, there is a very significant conceptual distinction. The *halakhah* views the charging of interest as completely illegitimate; the lender has no right whatsoever to that additional money. The *Shemittah* directive is fundamentally different. The lender does, in general, have a right to have his loan repaid. The *Shemittah* mandate is a shifting of the advantage towards the borrower, presumably reflecting the general likelihood that the borrower is in greater need than the lender. Nonetheless, this forced benevolence does come at a cost to that lender, one which transcends the usual standards of justice and may not be trivial in its impact.[81]

This distinction is reflected in a very concrete difference in *halakhah.* In the case of interest, the prohibition is absolute and extends to the borrower as well. The borrower may not agree to pay interest, nor may he voluntarily offer it afterwards (at least per rabbinic law), and interest that is paid must be returned after the fact. However, voluntary payment of the principal after *Shemittah* is treated completely differently. A borrower who chooses to do so is identified by the *mishnah* as

---

80. *Rashi,* s.v. *l'vitulei,* understands the view of Shmuel, who expressed a desire to uproot *Prozbol,* as relevant to a generation that is morally superior, and would not hesitate to lend; according to that position, such a situation is conceivable. However, this may itself be the issue under consideration. See the comments of *Pnei Yehoshua* there.

According to *Chatam Sofer (Chiddushim* to *Gittin*), the issue motivating the Talmud's question is whether or not the prohibition is what is being addressed; if so, he assumes, the enactment would certainly be made for all generations.

81. See also *Mishnah Rishonah, Shvi'it* 10:2, who notes the distinction is also relevant to the concept of *moser shtarotav l'beit din,* in that regarding prohibitions of interest and the like, no license is granted to the rabbinic court to act in a manner prohibited to the actual lender. However, in the case of *Shemittah,* the Torah specifically issued a restriction on the lender personally, rather than condemning the concept of collection itself as immoral.

acting in a praiseworthy manner. The lender is instructed to make clear his willingness to cancel the loan, but after having done so is permitted to keep the funds.[82]

R. Yosef Zvi Rimon puts forward a suggestion that is relevant to this distinction. Presumably, the intent of the Torah in mandating *shemittat kesafim* is to provide needed amnesty to the genuinely poor who may become intractably mired in debt. A borrower who is, however, in a position to reasonably repay what he has borrowed, and especially one who has been able to use those funds to invest and to generate profit, would be morally correct in repaying the loan.

Within that framework, the institution of *Prozbol* makes a valuable contribution. The borrower, when taking out the loan, does not know whether or not the lender will eventually write a *Prozbol*. Accordingly, he must make every effort to preserve his capacity to repay what he has borrowed, in the event that it comes due and is required to pay, even after *Shemittah*. Should it be that the borrower is indeed unable to repay and continues to be indigent, any lender of a decent and compassionate nature will presumably not insist on repayment. In such a manner, the *Prozbol* is able to create a balance between the needs of the poor to receive loans to begin with, as well as to be given amnesty when genuinely called for, together with the goal of giving the lender confidence to lend when he is able to and to be repaid when appropriate.[83]

Certainly, any effort to incorporate all the values of *Shemittah* is laudable. The primary purpose remains the continuing provision of financial assistance to the needy, and of course the realization of this purpose must be a priority. The utilization of the *Prozbol* does not prevent a lender from forgiving a loan when it is clearly a hardship on the borrower to repay, and all the more so its very enactment is an exhortation

82. *Mishnah, Shvi'it* 10:8–9. According to some authorities, this does not imply any *a priori* obligation to repay; accordingly, the praise recorded in the *mishnah* is for the general avoidance of unwarranted enrichment, or the resulting encouragement to lenders in the future. (Some interpret the *mishnah* as referring to one who returns the loan before the end of the *Shemittah* year.) However, R. Moshe Feinstein, *Resp. Iggerot Moshe,* CM, II, 15, understands that there is an absolute moral obligation to return the loan. See R. Dovid Gottleib, *Ateret Ya'akov,* 15.

83. *Shemittah,* pp. 374–375.

upon those with resources to proactively find ways they can to be of aid to those in need.

One theme that emerges consistently throughout the generations of discourse on this matter is that evading the purpose of *Shemittah* would be highly objectionable, even if it is technically possible. To the contrary, the Rabbis enacted their own observance of *Shemittah,* even when the Torah did not obligate it, and ordered that the remembrance of its themes be preserved. At each stage of the discussion, within each range of possibilities, *Prozbol* was deemed the option that was not evading *Shemittah,* but rather was engaging with it.

There is a particular irony to the perception that *Prozbol* represents a subversion of the intent of the Torah, and so much so that it displays unlimited rabbinic power of that nature. In addition to the contraindications noted above, R. Yitzchak Isaac HaLevi Herzog[84] noted an additional perspective. He asserted that in fact, *Prozbol* was not a necessary vehicle to achieve the end of overriding the loan cancellation; in fact, as referenced above, other tools exist with the halakhic system that could accomplish this purpose. If, however, the Rabbis had sufficed with those tools, the population, not fully appreciating the mechanisms and the elements involved, would have formed the impression that the Rabbis actually do have the power to circumvent any Torah mandate they deem problematic. Specifically to avoid that misconception, he maintained, the *Prozbol* was created, so that a tool connected to *Shemittah* would display the ongoing relevance of the *mitzvah.*

While the restoration of the full Torah commandment of *Shemittah* is anxiously awaited, in the meantime, the *Prozbol* has stood the test of time, winning full acceptance from the time of its illustrious original advocate to the present day rabbinic leadership. In light of the above, this can be well understood; it may be the best example of a halakhic alternative that justifies itself in letter, spirit, and in serving an urgent need.

84. *Techukah L'Yisrael Al Pi HaTorah,* II, p. 18.

Chapter 8

The Torah's Commandment of Inheritance and Contemporary Practice

One area in which there seems to be a wide distance between what is mandated in the Torah and what takes place is the area of inheritance. By Biblical mandate, upon one's death, his property automatically passes to his heirs. These heirs are first the sons of the deceased, with the firstborn (*bekhor*) receiving a double portion. Only if there are no sons, do the daughters inherit at all.

Nonetheless, for the past several centuries, methods have been found to distribute the assets differently, primarily to the end of including the daughters, to a partial or full degree. Sometimes, the double portion for the eldest is also eliminated.

This appears to be a complete circumvention of the Torah's rule and intent. Yet, this is not only widely done in all segments of the observant Jewish community, it is strongly advocated by great authorities of *halakhah*.[1] Understanding this phenomenon requires separate considerations of the letter and the spirit of the law.

THE LETTER OF THE LAW

As a general rule, Jewish monetary law is subject to modification by mutual agreement of the parties. However, inheritance is an exception;[2] as it is not merely a financial arrangement, but a *mitzvah*, it is a mandatory practice, identified by the Torah[3] as *Chukat Mishpat*, a "statute of justice." Further, it happens automatically; immediately upon one's death the assets become the property of the halakhic heirs.

As such, effecting any kind of alternative distribution faces obstacles both in terms of permissibility and of possibility. A number of approaches have emerged to address these challenges.

It should be noted that there are some authorities who have maintained that the simple execution of a civil will can indeed effectively serve these purposes, among them the preeminent decisor R. Moshe Feinstein.[4] Further, there were instances of great Chasidic rabbis who left such wills and expected them to be carried out.[5]

Of course, this position is not taken in simple disregard of Torah law. It is predicated on the belief that one or another of the methods that have been suggested for alternative asset distribution can actually

1. R. Shlomo Dichofsky, a prominent rabbinical court judge, writing in the journal *Techumin*, XVIII, p. 30, reports from his experience of thousands of estate cases in all circles of observant Judaism, that in not a single case was the intent for the estate to be distributed only to the sons and not to the daughters or the widow. See also *Resp. Mishpetei Aretz*, pp. 296–299.
2. *Bava Batra* 130a; *Mishneh Torah, Hil. Nachalot* 6:1; *Shulchan Arukh*, CM 281:1.
3. Num. 27:11.
4. *Resp. Iggerot Moshe*, EH I, 104 and 105.
5. For example, there is much discussion in the responsa literature regarding the will of the Sadigerer Rebbe; see *Resp. Maharsham* II, 224; *Resp. Maharia HaLevi*, II, 86; *Resp. Minchat Shai*, 75. See also the list of prominent wills in *Mishpat HaTzava'ah*, II, *biurim, nispach* 1.

be activated by the drafting of the civil will.[6] For example, R. Feinstein's approach draws on the fact that one can distribute his property in any fashion he wishes if he does so while he is alive. Given that the terms of the will certainly will be enforced by the civil authorities, it may be possible to consider the execution of the will as effecting the transfer of the property at that time, while the testator is still alive. Some have explained that this is accomplished through the halakhic recognition of the authority of civil law (*dina d'malkhuta dina*).[7] However, many authorities did not concur with this ruling and have advocated other approaches.[8]

It should be clarified here that the suggestion is not that *dina d'malkhuta* would mean that legal standards of inheritance would supplant halakhic ones; *dina d'malkhuta* does not override Torah law. This point is made forcefully in the *rishonim*[9] and halakhic codes,[10] where it is asserted that the application of this concept to inheritance law would both exceed its scope and negate explicit sections of the

6. See R. Aharon Ezriel's *Kapei Aharon,* I, CM, 12, citing R. Avraham Ashkenazi (1813–1880), who served as *Rishon L'Tziyon.* See also *Resp. Achiezer,* IV, 66, who considers the matter inconclusively. His reasoning is discussed below.
7. See the discussion in R. Herzog, *Techukah L'Yisrael Al Pi HaTorah,* pp. 143–147.
8. See *Resp. Chatam Sofer,* CM, 142; *Resp. Lev Aryeh,* II, 57; and *Resp. Minchat Asher,* III, 114. Among those also rejecting the validity of a secular will are *Resp. Minchat Yitzchak,* VI, 165, and, for practical purposes, R. Feivel Cohen, *MiDor L'Dor,* pp. 1–4. See also *Meishiv B'Halakhah,* I, 147; and R. Moshe Bransdorfer, *Heikhal Hora'ah,* IV, 184.
9. See *Beit Yosef,* CM 26, citing *Resp. Rashba.*
10. See CM 369:11 with *Rama* and *Sma. Resp. Pnei Moshe,* II, 15, does quote the opinion of a R. Yirmiyah Morgento that inheritance practices are governed by the *dina d'malkhuta,* but this has not been accepted at all by halakhic authorities. R. Herzog, p. 107, n. 8, while acknowledging the complete rejection of this view, asserts that a scholar of such stature was presumably not simply mistaken, and thus endeavors an explanation, correlating to some of the theories associated with *dina d'malkhuta.* One possibility is that the authority stems from the king's functional "ownership" of the land; since this matter concerns property, the king's opinions of its distribution should prevail. Alternatively, *dina d'malkhuta* may reflect the "consent of the governed." If so, perhaps it is considered as if the sons have agreed to divide their inheritance with their sisters.

Torah.[11] Rather, the suggestion is that when a will exists, civil recognition and enforcement of that will creates a reality that may accord with certain halakhic principles that would result in the practical validity of the will.[12]

Perhaps the most widely known approach is one that has been used for centuries, known as the *shtar chatzi zachar,* the "document of a half male [portion]," because it arranged for each of the daughters to receive a portion equal to half of that of what each son received.[13] More recently, as the prevalence is for all the children to inherit equally, the term *shtar zakhar shalem,* the "document of a complete male [portion]" has become more common.[14]

Some have understood that the "half" model is in deference to the Torah's depiction of inheritance, which does not equate sons and daughters.[15] R. Yitzchak Isaac HaLevi Herzog, the second Chief Rabbi of modern Israel, who devoted extensive attention to the ideal functioning of the nascent Jewish state, thought differently. In his writings, he observes that this does not seem to be the case. Rather, the allotments

---

11. R. Ovadiah Yosef makes this point in strong terms, with many citations, in his *Resp. Yechave Da'at,* IV, 65.
12. Some specific examples of this will be discussed further below.
13. A thorough history of the *shtar chatzi zakhar,* and related methods, "*L'Sh'eylat Yerushah Shel HaBat,*" was authored by Prof. Simcha Assaf and appears in *Sefer Yovel l'Y Freiman,* pp. 8–13. He traces the first appearances of this document to around the year 5160 (1400), and notes that it was soon in wide use in the major Jewish population centers. See also *Pitchei Choshen,* IX, ch. 4, n. 98. For another survey of the history, see *Mishpat HaTzava'ah,* II, *biurim,* ch. 20.

    R. Zalman Nechemiah Goldberg wrote an article in the journal *Techumin* (IV, pp. 342–351) advocating for renewed usage of the *shtar chatzi zakhar,* stating that it had fallen out of use (see *Resp. Maharsham,* II, 224:29). He explains the logic behind a number of its components, as well as suggesting various modifications in its composition and utilization.
14. *Ketzot HaChoshen,* 33:3, refers to this document as customary.
15. *Resp. Chatam Sofer,* EH, 147, who adds that the two-to-one ratio was used to echo the Torah's prescription for firstborn and other sons. See also R. Feivel Cohen, *MiDor LeDor,* p. 35. Nonetheless, R. Cohen does write (p. 36) that if a *shtar zakhar shalem* is called for in order to maintain family harmony, one should not hesitate to utilize it.

were calibrated to the perceived needs of the daughters, and need not be seen as the only acceptable ratio.

Usage of the "half" document, which functions the same way as the "whole" document, is recorded as customary by the *Rama*,[16] and is sourced in the writings of the *Maharil*.[17] It involves the father declaring that he has taken on a large debt to his daughter, which takes effect one hour before his death, and upon his death would pass on to his sons, as the halakhic heirs. If, however, the sons follow the father's instructions in distributing the assets, the debt will be canceled.[18]

It has also become customary to combine this with another method, namely to transfer the assets at the time of the writing, when the testator is still alive and can distribute his assets as he wishes.[19] The actual usage of the assets is stipulated to transfer following his death. One drawback, however, is that this is only effective for assets in his possession at that time. There are other limitations as well that make this method less effective and not applicable to all kinds of assets.

Versions of this document appear in earlier literature, largely associated with a desire to assist the daughters in marriage, first in providing a dowry[20] and then to enhance her status within marriage.[21] The history

16. CM 281:7 and 113:2.
17. *Resp.*, 88.
18. Two points of interest in the language of the *Maharil:* he, and others, use the term *shtarei yerushot*, or "documents of inheritance," despite the general avoidance of that terminology for gifts to daughters, as discussed below. The fact that the *shtarei yerushah* were the same as the *shtar chatzi zakhar* is evident from *Resp. Mahari Veil*, 15; the *Rama* copies his language, except that he uses the phrase *shtar chatzi zakhar*.

    Also, he uses the term *ha'aramah* – but not to describe the *shtar chatzi zakhar*, but rather to defend it (and the *Rama* records this language as well). The topic of his responsum is the impropriety of a man assigning additional assets to his wife, in an instance where this would detract from those that would be given to the daughter, per the contract. See *Nachalat Shivah* 21, n3. This issue, with the same language, was addressed at length by the *Chatam Sofer* in a responsum (EH, 147); and see also a different *ha'aramah* concern expressed in *Resp. Chinnukh Beit Yehudah*, 112.
19. See *Rama*, CM 281:7.
20. See *Resp. Maharam Mintz*, 47. *Resp. Maharsham*, VII, 12, argued that it should be limited to this context.
21. See *Nachalat Shivah*, 21:2; *Resp. Chatam Sofer*, CM, 183; *Resp. Minchat Yitzchak*, III, 135:2.

of these enactments traces back to the Talmud itself, which records a number of obligations the Rabbis incorporated into the process of marriage, directing increased assets towards wives and daughters.

Among these are the rule recorded in the *mishnah*[22] that upon a man's death, his daughters are entitled to support from the estate, until adulthood or marriage. This obligation is prioritized over the sons receiving their inheritance[23] and is a more inclusive obligation than a father's responsibility to sustain his daughter's during his lifetime.[24] A father could also direct assets to his daughters and their descendants through the establishing of a dowry (*nedunia*) on their behalf, which was also subject to additional enactments on behalf of her sons.[25]

A husband inherits the property of his wife,[26] although there is a dispute as to whether this is a matter of Torah law or rabbinic law.[27] Either way, this would indicate that the Torah's rules were impacted by rabbinic enactment. If the inheritance is rabbinic, that itself is the modification from Torah law; if the inheritance is by Torah law, then that law was modified by later rabbinic enactments that diminished the husband's portion.

The *Mabit*[28] maintained that the Torah's language of *Chukat Mishpat* precluded any possibility of rabbinic legislation altering the path of an inheritance. The modifications in the area of spousal inheritance, then, must function differently, as a result of knowing consent upon entering into a marriage. R. Herzog,[29] however, argued that it

---

R. Simcha Yonah Klein, *Piskei HaMishpat,* CM 281 n4, suggests an additional reason, noting the efforts extended by daughters on behalf of elderly parents, and citing as support *Da'at Zekenim,* Deut. 21:15. In that comment, it is put forward that the Biblical Jacob was justified in preferring his son Joseph over his firstborn son Reuben, in apparent violation of Torah law, because Joseph took better care of him.

22. *Ketubot* 4:6 (52b).
23. *Mishnah, Ketubot* 13:3.
24. See *Taz,* EH 112:2.
25. *Mishnah, Ketubot* 4:10.
26. EH 90:1.
27. See *Be'er Heitev,* 90:1, who cites the positions on this dispute.
28. *Resp.* II, 128.
29. *Techukah,* p. 145.

was evident from earlier sources[30] that it is indeed rabbinic authority that powered these changes.

There were innovations in the medieval era as well, including one associated with Rabbenu Tam. This addressed a situation in which a marriage lasted less than a year before the wife passed away. Rabbenu Tam, in recognition of the sorrow of a father who has to both bury his daughter, and also lose the property that he had given over as her dowry, enacted that in these circumstances, the dowry should be returned to the father.[31]

A later enactment was the *Takanat ShU"M* (Shpira [Speyer], Vermaiza [Worms] and Magentza [Mainz]), which dictated (among other policies) that if one spouse died within two years of marriage, half of the dowry goes to the heirs of the deceased.[32] This enactment was deemed to have spread to the extent that it was considered a condition of marriage even when not spelled out as such.[33] The enactment of *Tulitula* (probably Toledo) included the rule that if a woman died during her husband's lifetime, the husband and her heirs would split what remained of her dowry and her assets.[34] A number of other enactments existed as well, to different degrees of acceptance.

Following in the path of these earlier innovations, R. Herzog proposed[35] that the Chief Rabbinate of Israel should make an enactment that daughters should receive an equal portion instead of what was provided to them by the earlier, Talmudic enactments, and this should be written into the *ketubot* of their mothers.

In formulating his proposal, R. Herzog noted that it was difficult to determine why the Rabbis of the Talmudic era felt a need to put into place policies that were not considered necessary by the Torah itself.

---

30. See *Resp. Rosh,* 55.
31. This is codified in *Rama,* EH 53:3; see *Sefer HaYashar,* 579; *Resp. Maharam bar Baruch,* 934; *Resp. Shvut Ya'akov,* II, 125. Regarding the scope of the acceptance of this enactment, see *Arukh HaShulchan,* EH 53:18, and *Knesset HaGedolah* to EH 118. According to *Tosafot, Ketubot* 47a, s.v. *katav,* Rabbenu Tam reversed himself on this policy at the end of his life.
32. See *Rama* ibid.
33. See *Chelkat Mechokek,* EH 118:22.
34. See *Resp. Rashba,* III, 434; *Resp. Rosh,* 55, and Tur and *Shulchan Arukh,* EH 118.
35. *Techukah,* pp. 133–135, and discussed throughout.

Perhaps, he speculated, economic situations following the destruction of the Temple were so radically different that they necessitated new approaches; however, given that we do not know exactly when these policies were put into place, it is difficult to assume with confidence.

R. Binyamin Zvi Rabinowitz Teumim, in a lengthy essay,[36] discussed an enactment of this nature, and emphasized that the reality of the needs of women to support themselves is different today than it was in ancient times, essentially identical to that of men.[37] Accordingly, any such innovation is not an attempt to modernize the Torah or to imitate other cultures, but simply a response to the actual needs, in the sense that earlier enactments were calibrated to the needs of that time.

Nonetheless, he notes that there has long been opposition to any act that would fundamentally change the inheritance laws of the Torah in their totality, and thus maintained that an enactment would have to satisfy a number of conditions: a) it should not be imposed unilaterally as an act of *beit din (hefker beit din)*, as we have seen a historic refusal to utilize this tool in this way; b) it should be formulated in a way to protect the general structure of the Torah's inheritance laws; c) it should be connected, at least theoretically, to supporting the marriage of the daughters, as earlier enactments were; and d) it should be formulated as a gift, not as an inheritance.

Accordingly, he thought that a clause in the *ketubah* at the time of marriage, obligating a husband to gift to his daughters in a fashion equal to what the sons would inherit, satisfied all of the above purposes.

The *Chazon Ish*,[38] in a letter to R. Isser Zalman Meltzer, expressed his deep opposition to the suggestion of an enactment, and their disapproval, together with that of the Brisker Rav, R. Yitzchak Ze'ev Soloveitchik (also cited in the letter), was a significant factor in the failure of this proposal to become accepted.[39]

---

36. Printed in *Techukah L'Yisrael Al Pi HaTorah*, II, pp. 203–226.
37. As R. Mordechai Willig notes, the difference in economic realities is indicated by a statement in the Talmud (*Bava Kama* 15a) that indicates that men are involved with business dealings, and women are not, and suggests that a Torah law may have been addressed to that reality.
38. *Iggerot Chazon Ish*, I, 96.
39. See also *Meorot HaParshah*, pp. 461–462, and *Resp. Mishpetei HaTorah*, p. 298.

THE SPIRIT OF THE LAW

The wide utilization and advocacy of methods to create functionally egalitarian distribution of one's assets begs the question of Part (B) of the formula, spirit of the law. Even if it is granted that these methods are adequate from the perspective of the letter of the law – in both senses, that they are effective and are also permissible to utilize – it remains unclear how they satisfy the "will of the Torah." If, in the Torah's formulation, when there are sons and daughters in a family, the sons inherit and the daughters do not, does not the orchestration of any other result thwart the Divine intent?

It should be noted at the outset that there is a fundamental point of agreement among all authorities, regardless of their positions. The Divine and perfect Torah is not in need of change or modernization; nor is it to be cast as unjust or unfair, particularly in comparison with man-made systems.

This axiom manifests itself in a number of ways. To some, this means no deviation from the asset distribution the Torah describes, or at least not beyond that established by early rabbinic authorities. To others, the issue is more subtle; any modification must not be presented as a conceptual or moral challenge to the Torah's mandate, nor may it confuse the understanding of the intent of the Torah.

One manifestation of this – important for technical reasons as well – is the abjuring of the language of "inheritance" in the context of any policy directing assets towards the daughters. Rather, words such as *matanah* (gift)[40] or *chov* (debt) or *hoda'ah* (acknowledgement of a debt) are used.

In this vein, a number of statements in the *Mishnah,*[41] *Talmud Bavli,*[42] and *Talmud Yerushalmi*[43] make statements to the effect that any claim that sons and daughters inherit equally is "not to be listened to,"

40. R. Yona Reiss notes that there is a Biblical precedent for the usage of gifts to functionally modify the Torah's order of inheritance, i.e. the information that Abraham, while giving "all that he had" to Isaac (Gen. 25:5), also gave "gifts" (*matanot*) to the sons of the *pilagshim* (25:6). See also *Resp. Meishiv Mishpat,* III, p. 376, in fn.

41. *Bava Batra* 8:5.

42. *Bava Batra* 115b.

43. *Bava Batra* 8:1.

or is not saying "anything," and such claims are associated with Saducees and non-Jewish scholars.

Following this path, R Herzog,[44] in articulating his proposal, emphasized that his purpose was "not God forbid to follow the non-Jewish rules out of principle, but to prevent strife within the family."

Nonetheless, from a practical perspective, we have seen that the Rabbis of the Talmud did enact policies to the material benefit of daughters, even to a substantial degree. In that context, the Talmud[45] asks the very question of our concern: How could it be that the Torah decreed that sons should inherit and daughters do not, and yet the Rabbis create enactments whereby the daughters do inherit?

To this, the answer is given, that the motivation is also a Torah precept, in providing for the daughters the resources to incentivize and enable a marriage. A verse[46] is cited to this effect: "Take wives for yourselves and bear sons and daughters, and take wives for your sons, and give your daughters to husbands."

This citation cannot mean that the policy is Biblical in nature; the Talmud makes it clear that the subject is a rabbinic enactment. This leads the *Lechem Mishneh*[47] to comment that the citation is an *asmakhta,* an allusion to a Scriptural verse to connect to a rabbinic law.[48] It could also be understood that the citation is not meant to ascribe Scriptural authority to the specific enactment; rather, it is there to answer the question posed in the text: how could the Rabbis thwart the will of the Torah? To that, the answer is provided: the enactment itself is also motivated by a concern recognized by the Torah. As such, even if it impacts on one mandate of the Torah, it is serving the overall interests of the Torah, even if it is addressing a different specific need.[49]

---

44. *Techukah,* p. 171, 6:1.
45. *Ketubot* 52b.
46. Jer. 29:6.
47. *Hil. Ishut,* 20:1.
48. It is also relevant that the verse is not from the Pentateuch, but from the book of Jeremiah. If this would indeed be the source for the policy, it would be considered "*divrei Kaballah,*" a status describing rules that are Scriptural but not Pentateuchal, and subject to a debate among later authorities as to its level in relation to Torah law.
49. See R. Herzog, p. 100.

As such, this passage serves as a precedent for the balancing of the Torah mandate of inheritance with other recognized concerns. This seems to be the understanding of the *Netziv*,[50] who in a tentative[51] comment suggests that this passage is the foundation for the later adoption of the *shtar chatzi zachar*. It was more confidently stated earlier by the *Chatam Sofer*,[52] who wrote that the *shtar* came to replace the earlier enactments when it became a better fit for the purpose.[53]

To return to the Talmudic passage, it is noteworthy that the Talmud proceeds to question the fact that the enactment under discussion allowed for assets to transfer from the daughter to her sons, but not her daughters. The reason for this, the passage continues, is to maintain the Biblical format in which sons inherit but daughters do not. Here again, we find a functional redistribution that is limited by a concern to preserve the conceptual underpinnings established by the Torah.

In any event, the prevalence of such methods would imply that the conflict must not be as blatant as it seems. Any rabbinic adjustment, even if it falls short of equating sons and daughters, subtracts some amount from what the Torah bequeathed to the sons. As such, R. Herzog, in formulating his proposal,[54] dismisses the claim of undermining the Torah, noting that the Rabbis of the Talmud did enact and recognize at least some methods of modifying the inheritance process; accordingly, he asserts, any such objection lodged against contemporary approaches

50. *He'amek Shealah*, 21:1.

51. He prefaces the suggestion with "*lulei d'mistafina*," "were I not afraid...."

52. *Resp.*, EH, 147.

53. R. Moshe Shternbuch, *Resp. Teshuvot V'Hangahot*, II, 718, expresses some ambivalence about the *shtar chatzi zakhar* and its apparent subverting of the Torah, but ultimately appears to accept it. (He tentatively notes that, were it to be deemed appropriate, it could be formulated as a general policy announced to all marrying couples and thus incorporated into their agreements.) He suggests that given that historically, daughters were supported at the time of their marriages while sons were not, and in the modern era sons and daughters are treated equally at marriage, equal division at the time of the father's death developed to compensate for the change. He also suggests that this is not considered a *ha'aramah* because it is clearly a gift rather than an inheritance.

54. p. 145.

must be levied at them as well. As such, an effort must be made to consider the arguments for some degree of compatibility.

THE ROLE OF FAMILIAL HARMONY

It is clearly emphasized in much of the literature that familial harmony is an overwhelming consideration at play in this area. To be sure, *shalom* is a deeply cherished Jewish value, and its opposite, strife, is repeatedly denigrated in the sources of Jewish law and philosophy. This is all the more true within a family unit, in which the consequences of discord are particularly painful and even, in their extremes, tragic.

Without question, this reality, already self-evident, is acknowledged in the rabbinic literature. The sale of Joseph into slavery, a crime that reverberates throughout history as the paradigmatic interpersonal offense, is traced by the Talmud to Jacob's unequal treatment of his sons, and formalized there as a point of moral instruction and a cautionary tale.[55]

Historically, this referred to favoring one child over the other. In a modern cultural context, a similar result can occur through omitting the daughters, or giving a double portion to the first-born, especially if disregarding other factors. The *Rama*[56] explicitly mentions the desire to prevent strife as a motive for a father to plan the distribution of his assets.

R. Yechiel Michel Tukichinsky, in his work on issues surrounding the end of life, *Gesher HaChaim*,[57] stresses the importance of this through a cautionary tale. He relates the sad episode of a wealthy and pious man who was committed to leaving his property exactly as dictated by the Torah, thereby excluding his daughters. As a result, he actually bequeathed "hatred and competition and division" to his family, so much so that it was said about him that it would have been better had he not left any legacy at all.

Further, even Torah scholars disdained his actions, noting he had abandoned rabbinic wisdom, both in the specific sense of the enactments

55. *Shabbat* 10b. However, the Rambam, in codifying this passage (*Hil. Nachalot*, 6:13) assumes it to refer specifically to during one's lifetime.
56. CM 257:7, following *Resp. Rashba*, III, 118.
57. I, 1:5, p. 42.

put in place to benefit daughters, and the more general message of the Talmudic dictum that custom must at times dictate *halakhah.*[58]

An earlier work on the same subject, R. Aharon de Modena's *Ma'avar Yabok,*[59] makes a similar point, connecting the spiritual with the practical. How tragic would it be, he writes, for the soul of a father to bear the guilt of having caused, through his final acts, strife and discord among his children? By contrast, one who takes steps to create, through his foresightful instructions, an atmosphere of love and peace and brotherhood among his children, can be confident that his soul will enjoy great heavenly reward.

Accordingly, it seems possible to maintain that the vital importance of *shalom* plays a fundamental role in the acceptance and encouragement of strategies to equalize inheritance. This is conveyed explicitly in R. Herzog's writings as a primary motivation for his proposal, and he stresses in this context the Talmudic emphasis on the preservation of peace, even at the expense of other commandments.[60]

However, to posit that the Torah's intent is simply set aside in favor of *shalom* is unsatisfying. Aside from the problematic abandonment of a *mitzvah,* there is the question of why the Torah itself did not factor this into the original *mitzvah.* R Herzog[61] does offer the possibility of a decline in commitment over the generations, from an earlier point where perhaps the Torah's arrangement was accepted with equanimity and did not provoke strife.

It could be added that at least in the modern era, there are certain technical obstacles that make some kind of modification necessary, even should a father wish to have his property allocated exactly in accordance with Torah law. For one, civil law generally provides for all siblings to inherit equally. To avoid the enforcement of this principle, daughters (as well as non-first born sons) would need to voluntarily waive their rights, which may not happen, and may also face technical barriers. A daughter

58. *"Minhag mevatel Halakhah," Yerushalmi Yevamot* 13:1.

59. *Siftei Tzedek,* ch. 8.

60. *Techukah,* p. 110. For a survey of halakhic literature regarding the balancing of *shalom* with other halakhic mandates, see *The Right and the Good: Halakhah and Human Relations,* pp. 48–54.

61. p. 113.

who wishes to challenge the allocations legally has recourse to the civil court system, but that path involves Torah prohibitions both regarding the process and the result. Notably, a number of authorities maintained that the daughters, while not granted inheritance by the Torah, are nonetheless not obligated to waive their civil rights to inheritance, while others sharply disagreed, and still others staked a position in the middle.[62]

Integrating the practice with the spirit of the law in this case may be a two-step process. The first step is to ascertain to what extent the exclusive inheritance of males represents a Torah imperative or ideal, or, alternatively, is it more functional in nature and connected to societal circumstances.

Rishonim offer various understandings as to why the inheritance is, when possible, given exclusively to the males. The Ralbag understood it to be due to the desire one has to keep his property within his family, and the concern that a daughter, through her marriage, would remove the property to a different family. Similarly, the *Netziv* posits that daughters do not feel anguish at seeing their father's property transferred to their brothers, as they understand that the sons represent the continuation of the father's household. However, should there not be any sons, the daughters certainly would be dismayed to see the property removed completely from the family, and in that case the Torah dictates that they do inherit.

The Ralbag also writes that the Torah assumed that the brothers would take care of the needs of the sisters, at least towards marriage. It should be noted that, as a matter of *halakhah*, this is not left up to them and their generosity; as the *Shulchan Arukh* records,[63] it is taken as an enforceable condition of marriage (whether or not this is acknowledged in the written *ketubah*) that the portion of the estate necessary for the sustenance of the daughters be reserved for that purpose, even if this would leave so little remaining that the sons would be forced into poverty. As R. Chaim David HaLevi notes,[64] this arrangement resulted in the fact that in the majority of cases (i.e., when the estate was of average

62. For a survey of positions on this issue, see Appendix.

63. EH 112, 1 and 6.

64. *Resp. Mayim Chayim*, III, 50.

size, or smaller), the daughters benefitted more from this distribution than they would have had the Torah dictated that property be divided equally among the siblings. This is further the case because such equality would mean that upon the marriage of the daughters, their husbands, having shared their own inheritances with their sisters, would have less with which to support their new wives.

It is perhaps noteworthy that the exclusive inheritance of the sons is not mentioned explicitly in the Torah. Rather, it is taken for granted as a starting point. Beginning from that unexpressed premise, the verse[65] states "if a man dies without a son, you shall transfer his property to his daughter." The lack of an overt statement directing the inheritance to the sons might reflect a mandate that is more functional rather than conceptual.

The *Torah Temimah*[66] notes that the inheritance of sons is conceptually different from that of other heirs. The sons naturally occupy the space that has been filled by their fathers; as such, their receiving of the ancestral property is practically an automatic reality.[67]

Further underscoring the point, perhaps, is a striking midrashic statement characterizing the successful appeal of the daughters of the Biblical Tzlophchad in obtaining inheritance rights to their father's property, given that he had no sons. According to the *Sifri*, "They said: The mercy of man is not like the mercy of God. The mercy of man feels more for males than for females. But He who has created the world is not that way. His mercy is for both males and females. His mercy is for all, as is written:[68] "God is good to all and His mercy is for all His creations." While there are varying interpretations as to the intent of this *midrash*,[69] it seems at a basic level to be conveying that the policy is functional rather than a conceptual discrimination against the daughters.

One additional point to consider from the perspective of the spirit of the law is whether there is a distinction in the intent of the Torah

65. Num. 27:8.

66. Num. 27, #16.

67. See *Chavatzelet HaSharon al HaTorah* who suggests the same might be true regarding the inheritance of the daughters when there are no sons.

68. Ps. 145:9.

69. See *Ha'amek Davar* and *Torah Temimah* to Num. 27:18.

regarding daughters not inheriting on the one hand, and the double portion for the firstborn. In the case of the double portion of the firstborn, there may be an additional element. The Ramban[70] maintains that attempting to deprive the firstborn of his double portion constitutes a Torah prohibition.[71] This position is taken as a critique on the Rambam, who records no such transgression.[72] As such, even a technically successful effort in this area may be contradictory to the spirit of the law in a more overt fashion.[73] (R. Herzog, in discussing his proposal, was concerned with this and offered various suggestions to mitigate the problem, including securing an explicit or implicit waiver from the firstborn.)[74]

A second step in the process of reconciling spirit and practice would be to consider whether *shalom*, and in particular familial harmony, is a competing value, or could it instead be understood as a component value to the commandment of inheritance.

In expressing the purpose and intent behind the *mitzvah* of inheritance, the Rambam[75] asserts that the purpose of a *mitzvah* of inheritance is that good should not be held back from those who can and should benefit from it, in this case, the descendants. The *Sefer HaChinnukh*[76] highlights the kindness of God in allowing humans to benefit from the assets that they have acquired throughout their lifetimes. Given that

---

70. *Hasagot* on the *Sefer HaMitzvot, shikh'chat lavin,* 12, and Commentary to the Torah, Deut. 21:16–17. This is also the position of *Ohr HaChaim* to Deut.
71. *Avnei Miluim,* 111:4 (and also in *Ketzot HaChoshen,* CM 281:1), accepts this view and emphasizes that the Rabbis would not enact a policy that would subvert this prohibition; it is also accepted by *Resp. Shoel U'Meishiv, kama,* II, 104. See *Resp. Chatam Sofer,* CM 150.
72. This is also the implication of *Tosafot, Bava Batra* 130b, s.v. *lo yevaker.* See the discussion of the Rambam's position in *Resp. Iggerot Moshe,* EH, IV, 87:3.
73. By contrast, there is a view that de-emphasizes the aspect of the double portion for the firstborn, excluding it from the prohibition (discussed below) of disinheritance; see *Resp. Halakhot Ketanot,* II, 30; and *Kerem Shlomo,* CM, 282:1. See also *Resp. Teshuvot V'Hanhagot,* II, 720, who quotes R. Yitzchak Elchanan Spector to the effect that the priority is to execute a will that is halakhically effective, so that the other brothers will not be considered stealing from the firstborn.
74. *Techukah,* pp. 111–116.
75. *Moreh Nevukhim,* III, 42.
76. Commandment #400.

humans are mortal, they will eventually cease their personal usage, but they are able to transfer their assets to their families for their benefit.

Of course, the legacy of an intact family is far more valuable than that of the material property the individual leaves behind. As such, were the distribution of assets to tear asunder the family relationship, primary importance would be clearly undermined by the secondary.

THE *MITZVAH* TO FULFILL THE WISHES OF THE DECEASED

There are possibly additional components as well. Among them is the assumption that allowing one's assets to be distributed in accordance with their desires is itself a Torah value to some degree.

There is a Talmudic principle, *mitzvah l'kayem divrei ha-met,* "it is a *mitzvah* to carry out the wishes of the deceased."[77] From a technical standpoint, this rule by itself likely does not carry the load of reassignment of assets;[78] many *rishonim* (although not all) assume that it applies only to the disbursement of property that is already physically in the hands of a third party, rather than that which is in the control of the decedent, whose halakhic heirs automatically assume ownership upon his demise.[79]

Still, at least one prominent authority, R. Chaim Ozer Grodzinsky, did consider it feasible that this standard might be met by a civil will (at least after the fact), in that the enforceability by the civil courts should be considered equally significant.[80]

---

77. *Gittin* 14b.
78. See *MiDor L'Dor,* pp. 2–3.
79. *Tosafot, Gittin* 13a, *Ketubot* 70a and *Bava Batra* 149a, s.v. *d'ka; Shulchan Arukh,* CM 522:2. Among those who disagreed with this are the *Ramban, Ritva,* and *Ra'ah;* see *Beit Yosef* to 552. Some assume that the *rishonim* are not actually in dispute: the key factor is the recipient of the instructions; if the instructions were given to the heirs, or anyone directly empowered to carry out the wishes, no escrow with a third party is needed; see *Resp. Rama,* 48.
80. *Resp. Achiezer,* III, 34, and IV, 66. The matter had been debated in earlier generations. *Resp. Maharia HaLevi,* II, 86, opposed this understanding, noting it would require the daughters to pursue their civil rights legally, which the father should not assume would happen. However, *Resp. Minchat Shai,* 75, accepted this approach definitively (citing *Resp. Radbaz,* I, 67 as support); and in #79 printed a response to *Maharia*

Another approach leading to a similar conclusion was found in the responsa of a prominent British authority, R. Chanoch Padwa. He noted that at least in his home country of England, drafting a civil will means the appointment of an executor. As such, he suggests, this may meet the standard of the involvement of a third party.

Differently, R. Yitzchak Isaac Herzog[81] understood that this was the case due to *dina d'malkhuta dina*. He explained that the need for the third party possession was for the concern that the order did not represent the individual's final wishes, and some display of seriousness was required to dispel that concern. The knowledge that the civil law will enforce the request, he argued, accomplishes that purpose.[82]

Even assuming this principle does not suffice practically to create a redistribution, it may have conceptual relevance. The *Tashbetz*,[83] while acknowledging the technical limitations mentioned, further sharpened the concept by emphasizing that those on their deathbeds do not

---

HaLevi, and following his signature appended a note that *Maharia HaLevi* had then accepted his position and reversed his own view. See also *Resp. Binyan Tziyon, chadashot*, 24.

R. Shlomo Zefrani, in the journal *Moriah* (Vol. XX, 10–12, p. 122, in Tevet, 5756) relates the view of R. Yosef Shalom Elyashiv, who held that a civil will is ineffective, but that this question of the impact of *mitzvah l'kayem* is unresolved and accordingly a settlement should be negotiated between the parties. Ideally, though, a halakhic will should be executed to prevent any ambiguity. In R. Elyashiv's printed responsa, *Kovetz Teshuvot*, III, 225, in an earlier-dated letter (*erev Rosh HaShanah*, 5747), he makes a number of observations: a) that *Minchat Shai*'s claim of *Maharia HaLevi* conceding the point is not sustained by the latter's publication of his original objection in his own responsa at a later date; b) that a resolution between the two positions may hinge on the religious observance of the beneficiaries: if they would be likely to pursue their claims in a civil court, despite halakhic objections, the will may be considered as if deposited with a third party, while an observant beneficiary, who would not do so, would not create that reality; and c) a distinction may be drawn between moveable items and real estate, in that real estate can only be transferred through the involvement of the civil authorities.

81. *Techukah*, p. 144.

82. For an additional perspective on the purpose of the third party, see R. Zechariah Gelley, *Zekher Menachem*, 36.

83. *Resp.* II, 53.

automatically acquire some royal authority over others. Rather, it applies specifically to the distribution of their property.[84]

He understood this principle to be itself included in the *mitzvah* of inheritance; in other words, while the commandment that directs distribution of one's assets contains binding rules, an inherent goal of the commandment is the fulfillment of the wishes of the decedent.

This may open the door for a suggestion that the fulfillment of an individual father's specific desires in the allocation of his property after his death is not simply an additional value to be balanced against the *mitzvah* of inheritance, but is actually connected, at least in a conceptual sense, to that commandment itself. Even without extending that far, the notion of a Torah-validated respect for the wishes of the original owner of the property may soften somewhat the allegation that efforts to modify the distribution process run counter to the intent of the Torah.

It may be the case that the *Tashbetz*'s comments regarding this concept differ in theory from those of another *rishon,* the *Mordekhai.* In his understanding, the principle exists in order to address any emotional anguish that may be exacerbating the physical deterioration of an individual on his deathbed; reassurance that his wishes will be carried out, will, it is hoped, put his mind at ease.

Indeed, this is the rationale behind another rabbinic enactment, the *matnat schiv mera.* In that case, a tool was created to immediately transfer property from a dying individual to those he wishes to benefit, without the necessity of formal methods of acquisition. The Talmud explicitly states that this is in place in order to prevent mental distress that will be harmful to the physical condition.[85]

However, *schiv mera* and *mitzvah l'kayem divrei ha-met* seem (at least according to many commentaries) to be two distinct ideas. In the former case, the concept is only activated once an individual becomes ill, and is canceled if he recovers from that illness. This is not the case regarding the latter concept,[86] which is understandable within the *Tashbetz*'s association; if it is about the appropriateness of assigning

84. See also *Resp. Shvut Ya'akov,* I, CM, 168.

85. *Bava Batra* 147b.

86. CM 252:2. This is against the view of *Rivash* (217).

one's assets in accordance with the owner's desires, it is not necessarily connected to deathbed circumstances.

In addition to the view of the *Tashbetz,* the Tosafists also, albeit less explicitly, link the concept of "*mitzvah l'kayem*" to inheritance. The Klausenberger Rebbe, R. Yekutiel Yehuda Halberstam, went so far as to articulate this as reflecting a mandate to fulfill the wishes of the deceased "due to his ownership (*ba'aluto*) that remains on the property."[87] Given that the assets transfer to his heirs immediately upon death, presumably he is referring to moral influence over the property rather than legal ownership. Or, put differently, perhaps his ownership during his lifetime leaves an impact on the property, that is manifested in a mandate that his wishes should impact its disbursement.

An earlier authority, R. Shmuel Salant (1816–1909), had advanced a similar theory and incorporated it into a practical context.[88] R. Shmuel argued for the general upholding of wills, maintaining that this had been the attitude of halakhic authorities preceding him. He asserted that *mitzvah l'kayem* indicated that until the heirs designated by the Torah actually take physical possession of the estate, the ownership of the deceased continues to maintain an influence. Accordingly, the assets should be distributed according to his wishes, especially when there is some benefit to the deceased in doing so. It is particularly noteworthy that he relates to it as both a moral and technical principle. Because of the former, he explicitly considers it a value to uphold it as the latter. This position, which he acknowledges is unprecedented, has been strongly contested.[89]

---

87. *Resp. Divrei Yatziv,* CM, 28. A very similar approach is developed by R. Shmuel Rozovsky, *Chiddushei R. Shmuel, Gittin,* 15.
88. Published in *Torat Rabbenu Shmuel Salant,* III, pp. 31–38.
89. See pp. 39–43 of that volume for the response of R. Shmuel Heller. One particularly relevant issue for practical purposes is that of who is considered "*muchzak,*" or halakhically in possession: the Torah-designated heirs, by dint of that status; or whoever is in physical possession of the property; or perhaps the heirs designated by the will, due to the certainty of civil enforcement. This question will determine which party maintains the presumption when the ruling is in dispute. See *Mishpat HaTzava'ah,* III, *sha'ar* 8.

In attempting to find a Torah source for this principle of *mitzvah l'kayem,*[90] R. Yosef Shaul Nathanson[91] quotes the sermons of R. Yehoshua ibn Shuaib that cite the Ramban as tracing this value to the statement in the Torah[92] that Jacob's sons carried out his wishes regarding his burial. R. Nathanson challenges this assertion of the Ramban from a number of considerations, but concludes that the reference is unnecessary. The moral value of fulfilling the wishes of the deceased is clear, as a realization of the "true" kindness (*chesed shel emet*) involved in satisfying the wishes of those who cannot any longer act on their own behalf, or reciprocate. Likewise, R. Asher Weiss[93] understands this principle to be an expression of the justice and ethical values of the Torah.[94]

Similarly, the *Maharshdam*[95] asserts that even when the "*mitzvah* to carry out the wishes of the deceased" lacks technical efficacy, it carries moral weight, and it is appropriate to fulfill these wishes.[96] In this vein, R. Herzog argues, the enforcement of civil law, when relevant, comes not to contradict the Torah, but to act "in the spirit of the Torah."[97]

The *Ketzot HaChoshen*[98] makes a point that is relevant to our issue, whether *mitzvah l'kayem* is an enforceable mandate or a moral responsibility. He notes that there is no contradiction here to the Torah's rules of inheritance, because the rule does not trigger any automatic reassignment of property. The heirs receive the assets that the Torah grants to

---

90. Many assume that the principle is in fact rabbinic in origin; see *Tosafot, Ketubot* 86a, s.v. *priyat; Resp. Maharshdam,* YD, 173; *Resp. Teshurat Shai,* I, 433. See *Resp. Noda B'Yehudah,* II, 45, where it is implied this is a rabbinic principle. See the discussion in *Resp. Maharsham,* II, 224:12.

91. *Resp. Shoel U'Meishiv, tinyana,* 1:1. See also *tlitai,* II, 183.

92. Gen. 50:12

93. See *Resp. Minchat Asher,* III, 115.

94. See also R. Akiva Eiger, *Drush V'Chiddush,* I, *ketavim,* p. 90b.

95. *Resp.,* YD 203.

96. The context of this responsum is not about the distribution of assets but rather about a parent's wish to be buried in the Land of Israel.

97. *Techukah,* p. 144.

98. CM 248:5.

them, and only afterwards are confronted with a responsibility to use those assets in fulfillment of the father's wishes.[99]

R. Shmuel Rozovsky asserts that even though *mitzvah l'kayem* does not automatically transfer the property to the intended recipients, they are interested parties. In other words, the responsibility imposed on the instructed individuals is not simply a matter of conscience; the intended recipients have a moral claim on the assets.

This principle does seem to be primarily directed at the children of the deceased.[100] Accordingly, it does raise the question of the impact in this area of the mandate of *kibud av,* of honoring one's parents, even though that commandment is a distinct principle.

The Talmud rules, after some debate, that the obligation to serve one's parents is subsidized "*mi-shel Av,*" that is, the expenses of such services are paid for from the assets of the father, not from those of the child. This would be relevant in considering the question of whether the commitment to honor one's parents extends to fulfilling their wishes regarding the distribution of their assets.

While it is true that the obligation to honor one's parents extends even after their death, it is questionable to assert that this would require carrying out this particular wish. Even granted that the commandment obligates a child to carry out parental instructions in their absence – itself a disputed premise[101] – in this case, given that, following death, the property was immediately transferred to the heirs, it would seem that requiring them to allocate that property per the parent's instructions would contradict the Talmud's conclusion of "*mi-shel Av,*" as it would require the children to give away property that is rightfully their own.

---

99. He thus disagrees with the position of *Maharit,* CM, 6, that *mitzvah l'kayem* does not apply in a situation where there is an inheritance. See *Netivot HaMishpat,* 248:5 and 6.

100. See *Mordechai* and *Ramban, Gittin* 13a, s.v. *l'olam*. See also *Netinah L'Yitzchak, yerushah,* #10. *Resp. Minchat Elazar,* IV, 19, does assume *mitzvah l'kayem* to be applicable to enforce a will that would require a husband to cede property he had inherited from his wife (although that particular situation had additional complicating factors).

101. While this question is in general a debate in the *rishonim,* there would seem to be room to suggest that fulfilling a will is more likely to be included in *kibud av;* see *Mishpat HaTzava'ah,* III, *sha'ar* 8, *anaf* 9.

However, the great authority R. Akiva Eiger[102] was not sure that this was the case. It is true that the rule of *mi-shel Av* does not require a child to dip into his own pocket to pay for the services the parent requests. In this case, though, the assets in question are only available to the child because of the parent. As such, perhaps, the parent's wishes should indeed be respected.[103] While R. Eiger is ambivalent about the conclusion, *Resp. Kokhav M'Ya'akov*[104] was more confident, adding the logic that the father could have side-stepped the issue by legally transferring the property in his lifetime.[105]

Even if one does not accept that there is an obligation stemming from *kibud av,* the notion may still have relevance. In a responsum addressing the will of the Sadigerer Rebbe, R. Yitzchak Aharon Itinga,[106] while maintaining that "*mitzvah l'kayem*" is an insufficient validation, builds on the responsum of R. Akiva Eiger by noting that even if *kibud av* does not require a child to honor a father's instructions regarding asset distribution, a child who voluntarily chooses to do so is certainly in fulfillment of that cherished commandment.[107]

---

102. *Resp.,* 68.
103. R. Yitzchak Zilberstein endorses a similar approach in *Chashukei Chemed, Kiddushin* 32a. This is also apparently the underlying question in *Resp. Chavvot Yair,* 214, as understood by *Resp. Emek Shealah,* CM, 6 (in which case *Chavvot Yair* is concluding that *kibud av* does apply). See *Emek Shealah*'s analysis of the question, in particular in s.v. *Akh.* See also R. Yechiel Tauber, *Meishiv K'Halakhah,* I, 201, and n. 375, who assumes the consensus position to be that *kibud av* is in force, and adduces textual proof that the inheritance is considered as coming from the father's money.
104. I, 85.
105. If the conclusion is correct, however, it raises the question as to why *mitzvah l'kayem* is needed, when *kibud av v'eim* accomplishes these goals; R. Eiger, in his original responsum, suggests some differences between them. Similarly, *Maginei Shlomo, Ketubot* 86, to *Tosafot,* s.v. *pri'at,* assumes that "*mitzvah l'kayem*" is in place to expand the responsibility to those other than the children.
106. *Resp. Maharia HaLevi,* II, 86.
107. That will and the considerations of *kibud av* and *mitzvah l'kayem divrei ha-meit* are also analyzed at great length in *Resp. Maharsham,* II, 224, who notes that there is certainly a moral obligation of "you shall do the right and the good" (Deut 6:18). See also *Resp. Yashiv Yitzchak,* II, 43. See also *Resp. Minchat Shai,* 75, who considers *kibud av* to be operative in this case.

This issue resurfaced in a more recent debate between two esteemed British rabbinic figures, regarding the effectiveness of a civil will. R. Elyakim Shlesinger was of the opinion that the will has no halakhic validity whatsoever, and that a non-halakhic heir who collects is in violation of theft. Further, he maintains, even if the halakhic heirs would waive their rights, that would not change the situation, as they would presumably be doing so out of ignorance of their rights, and accordingly their consent is uninformed and thus invalid.

This last point was challenged by R. Chanoch Padwa.[108] He argued that the consent, even if not coming from a place of Torah knowledge, should not be deemed an error. Presumably, the willingness of the halakhic heirs to allow the distribution comes from a desire to honor the wishes of the parent. Given that the *halakhah* would indeed validate that instinct – if not as obligatory, certainly as meritorious – the consent should not be considered erroneous.[109]

It must be emphasized that the above points, which are all subject to vigorous debate, are not brought to question the widespread recommendation that a halakhic will be executed. Doing so would negate all controversy in practice and constitute the most straightforward path to both halakhic and familial harmony. Rather, they are brought to address the question of why the halakhic will, with its alternative distribution of assets, should not be considered an evasion of the intent of the Torah. The recognition of these additional aspects may help to provide a more complete picture of the components of that intent.

HA'AVARAT NACHALAH (DISINHERITANCE)

Another issue to contend with in ascertaining the spirit of the law regarding inheritance is that the Talmud identifies a specific prohibition of *ha'avarat nachalah* (*avurei achsanta* in Aramaic), or removing inheritance

108. *Resp. Cheshev HaEphod* II, 106.

109. He also asserts in this responsum that the authorities who would not require daughters to sign away their rights to assets granted them by civil law – which he regards as the majority opinion – would all the more so maintain that position when a will has been executed, indicating that this is consistent with the father's wishes. Compare also the related discussion, of a different scenario, in *Meishiv K'Halakhah*, 148.

from rightful heirs.[110] Apparently, it is contrary to the spirit of the Torah to disinherit all or one of one's sons; the Rabbis are unhappy with this behavior (*ein ruakh Chakhamim nocheh bo*).[111] This is codified in the *Shulchan Arukh,* where the *Rama* adds in the name of the *Mordechai,* that one who commands that his assets should be distributed "in the best possible fashion" is understood to mean to give them to his heirs, as there is nothing preferable to that.

One conceptual question, particularly for our purposes, is the issue of whether this represents an emphasis of the Torah's regulations regarding inheritance, or if this constitutes a separate principle highlighting the functional value of one's heirs receiving their property. The issue is significant because it impacts on whether one issue affects the other; in other words, if the Torah's rules would be technically satisfied, perhaps there is no concern of disinheritance. Conversely, if the two are not linked, even if the disinheritance could be justified – for example, because of an unworthy child – the Torah's mandate of distribution may still loom large.

To illustrate the point, R. Ovadiah Yosef wrote in a responsum that if one acts within the understood parameters of the disinheritance injunction, there is no worry that he is contradicting the Torah mandate of inheritance, disputing an earlier author[112] who had bifurcated the two.

That point was raised in the context of adjudicating a major subject of dispute, the question of whether any degree of dishonorable behavior can justify disinheritance. While the Talmud explicitly says one should not disinherit "even from a bad son to a good son," there is significant debate as to whether there are extremes that

110. *Ketubot* 53a, *Bava Batra* 133b. Compare also *Yerushalmi Bava Batra* 10:6.

111. There is some debate whether this constitutes a Torah prohibition, a rabbinic prohibition, or merely discouraged behavior (see *Rashbam, Bava Batra,* s.v. *mah* and s.v *ein; Resp. Rosh,* 85:3; *Resp. Divrei Malkiel,* I, 103; *Resp. Tzur Ya'akov,* II, 24; *Resp. Yabbia Omer,* VIII, CM, 9; *Resp. Meishiv Mishpat,* III, 52:11. R. Zalman Nechemiah Goldberg suggests a proof that there is no actual prohibition in an addendum to *Am Mordechai* to *Shulchan Arukh*). While the correct classification is significant, any of these is sufficient to present the question at hand.

112. R. Moshe Tzweig, *Ohel Moshe,* III, 21:3.

indeed justify such reallocation, and what other considerations may be involved.[113]

That particular fraught question is representative of a larger analytical point, as the linkage between the Torah commandment and the rabbinic statement against disinheritance has a number of implications. For example, many maintain that the rabbinic statement applies specifically to complete disinheritance, and the concern is avoided by leaving some significant property to go to these heirs. Further, the role of major charitable giving in this context is a dispute, with some arguing that such donations do not constitute disinheritance, and others less absolute on that point.[114]

The Talmud specifically includes in this prohibition transferring an inheritance from a son to a daughter,[115] thus initially calling into question the appropriateness of the *shtar chatzi zakhar* and related mechanisms.[116] The challenge posed by the conflict between practice and the simple reading of the Torah's commandment is intensified by this Talmudic passage, which has yielded much analysis together with practical applications.

One author who struggled most explicitly with this is R. Avraham David Wahrman (1770–1840), known as the Butzchacher Rav. In an essay in his commentary on the section of *Shulchan Arukh* dealing with disinheritance,[117] he asserts that "not even the most pious" have refrained from utilizing a *shtar chatzi zakhar,* and puts forward a two-pronged approach to reconcile the tension between this fact and the injunction against disinheritance.

113. See *Bava Batra* 133b, *Sma* CM 282:13, *Resp. Maharam Shik* CM 43, *Resp. Dovev Mesharim* I, 97; *Resp. Iggerot Moshe,* CM, II, 50; *Resp. Yabbia Omer,* VIII, CM, 10.
114. See *Ketubot* 67b; *Shi'iltot D'Rav Achai Gaon,* 62 and 64, and *He'amek She'alah,* 13; *Rama,* YD 249:1; *Chokhmat Adam,* 144:12.
115. See also *Resp. HaRosh,* 85:3.
116. See, in particular, *Beit HaBechirah* of the *Meiri* to *Ketubot* 53a, who warns against a father substantially increasing the money used for his daughter's dowries, out of fear of disinheritance. However, compare his commentary to *Bava Batra* 133b; see also *Resp. Shevivei Eish,* CM II, 111.
117. *Kessef HaKodashim,* CM, 282.

One part of this is accomplished through softening the conflict cumulatively, by suggesting a number of aspects that may satisfy the concern, either separately or collectively, that may or may not be in place. These elements will be enumerated and discussed below.

More fundamentally, however, he confronts the *ha'aramah* issue, including reference to the *Bekhor Shor*'s position on *mekhirat chametz,* and the possible distinction on this matter between Torah law and rabbinic law (and accordingly considers how to characterize disinheritance). Addressing the issue holistically, he maintains that a strategic, creative maneuver is not necessarily a *ha'aramah.* Instead, a *ha'aramah* is when there is a fundamental disconnect between one's actions and one's inner beliefs about those intentions.

This is conceivable, for example, regarding the sale of *chametz,* as one may execute a sale that is enforceable based on its explicit terms, despite the fact that one's internal attitudes toward the ownership of the *chametz* may differ, and place him thus at odds with the totality of God's commandment regarding *chametz.* It is this artifice, he maintained, that so offended the *Bekhor Shor.*

By contrast, when a father writes a *shtar chatzi zakhar* to benefit his daughter, he does so with full sincerity and complete commitment to the components of the system. Further, he does so out of a desire to act properly toward all involved, and to do so in the most righteous manner possible, and to follow in a path that was paved by holy and learned lights of earlier generations. Accordingly, he asserts, there should be no stigma of *ha'aramah* in this action.[118]

Another, earlier authority who categorically addressed the seeming tension between the *shtar chatzi zakhar* and disinheritance is the *Maharam Mintz* (1420–1482).[119] He argues that there is no conflict, as the *shtar chatzi zakhar* follows in the path of the Talmudic enactments whose purposes were validated in that context.[120]

---

118. Notably, he extends the same justification to efforts to address the prohibition of taking interest.
119. *Resp.,* 47 (the second one).
120. See also *Nachalat Shivah,* 21:2. However, see the qualifications in *Resp. Maharsham,* VII, 12. R. See also the discussion and suggestions on this point in R. Avraham Englard, *Resp. Imrei Avraham,* 66.

There are a number of other more specific approaches, some of which emerge from conceptual inquiries into the nature of this prohibition. Various suggestions are put forward as to why this specific rabbinic condemnation exists, among them: the deprivation of family members of what should be rightfully theirs; a neglect of the Torah's directives and their intent; or the inciting of jealousy and resentment between the siblings.

Building off of one or more of these postulates leads to a number of suggested parameters to this concern:

One question, crucial to the methodology of asset distribution, is whether there is any inhibition against giving away significant amounts during one's lifetime, which means *de facto* that those assets will not reach one's heirs, even though there is no overt disinheritance.[121] Extending that notion, even a bequest at the time of death that is formulated as a gift may not run afoul of this principle.[122]

Some posit that there is no issue of *ha'avarat nachalah* as long as there is some portion of the estate that is left to be handled according to the dictate of the Torah. Within this position, there are varied views as to what qualifies as an appropriate amount or percentage, and there are also various practices as to the most conducive way to accomplish this goal.

The position of the *Tashbetz*[123] was that even leaving a basic sum ("four *zuzim*")[124] to be distributed in the traditional fashion satisfied the injunction against disinheritance.[125] Finding a balance on this issue has challenged halakhic authorities. On the one hand, an absolute insistence on preserving every asset for one's halakhic heirs is clearly not the case; that would prevent one from ever giving away anything even during their

121. See *Resp. Chatam Sofer,* CM, 151.
122. See *Kessef HaKodashim,* CM, 282. See the discussion in *Resp. Shevivei Eish,* CM, II, 111, and *Resp. Lev Aryeh,* II, 56.
123. *Resp.,* III, 147, citing the *Ba'al HaIttur;* also cited in *Ketzot HaChoshen* 282:2.
124. There is some debate as to how to translate this figure into modern economic terms, as some see it as a nominal amount, and others see it as more significant.
125. This approach has received wide endorsement despite contradictory indications in some sources (such as *Ketubot* 53a and *Rashbam, Bava Batra* 133b), as the *Chatam Sofer, Resp.,* CM, 151 wondered; see *Pitchei Teshuvah,* CM 281:1, and see also the sources cited in *Mishpat HaTzava'ah,* p. 44, n. 1, and see, at length, in II, *biurim,* ch. 2. *Resp. Cheshev HaEphod,* II, 107, offers an approach to reconcile.

lifetimes, even to charity.[126] On the other hand, removing all, or almost all assets – even indirectly – from the scope of the disinheritance injunction would render it meaningless.[127] It is appealing to draw a distinction between that which is meaningful and that which is less so, but difficult to do so in an arbitrary, unsupported fashion.[128]

R. Moshe Feinstein, in two consecutively printed responsa[129] displays this tension in an effort to assess what would be the modern currency equivalent of the *Tashbetz*'s standard, as well as whether it is appropriate to rely on that standard. He suggests, in that context, that the injunction against disinheritance is defined by intent. One who is trying to deprive his heirs is acting inappropriately; one who is diverting his assets for a noble purpose, such as charity, may be acting meritoriously.[130]

As R. Mordechai Willig notes[131], an approach such as this is extremely significant for concerns of the spirit of the law, because it means that motivations such as harmony are not overriding the prohibition, but are not included in the prohibition in the first place.

A variation on the above focuses not on an amount that is left for traditional distribution but rather on certain categories of assets. For example, some advise leaving real estate to be distributed according to the Torah's rules, and others suggest that collections of holy books are appropriate for this purpose.[132]

---

126. See the citations of this question in *Resp. Meishiv Mishpat,* III, 52:2, including: *Levush HaOrah, Parashat Chayei Sarah; Resp. Agudat Ezov,* CM, 15: *Resp. Divrei Malkiel,* ibid; and *Yedei Eliyahu, Tikkun* 61.
127. Further complicating matters is a suggestion by the *Chatam Sofer,* ibid., that there are actually two different levels of condemnation involved (based on different formulations in the *Talmud Bavli* and *Talmud Yerushalmi*) and it is possible to satisfy one while still running afoul of the other.
128. As noted by *Resp. Minchat Yitzchak,* III, 135; see his broad discussion of the topic.
129. *Resp. Iggerot Moshe,* CM, 49–50; chronologically, the second one was written thirteen years earlier than the first.
130. *Meishiv Mishpat* cites a similar approach from R. Asher Weiss, as well as earlier authorities. See *Resp. V'Shav V'Rapha,* II, 100, and his extensive discussion of the topic.
131. *Am Mordechai* to *Shulchan Arukh,* p. 285. See this entire chapter (#55) for an extensive analysis of issues of contemporary inheritance.
132. *Pitchei Teshuvah,* CM, 281:12, records as customary the setting aside of both of these categories.

Different rationales have been offered for this particular policy. The *Nachalat Shivah* noted that these properties, each in their own way, are clearly and distinctly associated with their owners, and perhaps the thought of them transferring out of original family line through a son-in-law is particularly fraught with potential distress, and thus it may seem appropriate to distribute those specifically to the sons.[133]

The *Chatam Sofer*[134] puts forward a completely different approach, and in doing so uses the entry point of this detail of custom to articulate a somewhat radical theory of contemporary practices of asset distribution and their relationship to Torah law. Focusing on the notion of leaving real estate to be divided according to the Torah's dictates, he notes that it is actually real estate that is the context of the mandate of inheritance in the Torah. As such, it is the sole object of the explicit commandment.

This is significant, in his explanation, because it reflects the process that enables the *shtar chatzi zakhar.* The Talmud teaches that under certain circumstances, the Rabbinic leadership has the authority to modify Torah law.[135] As one would imagine, the parameters of this concept are highly delineated and debated in the texts. From the affirmative side, as the *Chatam Sofer* identifies in this case, it requires that the modification is "needed by the moment" *(she-ha'sha'ah tzrikhah l'kakh)* and that the Rabbis see the step as a necessary corrective to societal issues (*keivan she'rau tikkun ha-dor b'kakh*). On the negative side, there is a widely accepted view that no such modification can contradict the explicit directives of the Torah. Taken in balance, he is asserting that the *shtar chatzi zakhar* represents a rabbinic modification of the Torah's commandment, and as such must stop short of altering the overt body of that commandment, that real estate must

133. See *Pitchei Teshuvah,* ibid., for various distinctions flowing from these rationales. *Resp. Chinnukh Beit Yehudah,* 112, asserts that real estate actually refers only to the residence of the owner, noting that were that not the case, a father could commit a "*ha'aramah*" against the *shtar chatzi zakhar* by investing all his money in real estate and not leaving any assets to be included in the *shtar.*

134. *Resp.,* EH, 147.

135. See *Yevamot* 89b–90b.

be bequeathed to the sons and with recognition of the status of the firstborn.[136]

To avoid any overinterpretation or overapplication of this approach, it must be emphasized that the *Chatam Sofer*'s explanation is unique to him and boldly creative, and presumably leaves much unsaid, in terms of what other factors contributed to the justification of this development. One vital factor was mentioned earlier, that being the association he felt the *shtar chatzi zakhar* has with earlier Talmudic enactments that were themselves predicated on Scriptural support. Most significantly, the *shtar chatzi zakhar* is not actually functioning in violation of Torah law, but rather is orchestrating a result that seems to be at odds with its intent. It must be assumed that his analysis is dependent on that crucial distinction. Further, his theory is expressed only to explain a policy that had been in effect, with rabbinic approval, for centuries before his writing, and does not prescriptively lay out any framework for innovations in other areas.

Even these excepted asset categories, as R. Feivel Cohen[137] notes, may still add up to a substantial amount, and excluding the daughters from a share may still cause significant resentment. In that case, he advocates, it is preferable to include them as well in the *shtar chatzi zakhar,* as there is no actual prohibition to do so.

The *Rabdbaz,* in his work on the meaning behind *mitzvot,*[138] takes a largely mystical approach to understanding the commandment of inheritance, interwoven with practical components. Among those, he mentions the value to an individual in the ability to keep his property within his family. He notes that the scholars of other religions have often challenged Judaism for not providing for the daughters. His response to this was that the Torah understood the nature of humanity, which would lead to the brothers choosing to support their sisters and bring them to marriage in dignity.

---

136. He explains the exclusion of holy books differently, assuming they would be used primarily by the sons. Regarding the real estate, it would seem from his logic that it would include all land holdings, and not only the place of residence.
137. *MiDor L'Dor,* P. 36.
138. *Metzudat David, mitzvah* 530.

Accordingly, it may be possible to suggest that contemporary methods are further compatible with the intent of the Torah with a few additional points in mind. If the leadership perceived that the son's fraternal love for their sisters was proving insufficient to bring about that aspect of the vision, it would be necessary to institute societal tools to facilitate that goal. Further, it is noteworthy that some of the approaches are specifically designed to direct the brothers to share with their sisters, in particular the *shtar chatzi zakhar* and its variations.

Addressing the jealousy aspect, it is should be noted that the *Tur,* in his codification of the disinheritance injunction, does place the sowing of disharmony front and center in his formulation. Accordingly, there are some who argue the concern is mitigated whenever that risk is reduced or eliminated, such as if the siblings agree, or alternatively will not be aware of the discrepancy,[139] or perhaps if there is an inherently understandable reason for the differentiation.[140] More affirmatively, if the distribution is not only inoffensive to harmony, but actively designed toward its preservation, presumably this makes a strong argument that it is consistent with both the letter and the spirit of the law.[141]

The question of the concept and practice of inheritance in *halakhah* may be unique among our subjects in its particular mixture of widely accepted and encouraged policies that seem to deviate sharply from Torah law, and the degree of impact from areas of *halakhah* both external and internal to the subject at hand. Nonetheless, in its unusual manifestation, it may shed important light on the mechanisms and motivations of our broader subject as well.

139. See *Kessef HaKodashim,* ibid.

140. See *Chiddushei Chatam Sofer, Shabbat* 10b, who suggests that the admonition against different treatment within siblings does not apply when there is an understandable reason for the variance, and see the application of R. Yehoshua Heshel Adler, *Yeshuot Kohen al haTorah,* pp. 121–122. See also *Resp. Shevet HaLevi,* IV, 216.

141. See *Resp. Cheshev HaEphod,* II, 207. See also *Meishiv Mishpat,* III, 52:12, who demonstrates that concerns for harmony have traditionally overridden the issue of disinheritance. See also *Am Mordechai,* 55:1.

Chapter 9

Siyumim: Celebrating the Torah at Times of Restrictions

To turn attention briefly to an area of purely rabbinic law, in which an "avoidance" mechanism is subject to some controversy, it is instructive to consider the *siyum*. The notion of a celebration upon the completion of a tractate is found in the Talmud[1] and the *siyum* thus acquires the status of a *seudat mitzvah.*[2]

Accordingly, the completion of a tractate of the Talmud, or order of the *Mishnah*, and the accompanying celebration, is sometimes observed at a time of halakhic restriction, with the assumption that the festive commemoration suspends the restriction. This is widely done on the eve of *Pesach,* which is otherwise marked as a fast for first-borns, who may eat at the ceremony and then for the rest of the

1. *Shabbat* 118a.
2. *Yam Shel Shlomo, Bava Kama,* VII, 46, and *Rama,* YD, 246:26.

day as well. More controversially, *siyumim* are often conducted during the nine days between the beginning of the month of Av and the fast of the 9th of Av, when custom forbids the consumption of meat and wine, as part of the observance of mourning for the destruction of the two Temples. The assumption is that these restrictions are suspended during the *siyum,* although they revert to effect at the completion of that festive meal.

I. *SIYUMIM* ON THE FAST OF THE FIRSTBORN

Understanding the role of the *siyum* on *Ta'anit Bekhorot* requires having some understanding of that day itself, which is of somewhat mysterious origins. The idea of firstborns fasting on *erev Pesach* is mentioned in the minor tractate *Masekhet Soferim* (21:3) but is not brought in the Babylonian Talmud. In the *Talmud Yerushalmi,*[3] there is a passage that appears to both consider and reject the notion of *erev Pesach* being a time for firstborns to fast,[4] although the passage is the subject of both variant texts and alternative interpretations.[5] For example, the *Meiri*[6] records a widespread "custom" of fasting that is "not at all compulsory" (*ein bazeh srakh hekhrech klal*). The *Shulchan Arukh*[7] states simply that "the firstborns fast."

It is unclear why this should be, as the Jewish firstborns were saved during the final plague and would have no reason to treat the day as a sad one. There is even a suggestion in some writings that the text should be emended, and instead of "*ha-bekhorim mit'anin,*" the firstborns fast, it should read "*ha-bekhorim mit'angin,*" the firstborns enjoy themselves.[8]

3. *Pesachim* 10:1.
4. The *Ra'avyah* (#525) understands the *Yerushalmi* to be in conflict with the *Massekhet Soferim.*
5. See *Ran, Pesachim* 16a in pages of the *Rif,* s.v. *Yerushalmi,* citing *Ramban; Rosh,* 10:19 and *Korban Netanel.*
6. *Pesachim* 107b.
7. OC 470:1
8. Attributed to R. Zvi Hirsch of Zidotchov, cited in *Resp. Minchat Yitzchak,* II, 93 and elsewhere. However, see *Nimmukei Orach Chaim,* 470, who is harshly critical of relying on such a suggestion as a basis for leniency.

One particularly creative suggestion was put forward in recent generations by scholars[9] who noted that the firstborn indeed have more of a reason to celebrate than others do, as they were saved from the plague in addition to the redemption from slavery, and all of that should presumably focus on Pesach night, not the day prior. Accordingly, they suggest that fasting on *erev Pesach* is actually an extension of the general restraint in eating, and complete abstention from *matzah*, that is expected from everyone on that day in order to increase the appetite and appreciation for the *seder* meal. As beneficiaries of an expanded miracle, they are expected to intensify the commemorative experience.[10]

In any event, there is a tradition of efforts to avoid the fast, and of rabbinic disapproval of those efforts. R. Yechezkel Landau, the *Noda B'Yehudah,* in one responsum,[11] is harshly critical of a practice that had developed to delay the *brit* of a newborn boy until *erev Pesach* so that the festive meal for that event could cancel the fast.[12] While much of that opposition came from the unacceptable postponement of that *mitzvah,* R. Landau was also opposed to the *siyum* on that day, as reported by

9. R. Eliyahu Baruch Finkel, *MiShulchan Rebbi Eliyahu Baruch, Mo'adim* I, pp. 10–15; and R. Shlomo Zalman Shmayah, *Birkat Mo'adekha, Pesach-Shavuot* #9. A similar approach is taken by R. Eliyahu Levine, in the journal *Orayta,* VI, 5759, 2, pp. 91–92; R. Eliav Silverman, *Meishiv Nefesh,* III, 65, cites this and discusses extensively the ramifications of whether the fast is functional or commemorative.
10. R. Finkel notes a support for this position in the view of R. Yechiel, cited in the *Mordechai* (*Pesachim* 10:122), that allows light eating on this day, as opposed to a total restriction. Regarding the position of R. Yechiel, it is noteworthy that the above mentioned passage from the *Talmud Yerushalmi* creates ambiguity here as well, with the *Maharil* (Resp., 157) citing it as a refutation of R. Yechiel and *Bigdei Yesha* (commentary to the *Mordechai*) quoting it as support. The *Beit Yosef* records that the practice is not in accordance with R. Yechiel, although the *Mishnah Berurah* (470:2, and *Sha'ar HaTziyun,* 6) recommends the approach as an alternative for those who find the fast difficult or counterproductive. See *Darkei Shmuel: Halakhah U'Minhag,* p. 252, n. 8. See also the additional sources, positions, and explanations cited in R. Shlomo Schneider, *Resp. Divrei Shlomo,* IV, p. 364.
11. *Tinyana,* YD, 167.
12. As for a *brit* that is appropriately held on *erev Pesach,* the *Magen Avraham* (OC 470:1) cites the view of *Maharash HaLevi* that it is permissible to eat, but also praiseworthy to be stringent, an attitude that, reports the *Magen Avraham,* prevailed in his locale.

his student, R. Eliezer Fleckes.[13] Similar opposition has been relayed in the name of the *Chatam Sofer,*[14] and was echoed by his descendant R. Shimon Sofer.[15]

Even for those who approved the *siyum* on *erev Pesach,* there were disputes over aspects of the event. A number of authorities asserted that while the one completing the tractate could eat, there was no justification to invite others who had not been a part of the study.[16] Nonetheless, the contemporary custom is to invite others to the *siyum.*[17] The *Arukh HaShulchan* assumes this to be a concession due to weakness.[18]

THE SPIRIT OF THE LAW

As far as the spirit of the law, one point to consider is a general mismatch between the 14th of Nissan and a fast day, and thus perhaps a greater readiness to see the fast overridden. In addition to the questionable appropriateness of a fast on *erev Yom Tov,* it is actually the case that the 14th has its own special status in its own right.[19] Further, to enter the *seder* in a compromised state due to fasting detracts from that obligation in a

13. *Resp. Teshuvah MeAhavah,* II, 281, and III, 376.
14. See *Likutei Beit Ephraim,* #29; and *Resp.,* CM, 148, where it is clear the expectation in his time was that a firstborn would fast on *erev Pesach.*
15. *Resp. Hitorerut Teshuvah,* II, 245. Note that the questioner does assume a *siyum* is effective for eating meat during the Nine Days, and the response does not note an objection to that.
16. See *Resp. Teshuvah MeAhavah,* II, 266.
17. As acknowledged by the *Mishnah Berurah* and the *Arukh HaShulchan.*
18. Regarding the question of delaying a *siyum* so that it occurs on *erev Pesach* (an issue discussed more extensively below regarding the Nine Days), there appears to be contradictions in the writings of R. Shlomo Kluger. In his *Resp. HaElef Likha Shlomo,* 317, he disallows delaying a *siyum* until *erev Pesach.* However, later on (#387), he is more open to it, providing the learning accomplishment is significant enough. Compare also his statements in his *Resp. Shenot Chaim,* 52, 173, 245, modifying an earlier statement in *Sefer HaChaim,* OC 581, where he suggests that pushing off a *siyum* to "a fast day" is actually an enhancement, in that it will increase one's appreciation for the *siyum.* See R. Yitzchak Tesler, in the journal *Orayta,* XX, p. 170, and R. Yechiel Avraham Zilber, *Birur Halakhah, telita'ah,* p. 205. R. Yedidyah Taiah Weill, in his responsa, OC 38, allows this delay.
19. See *Mishneh L'Melekh, Hil. Klei HaMikdash,* 6:10.

problematic fashion.[20] Also, the fact that this fast at most only applied to a small minority of the population plays a role as well. Accordingly, the spirit of the law of "the 14th of Nissan" may be a factor in the attitude here.[21] This is all combined with the fact, noted above, that both the origins of the fast and its binding nature are somewhat open to question.[22]

An attitude that de-emphasizes the importance of the fast may be evident in some rulings regarding the question of listening to a *siyum* over the telephone. From the perspective of the internal logic of the concept, it is difficult to permit this.[23] Separate and apart from the debate regarding the status of *mitzvot* performed over electronic media, this is not a commandment based on "hearing"; it would seem that actual, physical

---

20. See *Resp. HaElef Likha Shlomo,* OC 316. Interestingly, as noted above, he is stringent regarding this fast in not allowing the timing of a *siyum* to be manipulated to cancel it, but allows it to be abandoned by one who feels he is weak and it will interfere with the *seder.* Presumably, for such an individual, even an "artificial" *siyum* should improve the situation, especially if, as discussed below, the *siyum* offers some affirmative benefit. See also *Resp. Ohr LeTziyon,* II, 12:1, who considers the concern for the *seder* a major component in justifying leniency, without which he advocates stringency.
21. See *Pitchei Teshuvah* to *Orach Chaim,* 470:1, and the sources cited there.
22. See, in particular, R. Yosef Mashash, *Resp. Mayim Chaim,* 179. See also R. Yosef Shaul Nathanson, *Yosef Da'at,* YD 399, who invokes the combination of factors in explaining his own lenient practice.

    R. Moshe Shternbuch, *Resp. Teshuvot V'Hanhagot,* II, 210, assumes that it is only custom together with a lack of clear sourcing for the fast that can explain the lenient attitudes that prevail, noting that the objections of earlier authorities as well as conceptual analysis would have indicated otherwise. In particular, he highlights the allowance of a limited offering of cakes and fruit, rather than a genuine meal including bread, as reflective of this leniency.

    Similarly, R. David Taharani, *Resp. Divrei David,* III, 20, relies on this attitude to allow a *siyum* on Thursday when *erev Pesach* is on *Shabbat,* despite various logical inconsistencies noted by earlier authorities. (Regarding this issue, see *Chidushim U'Biurim al HaShas* of the Lubavitcher Rebbe, 15.)

    A variation on the emphasis on the customary nature of the fast is not necessarily to see it as inherently less stringent, but rather to assume that the acceptance of the custom was predicated on excluding a *seudat mitzvah* from its scope. See *Pri Chadash,* OC 470:2; R. Ovadiah Yosef, *Meor Yisrael, Pesachim* 108a; and *Ratz KaTzvi, Pesach/Shavuot,* 6:7.
23. Indeed, R. Yisrael David Harfenes, *Resp. Mekadesh Yisrael, Pesach,* II, 256, does not permit this.

participation in the meal is the only basis to consider one a part of the celebration.[24] In fact, in the context of a *siyum* during the Nine Days, meat and wine is not only limited to the *siyum* meal, but to the physical location of the meal.[25] Nonetheless, regarding the *Ta'anit Bekhorim siyum*, many authorities have allowed telephonic participation.[26]

Reflective of this general approach, the *Arukh HaShulchan*[27] records that for many generations already it has been the practice to be extremely lenient with this fast, and to conduct a *siyum*, in which not only the one who learned the text can eat, but all the firstborns are invited, and that this practice is widespread, and that it is unclear why this attitude of leniency has been accepted, although it is indeed the case that great rabbis have not objected.[28] In fact, some contemporary authorities assume that the attitude of negation towards the fast has taken on the status of an accepted custom, and accordingly, even a mourner in the middle of the *shivah* period who may not attend a *siyum*, still does not fast (although he should make a charitable donation in its place).[29]

---

24. This position is expressed by R. Yisrael Belsky, *Resp. Shulchan HaLevi*, 13:1. See the discussion in *Resp. Maharam Brisk*, I, 133, and see the contrasting views brought in *Ma'adanei Yom Tov*, IV, p. 581.
25. *Mishnah Berurah* 551:75; see also *Rama*, OC 565:2.
26. See R. Asher Bush, *Shoel B'Shlomo* (5778), 44. R. Noach Isaac Oehlbaum, *Resp. Minchat Chen*, III, 30, recommended relying on this opinion in the early days of the COVID-19 pandemic, when gathering in person for a *siyum* was prohibitively dangerous. (If no *siyum* at all was available, he advocated not fasting under these circumstances.)
27. OC 470:4.
28. See also *Resp. Teshuvot V'Hanhagot* II, 210, who notes other leniencies as well that have become associated with this fast. See also *Resp. Even Pinah*, I, 33.
29. See *Nitei Gavriel*, 43:19, and *Resp. D'var Yehoshua*, II, 81. See also *Ratz K'Tzvi, Pesach-Shavuot*, 6 (and see as well his discussion as to the impact of a *siyum* on other customary fasts throughout the year). The *D'var Yehoshua* actually assumes that the custom to fast has been abandoned in favor of the alternative commemoration of a *siyum*, which therefore does not override the fast through its performance but simply replaces it. Accordingly, one who is unable to attend a *siyum* is nonetheless not obligated to fast. (He also indicates that the *siyum* does not require a joint meal, but rather allows for the participants to go home and eat separately; see also *Resp. Avnei Derekh*, I, 76.) However, compare *Resp. Pri HaSadeh*, IV, 57, who forbids a mourner from attending a *siyum*, and does not permit him outright to eat nonetheless (unless he is particularly weak). Regarding the general question

What may also be relevant is the question of the spirit of the fast itself. If, indeed, the day does not merit a practice reflecting sadness, it may be that the fast has a different purpose. A number of commentaries see the fast as a "*zekher l'neis*"[30] or a publicizing of it (*Pirsumei Nisa*).[31] In one later formulation,[32] it is understood as a reenactment of the original event, in the sense that at that point, the Jewish firstborns had to establish their worthiness to be spared. (This would thus be comparable to *Ta'anit Esther,* the day before Purim, when a fast is observed to commemorate the fast and prayers undertaken to thwart the plot of Haman.)[33] Similarly, contemporary firstborns fast to evoke the repentance and prayer of their ancient counterparts.[34]

R. Zvi Hirsch Frimer, the Kozhaglover Rav, drew on this notion to explain a distinction between the fast of the firstborn and the Nine Days regarding the *siyum,* in that in the former case, following the *siyum,* the fast is abandoned, while in the latter case, meat and wine can only be consumed during the *siyum* itself. He posited that this is a function of *Ta'anit Bekhorim* not being a standard fast day, but rather a reenactment of the original event.

To complete the explanation, it may be suggested that the purpose of the observance is to highlight the need for the Jewish people to earn the survival of their firstborns through merit, not merely as recipients of Divine favor. The initial path to do that is through prayer and penitential fasting. However, perhaps there is an alternative, maybe even a superior

---

of a mourner attending *siyumim,* see also R. Eliyahu Bakshi Doron, *Resp. Binyan Av,* V, 54.

30. Tur, OC 570, from *Massekhet Soferim.* See also Meiri to *Pesachim* 107b.
31. See *Birkei Yosef.*
32. R. Yehudah Greenwald, *Resp. Zikhron Yehudah,* 133. However, *Darkei Shmuel: Halakhah U'Minhag,* p. 251, n. 4, notes the contrary implication of *Resp. Maharil,* #110, who states that since the miracle happened at midnight of the 15th, observance of the fast on the 14th is a concession to necessity and only commemorative. See also R. Shlomo Schneider, *Divrei Shlomo,* V, 1129.
33. See *Chatam Sofer, chiddushim* to *Pesachim* 108b, and note the critique of *Birkhat Mo'adekha,* ibid.
34. See also R. Yosef Tzvi Salant, *Be'er Yosef,* II, *inyanei Pesach,* pp. 329–333, for an elaborate version of this approach; see also the addendum from the son of the author, pp. 333–342.

route: embracing the new mission of the Jewish people, the study of the Torah, and in fact doing so with enthusiasm.[35] In such a manner, it could be suggested that *minhag yisrael* has developed to see the *siyum* on *Ta'anit Bekhorim* as a more appropriate reflection of the theme of the day, given all the elements, then fasting would be.

It should be noted that according to the view cited above, that the purpose of the fast is to intensify the experience of eating *matzah* later that night for the firstborns who owe increased gratitude, an exemption due to participating in a *siyum* is particularly difficult to understand. Unlike a day of sadness, which may yield in its atmosphere to the *mitzvah* meal, in this case the fast comes from a practical consideration to preserve appetite. R. Eliyahu Baruch Finkel, one of the proponents of the "appetite" theory, suggests that the fast for this purpose is observed as an enhancement (*hiddur*) of the *mitzvah*, undertaken as a general policy to preserve preparation for the later *mitzvah*. As such, a meal that is itself a *mitzvah* is understandably excluded from this policy.[36]

---

35. R. Shlomo Zalman Auerbach (quoted in the journal *Mevakshei Torah, Pesachim* II, p. 562) notes that the firstborn were sanctified to serve in the Temple on the night of the Exodus, but later lost that privilege due to the sin of the golden calf. Accordingly, that day approaching *Pesach* night has taken on an aspect of sadness for the firstborn. (Similarly, R. Moshe Shternbuch, *Mo'adim U'Zmannim*, VII, 69, suggests that for this reason it has become a day of fasting and repentance.) R. Auerbach posits that since Torah study is even greater than the priestly service, the practice developed to study Torah and joyously commemorate that study on that day, as a comfort to the firstborn.

    R. Moshe Greenwald, in his *Resp. Arugat HaBosem*, OC 139, in the middle of a paragraph where he is actually harshly critical of attendance at an *erev Pesach siyum* by those who have no connection to the scholar or to learning in general, makes a fascinating statement that can also be incorporated into the above perspective. Addressing a comment of the *Magen Avraham* that in his day, they were lenient to eat on *erev Pesach* for a *siyum* but not for a *brit milah*, he offers a novel suggestion to explain the distinction. A *brit*, which generally must be at a set time, would conceal the existence of *Ta'anit Bekhorim*, were people to be eating then. By contrast, the *siyum* has no inherent need to take place at that time. The fact that one is being arranged at that specific time will itself serve the purpose of publicizing the occasion, and thus is, apparently, more in harmony with the spirit and intent of *Ta'anit Bekhorim*. See also the objection of *Resp. Maharam Brisk*, I, 133.

36. *MiShulchan Rebbi Eliyahu Baruch*, ibid., pp. 14–15; see there also for his explanation as to why this *mitzvah* meal cancels the fast for the rest of the day that follows as well.

More broadly compatible with the theories mentioned above, his understanding is that this effort to intensify the *mitzvah* of *matzah* serves as an additional merit for the firstborns. As such, the *siyum* meal, together with the learning that prompts it, is effective as an alternate, perhaps even preferable, source of merit.[37]

II. THE NINE DAYS SIYUM

Regarding the period of the "Nine Days," from the beginning of the month of Av until after the fast of the ninth (practically, until midday on the tenth), the *siyum* receives an even more mixed reception.

There is some discussion in the literature as to the relative severity of the erev *Pesach* fast and the prohibition of meat and wine during the Nine Days. In some responsa, the accomplishment in learning necessary to justify a *siyum* is held to a higher standard for *erev Pesach* than for the Nine Days.[38] One explanation provided for this is that the fast on *erev Pesach,* as noted above, has some sourcing in early Rabbinic literature, while the Nine Days restrictions, as will be noted, are a function of custom.[39]

Nonetheless, it is clear that in the aggregate and certainly in contemporary attitudes, a *siyum* during the Nine Days is met with significantly more resistance and limitations than one on *erev Pesach.*[40] This would appear to emerge from the perception that as far as the spirit of the law is concerned, circumventing the *erev Pesach* fast can be understood to be more tolerable than what amounts to interrupting the mourning over the destruction of the Temple.

---

37. Similarly, as noted there, R. Velvel Soloveitchik of Brisk was asked regarding a father who was fasting on *erev Pesach* on behalf of his minor son who was a firstborn. The son, however, completed a tractate that day, although the father did not attend the *siyum.* R. Soloveitchik responded that the father need not fast in this instance (cited in *Haggadah MiBeit Levi*). Apparently, the goal is to provide a source of merit as a protection, and the scholarship of the son is as effective as the fast of the father.
38. R. Shalom Yosef Feigenbaum, *Resp. Meishiv Shalom,* 230, records this as common practice in his experience.
39. *Resp. Beit Avi,* II, 52. R. Yechiel Avraham Zilber considers both sides of the question of which is more stringent in his *Birur Halakhah, telita'ah,* pp. 204–205.
40. See *Resp. Minchat Yitzchak,* II, 93:4, who notes a shift in this area away from the attitudes of earlier authorities who had been more stringent regarding *erev Pesach.*

An example of the concern for the spirit of the Nine Days can be found in the words of the *Arukh HaShulchan,* who bemoans the "embarrassment" of Jews who are unable to abstain from meat and wine for this brief part of the year in recognition of the devastating spiritual loss, while people from all walks of life voluntarily refrain from meat and wine for much longer, without comparable motivation. (In this section, he is not addressing the circumstance of a *siyum,* but rather those who are lax in this custom with no license whatsoever.)

The abstaining from meat and wine that is found in the Talmud is limited to the hours preceding the fast of *Tishah B'Av.*[41] By custom, this has been extended to a longer period,[42] with the prevalent Ashkenazic practice of observance from the first day of Av until *Tishah B'Av,*[43] generally nine days, although the fast often falls on *Shabbat* and is then pushed to the tenth (the prevalent Sefardi custom is to observe the restrictions in the week of *Tishah B'Av*). This custom is mentioned by the Rambam[44] and is treated with great severity in the earlier sources, with the *Beit Yosef* citing the words of the *Ramban* and the *Rashba*[45] that one who disrespects this custom is breaching the structure established by those who came before. The *Arukh HaShulchan* understands the commitment to be on the level of a vow taken with public awareness (*al da'at rabbim*) which is not subject to repeal, and thus binding on a Torah level.

The *Rama*[46] adds that "at a '*seudat mitzvah,*' including a "*siyum masekhet,*" all of those who are "relevant to the meal (*kol ha-shaykhin l'seduah*)" eat meat and drink wine. The first indication that there is something uncomfortable about this celebration during the time of national mourning is in that same gloss of the *Rama,* who adds that one should "minimize" (*l'tzamtzem*), and "not add," presumably referring to

41. *Mishnah, Ta'anit* 26b and *gemara* 30a; the reference is either to the last meal before *Tishah B'Av,* or the entire afternoon.
42. The *Shulchan Arukh* (OC 551:9) records three possibilities: from the 17th of *Tammuz;* from the first of *Av;* the week of *Tishah B'Av.*
43. *Rama,* ibid.
44. *Hilkhot Ta'anit* 5:6; see *Hagahot Maimoni.*
45. *Resp.* I, 306.
46. OC 551:10.

the guest list; and during the actual week of *Tishah B'Av,* when there is greater stringency, only an exact *minyan* should be present.[47]

Some went further than the *Rama,* and challenged the conducting of the *siyum* at that time at all. For example, R. Eliezer Fleckles[48] notes that the other examples listed as a *seudat mitzvah-* a *brit milah,* a *pidyon haben* – are limited to specific times and dates. A *siyum,* by contrast, can be delayed until a time that is "appropriate to hold a meal."[49] As the nine days are certainly not such a time, it would seem that the *siyum* should be moved away from them. At a minimum, he asserts, a *siyum* should not be held during the week of *Tishah B'Av.* R. Ya'akov Shalom Sofer, in his *Torat Chaim,*[50] responded to this assertion, noting that while a *siyum* can be moved to allow for a more elaborate affair, that does not mean that it needs to be moved from its natural date, once we have established that it can indeed take place during these days.

The essential license of the *Rama,* to consume meat and wine during this period at a *siyum,* has been endorsed by major codifiers.[51] Nonetheless, a number of qualifications have been advocated and discussed. Some have argued that a *siyum* with meat is only justifiable if the one involved would otherwise conduct a *siyum* of that standard, at a different time of the year, or at least would enhance the event to some recognizable degree.[52] The *Torat Chaim* challenges this point as well, asserting that only the attitude at the moment should be of significance.[53] Others suggest that the limitation would only apply to one who has come to the intellectual decision not to make celebratory *siyumim*

47. See also his comments in *Darkhei Moshe,* 551:10.

48. *Resp. Teshuvah MeAhavah,* II, 273, gloss to OC 551.

49. See *Shakh,* YD 246:27, citing *Maharam Mintz.*

50. OC 551, #27.

51. See *Chayei Adam,* 133:16; *Arukh HaShulchan,* OC, 551:27; *Derekh Chaim,* 12; *Kitzur Shulchan Arukh;* 122:8. It is related that R. Yehoshua of Kutno would eat meat on the night following *Tishah B'Av* (when the restrictions still apply) on the strength of his *siyum* on the book of Lamentations (which is read on *Tishah B'Av*).

52. See *Elyah Rabbah,* 551:27, s.v. *efshar.*

53. See *Resp. Yedidyah Taiah Weill,* OC 35, p. 41, s.v. *akh,* who related that his father, the *Karban Netanel,* would make a *siyum* at this time, even though he normally did not.

as a policy, not to one who recognizes their value, but does not always go to the effort or expense.[54]

Further, even if a *siyum* need not be moved away from the Nine Days, moving one *into* the Nine Days – either through speeding up the learning, or intentionally delaying it – is another matter. The *Elyah Rabbah,*[55] cited by the *Mishnah Berurah,*[56] forbids this, an objection shared by many others.[57] Among these is *Arukh HaShulchan,* who calls such manipulation a "*davar mekhuar,*" a distasteful act. However, it is noteworthy that he is less condemnatory towards one who would begin a tractate with the intention of completing it and making a *siyum* during this time period. Apparently, as he indicates, the net gain to the study of Torah is a possible salvation.

Similarly, there are those who drew a distinction between delaying and accelerating. R. Ya'akov Emden, in his *siddur,* wrote that quickening the pace is praiseworthy as an expression of enthusiasm, as long as understanding is not sacrificed. R. Yosef Mashash,[58] responding to the concern that speeding up the pace of the learning could constitute a *ha'aramah,* wished that all *ha'aramot* could be of this nature, as they increase the study of Torah. In fact, he asserted, one who does not accelerate should be charged with a *ha'aramah,* as he fools himself into believing he fulfills his obligation of Torah study with less than he is capable of![59]

Despite the strongly expressed opposition, there were a number of authorities who did tolerate pushing the completion of the learning into the Nine Days to enable the *siyum* then.[60]

---

54. See *Resp. Yabbia Omer* I, OC, 26; this is also the conclusion of a lengthy analysis of the lenient practice on this issue, by R. Yeshaya Slomovitz, in his *Avnei Shoham, Bein HaMetzarim,* 48, who draws comparisons to similar statements in other areas of *halakhah. Resp. Mekadesh Yisrael, Bein HaMetzarim,* #142, takes a stringent stand on this.
55. #26.
56. #73.
57. See also *Resp. Chesed L'Avraham, Kama,* 56; *Resp. Ezriel Hildesheimer,* 90; *Resp. Ramatz,* I, 41 (who makes an exception for the night following *Tishah B'Av*); *Resp. Nishal David,* OC 22.
58. *Resp. Mayim Chaim,* ibid. The responsum is addressing *erev Pesach.*
59. Presumably, he means this homiletically, as it is very possible the individual is learning to his full capacity in other areas of Torah.
60. See, for example, *Kaf HaChaim,* OC 551:161; R. Avraham Yudeliwitz, *Resp. Beit Av,* OC 82:1; R. Ovadiah Yosef, *Resp. Yabbia Omer,* I, 26 (although in *Resp. Yechave Da'at,*

The debate around deferring a *siyum* until the nine days reflects, if not always explicitly, some of the general *ha'aramah* debate, together with aspects specific to this issue. There are a number of components to the discussion: one is a general *mitzvah* question, the permissibility of reaching the end of a *mitzvah* project and then pausing, trading an expeditious completion for one at a more opportune moment. Many point to a Talmudic passage[61] that indicates that this is a justifiable calculation, at least in general.

However, this addresses only the "letter of the law" question. It is clear that there is an additional tension here, that emerges from the apparent desire to subvert the goal of experiencing the mourning through abstaining from meat and wine. This would clearly be more objectionable if it results from some artificial manipulation. In this, there is a spirit of the law consideration which would not be addressed by the Talmudic proof text allowing the general delay of a *mitzvah* completion.[62] Beyond that, if the delay is significant, there may develop an additional "letter of the law" consideration, as the *siyum* could theoretically be considered completely detached from the actual learning, and thus unwarranted.[63]

I, 40, he writes some significant limitations); *Resp. Minchat Yitzchak,* II, 93; *Yesodei Yeshurun,* VI, p. 39; *Mo'adei Yeshurun* p. 132:11b, and 155:66; *Resp. Mishneh Sakhir,* II, OC 144; *Resp. Sheilat Yitzchak, tinyana,* 56. See Tesler, pp 170–173. R. Yisrael David Harfenes, *Resp. Mekadesh Yisrael,* acknowledges that the custom is to allow timing specifically for a *siyum,* but regarding delaying, he notes the difference between one who finishes early and simply waits until the Nine Days to formally finish and make a *siyum,* on the one hand, as opposed to one who realizes he will finish earlier and therefore slows down the pace in order to actually finish during that time period. He considers the latter approach vastly preferable and thus recommends doing so.

61. *Moed Katan* 9a. The implications of this passage are debatable and have been the basis for conflicting claims in this controversy; the same can be said of a responsum of the *Maharam Mintz* (#119) that is cited by many of the later authorities. See the analysis of R. Shmuel Heller, *Resp. Shem MiShmuel,* 7.
62. *Chesed L'Avraham,* ibid., in his stringent position, essentially combines the points, noting that delaying the completion of a *mitzvah* can only be justified by the motivation of pushing it to a more appropriate time. Without that element, there is no permission to wait; and certainly to delay to a time which is, in his understanding, a less appropriate time, is a complete inversion and should not be tolerated.
63. See *Shoshanat Yisrael,* 3:14, n. 21.

It is also worth noting that some go so far as to define the act according to the intent. R. Yitzchak Weiss, in his *Resp. Minchat Yitzchak,*[64] asserts that a *siyum* motivated by a desire to eat meat is not only inappropriate, it is actually ineffective.[65] This is certainly a strong formulation, and it too draws upon the general debate about *ha'aramot.* In that context, while the concern of a sham process has often been expressed, many argued that motivation was not disqualifying once one committed to the genuine performance of the relevant action. Arguably, this should be especially true about Torah study, regarding which the Talmud teaches one should engage in "even not for its own sake."[66]

Interestingly, an earlier authority, R. Shlomo Kluger,[67] had invalidated learning done for the sake of the *siyum,* but conceded that this could be overcome by an enhanced accomplishment; one who undertook to learn a large tractate would generate enough genuine joy to qualify, even under those circumstances.[68]

An additional consideration, driven by the tension inherent in this practice, is the threshold that justifies the participation in the *siyum* by those who have not themselves completed the learning.[69] Many of the codifiers, expanding on the language of the *Rama,* maintain that those invited must have a connection, familial or otherwise, to the one making

64. II, 93.
65. *Avnei Shoham,* 48, cites a similar idea from the work *Chayei Moshe.*
66. R. Aharon Miasnik, *Minchat Aharon,* p. 25 and p. 107, explains a similar position in a different fashion: The permission to consume meat at a *seudat mitzvah* is not an exception to the prohibition; rather, such a meal is not classified with the category of inappropriate rejoicing at all. Accordingly, a participant in the meal who is motivated by his personal enjoyment would not be covered at all by the warrant of the *siyum.*
67. *Resp. HaElef Likha Shlomo,* OC 386.
68. Some have argued, based on the language of his responsum, that R. Kluger was distinguishing between Talmud, which would justify a *siyum* regardless of motivation, and Scripture, on which one could make a *siyum,* but only if the learning was undertaken for its own sake. See *Resp. Beit Avi,* ibid., and R. Shlomo Wahrman, *Orot Yemei HaPesach.*
69. It is agreed upon that guests may be invited to the *siyum* (see *Biur Halakhah,* s.v. *siyum,* citing *Magen Avraham* and *Elyah Rabbah*); the question is what parameters apply.

the *siyum.*[70] Complete strangers, however, would have no justification to attend or be invited, with the Maharil going so far as to term their presence a *mitzvah ha-ba'ah ba-aveirah,* a *mitzvah* tainted by performance through a transgression.

This consideration would seem to call into question the widespread practice of hosting *siyumim* in summer camps, and through that serving meat meals to all the campers. However, many cite a lenient ruling by R. Moshe Feinstein,[71] who understood that the camp environment, while it lasts, creates its own social circle, which qualifies as a guest list for this purpose. He applies the same logic for adults and families who spend their summers together in a bungalow colony.[72]

R. Ovadiah Yosef[73] goes farther and notes a number of advantages to a larger audience at a *siyum,* even of strangers, including: greater

---

70. See *Taz,* 12, and *Mishnah Berurah,* 75. R. Ya'akov Emden, in his *siddur,* allows inviting a large group if they are somehow supportive of the learning, but strangers invited merely to expand the crowd would be forbidden. See Tesler, pp, 173–178.

71. Quoted in *Kitzur Hilchos Bein HaMetzarim,* p. 8, #9, and *Nit'ei Gavriel, Bein HaMetzarim* 41:4.

72. Still, assumes R. Yisrael David Harfenes, *Resp. Mekadesh Yisrael, Bein HaMetzarim,* #136, R. Feinstein would presumably not extend his leniency to a hotel that hires a scholar to conduct a *siyum* in the presence of the hotel guests, as they are complete strangers to him (see also ibid., #137). However, R. Aharon Felder, *Mo'adei Yeshurun,* p. 155, n. 65, reports hearing from R. Feinstein that the contemporary custom is to allow the presence of even those with no acquaintance to the one conducting the *siyum.*

These considerations are relevant to the contemporary phenomenon of restaurants that solicit students to conduct *siyumim* throughout the nine-day period. This would certainly seem to be inconsistent with the standard that many of the authorities required of an actual connection to the event.

There is, though, an additional aspect to consider. There is a significant literature addressing the question of whether meat restaurants should be kept open during the Nine Days (and serve meat), whether for those who may have license to eat meat during this time, or, more pointedly, for those who are nonreligious and would otherwise eat non-kosher meat if the kosher variety were not available (see the discussion in *Ratz KaTzvi, B'Ma'agalei HaShanah,* II, 21). For those who allow such service, presumably the addition of even a substandard *siyum* would be an enhancement. However, there is a strong counterargument to this in that the substandard *siyum* may entice religious people who would not have otherwise eaten meat then.

73. *Resp. Yabbia Omer,* I, OC 26:8.

honor for the Torah, support for the scholar, inspiration and motivation for others. In his view, only those who have no appreciation for Torah or capacity to grasp the significance of the occasion would be inappropriate guests.

A POSSIBLE PERSPECTIVE

In attempting to understand the attitude that is more receptive to *siyumim* during the Nine Days, it is noteworthy that abstaining from meat and wine is not in and of itself a mourning practice; a mourner in the period of *shivah* is permitted to have meat and wine.[74] Only during the more intense period of *aninut* – between the death and the burial – is meat and wine prohibited. The hours immediately preceding *Tishah B'Av*, which parallel that intensity, have this prohibition. By custom, it is extended to the Nine Days. The nature of this extension, however, requires explanation.

One approach is to note that there is an aspect to personal mourning that is not present in the national mourning over the destruction of the Temple. A private *shivah* is not only for the expression of grief, but also for the comforting of the mourners. This creates a counterbalance to the mourning practices. Wine, in particular, is held up as a source of comfort to those in grief, and thus has an affirmative role in the *shivah* process. In other words, perhaps it would have been logical to prohibit meat and wine during *shivah*, but there is a reason not to. This dynamic is, though, not applicable to the Nine Days.[75]

One reason for this difference relates to an observation made by R. Joseph B. Soloveitchik. He pointed to the fact that structurally, the personal mourning process for a deceased relative, and the national mourning over the destruction of the Temple, are inverses of each other. The phases of personal mourning, beginning with *aninut* and closing, in the case of a parent, with the twelve month mourning period, gradually decrease in intensity. In contrast, the national mourning, starting with

74. See YD 348:8.

75. An approach along these lines can be found in R. Aharon Miasnik, *Minchat Aharon: Bein HaMetzarim*, p. 107, although his rationale for the distinction is different from that posited below.

the "Three Weeks" and closing with *Tishah B'Av* itself, increases in intensity. The reason for this differentiation is connected to the reality that an individual grieving a freshly lost loved one is naturally consumed by sadness, and needs to be comforted through a process that gradually leads him out of mourning. In the case of the mourning over the Temple, the individual is asked to emotionally connect to the loss of something he never experienced in any other form, that happened hundreds of years before. In that case, the emotion of grief needs to be evoked, and thus the process is designed to gradually deepen the experience.

Accordingly, the national mourning over the Temple is distinct from the experience of *shivah* in that it requires external enhancement in order to reach the necessary level. This is evident as well in a ruling of the *Tur,* who dismisses an opinion that chicken is permissible in the meal preceding *Tishah B'Av,* as chicken is not deemed a sufficient vehicle of "*simchah*" in the laws of *Yom Tov.* This view is rejected because it is not only active *simchah* that must be avoided; there is also a need to proactively add a conscious awareness of mourning. Thus, wine, despite its compatibility with *shivah,* is forbidden at this time.[76]

Still, this is the rule for the eve of *Tishah B'Av,* not the entire period of the Nine Days, in which meat and wine are prohibited by dint of custom. One related suggestion[77] is to understand the custom as a decision to equate the entire Nine Days to *erev Tishah B'Av* in intensity, infusing all of it with an atmosphere comparable to *aninut.* In that stage, denoted in the literature as *meito mutal l'fanav* – "the newly deceased loved one is lying in front of him" – the emotion is experienced in its most powerful form. However, such an extension would seem to defeat the purpose that R. Soloveitchik had perceived in the structure of this time, that of escalating intensity.

It is also possible to posit an alternative explanation to the abstinence from meat and wine during this time. Meat and wine both played important roles in the sacrificial service in the Temple. Accordingly, the

76. This may also explain the view of those who maintain that *Shabbat* garments should not be worn on *Shabbat* during the Nine Days, even though this is not the rule for an individual in *shivah.*

77. See *Minchat Aharon,* ibid.

Talmud[78] relates that following the Destruction, there were some ascetics who decided to abstain from meat and wine. R. Yehoshua challenged their behavior, noting that their logic would lead to abstaining as well from bread, fruit, and even water, and that mourning practices must be proportionate and sustainable. Apparently, while a permanent ban on meat and wine was discouraged, a custom for the period closest to *Tishah B'Av* developed and was deemed manageable and appropriate.[79]

With that background, it may be possible to understand the *siyum* not as a distraction from the message of the Nine Days, but rather as an emphasis of it. During this time, there is a yearning for the days in which meat and wine were utilized in the context of a holy purpose. In the modern era, with the Temple absent, other methods are sought to elevate the consumption of meat and wine from the indulgence of a material desire to the tool of enhancing holiness. In other words, the goal is not only to avoid meat and wine out of mourning for the Temple, but rather to declare that we will forgo the mundane consumption of these luxuries and strive to utilize them only in the context of *mitzvah*, itself a testament to the time when that usage was so central to our spiritual existence.[80]

---

78. *Bava Batra* 60b.

79. The *Arukh HaShulchan,* ibid., writes that the custom is "a testament to the sacrifices and libations that were canceled, due to our sins." The alternate practice to abstain from the 17th of Tammuz, he explains, is because that was the date on which the *tamid* sacrifice ceased. See also R. Aharon Leib Shteinman, in *Ka'Ayal Ta'arog,* pp. 273–274.Understanding the abstention as a recognition of the absence of the Temple, rather than specifically as a mourning practice, may also explain the continuation of the policy up to midday on the tenth of Av. From a mourning perspective, this is somewhat anticlimactic as it is past *Tishah B'Av.* On the other hand, as the Temple was still burning at that time, recognizing that fact is appropriate. See the discussion in R. Moshe Druk, *Birkat Moshe,* 59.

80. Note also *Nit'ei Gavriel, Hilkhot Bein HaMetzarim,* p. 250, who cites the custom of Gur to eat meat and drink wine at the *siyum* because the learning is considered "as if one brought sacrifices," per *Menachot* 110a.

Understanding the siyum as an expression of the theme rather than a hiatus from it also indicates that the relationship of the meal to the learning be apparent. See *Mekadesh Yisrael,* #134, who requires that the meal take place in the same room as the public completion of the learning (and see also #135, where he recommends the usage of special tablecloths).

There are, indeed, a number of positive themes that some rabbinic voices have found within the Nine Days *siyum,* that have been offered as a complement to the atmosphere of the period rather than a contradiction to it. For some, particularly in Chasidic circles, these motifs have been sufficient for the affirmative endorsement of *siyumim* during this time as an ideal, rather than a concession.[81]

Among these is the observation that the Talmud[82] attributes the Destruction to "the abandonment of the Torah."[83] The Klausenberger Rebbe, R. Yekutiel Yehudah Halberstam, stressed that a reduction of Torah study was both a cause and an effect of the exile, and accordingly lifting the banner of the Torah in celebration is a corrective. He notes in this vein the interpretation of the verse,[84] *tachat asher lo avad'ta... b'simchah u'v'tuv levav,* "[punishment will come to the Jewish people] because you did not serve God... with rejoicing and gladness of the heart."

A great emphasis on *siyumim* at this time was made by the Lubavitcher Rebbe, who directed his followers to make one on each of the Nine Days, although not necessarily with meat and wine. This would activate the value of *Pekudei HaShem yesharim m'samchei lev* (Ps. 19:9), "God's commandments are straight and gladden the heart." He recommended the *siyumim* should be in front of large crowds, and should possibly involve material that is shorter and easier for the public to understand.[85]

---

81. See *Nit'ei Gavriel,* 41:6, and n. 12, quoting many sources to this effect. This attitude is in particular associated with the students of the *Ba'al Shem Tov.* R. Yisrael of Rozhin is cited in *Orchot Chaim,* 551:35, and *Ta'amei HaMinhagim, inyanei Tishah B'Av, kuntres acharon,* as instructing his followers after the fast of *Tishah B'Av* to learn a tractate of *mishnah,* make a *siyum,* and eat meat. (*Resp. Afarkasta D'Anya,* I, 154:2 records this occurring during *shavuah she-chal bo,* but the *Ta'amei HaMinhagim* mentions *motza'ei Tishah B'Av.*) See also *Mekadesh Yisrael,* 138. See also the comments of the *Minchat Elazar* in *Sha'ar Yisachar, Tamuz-Av,* 8.
82. *Bava Metzia* 85b, *Nedarim* 81a.
83. See *Divrei Emet,* p. 147, citing the *Chozeh* of Lublin; see Tesler, pp. 179–187.
84. Deut. 28:47.
85. This is related in many of his writings, some collected in *Shulchan Menachem,* OC, III, pp. 59–62.

This approach requires some explanation. Mourning, at least in the personal version, is the time when Torah study is actually forbidden, due to the "gladdening" aspect identified in that verse. Similarly, in the context of the national mourning, Torah study is forbidden on *Tishah B'Av* for that reason. As such, it may seem surprising to invoke this verse specifically as a reason to celebrate Torah study during this period (even if not on *Tishah B'Av* itself). It seems that the Rebbe was understanding that an imperative of this period is to correct the historic mistakes associated with it and to transform the atmosphere from one that underappreciated Torah to one of esteeming the Torah and finding it glorious. In this vein, there is reference to a homiletic reinterpretation of the Mishnaic phrase "*MiSheNichnas Av m'ma'atin b'simchah*"[86] as, "when the month of Av begins, its negative nature should be reduced through appropriate rejoicing."[87]

R. Dovid Sperber, in his *Resp. Afarkasta D'Anya*[88] goes so far as to suggest that even learning without understanding the material "well" will have this uplifting effect, through exposure to the material, that is thus worthwhile.[89]

In addition to the symbolism of valuing Torah study, the gathering itself, with communal rejoicing, is significant. The *Chiddushei HaRim*[90] pointed to this element as corrective to the "baseless hatred" (*sin'at chinam*) the Talmud associates with the Destruction.

In the month of Tammuz, 5700 (1940), as the horrors of the Holocaust raged, R. Yissachar Shlomo Teichtal addressed a number of his followers, in Pishtian, Czechoslavakia, with whom he had completed learning a tractate, *Masekhet Megillah*. These followers felt that, given the state of the world and European Jewry at that time, a *siyum* celebration was inappropriate; if they have one at all, perhaps it should

86. *Ta'anit* 26b.

87. See *Shulchan Menachem*, ibid., p. 61, n5 with asterisk note.

88. I, 154:2

89. This responsum is sometimes cited in later literature as a source requiring understanding the material. However, while he includes that caveat at the beginning, he apparently deemphasizes the need for (at least complete) understanding with this statement afterwards.

90. Cited in *Siach Sarfei Kodesh*, I, #492.

be very restrained in terms of participants, and perhaps meat and wine should not be served. R. Teichtal, who would later author the major Zionist work *Eim HaBanim Semeichah* before being taken to Auschwitz and then murdered on a transport train, wrote a lengthy responsum on the importance of the *siyum*.[91] He asserted that it is especially during a time of crisis that the *siyum* assumes greater importance, and that it should be conducted with no diminution whatsoever, with meat and wine, and with guests invited.

R. Teichtal recorded that with the onset of World War II, traditional *seudot mitzvah* had ceased, with former participants feeling such meals were inappropriate and undesired. He notes that he strongly objected to this trend, arguing that these meals were a source of merit to protect from the threats of the time. He reflects on the usage of the word *siyum* for the meal, when literally it should connote "completion," referencing the learning itself. He asserts that the *siyum* is not merely a means but an end into itself, in that the importance of a *mitzvah* is reflected in the joy that surrounds it. R. Teichtal's letter does not address the Nine Days specifically, but does call attention to the themes within the *siyum* that make it well-suited to address the national shortcomings that have caused and prolonged the Exile.

The broad variance in views regarding *siyumim* during the Nine Days reflects a divergence of attitude, interpretation, and situational assessment. As such, there remains considerable disagreement as to if, when, and under what circumstances, they should take place. What is not in question, however, is the importance of preserving the Nine Days as a time of profound awareness of the gaping hole at the center of contemporary Jewish life, and the continuing need to strive mightily to address what is lacking internally that keeps that which has been lost from being restored. With or without a *siyum*, the call of the moment must remain in clear focus.

---

91. *Resp. Mishneh Sakhir*, OC, II, 18.

Chapter 10

The Plight of the *Agunah,* and Halakhic Pre-Nuptial Agreements

One who encounters, as we have done, the many areas of Jewish law in which challenges have been met with some kind of accommodation or alternative arrangement, may be left with profound unease. Apparently, many methods have been found over the centuries, and some with significant rabbinic endorsement, to locate a path within the halakhic system to alleviate situations of individual suffering, societal hardship, religious values in conflict, and financial loss. And yet, one circumstance that may combine all of these elements, or, at least the most painful of them, appears to go unresolved: the plight of the contemporary *agunah.*

The classic *agunah,* or chained woman, discussed in the Talmud, referred to a wife whose husband is missing, and conclusive proof of his death is unavailable. Absent such proof, the wife is unable to remarry. In the Talmud and later rabbinic literature there is much codification and analysis regarding what kind of evidence could suffice, including the records of great efforts exerted by authorities to marshal all resources possible to establish the death halakhically and allow the widow to remarry.

In contemporary usage, the term *agunah* is also used to describe a woman whose husband is very much alive, but, despite the functional end of their marriage, is refusing to cooperate through the voluntary granting of a *get,* a Jewish bill of divorce. This circumstance creates the same result as the situation in which the husband is missing, in that the wife cannot remarry.

By dint of a rabbinic enactment first put into place by Rabbenu Gershom (c. 960–1040), the husband may also not remarry until the situation is resolved.[1] Further, also due to Rabbenu Gershom's enactments, should the wife refuse to accept a *get,* the marriage is not dissolved, and, again, neither party may remarry.[2] Accordingly, in one sense, it would be accurate to say that both spouses have the ability to impede the formalization of the divorce. However, in practice, the situation of a wife in this circumstance is not identical to that of the husband, as will be discussed below.

For most intents and purposes, the dilemma is a bilateral one; a man or a woman can be trapped in a nonfunctional marriage by the recalcitrance of the other. Caught in such a situation, one is subject to intense emotional anguish, possibly over the course of years or even decades. Together with the personal suffering, from the perspective of religious fulfillment and obligation, there is complete paralysis in many ways here as well. Given the substantial history of successful negotiation of halakhic challenges of lesser impact, one would expect that a solution would be also found here; there is no question the need is as great, if not far greater, than the other contexts that we have examined.

However, need, as extreme as it is, is but one part of the equation. The first step in the formula is assessing compliance with the letter of the law, and in this case, this aspect is particularly challenging. Issues of marital status, known as *davar she-b'ervah,* are treated with unusual severity in Jewish law, in terms of standards of evidence, but far more

1. See *Resp. Rashba,* III, 446, and *Shulchan Arukh,* EH, 1:10.
2. See *Rama,* EH, 119:6, and *Chiddushei R. Akiva Eiger,* s.v. *avar.*

so in terms of tampering with the reality of the status, and the ensuing implications. For a woman with the status of "married" (*eishet ish*) to take another husband constitutes a capital crime, with permanent consequences such as illegitimacy of any future offspring, and prohibited status to the first husband as well as to any others who are involved while that first marriage is in effect. The *halakhah* only recognizes, essentially, two methods of terminating a marriage: the death of one spouse, or a formal *halakhic* divorce, effected through the willing granting of a *get* from the husband to the wife.[3]

In one sense, the classic *agunah,* whose husband is missing, faces challenges of a similar nature, and her situation certainly has tremendous difficulty associated with it. Nonetheless, there is a voluminous literature attesting to the successful efforts of rabbinic authorities to find solutions in individual instances, and, even more significantly, broad policy implementations that reflect the stated principle of "in matters of *'igun (agunot),* the Rabbis were lenient."[4] As such, one may wonder why the results have not been similar in situations where husbands are not actually missing, but merely recalcitrant.

Despite the external similarities, the two situations are fundamentally different. In medicine, for example, two diseases may be equally fatal, but one disease has a discovered cure, due to its manageable causes, while the other has no cure. So too, the wives in both cases are suffering equally, and both are confronted with the severity of binding marital status. However, crucially, in the case of the missing husband, all parties involved are convinced that he is actually deceased, and that the marriage in actuality has in fact ended. The challenge is establishing this fact conclusively within the standards of the halakhic system. Accordingly, the Rabbis are able to find tools within the system to accomplish this goal. It is true that the human suffering associated with the situation is a major factor in driving the recourse to these tools, but they are, still, tools that exist independently.

The recalcitrant spouse constitutes a far greater "letter of the law" challenge. In this case, there is (usually) no question that the husband

---

3. *Kiddushin* 2a.
4. *Yevamot* 88a.

is indeed alive, and, therefore, without a divorce, the marriage remains completely in effect. Accordingly, there is very little space for effective alternatives, assuming the husband is not willing (or, by rabbinic law, if the wife is not willing to receive). Logically, it would seem there are only two possible paths: convince the recalcitrant spouse to relent, or somehow abrogate the marriage without the consent of the husband, if that were to be possible.

Annulment, within the system of Jewish law, is particularly elusive. This is partially for structural reasons: unlike, for example, marriage within the Church or civil law systems, no external authority formalizes the marriage, and consequently no such authority is empowered to revoke its approval. In a Jewish marriage, the groom marries the bride, with her approval, and the officiating rabbi is there only to supervise and guide.[5]

It is true that the Talmud does posit that every groom does carry out the marriage with the understanding of the approval of "the Rabbis," and thus certain fundamental flaws have provided the basis for a nullification of those marriages.[6] However, while efforts have been made to utilize this principle in the modern era, it is difficult both conceptually and textually to equate any contemporary rabbi or a group of rabbis with that level of authority, such that it can be credibly maintained that the initial marriage was contingent on their approval. Further, even in the Talmudic era, this principle was associated with certain generalized violations which add an additional distinction that frustrates any effort to equate contemporary circumstances in individual situations with the classical application.

Another avenue explored in the vein of nullification is a claim of "a mistaken transaction" (*mekach ta'ut*). This would describe a situation in which one entered into a marriage essentially under false pretenses, missing information that would certainly have kept them from going forward. If that is indeed the case, the marriage would be null and void, without need for a divorce.

---

5. See R. Gedalyah Felder, *Nachalat Tzvi*, pp. 100–101.
6. *Ketubot* 3a; *Gittin* 33a, 73a; *Yevamot* 110a; *Bava Batra* 48b.

While theoretically this is a viable approach, the gap between theory and practice in this case is wide. Given the severity of the issue, and the reality that a decision to invalidate the marriage would greatly impact the rights of both parties, the threshold is extremely high. To qualify for this status, the flaw that was concealed must be objective, extreme and undeniable in consequence, and demonstrably present at the time the marriage took place. There are instances in which great authorities have approved of such decisions, but they are few and far between, given the requirements.[7]

Further, the situations in which this plan would be applicable either are present or are not; they could not develop afterwards if they were not in existence at the time of the wedding. This would be true also for any effort to invalidate any marriage on procedural grounds, i.e., if the wedding was performed in a fashion that was ineffective halakhically (e.g., in the absence of valid witnesses).

Accordingly, ending a marriage without the consent of the spouses is, as a practical matter, very rarely an actual possibility.

It must be acknowledged that the situation of the husband's recalcitrance is not equal to one in which the wife refuses to cooperate. Given that the prohibitions for a husband to divorce without his wife's consent, or alternatively to remarry regardless, are rabbinic in origin, there are significant differences in consequences. Rabbenu Gershom, the original promulgator of these regulations, incorporated an exclusion for extreme circumstances.

This exclusion, termed the *hetter meah rabbanim,* allowed for an exception if one hundred qualified rabbis, in at least three different countries, would each investigate the situation and determine that the circumstances warranted a dispensation. Given the challenging standards surrounding it, the *hetter meah rabbanim* is meant to be utilized in extremely rare circumstances, and even then only with a *get* put into escrow for the wife to receive when she is willing.

7. There is an extensive literature about this; for some examples and discussions in the writings of R. Moshe Feinstein, see *Resp. Iggerot Moshe,* EH, I, 79 and 80; III, 45; IV, 52, 83, and 113.

The sad fact that some have scandalously issued decrees of this category that do not meet the halakhic requirements is disgraceful, and does not reflect the values of *halakhah* or its arbiters. In fact, going to the other extreme, R. Joseph B. Soloveitchik has written that as a matter of policy, he never participated in any *hetter meah rabbanim.*[8]

One effort to thread the needle between the husband's recalcitrance and some degree of his consent is to explore the possibility of some kind of conditional marriage, that would be retroactively declared null and void under certain circumstances. However, attempts to utilize an approach of this nature have not won acceptance. Reasons for this include the significant difficulty of formulating a stipulation that would be both applicable and agreed to in advance, and, crucially, the question of whether a marriage that has been consummated is susceptible to conditional validity.

What remains, then, is the question of convincing the spouses to divorce willingly. The last modifier is crucial as the *halakhah* requires that the husband must give the *get* completely of his own free will.[9]

The Talmud does grant the possibility of circumstances in which a *get* can be coerced.[10] The Rambam's explanation of how this can be reconciled with the free will standard is widely quoted, and is actually invoked in other areas of *halakhah* as well, including many of the methods we have discussed in previous chapters.[11]

The Rambam[12] asserts that in essence, every Jew wishes to act in accordance with God's will. When he fails to do so, it is because of external distractions and misguided attitudes that overwhelm him.

8. *Community, Covenant and Commitment: Selected Letters and Communications,* p. 217.
9. *Gittin* 49b, *Yevamot* 112b. As to the scriptural source, see *Mishneh Torah, Hil. Gerushin,* 1:1–2, and *Rashbam, Bava Batra,* 48a.
10. *Ketubot* 77a–b; *Arakhin* 21a–b.
11. See, among other examples, *Resp. Yashiv Yitzchak,* XXVII, 12, regarding the sale of *chametz.*
12. *Hil. Gerushin,* 2:20.

Accordingly, the "coercion" is actually a method of realigning the individual's inner will with the practical demands of the *halakhah*.[13]

A crucial component of that explanation is ascertaining that the *halakhah* does justify the coercion. The Talmud provides a number of examples of what situations qualify, and the later codifiers debate the question of what meets that standard.

However, even when coercion is halakhically justified, there are still issues that must be addressed. Not everyone is susceptible to coercion by a rabbinic court, and this is especially the case in the contemporary diaspora, where rabbinic courts lack enforcement authority, or even the ability to exert jurisdiction on the case.

Further, a rabbinic assessment allowing coercion still must be carried out by the rabbinic court or its agents. A divorce extracted by civil authorities, even when otherwise warranted by the circumstances, is considered involuntary and thus invalid.[14] This reality has been a major complicating factor in efforts in a number of American states, and in other countries, to enact legislation to compel the granting of a *get.*

There are, however, methods of influencing the spouse to do what is proper in this case that do not constitute invalid compulsion. The great medieval authority R. Ya'akov ben Meir, known as Rabbenu Tam, was associated with a slate of policies known as his *harchakot,* or "distancings."[15]

These protocols, at least as they are often understood in contemporary application, make clear to a recalcitrant spouse that as long as the situation persists, he is unwelcome in local synagogues, schools, business dealings, and social settings. The policy is publicized throughout the community, which collectively conveys its rejection of this behavior.[16]

---

13. For alternative perspectives among the *rishonim* in explaining the effectiveness of coercion, see *Rashbam, Bava Batra* 48b; *Tosafot* ibid; and *Resp. Radbaz,* I, 228 (157). For specific challenges to the position of the Rambam, see *Resp. Chavvot Yair,* 55. See also, at length, the introduction to R. Yosef Goldberg's *Eilu Kofin L'Hotzi.*
14. *Shulchan Arukh,* EH 134:5 and 7.
15. See *Mordekhai, Ketubot* 204; *Resp. Maharik,* 135; *Sefer HaYashar, chelek hateshuvot,* 24; *Beit Yosef,* EH 154: *Rama,* EH 154:21.
16. See *Resp. Teshuvot V'Hanhagot* I, 789, in explaining the permissibility of this apparent embarrassment.

While this treatment certainly is unpleasant for the targeted individual, it does not constitute coercion. If the spouse wishes to remain recalcitrant, he can always search for a different community in which he is more comfortable.[17] If he chooses to agree to the divorce, it is his decision to comply with communal standards.

These "distancings" have proven successful many times over the course of Jewish history, and in recent decades.[18] In order to be effective, however, it requires a coordinated, cohesive communal effort, which is not always attainable. When it is, it requires embroiling the community in the sordid details of the marital dispute, which of course is highly undesirable. And, there are some recalcitrant spouses who are impervious to any degree of social pressure.

As such, it would be preferable if another approach can avoid these aspects. Fortunately, in recent years another path has emerged.

HALAKHIC PRENUPTIAL AGREEMENTS

One suggestion that has increasingly found significant rabbinic endorsement is the utilization of Halakhic prenuptial agreements. While there are, as will be noted, detractors to this as well, the broad support that does exist for these arrangements has provided a foundation for great effectiveness and promise for the future.

One such agreement is associated with the Beth Din of America (BDA) and was drafted in 1992 by R. Zalman Nechemiah Goldberg[19]

---

17. See *Resp. Maharik,* ibid; *Biur HaGra,* EH 154:67.

    One may wonder if this continues to be the case in the era of the internet and social media, as it would seem that there would now be no escape, anywhere in the world, from the communal opprobrium. However, in actuality, the problem is its own solution. The same technology that publicizes the social sanction also allows the recalcitrant spouse to find alternative communities, physical and virtual, of like-minded people in which to find refuge.

    Also, R. Zalman Nechemiah Goldberg, *Mishnat Nechemiah,* 7:8, assumes it is "obvious" that the husband's ability to escape the sanctions is not crucial to their permissibility.

18. There has been some controversy as to their application; see, for example, *Pitchei Teshuvah,* 154:30 citing the *Gevurot Anashim* of the *Shakh* that they should no longer be used.

19. The agreement is described in *Mishnat Nechemiah,* 7:9.

together with R. Mordechai Willig, and has been endorsed by prominent rabbinic experts such as R. Ovadiah Yosef, R. Chaim Tzimbalist, R. Yitzchok Leibes, R. Hershel Schachter, R. Asher Weiss, and R. Gedalyah Dov Schwartz, and many others.[20]

There are two major components to this prenuptial agreement. The first is essentially uncontroversial: an agreement to arbitrate the terms of the divorce in a predetermined *Beit Din* (rabbinic court). This component in and of itself would go a tremendous distance in eliminating the *agunah* problem.

This is because, as experience indicates, the vast majority of intractable Jewish divorce situations are, at a basic level, venue disputes. Most recalcitrant spouses are not admitting to a strategy of permanent intransigence. Rather, they are maintaining that the other spouse's preferred authority – be it a specific *Beit Din* or civil court – is biased against them. Once the case is moved to a "fair" venue, they will promptly cooperate. Accordingly, designating a mutually acceptable venue in advance, through a legally binding agreement, removes what is very often the major obstacle and can in a great many cases lead directly to a speedy resolution.

This first component, the agreement to arbitrate, has been proposed and utilized by many authorities and is an extremely valuable tool in this area. R. Moshe Feinstein, in a brief responsum[21] written in 1979 to R. Yechiel Perr, endorsed the suggestion that a clause be placed into the *t'na'im* (marriage commitment document). This clause would state that in the event of a separation, the husband agrees to provide a *get,* and the wife to accept one, when so ordered by an identified *beit din.*

R. Feinstein noted that such a clause would be enforced by the civil courts, and yet would not be considered a forced *get.* This addition, he wrote, would be of great benefit and would save wives from suffering the status of *agunot.* (However, he added that the officiant should assess the personalities of the bride and groom, to ensure that this step will not itself inject contentiousness into their relationship.)

---

20. These and other endorsements are available at the website theprenup.org.

21. *Resp. Iggerot Moshe,* EH, IV, 107.

The second component is monetary in nature, and has been the subject of some debate. The gist of this component is to formally recognize that until the *get* has been given by the husband and accepted by the wife, the marriage continues to be in effect. As such, the husband continues to be obligated in financial support of his wife.

Of course, given that they are separated, it is no longer true that "two can live as cheaply as one." The agreement establishes a rate of support that is within a realistic range, indexed to fluctuations in the cost of living. Practically speaking, the burden of paying out of pocket for this support of a spouse one no longer wants to live with will generally motivate the husband to end the marriage in short order.

There are historical precedents for arrangements such as this. One is associated with the *Takanat ShU"M* (Shpira [Speyer], Vermaiza [Worms] and Magentza [Mainz]), recorded in the classical collection of documents known as *Nachalat Shivah.*[22] In this version of the *t'na'im,* there is an explicit provision that in the instance of strife between the spouses, the husband will provide a sum of money to sustain his wife during their time of separation.[23]

Similarly, R. Ya'akov of Lisa, the author of the *Netivot HaMishpat,* in his *Torat Gittin,*[24] discusses a plan in which a husband would waive all marital rights, and yet commit to continue support of his wife. Given the imbalance, the husband will soon choose to divorce. Nonetheless, there is no monetary obligation directly associated with the giving of the *get,* and accordingly, he concludes, this would not be considered a forced *get.*[25]

22. #9. Although the assumption is that this clause is from *Takanat Shu"m, Nachalat Shivah* in his comments (#14) expresses difficulty in locating this in the original enactment, and suggests an explanation as to its history. See also *Tiferet L'Shivah,* #38–40.
23. R. Asher Weiss, in his letter endorsing the pre-nup, nonetheless questions the association with *Takkanat Shu"m,* asserting that the earlier enactment was meant only to provide for the wife during the separation, not to promote a divorce. In the comments of *Nachalat Shivah,* he indicates that the purpose is to encourage a reconciliation.
24. EH, 134:4.
25. See also the analysis in *Resp. Chelkat Yoav,* I, *dinei ones, anaf* 5. See also the objections of *Chazon Ish,* EH, 99:6.

It is crucial to appreciate that this is not formulated as a penalty. Rather, it is expressed as the natural consequence of choosing to remain in the marital relationship. This point is central to some of the opposition that the BDA prenup has encountered. Some contemporary authorities have argued that the financial element is punitive in nature, and thus constitutes a coercive impact that would invalidate any *get* that would result.[26]

The question of financial pressure and its impact on the voluntary status of the *get* is the subject of some debate,[27] and this issue has also cast a cloud on some of the legislative efforts that have been associated with this cause.

Accordingly, the BDA prenup is deliberate in avoiding the character of a financial penalty. The rate of support is calibrated to a plausible cost of living. The accuracy of this claim is a component of the controversy, and of course cultures and communities differ as to

---

26. One prominent opponent of the prenup is R. Moshe Shternbuch, who (in a letter later published in *Resp. Teshuvot V'Hanhagot*, VII, 165) disputes the reasonableness of the rate of support, and argues that this is proof of the punitive nature he understands to characterize the agreement.

27. The *Rashba,* in a responsum (IV, 20) cited by *Beit Yosef,* EH, 134, ruled that financial pressure can constitute undue coercion that could invalidate a *get,* and attributed this view as well to R. Chananel and the *Raavad*; this is also the position of *Tosafot, Bava Batra* 48a, s.v. *amar Rava.* Similarly, *Ritva, Kiddushin* 50a, s.v. *ha,* equates monetary coercion to physical coercion. By contrast, Rabbenu Yerucham, *Netiv* 24, *chelek* 1, (also cited by *Beit Yosef*) indicates such a *get* would be valid. *Rama,* CM, 205:7, equates monetary coercion to physical coercion.

    Rashba, in his stringent position, further rules that financial pressure would disqualify even when it comes as a result of a commitment that the husband himself had earlier undertaken. *Rama,* EH, 134:4, quotes two opinions on that matter, and concludes that it is advisable to account for the stringent position, while after the fact the lenient view (*Maharik, shoresh* 63; *Resp. Ritva,* 96 in *Mossad HaRav Kook* edition; *Resp. Radbaz,* III, 610, and others) can be relied upon; see also *Chazon Ish,* EH 99:5. However, *Pitchei Teshuvah,* 10, cites views that the lenient position is being misapplied and cannot be relied upon even after the fact. See *Arukh HaShulchan,* EH, 134:26–29. See also the sources cited in support of both sides in R. Nehorai Yosef Ochana, *Mishpat HaGet,* 134:33, who assesses that the consensus is in agreement with the lenient view.

    Also significantly relevant to this issue is the position of some authorities that even if financial pressure could invalidate the *get,* this would not hold true for a sum that the husband could choose to absorb if he genuinely wished to stay married; see for example, R. Yitzchak Isaac HaLevi Herzog, *Resp. Heikhal Yitzchak,* I, 1:52.

what is reasonable. Still, the formulation is specifically as support, and not as a coercive penalty.

This can be clearly demonstrated by the writings of one the primary authors of the prenup, R. Z. N. Goldberg. In a published essay,[28] R. Goldberg assumes a strict stance on financial coercion, going so far as to invalidate a *get* that the husband had himself committed to at an earlier date, under the penalty of monetary loss should he fail to comply at the time of relevance. This "self-imposed penalty," assumed R. Goldberg, is no more acceptable than a penalty imposed by a third party.[29] Clearly, R. Goldberg would not have approved, and in fact authored, an agreement premised on a principle he took as invalid.

A related objection to this prenuptial agreement is that the financial obligation constitutes an "*asmakhta,*" a commitment that is unenforceable due to the party having agreed only with the expectation the situation would not arise.[30] Because of this concern, R. J. David Bleich has proposed an alternative agreement[31], one in which the husband agrees at the time of marriage to an obligation of support (*mezonot*) at a significantly increased rate. This obligation would cease at the time the marriage ends, or at the point at which the husband declares his willingness to immediately provide a *get.* More significantly as far as *asmakhta* is concerned, the obligation begins immediately upon marriage and is not contingent upon anything. However, the wife will presumably choose to waive the increased obligation as long as they are happily married and will accept in its place the standard support obligations associated with marriage.

There are several responses to the *asmakhta* concern regarding the BDA prenup, including the inclusion of technical language and components that are recognized as neutralizing the issue of *asmakhta.*[32]

---

28. *Divrei Mishpat,* II, pp. 110–122.
29. See *Shulchan Arukh* and *Rama,* EH 134:5.
30. R. Yosef Shalom Elyashiv, *Kovetz Teshuvot,* II, CM, 163 invokes this concern (although his responsum involves an arrangement with differing details), as does R. J. David Bleich, *B'Netivot HaHalakhah,* pp. 21ff.
31. *B'Netivot HaHalakhah,* I, pp. 3–20.
32. See *Shulchan Arukh,* CM 207:14–15. See, regarding *asmakhta* in general, *Am Mordechai* to *Shulchan Arukh,* 54.

More fundamentally, every Jewish marriage must include a *ketubah,* which would seem to be subject to the same concern, if it is indeed well-founded.[33] (This would especially impact the *tosefet ketubah,* additional sums a husband chooses to commit to his bride.) In fact, the question can be raised in the reverse: perhaps the prenup is redundant, in that the *ketubah* itself mandates the husband's support of his wife as long as they remain married.

There is some truth to this, in theory. However, in practice, it is difficult to apply the *ketubah*'s demands to contemporary spousal disputes. The *halakhah* distinguishes in this area based on which spouse is deemed responsible for the separation.[34] In practice, the time and process required to establish that element will neutralize its relevance for this purpose, even if the facts would support the wife's position. Essentially, the prenup accomplishes what the *ketubah* is already designed to do, but in a fashion that gives it broader effectiveness in a contemporary context.

To be clear, the prenup as well factors in issues of responsibility for the impasse. The agreement is nullified in the event that the wife declines to appear in the *Beit Din,* or to follow its instructions. Further, the obligation does not begin until the wife affirms her intention to collect the contracted sum.

The agreement described above is a unilateral one that functionally obligates the husband in the event that he refuses to provide a *get.* As noted, it is also possible for the wife to impede the process by refusing to accept a *get.* As such, there has also emerged a bilateral prenuptial agreement, in which the wife also commits to paying a stipend should she be the recalcitrant spouse.

While this agreement is viable,[35] and would indeed address the situation of the wife's noncooperation, it should be noted that this differs in concept and in pedigree from the unilateral agreement. In this case, it is more difficult to frame the commitment as a natural extension of the marital obligations, and to thus avoid the appearance of a penalty. Nonetheless, a penalty imposed on the wife would not invalidate the *get,*

33. R. Elyashiv addresses this issue briefly in *Kovetz Teshuvot* I, 163.

34. See *Shulchan Arukh* and *Rama,* EH 70:12.

35. From a halakhic perspective; legally, there may be some complications.

and accordingly that aspect does not carry the concern that a coercive penalty on the husband would bear.

THE SPIRIT OF THE LAWS

The above summary makes no claim at exhausting all the suggestions that have been put forward in this vexing area, or of sufficiently analyzing the strengths and weaknesses of those that have been mentioned. Nor is the section addressing the prenuptial agreement a complete treatment of all considerations of the concept, of its history, or of the arguments on both sides of its acceptance. For that matter, it also does not, for the most part, discuss other prenuptial agreements that have been proposed or utilized, and their relative advantages and disadvantages.

That being said, the BDA prenuptial agreement has garnered widespread endorsement of premier Torah scholars, and has proven greatly effective in removing the threat of *igun* when it is utilized. Impediments to its success can be imagined – for example, a spouse either too wealthy or too indigent to be motivated by financial impact, or one that vanishes without a trace. In practice, though, much potential suffering has been averted through the utilization of this agreement.

Further, the agreement has been tested in civil courts, and emerged validated. Alternative versions have been developed for states and countries with laws that impacted the viability of the agreement. Similarly, from a halakhic perspective, communities which had not adopted the original prenuptial agreement have begun to develop versions that are more compatible, with modifications as appropriate.

It is worth considering why the prenuptial agreement has had wider success than other efforts in this area. To be sure, the combination of halakhic grounding, legal validation, and practical results plays a major role. Further, though, a significant and underappreciated aspect has to do with the spirit of the laws involved, in multiple senses.

As noted above, the motive of the prenup, in bringing a resolution to a paralyzed process of ending a nonfunctional marriage, is firmly within the realm of appropriate rabbinic involvement. The massive human suffering, and the concurrent spiritual devastation, certainly warrants attention. The specific goal is clearly within the Torah's intent:

great halakhic authorities such as R. Moshe Feinstein[36] and R. Yosef Eliyahu Henkin,[37] have ruled that when a marriage is no longer viable or of interest to the parties, it is an obligation on both husband and wife to agree to a divorce.

R. Henkin added that a husband who exploited the situation for monetary gain was a thief, but no ordinary thief; the impact of his villainy placed him in the broader category (*abizrayhu*) of a murderer. Further, R. Feinstein[38] even considered it plausible that in the instance a husband was resigned to the marriage having ended, but was prolonging the process to extract concessions, it would be acceptable to coerce a *get* and such a divorce would be valid. He was not prepared to rule conclusively based on this postulation, and indeed no plan is premised upon it, but it speaks to the justice of a more grounded plan that brings a speedy resolution to such a situation.

Some have opposed the prenup under the claim that it encourages divorce.[39] To be sure, marriage is a religious value, counted by many as a *mitzvah,*[40] and to allow a marriage to fail when it could reasonably have been restored to a genuinely harmonious state is a tragedy;[41] according to some, it may even constitute a transgression.[42]

However, a marriage that has completely ceased to function brings no value, and much suffering. Divorce is also classified as a *mitzvah,*[43] and while commentaries differ as to the significance of that label, one perspective is that it is a *mitzvah* in the service of marriage. For example, the Abravanel, commenting on the Biblical verse[44] that describes divorce, details at great length the great blessings that marriage can bring. However, at times those benefits are inaccessible because a

---

36. *Resp. Iggerot Moshe,* YD, IV, 15.
37. *Eidut L'Yisrael,* #46, in *Kol Kitvei HaRav Henkin,* I, p. 115.
38. *Resp. Iggerot Moshe,* EH, III, 44.
39. R. Moshe Shternbuch registered this objection as well.
40. *Mishneh Torah, Ishut* 1:1; *Sefer HaChinnukh* #552.
41. See *Gittin* 90b.
42. See *Resp. Rashba,* I, 18; and *Mishneh L'Melekh, Gerushin,* 10:21.
43. See *Rambam, Sefer HaMitzvot,* positive commandments, 222; *Sefer HaChinnukh,* 579; *Sma"k,* 184; *Sma"g,* positive commandments, 50.
44. Deut. 21:24.

non-functional union is blocking the path; in those situations, he asserts, it is a *mitzvah* to allow for a truly beneficial marriage to take its place. As R. Bleich notes[45], that cost of any increase in divorce associated with these agreements is dwarfed by the suffering of *agunot* that persists without them.

Of great significance is the fact that the prenuptial agreement does not undermine the value of marriage, by rendering it conditional, incomplete, or vulnerable to external nullification. It does not compromise the autonomy or the recognized rights of either spouse.

Equally important to what the agreement does not do, is what it does do. It strengthens the existing responsibilities of marriage. Far from the exploitation of a loophole, this approach instead forecloses the possibility of abusing extant laws, and reinforces their applicability.

Further still, the agreement addresses one of the core drivers of the current crisis. In Talmudic times, Jewish communities had greater autonomy and centralization. Divorce cases could be addressed by a recognized rabbinic court with acknowledged jurisdiction, and the powers of enforcement to give meaning to their rulings. They could impose settlements and, when appropriate, command and even coerce a *get* that would be valid.

Centuries of exile and dispersion have dismantled this structure, greatly exacerbating, if not creating, the intractable torments of today. The prenuptial agreement takes a few important steps in the direction of rebuilding it.

Most fundamentally, it joins at least the husband and wife within one rabbinic jurisdiction. No longer can each spouse maintain a separate allegiance that makes answering to a common ruling – or even entering a common venue – impossible.

More significantly, as it grows in popularity, the agreement solidifies entire populations into integrated communities. Even if it does not centralize the populace around one specific *Beit Din,* it materializes the notion of a common jurisdiction, and allows for the networking and cooperation of rabbinic courts across segments of the population.

45. *B'Netivot HaHalakhah,* I, p. 16.

Just as the "distancing" protocols of Rabbenu Tam depend on communal cohesion, the prenuptial agreement, with far less unsavory entanglement, expands in efficacy with the tightening of communal involvement. In turn, the notion of a common halakhic community is itself reinforced.

Ultimately, the agreement finds its greatest success in early prevention, in the clear establishment of a public standard of behavior and respect. Young couples sign the agreement as a signal to each other and to their social circles that they subscribe to an ethic that places their human challenges in the hands of a mutually recognized responsible halakhic community. Increasingly, couples married long before are signing comparable "postnuptial" agreements that message to the next generation their voluntary embrace of this value system.

The solidification of a communal standard is itself an expression of values. Ideally, broadly based educational efforts will lay the groundwork to prevent conflicts of this type from taking root and escalating in the first place. When issues do develop, the shared message can promptly emerge.

As noted, the Rambam understood that when a *get* may be compelled, it is because there is a self-evident *mitzvah* that is imposing its mandate. One possibility is this is the directive of adhering to rabbinic authority.[46] Another is that it is the core obligation of "Love your fellow as yourself."[47] In either case, arrangements such as the prenuptial agreement, and the consensus that forms around it, allow for these principles to be honored before they can be breached.

---

46. See *Bava Batra* 48a.
47. See *Resp. Chatam Sofer,* EH II, 144; and note the objections of *Resp. VaYa'an David,* II, 202.

Chapter 11

Conclusion: The Soft Voice of the Spirit

By its nature, the subject at hand is one that is hard to analyze objectively. A combination of custom, rabbinic enactments, communal practice, and individual innovation, the approaches discussed here have received widely different receptions. Seeking consistency within this environment is an impossible and perhaps undesirable goal. We have attempted to suggest a framework in which to understand those variances, but it is hardly an exact science. Much of what we have seen here is subject to intense debate, and some of it is overtly speculative.

There are some things we can say with confidence. The mission of the Jew in this world is to live by the word of God in all his deeds, to walk a path completely faithful to Divine instruction. However, it is not only the word that commands, it is also its meaning, the message within. At times, perhaps often, discerning that message demands that we engage in speculation, for refusing to do so is to constrain ourselves only to what it is written. And, it seems abundantly clear that is not enough.

Many of the giants of Jewish thought have written of the imperative to fulfill the intent of the Torah as well as its explicit command. On one level, this has been suggested as the basis for rabbinic legislation; the assumption is that the Rabbis intuited, through their broad sweep of the totality of the revealed Torah, what is beneath the surface, and formalized it, as was their mandate.

We need not, however, wait for the Rabbis to legislate. As individuals, we are required to listen to the voice of the Torah speaking broadly, not just to the words. This is what is conveyed by the verse,[1] "I have listened to the voice (*b'kol*) of the Lord my God, and have done according to all that you have commanded me." Commentaries,[2] building off the writings of the Rambam, explain the seeming redundancy here, and emphasize that it is not only the explicit commandments that are to be followed, but it is the totality of the message within the voice.

This is expressed by specific commandments of the Torah as well. *Kedoshim Tihyu*, "You shall be holy," commands the Torah, and Nachmanides comments on both the vagueness and the redundancy of its instruction. Its message, he explains, is to adhere to a holiness that is not limited to the words of the text, but emanates through it; one that imprints itself upon the reader of all of the sentences even when it is spelled out in none of them. So, too, in the interpersonal realm: "You shall do the right and the good, *hayashar vi-ha-tov*."

Ascertaining the Divine will through the study of the explicit details of the text has, in the opinion of great rabbinic authors, yielded concrete obligations within existing commandments;[3] in generating new obligations;[4] and in imposing responsibilities of the moment on specific individuals.[5]

Even more fundamentally, it was the primal search for an understanding of the Divine will on the part of our forefathers that led them to observe the principles of the Torah even prior to the issuing of its

1. Deut. 26:14.
2. See, for example, *Shem MiShmuel, Parashat Ki Tavo*, 5672, p. 166.
3. See *Arukh HaShulchan*, OC 675:18)
4. See *Minchat Asher al HaTorah*, Deut. 51, and *Chamudei Yitzchak*, Gen., *simanim*, #17.
5. See *Emet L'Ya'akov*, I Kings 1:11–13.

formal command upon their descendants at Mount Sinai.[6] That subsequent binding covenant formalized the pre-existing commitment of the Jewish nation to carry out a message now put into rules.

The approaches we have examined in this volume have, at times, strained the limits of the spirit of the law, and indeed some have been resisted or rejected for that reason. However, in other cases – or sometimes other versions of the same approaches – the motive was actually to restore the spirit of the law, or to realign letter and spirit.

Sometimes, it is the spirit of other laws that call for alternatives, and it is attention to those calls that drives the innovation. Advocates of such actions carefully evaluate the conflicting ideals, choose priorities, and continuously reassess the wisdom of each path.

Careful attention to the topics at hand yields powerful insights into the thinking of rabbinic leadership over the long sweep of Jewish history. The delicate balancing of the communal and the personal, the ideal with the necessary, spiritual integrity with material sustenance, has occupied great rabbinic minds throughout, and the integration of superior scholarship with profound communal responsibility is a source of lasting inspiration. One may disagree with the conclusions, but to read the expressed concerns and sensitivities of the *Mas'at Binyamin* searching for ways to save the *chametz* necessary for the livelihood of his followers; of R. Shlomo Kluger writing about the collective sale; of the *Chelkat Ya'akov* writing of the need for the *hetter iska* or for the sale of *chametz* of nonobservant store owners; of R. Kook and later Chief Rabbis of Israel grappling with *Shemittah* and the *hetter mekhirah;* of R. Yonatan Eibshutz writing about *Prozbol;* of the *Kessef HaKodoshim* writing about the *shtar chatzi zakhar;* is to be lifted on the wings of leaders who knew they carried the weight of the Torah and of the Jewish Nation at once.

At times, the voice of the spirit of the law will be barely audible, as the apparent exigencies of the moment crowd it out, seemingly stifling the eternal to allow for the efficient, a hollow structure stripped of any significance. And yet, here as well, that still small voice can be discerned by those possessed of the long view. That structure is far from hollow; it is a bridge, allowing the essentials of the halakhic system to

6. *Yoma* 28b; see *Resp. Rashba* I, 24.

stretch from one generation to the next, passing safely over the raging currents of the many challenges and obstacles to the survival of observant Judaism. As the crashing tides of ignorance, persecution, economic crisis, exile, apathy, and changing cultural contexts scream below, wise and devoted engineers provide safe passage to the letters of Torah law until they can be reunited with its values.

There, too, the spirit speaks, with the long past and future of the Jewish people firmly in sight. In time, a *hetter mekhirah* will yield to a flourishing Land of Israel where *Shemittah* is fully honored, as *Prozbol* has given way to a society of generous benefactors confidently assisting the poor, with no wish of repayment. These borrowers will receive their loans without any hint of interest, from caring lenders who have succeeded in balancing the commercial with the compassionate. Merchants who transacted in *chametz* they claimed to have already sold will turn more genuinely to an observant community that strove to include them, however weakly, in their annual rites of redemption. And a rebuilt *Beit HaMikdash* will sanctify the use of meat and wine, while the Torah is studied, completed and celebrated for its own sake.

In the meantime, the towering scholars and compassionate souls who author the living texts of the *halakhah* will continue their noble efforts to bring harmony, integrity, and continuity to a conflicted world that welcomes none of those. And they will draw the strength to persevere from the knowledge that even when the spirit of the Torah cannot be perceived in their concessions, it lives securely in their consciences.

As we have acknowledged, much of what we have discussed is debatable, speculative, or both. However, it is hoped that there is value in that subjective speculation. In a departure from the standard approach to scholarship, we might suggest that this discussion be more prescriptive than descriptive. It is incumbent upon serious Jews to consider sincerely and meaningfully the approaches taken to the actual practice of Judaism, to consider how both the letter and spirit of the law can best be given maximal expression within the challenges of daily life in the real world. To do so requires not only the necessary study of rabbinic perspectives, and an honest examination of the halakhic foundations, but also a constant evaluation of one's own motivations and efforts in light of the competing factors that are so often brought to bear.

One more thing can be said for certain: an attitude of cynicism is corrosive to the soul and damaging to the commitment needed to bring the Divine word to life. To the extent one feels that his practice is not only rote but is insincere, that the rules of Jewish law are simply regulations devoid of meaning or message, the negative impact will be felt in every area of spiritual life.

An alternative approach that may have impeccable rabbinic backing nonetheless fails for the individual who lacks confidence in its validity, or in his own commitment to it. Sincerity, ultimately, lies within ourselves. We may sell our *chametz*, our utensils, maybe even, temporarily, the Holy Land itself, but we need not sell our souls.

The first step towards a religiously meaningful existence begins with a genuine desire to navigate the challenges of functioning in a complex world in a way that honors both laws and values, even if that requires imposing an understanding that resonates as authentic to the individual, independent of the range of opinions and arguments that abound. All the rest, as important as it is, is commentary.

Appendices

I. OPINIONS IN SUPPORT OF OR IN OPPOSITION TO THE *BEKHOR SHOR*'S STANCE ON *HA'ARAMOT* AND TORAH LAW

The *Bekhor Shor* maintained that the use of *ha'aramot* was acceptable only regarding rabbinic law, but not Torah law. Among those who disagree with the *Bekhor Shor* on this premise (those who dispute the *Bekhor Shor* specifically on points regarding *mekhirat chametz* are discussed in that section) are R. Ya'akov of Lisa, *Resp. Nachalat Ya'akov,* 1 and *Mekor Chaim,* 448 *biurim* 11; and R. Moshe Sofer, *Resp. Chatam Sofer,* OC, 63, who displays that the factors that influence the acceptability of a *ha'aramah* are very diversified and do not correlate at all to the origin status of the relevant *mitzvah.* Others who disagree include *Resp. Oneg Yom Tov,* 28 (his disagreement is addressed at both points in combination; sales mechanisms are not considered a *ha'aramah,* and are effective on a Torah level); *Resp. Neta Sorek,* YD, 42; *Resp. Tzemach Tzedek* (Lubavitch, YD, 102) who notes that his grandfather, the *Ba'al HaTania,* writes as well in the *Shulchan Arukh HaRav* (YD 48) that a *ha'aramah* "is not effective at all by Torah law," but nonetheless notes that the implication of the Talmud is against this (however, the seventh Rebbe, R. Menachem Mendel Schneerson, does seem to accept the premise in an essay published in *Shulchan Menachem,* OC II, 226; see footnotes there); R. Naftali Hertz Landau, *Cheker Halakhah,* II, *ot chet,* 21; *Resp. Binyan Olam,* OC, 21; R. Meir Tzvi Vitmeir, *Resp. Ramatz,* YD 86:5; R. Avraham Teomim, *Resp. Chesed L'Avraham,* YD 112; R. Yehoshua Babad, *Resp. Sefer Yehoshua, pesakim u'ketavim,* #417 (although he agrees to maintain his conclusion regarding selling animals for Pesach); R. Moshe Yehudah Leib Zilberberg, *Zayit Ra'anan*, OC 441, 13; *Resp. Mahari haKohen*, OC. 17 and YD, 35; *Resp. Shevet HaLevi*, IV, 49 and IX, 112; and *Resp. Minchat Asher*, II, 45:4. See also *Resp. Beit Shlomo*, OC 72, and the comments of *Resp. Zekher Yehosef*, III, 160:3. R. Ovadiah Yosef, *Resp. Yabbia Omer*, X, YD 38:3 (and also in *Chazon Ovadiah:Prozbol/Shvi'it, Ha'aramah B'Mekhirat Karkaot*, sec. 2–3), surveys much literature on the topic and is inclined to disagree with the *Bekhor Shor* on all of his assertions, maintaining that "all of the *acharonim*" have refuted his view and accept *ha'aramot* even in areas of Torah law. R. Ya'akov Breisch (*Resp. Chelkat Ya'akov*, EH 24; III, 93 in older editions), in addition to arguing based on prooftexts and sources, also establishes a definition of *ha'aramah* as something that is inherently false, rather than simply motivated by ulterior considerations (e.g., a sincere conversion to Judaism, initially prompted by a desire to marry a Jewish spouse, would not be a *ha'aramah*).

Those who agree with the position of the *Bekhor Shor* include his grandson, R. Ephraim Zalman Margolios, *Resp.Beit Ephraim*, OC 33 (and note his detailed analysis of the relevant prooftexts), as well as a separate essay on the topic entitled *Makneh U'Kinyan*; *Yeshuot Ya'akov*, OC 13:4; R. Shmuel Yitzchak Shur, *Resp. Minchat Shai*, I, 68; *Resp. Arugat HaBosem*, YD, 121 (at least as a worthy concern); R. Avraham David Wahrman of Butzchash, in a letter printed in the beginning of *Resp. Neta Sha'ashuim*, sec. 3 (and see also his comments in *Kessef HaKodashim*, CM, 282); *Resp. Yehudah Ya'aleh*, OC 99 and 125 (and see also YD 341); R. Zvi Hirsch Chajes, glosses to *Bava Metzia* 90b; R. Shlomo Kluger, *Chokhmat Shlomo*, OC, 448:7 (although he also notes there a contradictory proof), and elsewhere; R. Chaim Berlin, *Resp. Nishmat Chaim*, 100; *Resp. Teshuvot V'Hanhagot*, I, 764, and IV, 95. R. Yosef Landa, *Resp. Birkat Yosef*, OC 13, defends the logic of the *Bekhor Shor* against technical objections through conceptual analysis. R. Ya'akov of Karlin, *Resp. Mishkenot Ya'akov*, OC 38 (misnumbered; it is actually #37), independently takes it as a given, based on Talmudic passages, that *ha'aramot* are only acceptable in regards to rabbinic law. R. Yerucham Fishel Perlow, Commentary to *Sefer HaMitzvot* of R. Sa'adya Gaon, III, p. 228, inclines towards this position after considering prooftexts for both sides. In 5763

(2003) a volume was produced by R. Yitzchak Eliezer Yakab, rabbi of the *Beit HaMidrash Tevuot Shor*, entitled *Tevuot B'Koach Shor,* to analyze and defend the position of the *Bekhor Shor* on this issue.

R. Natan Gestetner, *Resp. L'Horot Natan,* VI, 97, and XIII, 64, works within the premise of the *Bekhor Shor* without indicating explicitly his acceptance. R. Zvi Hirsch Frimer, *Resp. Eretz Tzvi,* 84, also works within the *Bekhor Shor*'s premise, and expands upon it creatively; however, in a footnote appended to the beginning of the responsum, the assertion is that need is the only factor, whether Torah law or rabbinic law is involved.

The *Arukh HaShulchan* (OC 448:13) maintains that the *Bekhor Shor* is essentially correct, but establishes his position somewhat differently, based on a close reading of the Talmudic prooftext (*Shabbat* 139b). Accordingly, he assumes that a "*ha'aramah d'mukhach,*" that is evident, is unacceptable when dealing with Torah law. This is the case with the specific situation addressed by the *Bekhor Shor,* that of selling one's animals to a non-Jew and allowing them to be fed *chametz* over *Pesach.* In that instance, the animal is clearly in every sense remaining in the possession of the Jew, and thus the *ha'aramah* is overt and obvious. This would not be a problem, however, for the sale of *chametz* itself as it is generally conducted (the *Bekhor Shor* had explained the difference between the sale of the animal and that of the *chametz* differently, as discussed in more detail elsewhere.) The same general distinction between types of *ha'aramot* is adopted by *Resp. Maharsham* V, 71; a number of others include this distinction as well, with less explanation. Interestingly, another grandson of the *Bekhor Shor,* R. Yitzchak Eizek Shor, *Resp. Mei Be'er,* 43, writes that "only a *ha'aramah nikeret* (recognizable *ha'aramah*) was prohibited regarding Torah law," and he attributes this position to his grandfather.

R. Yehudah Leib Graubart, in an essay published in his *Chavalim B'Ne'imim* (I, *sugya* 20) asserts that a *ha'aramah* is acceptable in the area of Torah law, as long as the transfer involved is complete and sincere. However, it is difficult to position this as oppositional to the *Bekhor Shor,* because, as noted, it is the sincerity itself that the *Bekhor Shor* questioned. R. Graubart continues to posit that regarding rabbinic law, there is additional latitude for actions that are prohibited, but there exists permissible methods that are connected to intent, as long as the contrary intent is not externally evident. When there is no such avenue, he argues, the acceptability of a *ha'aramah* in rabbinic law is subject to dispute.

Regarding the *Bekhor Shor*'s specific objection to the sale of animals before *Pesach, Resp. Divrei Chaim,* OC, I, 18, accepts the distinction but with a different rationale. See also R. Yechezkel Paneth, *Resp. Mareh Yechezkel,* 21; R. Chaim Rappaport, *Resp. Mayim Chaim,* 8; *Resp. Ateret Chakhamim,* YD, 14; *Resp. Teshuvah M'Ahavah,* II, 258; and *Zayit Ra'anan,* ibid. R. Matityahu Madanitzsky, *Resp. Matat Yado, tinyana,* OC 32, asserts that a *ha'aramah* is permitted in all areas, as long as it is executed prior to the prohibition taking effect; accordingly, he permits the sale of the animals. A similar theory is developed at length by R. Zvi Hirsch Orenstein, *Resp. Birkat Retzeh,* 80. *Resp. Maharsham,* IV, 66, recommends selling the *chametz* and the animals to a single purchaser, arguing that in that case one transaction will validate the other. R. Zvi Hirsch Bisko, *Tiferet Zvi/Resp. Maharatz,* 20, was inclined to permit, but was also ready to defer to the *Bekhor Shor* if that was the practice. See also *Resp. Shevivei Eish,* OC 31, and see R. Nachaman Kahana, *Orchot Chaim,* OC, 448:21.

See also the responsum of R. Aharon Moshe Toibesh printed in *Resp. Uri V'Yishi,* 121, who considers proofs for and against the *Bekhor Shor*'s position, and asserts that *mekhirat chametz* is given special license because of the monetary loss involved.

II. OPINIONS REGARDING WHETHER ONE IS OBLIGATED TO FORMALLY WAIVE CIVIL RIGHTS TO INHERITANCE THAT ARE NOT RECOGNIZED BY *HALAKHAH*

R. Yosef Shaul Nathanson, in a number of his responsa, quotes R. Moshe Benveniste, *Resp. Pnei Moshe,* II, 15 to the effect of allowing the daughters to decline to sign away their civil rights [he actually quotes this view from *Mahari Bason,* while also noting dissenting views in both directions: the *Maharit* who does not allow this, and another view that deems the civil allocation to be binding], and thus asserts that the daughters can use this fact to push for a settlement that includes them; while the legal allotment may not be in accord with Jewish law, the daughters did not actively cause this, and it is not their obligation to take affirmative steps to negate the possibility; see also *Resp. Mahariya HaLevi,* I, 4. See *Resp. Shoel U'Meishiv, tinyana* 1:1, 3:110; *telita'ah* 1:78, 265, 3:45; in *shi'itai,* 59, he indicates that while it would be wrong for the daughters to pursue their case in the secular courts, they can legitimately use the possibility of doing so as a negotiating tool; see also *Resp. Harei Besamim,* I, 129, and II, 99. An additional point of contention is the point asserted by some authorities that even if the daughters are permitted to negotiate for compensation, this would not amount to them receiving an equal share, but rather a settlement equal to a fraction of what civil law would have mandated (see *Resp. Rav Po'alim,* II, CM, 15, and *Mishkan Shilo,* p. 301–302).

R. Alexander Shmuel Halperin, *Resp. Maharash,* 52, maintains that the daughters are obligated to formally waive their rights, as he assumes that they have nothing to gain by refusing and thus avoiding "*midat Sedom*" obligates them to cooperate; however, the premise of R. Nathanson (whom he quotes to refute) is that they would have potential benefit in declining. R. Yisrael Grossman, *Resp. Netzach Yisrael,* 23, considers the *Sedom* argument at some length before allowing the daughters to hold out for a settlement, at one point drawing the comparison to a celebrity whose autograph is valuable and should therefore be entitled to share in whatever profit comes from providing it. See also *Resp. Maharsham,* V, 40. Some feel that at least to some extent, there is an aspect of *hashavat aveidah* (returning lost property) obligating the daughters to assist the brothers in obtaining their inheritance (see *Resp. Shevivei Eish,* CM II, 112; for an analysis of the applicability of *hashavat aveidah* to this situation, see *Resp. Meishiv B'Halakhah,* II, 243, n, 13). *Resp Mahariaz Enzil,* 28, goes further than this, arguing that *hashavat aveidah* understates the case; the daughters are guilty of theft or extortion, illegitimately holding on to the property of others, and are obligated to sign in order to fulfill the Torah's will that the inheritance be assigned to the legacy of the father. Similarly, *Resp. Beit Shlomo* (I, OC, 85:3; CM, 109; II, YD, 79) unequivocally obligates the daughters to sign, and finds the differing opinion shocking.

R. Asher Weiss, *Resp. Minchat Asher,* III, 117, is initially sympathetic to the arguments that the daughters are obligated to sign, a view that he considers both more just and the position of the majority.

However, he concludes that given that contemporary practice is in any event to come to a settlement of inclusive distribution, and there are views allowing the daughters to hold out for such a settlement, they have justification in choosing to do so and cannot be compelled otherwise. See also *Resp. Tzitz Eliezer,* XV, 60, and see the objections to his position in *Mishkan Shilo,* p. 298–302. See also *Resp. Divrei Chaim,* CM, II, 3; *Resp. Minchat Yitzchak,* II, 95; *Netinah L'Yitzchak, yerushah,* #2. An extensive, point by point analysis of the issues in this debate, authored by R. Pinchas Rosenbaum, can be found in the journal *Beit Aharon v'Yisrael* (#65, pp. 90–95; #66, pp. 70–81).

III. HALAKHIC, CONCEPTUAL, AND PHILOSOPHICAL APPLICATIONS OF THE RAMBAM'S POSITION ON A COERCED *GET* AND THE "INNER JEW"

We have seen, throughout the *ha'aramah* literature, a number of references to an innovative and impactful explanation of the Rambam, one that been utilized to justify a very generous approach to questions of insincerity or ignorance in some of the approaches discussed.

In his *Mishneh Torah,*[1] the Rambam addresses the apparent contradiction between the fact that a divorce can only be executed through the free will of the husband, and yet, under certain circumstances, a valid *get* may be coerced by a rabbinical court.[2]

In the Rambam's words: "Why is this *get* not void, as he is being compelled – either by Jews or by gentiles – [to divorce] against his will [and a *get* must be given voluntarily]? Because the concept of being compelled against one's will applies only when speaking about a person who is being compelled and forced to do something that the Torah does not obligate him to do – e.g., a person who was beaten until he consented to a sale, or to give a present. If, however, a person's evil inclination presses him to negate [the observance of] a *mitzvah* or to commit a transgression, and he was beaten until he performed the action he was obligated to perform, or until he dissociated himself from the forbidden action, he is not considered to have been forced against his will. On the contrary, it

1. *Hil. Gerushin* 2:20.
2. *Gittin* 88b.

is he himself who is forcing [his own conduct to become debased]. With regard to this person who [outwardly] refuses to divorce [his wife] - he wants to be part of the Jewish people, and he wants to perform all the *mitzvot* and eschew all the transgressions; it is only his evil inclination that presses him. Therefore, when he is beaten until his [evil] inclination has been weakened, and he consents [to the divorce], he is considered to have performed the divorce willfully."[3]

Following his formulation, it has at times been extrapolated that, in other areas of Jewish law, non-observance should not be assumed to be noncompliance with a given practice; any Jew can be presumed, at the core, to wish for the most halakhically appropriate path, whenever possible.

The Rambam's words, an apparently mystical and spiritual concept expressed in a technical halakhic context of tremendous practical consequences, have appeared frequently in Torah literature in a wide range of contexts, including halakhic rulings, conceptual analysis, philosophy, textual interpretation, and homiletics.

Source. The notion, which in the Yiddish expression would be termed "the Pintele Yid" (the small [inner] Jew), would likely have been taken as a chasidic concept had it been introduced many centuries later. As it is, the origin of the idea has prompted much speculation.[4]

According to some, the basis of the Rambam's position is an explicit Talmudic statement on the topic,[5] which (possibly tentatively) attributes the justification for coercion to the "*mitzvah* to listen to the Rabbis."[6] However, the alignment of that statement with the Rambam's position is subject to interpretation, both of the Talmud and of the Rambam.[7] That is to say, an association of the Rambam's position with

3. Sefaria translation, slightly modified.
4. Notably, the primary Talmudic passage invalidating a coerced *get,* unless under the proper circumstances (*Gittin* 88b), does not indicate this explanation; see Yaakov Levinger, *Darkei HaMachshavah HaHalakhatit shel HaRambam,* pp. 165–166.
5. *Bava Batra* 48a.
6. See *Maggid Mishneh,* and note the objections of *Lechem Mishneh.* See also R. Chaim Shmuelevitz, *Sha'arei Chaim, Kiddushin* 6:2.
7. See, for example, *Resp. Chut HaMeshulash,* 16; R. Yitzchak Yedidyah Frankel, *Derekh Yesharah,* II, 34; *Natan Piryo, Sugyot,* 42.

this passage may mean, rather than the assumption of a subconscious desire that overrides the explicit resistance, that the individual ultimately comes to recognize the religious obligation and thus acquiesces. This would be consistent with the explanation of *Rashbam* to that passage.[8] However, the more prevalent understanding of the Rambam in the broader literature is the former reading.

More philosophically, the notion of a struggle between internal spiritual striving and weakness of will is reflected in the Talmudic passage[9] that relates the prayer of R. Alexandri, who would declare that his wish is to perform God's will, but the "yeast in the dough" – symbolizing the evil instinct, as Rashi comments – interferes. R. Tzadok HaKohen of Lublin[10] and R. Yitzchak Hutner[11] are among those who connect this to the Rambam's position.[12] R. Shlomo Eiger[13] connects the notion to another passage,[14] which teaches that one only sins if he has been taken over by a *ruach shetut*, a spirit of insanity.[15]

Similarly, both the power and assumption of *teshuvah*, repentance, have been associated with this position, with the *Shevet HaLevi*, R. Shmuel HaLevi Wosner[16] connecting it to the language of the verse[17] that promises that repentance is "very near to" the Jews. Later[18] he associates the position with the verse in Malachi (3:1) that, in reference to a future redemption, describes the Jews as "*mevakshim*," seekers, explaining that the forces that pulled them away from observance will have been weakened.[19]

---

8. See *Dibberot Moshe, Gittin*, ch. 2, p. 23, and R. Mordechai Yitzchak Toldeano, *MiTal HaShamayim al haTorah*, IV, 24
9. *Berakhot* 17a.
10. *Divrei Soferim*, 21, 23; *Poked Akarim*, p. 18 and p. 44; *Resisei Lailah* p. 107 and 133.
11. *Iggerot Pachad Yitzchak*, 12.
12. See also the comments of R. Yehudah Segal in the journal *Noam*, VI, p. 254.
13. *Sefer HaIkkarim*, I, p. 179.
14. *Sotah* 3a.
15. Compare also *Resp. Mishneh Halakhot* VII, 115.
16. *Derashot*, p. 86.
17. Deut. 30:14.
18. P. 86.
19. See also R. Chaim of Volozhin, *Nefesh HaChaim, sha'ar* 1, ch. 18; and see R. Tzadok HaKohen, *Yisrael Kedoshim*, p. 86. In *Machshivot Charutz*, p. 84, and *Resisei Lailah*, p.

Further, R. Tzvi Hirsch Fromer, the Kozaglover Rav,[20] asserted that the principle was reflected in the dictum[21] that *teshuvah mei-ahavah* (out of love) has the capacity to convert one's transgressions into merits.

As R. Yosef Goldberg[22] notes, there are actually two components to the Rambam's position: the idea of the inner purity of the Jew, and that of the restricting force of evil inclination. Regarding the second, he references the Talmudic passage[23] that speaks of God creating the evil instinct, as well as its remedy, the Torah. Consequently, one is advised to engage in the study of Torah so as not to be "given into the hands" of the evil instinct.

Beyond a textual source, the question must also be raised as to a different kind of source, i.e., the origin of this inner will itself upon which Rambam relies.

R. Soloveitchik[24] traces this inner will to the Torah that is taught by the angel in the womb before birth, and then forgotten.[25] Many others assume the source is the collective acceptance of the Torah by the Jewish people at Mt. Sinai, which raises a number of issues.[26]

Textual challenges. One Talmudic text is invoked in some of the halakhic literature as both a possible basis for or a challenge to the Rambam's position.

In describing the receiving of the Torah, the Talmud[27] provides background that seems to modify the people's recorded response of *naaseh v'nishma.* Despite that declaration, apparently, the Jews were not fully ready to accept the Torah, and they had to be coerced into doing so. As such, continues the Talmud, there exists a "*moda'ah rabbah l'Orayta*"; as Rashi explains, a justification for not observing the Torah's

84; he associates the Rambam's words with the Talmudic dictum (*Sanhedrin* 44a), "*Yisrael af al pi she-chata, Yisrael hu,*" a Jew remains a Jew even when he has sinned.

20. *Resp. Eretz Tzvi,* II, p. 398.
21. *Yoma* 86b.
22. *Eilu Kofin L'Hotzi,* introduction.
23. *Kiddushin* 30b.
24. Cited in *Eretz HaTzvi,* p. 300.
25. *Niddah* 30b.
26. See also R. Alter Hilewitz, *Chikrei Zemanim,* IV, p. 150, and p. 340, and compare pp. 432–433.
27. *Shabbat* 88b.

commandments, as they were not accepted willingly. However, at a later date, following the miracle of the salvation of Purim, the Torah was willingly accepted by the Jewish people.

Halakhic authors applied this passage to the Rambam's position in conflicting ways. To some, the very premise of the "*moda'ah rabbah l'Orayta*" was a contradiction to the Rambam's thesis; if coercion is valid when it reflects God's will, it should have been valid and binding in this case as well. In fact, for this and other reasons, *Resp. Chemdat Shlomo*[28] offers a complete reinterpretation of the phrase, at variance with that of the *rishonim.*[29]

For others, the question was shifted. If the "inner Jew" was actually created at Mount Sinai, it would indeed make sense that an acceptance under duress would call the concept into question, together with compromising the acceptance itself (the "*moda'ah rabbah l'Orayta*"). In this vein, *Resp. Chatam Sofer*[30] asserts that the Rambam's principle could not have been effective until that later point in history, after the Purim miracle, when the Torah was accepted willingly.[31]

However, *Chatam Sofer* does indicate, without explanation, that this need not be true according to the explanation of the *Midrash Tanchuma.*[32] That source reconciles the coercion with *na'aseh v'nishma* by asserting a distinction. The Written Torah was indeed accepted enthusiastically. The Oral Torah, however, which contains many extra rules and stringencies, was not accepted, until God forced it upon the Jews.

---

28. CM 13.

29. See also his *Chiddushim,* in *petichah;* and see also R. Yom Tov Krispin, *Bigdei Yom Tov,* I, 3. See also the homiletic interpretation of *Zivchei Shlomo,* p. 168 and note also the interpretation of *Meshekh Chokhmah,* Ex. 19:17.

    Similarly, R. Ephraim Tchursh, *Hadrat Ephraim,* p. 150, invokes the Rambam in explaining why the oath at Mount Sinai was binding, even though it was apparently imposed on the Jews by Moses.

    Another possible reconciliation is noted by R. Yosef Goldberg (*Eilu SheKofin L'Hotzi,* p. 24): it is possible to say that the acceptance was binding, but, per the Rambam's rulings elsewhere (*Hilkhot Teshuvah,* 5:3), a commitment under circumstances such as these would not have warranted punishment for its neglect.

30. OC, 185.

31. See the approach to this question in R. Yisrael Algaze, *She'erit Ya'akov,* p. 11.

32. *Parashat Noach.*

Accordingly, there was at least some degree of willing acceptance at Mount Sinai, and this provided the framework for coercion to be effective on the rest of the Torah.

This explanation is well aligned with the Rambam's position. It emerges that the "inner Jew" is indeed established by the willing acceptance of the Written Torah, while the obstacle to acceptance of the Oral Torah is its seemingly burdensome nature; that is to say, the tension between the inner spiritual commitment and the external "*yetzer hara*" described by the Rambam in reference to a *get.*

This distinction may address a difficulty that some have raised regarding another Talmudic passage[33] that relates that God offered the Torah to all the nations of the world, and they all refused. Why, it is asked, did God not coerce them to accept the Torah as he did with the Jews (the Talmud records that this question was asked by the non-Jewish nations themselves). If coercion is only effective with some level of prior willing commitment, the special treatment for the Jews can be understood.[34]

Others attribute the distinction between the Jewish nation and others to the seven Noahide commandments applicable to all of humanity, which the Jews observed but the other nations did not.[35]

R. Yosef Goldberg[36] takes a different approach to the Talmudic passage regarding the giving of the Torah at Mount Sinai. Addressing the question of the contradiction to *na'aseh v'nishma,* the *Tosafot*[37] suggest that the Jews indeed accepted the Torah willingly, and the threat of the overturned mountain was to prevent any later reversal of the agreement. Building off of this premise, it is possible to find both halves of the Rambam's principle harmoniously integrated within this passage. The "inner Jew" was displayed by the enthusiastic acceptance of

33. *Avodah Zarah* 2b.

34. See *Masa Yad Al HaTorah,* III, pp. 636–637; and *Eish Dat* of the Ozever Rebbe. Similarly, this logic explains why one cannot be coerced to convert to Judaism; see *Resp. Yachel Yisrael,* I, 25. See also *L'Horot Natan al HaTorah,* Lev., pp. 32–34.

35. See R. Raphael Hamburger, *Marpei Lashon,* p. 86; see also R. Yosef Azoviv, *Yamim Echadim, drush* 8. Similarly, R. Chaim Yaakov Varshno, *Toldot Ya'akov, Parashat Bo* and *Parashat Ki Tisa,* credits the ancestry of the forefathers.

36. *Eilu SheKofin,* pp. 2–5.

37. 88a, s.v. *kafah.*

the Torah by the Jewish people. Nonetheless, at the same time, there existed the fear that the commitment would fade and elapse, and enforcement was necessary to prevent that. This reflects the influence of the *yetzer hara* on observance, and the role of authority in preventing it from prevailing.

Interpretations. The *Malbim,*[38] in explaining the possibility of effective coercion, draws a distinction between two Hebrew words that both seem to indicate a desire toward something, *chefetz* and *ratzon*. The former, he asserts, is an emotional, instinctive desire, while the latter is more intellectual and rational in nature. Accordingly, it is possible that one would not "desire" to give a *get,* yet could make an intellectual decision to do so. At the end of his explanation, the Malbim notes that it is "similar" to what the Rambam writes in *Hilkhot Gerushin.*

Presumably, he is asserting that despite one's current inclinations, it is a rationally correct decision to give a *get* when it is halakhically required to do so. Coupled with the assumption that the inner desire is to act consistently with *halakhah,* it can thus be cogently argued that the actual will is compliance, and the refusal to comply is merely the result of the interference of misguided instincts.

The *Chavvot Yair*[39] objected to the premise of the Rambam that the physical coercion imposed thus far had removed the influence of the evil inclination. It is not the pressure that has been exerted already that has been effective, he maintained; it is instead the fear of any future pressure that causes the husband to relent. Were he to be confident that no such pressure would be exerted, he would remain steadfast in his refusal. Accordingly, *Chavvot Yair* rejects the interpretation of the Rambam and offers an alternative.

In disputing the *Chavvot Yair,* R. Yosef Goldberg[40] offers a parable to explain the reasoning of the Rambam. He describes an individual who is taken captive, and cannot escape until his associates arrive and attack his jailers. At that moment, the captive is able to run away, and even if his associates cease their assault on the jailers, who may yet

38. Lev. 1:3, s.v. *karov.*

39. Resp., 55.

40. *Eilu Kofin L'Hotzi* pp. 13–14.

recapture him, as long as that has not yet happened, the former captive it is nonetheless liberated. Should he become recaptured, that will return him to an involuntary state. Accordingly, regarding the coerced *get*, even should the husband be unwilling in the absence of additional pressure, that simply means that he has returned to "captivity" and this does not negate the assessment that what takes place during the moments of pressure is, perhaps paradoxically, reflective of his true will.

Practical Ramifications. The *Maharik*[41] conceded to a correspondent that according to the Rambam's explanation, a *meshumad,* one who has abandoned the Jewish faith, would not be able to be effectively coerced to give a *get*. Since that does not seem to be the case, he tentatively puts forward a different explanation for the efficacy in that situation.[42] Similarly, *Resp. Maharit Tzahalon,* 83, invalidates the coerced *get* of an apostate for this reason.[43]

Nonetheless, there were many who felt that the logic could be applied to an apostate as well.[44] For example, *Chazon Ish*[45] understands the phrase that indicates that the husband wants to fulfill the Torah to refer to his ideal inner desire, not to a current explicit desire that happens to exclude this one commandment relevant at the moment. Notably, the *Chatam Sofer,*[46] explaining the view of Rabbenu Tam against the use of a non-Jewish name in a *get,* asserted that in the case of an apostate a *get* is often coerced, and at that moment even one estranged from Judaism returns to his roots and wishes to use his Jewish name.

The issue of a *meshumad* arises in the literature in a different way as well. R Eliyahu Mizrachi[47] considers the question of a deathly ill man who wishes to issue a *get* to his wife before he dies so she will not be subject

41. *Shoresh* 63.
42. See, alternatively, *Resp. Chelkat Yoav,* I, *dinei ones, anaf* 5.
43. See also *Resp. Shem Aryeh, Hosafot,* 3. See also *Resp. Machaneh Chaim,* IV, 1, who asserts that due to the Rambam's explanation, coerced divorce cannot be confidently applied to the non-religious.
44. This is evident from the view of *Riaz* cited in *Shiltei Giborim, Gittin* 49a in pages of the *Rif,* #5.
45. *Gittin* 99:1.
46. *Resp.,* EH, II, 38.
47. *Resp.,* 68.

to *yibum,* especially considering that his brother is an apostate. However, his wife is not available to receive the *get,* and thus the question is can it be acquired on her behalf, and presumed to be in her interest. Invoking the Rambam, the argument is made (among many others) that the religious undesirability of marriage to an apostate ensures that the wife would agree to become divorced before becoming consigned to such a situation.

The Talmud[48] teaches that even when there are grounds to coerce a *get,* the process cannot be carried out by non-Jewish authorities. The Maharam Shick, in his commentary, explains this as the result of the interaction between the Rambam's principle and the prohibition to litigate in secular courts. When that prohibition is violated, the "inner Jew" no longer consents to a process that is contradictory to *halakhah.*[49]

Going beyond *gittin, Radbaz*[50] validates a commitment an individual made under duress not to return to a specific profession, if the circumstances were such that he was indeed inappropriate for that position and would have been contradicting some halakhic value by returning to it. The transgressive nature of him occupying that position renders his commitment not to do so as voluntary.[51]

Applications to other concepts. The Rambam's principle makes frequent appearances in the literature of conceptual analysis, utilized to explain various Talmudic notions. There is a reciprocal benefit that emerges: the principle is helpful in explicating these ideas; in turn, the ideas serve as further support for the Rambam's principle.

It is not surprising that the principle is utilized in clarifying the parameters of coercion regarding *mitzvot* in general. It is invoked to explain the validity of a *mitzvah* (specifically *matzah*)[52] performed under coercion.[53]

---

48. *Gittin* 88b.
49. See similarly the Lubavitcher Rebbe, R. Menachem Mendel Schneerson, *Likkutei Sichot,* III, p. 981 n 13; and IV, p. 1130 n 52.
50. *Resp.,* #2, 145.
51. For a related responsum of *Radbaz* that does involve *gittin,* see #982.
52. *Rosh HaShanah* 28a.
53. See R. Shlomo Eiger, *Sefer HaIkkarim,* I, p. 154; R. Zelig Reuven Bengis, *Chiddushim,* II, 66; R. Yosef Dov Levine, *Yad HaLevi, drushim,* p 32, in fn.; *Minchat*

Resp. Yad Sofer[54] applied it to the policy of confiscating money from debtors in order to pay creditors (*tofes l'ba'al chov*). Given that repayment of loans is a *mitzvah*, it can be assumed that the assets are given over willingly.[55]

R. Yitzchak Hutner[56] explained accordingly the teaching[57] that coercion is not applied to a *mitzvah* that is explicitly connected to a reward; that motivation supplants the sincerity of the "inner Jew."[58]

More notable is the fact that the principle is used to explain Talmudic concepts in other areas with no obvious connection to either coercion or *gittin*.

R. Shlomo Eiger[59] explains thusly the rule of *i avid lo mehani*, which invalidates any action that is accomplished in a prohibited manner. Given the transgression involved, it can be assumed that the actual intent of the actor is lacking in the action.

R. Aharon Weinstein[60] explains the principle of *hefker Beit Din hefker*, which allows a rabbinic court to declare private property ownerless, as emanating from the assumption that the original owner would accede to the will of the rabbinic leadership because of the religious obligation involved.[61]

Malbim, in his halakhic work *Artzot HaChaim*,[62] draws on the Rambam to explain one scenario in which it is assumed that one is willing to have a *mitzvah* performed on behalf of another even at a loss (*nicha lei l'inish l'me'abad mitzvah b'mamoneih*).[63]

Machvat, I, 33, explaining *Sefat Emet* to *Rosh HaShanah*. See also *Sarei HaMeah*, II, p. 306.

54. P. 139.
55. Compare *Resp. Rabbenu Yosef M'Slutzk*, 91.
56. *Iggerot Pachad Yitzchak*, 12.
57. *Chullin* 110b.
58. See also *Resp. Shem Aryeh, Hosafot*, 3.
59. *Sefer HaIkkarim*, p. 179.
60. *Darkhei Aharon*, I, p. 67.
61. See also p. 50 regarding *matzah*.
62. *Eretz Yehudah*, 14:3.
63. Compare also R. Avraham Yitzchak Kook, *Mitzvot Ra'ayah*, 437:2.

The *Maharsham*[64] invokes the Rambam to explain the dynamic as to why *kibud av* does not override the observance of *Shabbat*; presumably, the parent does not actually want their instruction to be carried out if it would contradict the will of the Torah.

R. Shlomo Gross, *Resp. Mishnah Shleimah,*[65] explains thusly the view of some *rishonim* (possibly including the Rambam), that *bitul* is not effective for *chametz* that is known to the owner. Given that the desire of the Torah is that the owner actually destroy that *chametz,* a declaration of *bitul* must be assumed to lack sufficient intent.

R. Meir Meiri[66] notes that *yibum* and *chalitzah* appear to be diametrically opposed in terms of requirements for intentionality, with *yibum* requiring the least, and *chalitzah* requiring the most. He suggests that this can be explained by the Rambam's principle, taken together with the fact that the desire of the "inner Jew" is for *yibum* to be performed, while *chalitzah* is considered a rejection of the actual obligation. Accordingly, the first option can assume the intent of the "inner Jew," while the latter, as contradictory to it, requires explicit intent of its own.[67]

Applications by *Poskim*. Even more noteworthy than the above is the fact that the Rambam's principle has been incorporated into practical responsa by halakhic authorities in other areas of Jewish law (albeit sometimes tentatively, and in conjunction with other arguments.)

Often, this has been towards addressing whether a given mechanism, such as those we have discussed in this work, can be effective if one or both parties is ignorant of its fundamental aspects, or even resistant.

One example of this is *mekhirat chametz.* R. Ya'akov Breisch, *Resp. Chelkat Ya'akov,*[68] argues that the Rambam's principle should certainly be applicable to validate this procedure for a non-religious seller, given that it is already applied in the case of divorce, where the stakes are even higher (possible adultery and illegitimacy of offspring), and in

64. *Resp.*, II, 224:17.
65. 46:6.
66. *Ezrat Nashim*, III, p. 269
67. For additional applications of this nature, see *Mishnat Avraham* to *Sefer Chasidim*, I, p. 154; and *Resp. R. Nachum Tributsch*, 58.
68. OC, 194.

that case the husband has vocally declared his noncompliance. However, elsewhere[69] he does note that there is a complicating factor in the sale of *chametz* (and *bekhor,* which he assumes is similar), in that a non-Jew is also involved, and the "inner Jew" factor would not address any deficiencies in his commitment.[70] R. Yitzchak Zilberstein suggests the Rambam's principle is the reasoning behind a responsum of the *Divrei Chaim*[71] that validated the *chametz* sale of a nonobservant Jew who described his own sale as superficial.

Chelkat Ya'akov also applies his above arguments to a *hetter iska* executed under similar circumstances, here noting that they are even more compelling than with the sale of *chametz* or *bekhor,* as only Jews are involved. He acknowledges, however, that it is a weaker case when the lender is not interested, and it is only the borrower who is attempting to execute the loan in a permissible fashion.

R. Azriel Eiger, in his original proposal for a "*hetter iska klalit,*"[72] invoked the Rambam in a modified way. His proposal was primarily meant for a generally observant Jew who may nonetheless forget to utilize a *hetter iska* or lending money. He posited that given that "the inner Jew" wishes to act correctly, if he is distracted and forgets to do the right thing, his intent can be defined by any previous statement in which he expressed the desire to act properly.

It is noteworthy that not only do these examples constitute an expanded application of the Rambam's principle, some are also at odds with those views expressed above, in the context of *gittin,* that assumed the principle would be limited to those who are otherwise observant.

More broadly, authorities argued as to whether the Rambam's position granted a *chezkat kashrut,* a presumption of righteousness or innocence, to Jews in general. The Satmar Rav[73] asserted that it did not. Given that the Rambam specifically described someone being coerced,

69. YD, 69.

70. Others who consider the principle in this context include R. Yitzchak Shmuel Schechter, *Resp. Yashiv Yitzchak,* XXVII, 12; *Mo'adim L'Simchah,* IV, pp. 176–178; and R. Yitzchak Zilberstein, *Chashukei Chemed, Pesachim* 10a.

71. II, OC 46,

72. *Drushim,* I, part 2, 38:1, published by the *Agudath HaRabbanim* of Poland,

73. *Resp. Divrei Yoel,* YD 34:6.

the implication may be that at all other times that same individual is not necessarily acting properly. Nonetheless, the *Divrei Chaim*[74] implies that there is a general *chezkat kashrut*, citing the Rambam.[75]

Homiletic Applications. Unsurprisingly, the Rambam's principle has been harnessed for homiletical ends. R. Moshe Feinstein[76] invokes it to make the point that one should not give up on the possibility of any Jew repenting, and also[77] to explain the Talmudic dictum that "one should always engage in Torah and *mitzvot* even not *l'shmah* (for their own sake), because *l'shmah* comes from that which is not *l'shmah*." He explains that the point is not, as commonly understood, that such actions with ulterior motivations will lead eventually to one performing them for the proper reasons; rather, it is that even when they are apparently motivated by other factors, the "inner Jew" is performing them for noble reasons. R. Tzadok HaKohen of Lublin explained similarly Talmudic statements[78] that one who gives charity for ulterior reasons, or even without any intentionality at all, is considered "completely righteous."[79] The Kozaglover Rav[80] understood that the Rambam's principle rendered even awareness completely unnecessary, so much so that even an eight day old baby can be credited with his own circumcision.[81]

It should be noted that some of the usage of the Rambam's principle in the context of *ha'aramot* has been credited to the precedent of the writings of R. Eliyahu Kalatzkin (1852-1932). A deeply respected Lithuanian rabbinic scholar, he discussed this idea a number of times, among them in the context of an exposition published in his *Even Pinah* (#11; see also *Miluei Aven*, 13), crucial to the *chametz* and *hetter iska*, he acknowledges the discomfort inherent in the

74. *Resp.*, EH, II, 90
75. See also the comments of R. David Klein, *Kriat Sefer, Parashat VaYechi*, p. 278.
76. *Darash Moshe*, Lev. 13:59.
77. There and Lev 11:45.
78. e.g., *Pesachim* 8a-b.
79. *Divrei Sofrim*, ch. 21, and see also in *Yisrael HaKedoshim*, p. 131). See also *Ot Hi L'Olam, ma'arakhet ha-heh.*
80. *Eretz Tzvi*, II, p. 363.
81. See also p. 300.

appearance of an artifice against the commandments of the Torah. Nonetheless, he argues, these actions are not summarily condemned; they rise and fall completely with the sincerity of the actor. He sees this as consistent with the verse (*Hosea* 14:10), "For the ways of God are straight (*yesharim*); the righteous walk on them, while sinners stumble on them." It is no different, he maintains, than prayer; that is not devalued simply because there are those who utter the words with no intent or meaning.

To this end, he draws upon the words of the Rambam in his principle. Deep down, every Jew is sincere, and wishes to carry out God's will. Accordingly, at least without significant evidence to the contrary, it should be assumed that these mechanisms are being executed genuinely and without artifice. In this light, he interprets the statement of the *Talmud Yerushalmi* (*Ma'aser Sheni* 4:3) that explains the *mishnah's* (*Ma'aser Sheni* 4:4) advocating of a *ha'aramah* regarding *ma'aser sheni* as connected to the Torah's identifying that *mitzvah* with a "*berakhah*" (see pp 20-23). If the default assumption is that a Jew will act towards *mitzvot* with sincerity, this is all the more so when a *mitzvah* is highlighted as involving a particularly cherished blessing. In that case, the sincerity is guaranteed, and there need not be any fear of impropriety associated with a *ha'aramah*.

The Rambam's principle has occupied a perhaps unique place within halakhic codification. It is provided as an explanation for a formal practical rule of tremendous consequence and implication, and rests on a premise that is either a broad psychological assumption or a supernatural spiritual reality, depending on interpretation. Analysis of his position yields not only varying applications of the rule in its original context, but impacts upon both practice and theory throughout the corpus of *halakhah*. It has been subject to various understandings as far as its origin both textually and conceptually, and also as to its scope, most notably the issue of whether it includes only those who are generally observant and committed to Jewish identity, or even extends to those who may be far from that description. The latter possibility in particular has, at least to some, opened unexpected doors in areas of public policy, as well as provided the foundation for, and belief in, the potential for individual and communal repentance and growth. As such, it has inspired Jewish thinkers of all types in both the boundless spiritual potential of each member of the Jewish people, and of the corresponding obligation of leadership to enable that promise to endure and to flourish.

List of Sources

Dates and cities listed refer to one edition, not necessarily the first or the most recent. Some dates are approximated from the Hebrew dates. An indented listing is a coemmentary to the work listed immediately before it.

A. THE BIBLE AND COMMENTARIES

These works are arranged as commentaries to the Torah and/or *Nevi'im* and *K'tuvim*.

Alshich. R. Moshe Alshich (1508–1593), author of *Torat Moshe* and other Biblical commentaries, as well as other works.

Be'er Yosef. R. Yosef Zvi Salant. Jerusalem, 2009.

Birkat Yechekzel. R. Yissachar Dov Kaminsky. Halakhic essays arranged on the *parshiyot* of the Torah. Lakewood, NJ, 2022.

Chamudei Yitzchak. R. Yitzchak Chaim Fus. To Gen. Also authored *Imrei Yitzchak* to *Chafetz Chaim* and other works. Jerusalem, 2021.

Chavatzelet HaSharon al haTorah. Halakhic and Talmudic essays arranged on the *parshiyot* of the Torah. R. Mordechai Carlebach. Jerusalem, 2004.

Chelkat Betzalel. R. Betzalel Blidstein. Halakhic essays arranged on the *parshiyot* of the Torah. Bnei Brak, 2018.

Darash Moshe. R. Moshe Feinstein (see *Iggerot Moshe,* Sec. G). Bnei Brak, 1988.

Eish Dat. R. Moshe Yechiel Epstein (1889–1971), Ozharover Rebbe. Tel Aviv, 1978.

Emet L'Ya'akov: Iyyunim B'Mikra. R. Ya'akov Kaminetsky (1891–1986). Edited by Daniel Yehudah Neustadt. New York: *Makhon Emet L'Ya'akov,* 1990. Rosh Yeshivah of Yeshivah U'Mesivtah Torah VoDa'ath, Brooklyn, NY. His Talmudic lectures have also been published in volumes of the same name, *Emet L'Ya'akov.*

Ha'amek Davar and *Harchev Davar.* R. Naftali Tzvi Yehudah Berlin (1817–1893). Known as the *Netziv,* he was Rosh Yeshivah of the Yeshivah of Volozhin and also authored *Ha'amek Shealah* to the *Sheiltot D'Rav Achai Gaon, Meromei Sadeh* to the Talmud, and *Resp. Meishiv Davar* (see individual listings), as well as other works.

HaKtav VeHakabbalah. R. Ya'akov Tzvi Mecklenberg (1785–1865). Frankfort, 1880. Chief Rabbi of Koenigsberg, Germany.

Kriat Sefer. R. David Klein. Author of *Beit Arazim* to *Shulchan Arukh* and other works. Jerusalem, 2004.

L'Horot Natan. R. Natan Gestetner (see Sec. G).

Likkutei Sichot. R. Menachem Mendel Schneersohn (1902–1994), Crown Heights, Brooklyn, NY. Brooklyn: Kehot (*Karnei Hod Torah*) Publication Society. Seventh Rebbe of Lubavitch (Chabad). His ideas are also printed in the form of *Sichot, Chiddushim L'Shas,* and *Biurim L'Pirkei Avot,* and Responsa.

Malbim (HaTorah V'HaMitzvah). R. Meir Leibush ben Yechiel Michel Weiser (1809–1879). Classic commentary combining linguistic, philosophical, and conceptual interpretation. Machon Mosdot Alexander, Bnei Brak, 2020

Masa Yad. R. Yaakov David Ilan. Halakhic essays arranged on the *parshiyot* of the Torah. Jerusalem, 2020.

Meorot HaParshah. R. Elyakim Devorkes. Halakhic essays arranged on the *parshiyot* of the Torah. Author of many similar volumes under different titles. Jerusalem, 2008.

Meshekh Chokhmah. R. Meir Simchah HaKohen of Dvinsk (see *Ohr Sameach,* Sec. E). Jerusalem, 1974.

Mikra HaEdah. R. Eliyahu Grintzweig. Halakhic essays arranged on the *parshiyot* of the Torah. Jerusalem, 2020.

MiTal HaShamayim. R. Mordechai Yitzchak Toledano. Halakhic essays arranged on the *parshiyot* of the Torah. Machon Yabbia Omer, 1991.

Moshav Zekenim. Collection of commentaries of the Tosafists on the Torah.

Ohel Moshe. R. Moshe Scheinerman. Brooklyn, 2007.

Ohr HaChaim. R. Chaim ben Moshe Attar (1669–1743). In standard *Mikraot G'dolot* editions.

Pardes Yosef and *Pardes Yosef HaChadash.* R. Yosef Patzanofsky. Commentary to *Bereishit, Shemot,* and *Vayikra,* containing citations from sources in all areas of Torah study. Loch, 1900. R. David Avraham Mandelbaum (contemporary) printed a new edition of this work, adding to it his own *Pardes Yosef HaChadash* to *Bamidbar* and *Devarim,* maintaining the eclectic style of the original and entitling the set *Pardes Yosef HaShalem.*

Peninim MiBei Midrasha. R. Chaim Leib ben Dov. Halakhic and Talmudic comments on the verses of the Torah. Jerusalem, 1991.

Radak. R. David Kimchi (1160–1235). To the *N'vi'im.* In standard *Mikraot G'dolot* editions.

Ramban. R. Moshe ben Nachman (1194–1270) of Verona, Italy. Also authored *Chiddushim* to the Talmud and many other works. In standard *Mikraot G'dolot* editions.

Rashi. R. Shlomo ben Yitzchak (Yitzchaki) (1040–1105) of Troyes, France. Printed in most Hebrew editions of the Torah. Preeminent biblical and Talmudical commentator; also authored responsa.

> *Gur Aryeh.* R. Yehudah Loew (1525–1609). Known as the Maharal of Prague, he was the author of many halakhic and philosophical works, including *Netivot Olam* and *Derekh Chaim.*

Shevivei Eish al HaTorah. R. Shmuel Eliezer Stern. Halakhic essays arranged on the *parshiyot* of the Torah. Bnei Brak, 2006.

Shem MiShmuel. R. Shmuel Borenstein (1855–1926) of Sochatchov. Son of *Avnei Nezer,* who is frequently quoted in this work. Jerusalem, 1962.

Shiurei Leil Shishi. R. Yehudah Cohen. Halakhic essays arranged on the *parshiyot* of the Torah. Yeshivat Birkat Yitzchak.

Toldot Ya'akov. R. Chaim Ya'akov Varshno. Saloniki, 1762.

Torah Temimah. R. Baruch Epstein (1860–1942), Biblical commentary intended to display the unity of Oral and Written Torahs, citing most Talmudic and midrashic passages relevant to verses and adding a commentary analyzing the relationship. Also authored the biblical commentary *Tosefet Brakhah,* and *Baruch She'amar* to *Pirkei Avot* and a prayerbook. New York: Hebrew Publishing Co., 1925.

Yeshuot Kohen. R. Yehoshua Heshel Adler. Bnei Brak, 2023.

R. Samson Raphael Hirsch. (1808–1888) rabbi of the German Orthodox Community of Frankfurt Am Main and founder of the Torah Im Derekh Eretz Philosophy. Author of many other works. Feldheim Publishers, Jerusalem, 2010.

B. THE TALMUD AND COMMENTARIES–*RISHONIM*

The following commentators wrote on the Talmud (either directly or indirectly) and lived in the medieval era, preceding the *Shulchan Arukh.*

Ba'al HaIttur. R. Yitzchak ben Abba Mari (1122–1193) of Marseille, France.

Kaftor VaFerach. R. Ishtori HaParchi (1280–1355).

Maharam Chalavah. R. Moshe Chalava (d. c. 1370). Student of *Rashba.* Commentary to *Pesachim.*

Meiri. R. Menachem ben Shlomo HaMeiri (1249–1316), of Provence, France. Talmudic comments in *Chiddushei HaMeiri* and *Beit HaBechirah.*

Mordechai. R. Mordechai ben Hillel HaKohen (1240–1298) of Germany. In Vilna editions.

> *Bigdei Yesha.* Glosses of R. Yeshayahu HaLevi Horowitz, the *Shlah* (see Sec. M.).

Ohr Zarua. R. Yitzchak ben Moshe (c. 1200–c. 1270) of Vienna. Student of *Ra'avyah* and others.

Ra'avad. R. Avraham ben David (see Section E). Commentary to the *Rif* and to *Torat Kohanim.*

Ra'avyah. R. Eliezer ben Yoel HaLevi (1140–c. 1225) of Bonn.

Rabbenu David. R. David ben Reuven Bonfid (13th century). Student of Ramban. To *Pesachim.*

Rabbenu Yerucham. Rabbenu Yerucham ben Meshulam (1290–1350). Author of the *Sefer Toldot Adam V'Chavah.*

Rambam, Perush Mishnayot. R. Moshe ben Maimon (see Sec. E). Commentary to the *Mishnah.* In Vilna editions.

Ramban. R. Moshe ben Nachman (see Sec. A).

Ran. R. Nissim ben Reuven Gerondi (c. 1315–1376). Author of major commentaries to both the Talmud and to the Rif.

Rash MiSanz. R. Shimon ben Avraham (1150–c. 1214), prominent Tosafist and commentator to the *Mishnah.*

Rashba. R. Shlomo ben Adret (1235–1310) of Barcelona. Student of *Ramban* and *Rabbenu Yonah.* Also authored extensive responsa.

Rashbam. R. Shmuel ben Meir (1085–1158), grandson of Rashi. Troyes, France. One of the leading Tosafists, a running commentary of his is printed in the Vilna edition of tractates such as *Pesachim* and *Bava Batra.*

Rashi. R. Shlomo ben Yitzchak (see Sec. A). Printed alongside the text in standard Vilna editions.

Rif. R. Yitzchak Al Fasi (1013–1103) of Fez, Morocco. Authored a code of the halakhically relevant portions of the Talmud.

Ritva. R. Yom Tov ben Ishbilli (1250–1330). Also authored responsa.

Rosh. Rabbeinu Asher ben Yechiel (1250–1327), Germany. Code to halakhically relevant sections of the Talmud, and running commentary to *Masekhet Nedarim*. Father of the *Tur*.

> *Korban Netanel*. R. Netanel Weil (1687–1769).

Sefer HaTerumah. R. Baruch ben Yitzchak (c. 1140–1212), one of the Tosafists.

Sefer HaYashar. R. Yaakov ben Meir (1100–1171) known as Rabbenu Tam, grandson of Rashi and one of the most prominent of the Tosafists.

Shiltei Gibborim. R. Yehoshua Boaz; commentary to the *Rif* and the Mordechai.

Shittah Mekubetzet. Opinions of many *rishonim*, compiled by R. Betzalel Ashkenazi (d. 1592).

Tosafot. Talmudic comments of eleventh- and twelfth-century French and German scholars, printed alongside the text in the Vilna Talmud.

> *Maharam Shif*. R. Meir ben Yaakov HaKohen Shiff (1608–1644).

C. CODES OF MITZVOT AND HALAKHIC CODES OF *RISHONIM* AND *ACHARONIM*

Halakhot G'dolot. R. Shimon Kayyara (ninth century Babylonia).

Kol Bo. R. Aharon HaKohen (fourteenth century) of Luneil.

Metzudat David. Radbaz (see Sec. G).

Mitzvot Ra'ayah. R. Avraham Yitzchak HaKohen Kook (see *Mishpat Kohen*, Sec. G).

Sefer Chasidim. R. Yehudah HaChasid (1150–1217) of Regensberg Jerusalem: Mossad HaRav Kook, 1964.

Sefer HaChinnukh. Anonymous, but believed to be R. Aharon HaLevi of Barcelona.

Minchat Chinnukh. R. Yosef Babad (1800–1875) of Tarnopol.

Sefer HaMitzvot L'R. Sa'adiah Gaon. R. Sa'adiah Gaon (882–942).

Biur. R. Yerucham Fishel Perlow (1846–1934). Three volumes, Jerusalem: *Keter: Keren Sefarim Toraniyyim,* 1973.

Sefer HaMitzvot L'Rambam. R. Moshe ben Maimon; printed with most editions of the *Mishneh Torah.*

Ramban. R. Moshe ben Nachman (see Sec. A). In standard editions. Includes additional *mitzvot* the Rambam omits.

Sefer HaMitzvot Maharam Shik (see Sec. G).

Sefer Mitzvot Gadol. R. Moshe of Coucy (early thirteenth century). Known as the *Semag,* this work is divided into two sections, *Lavin* (prohibitions) and *Essin* (positive commandments).

Mishnat Avraham. R. Avraham Price. Three volumes, Toronto: *Yeshivat Torat Chaim,* 1972.

Sefer Yereim. R. Eliezer of Metz (ca 1115–1198). A discussion of the mitzvot following the listings of R. Yehudai Gaon and the *Ba'al Halakhot G'dolot,* divided into seven *amudim* (pillars). Also known as the *Re'em.* A French tosafist and student of Rabbeinu Tam.

Shi'iltot D'Rav Achai Gaon. R. Achai MiShabcha (680–760).

Ha'amek She'alah. R. Naftali Tzvi Yehudah Berlin (see *Ha'amek Davar,* Sec. A).

D. TALMUD COMMENTARIES–*ACHARONIM*

Commentaries to the Talmud written in the centuries after the *Shulchan Arukh.*

Ayn Ayeh. R. Avraham Yitzchak HaKohen Kook (see *Mishpat Kohen,* Sec. G).

Bartenura. R. Ovadiah (c. 1445– c. 1525) of Bartenura, popular commentator to the *Mishnah.*

Bekhor Shor. R. Alexander Sender Shor (1673–1737). Author of the *Tevuot Shor* to the laws of *Shechitah* and *Treifot.* Zolkova, 1840.

Chashukei Chemed. R. Yitzchak Zilberstein. 2007. Prominent contemporary halakhic authority.

Chatam Sofer. R. Moshe Sofer (see Sec. G). Pietrokov, 1903.

Chazon Yechezkel. R. Yechezkel Abramsky (1886–1976), student of R. Chaim Soloveitchik and head of the London Beth Din from 1934–1951. To the *Tosefta.* Jerusalem, 1948.

Chemdat Shlomo. R. Shlomo Zalman Lifshitz (1765–1839), first Chief Rabbi of Warsaw. Also authored responsa and published sermons under this title. Warsaw, 1851.

Chiddushei HaRim. R. Yitzchak Meir Alter (1789–1866). First Rebbe of Ger. Beit Shemesh: 1997.

Chiddushim U'Biurim al HaShas. R. Menachem Mendel Schneerson (1902–1994), seventh rebbe of Lubavitch.

Dibberot Moshe. R. Moshe Feinstein (see *Iggerot Moshe,* Sec. G).

Drush V'Chiddush. R. Akiva Eiger (see Sec. G).

Einayim L'Mishpat. R. Yitzchak Arieli (1896–1974), commentary expanding on citations of halakhic codifications of Talmudic passages. Jerusalem, 1994.

Geresh Yerachim. R. Aryeh Leib Tzintz (1768–1833). Petersburg, 1899.

Gilyonei HaShas. R. Yosef Engel (see *Otzerot Yosef,* Sec. H).

Hagahot Maharatz Chajes. R Zvi Hirsch Chajes (1805–1855), best known for his Introduction to the Talmud.

He'arot. R. Yosef Shalom Elyashiv. (see *Kovetz Teshuvot,* Sec. G).

Hon Ashir. R. Immanuel Chai Ricchi (1688–1743) of Italy. To the *Mishnah.*

Kehilot Ya'akov. R. Yisrael Ya'akov Kanievsky (d. 1985) of B'nei Brak, Israel. Known as the "Steipler Gaon" (after the town of Hornsteiple), he authored *Sha'arei Tevunah* in his youth, and his Kehilot Ya'akov, originally a ten-volume collection of essays, was later rearranged, revised, and expanded according to the tractates of the Talmud. Also authored *Birkat Peretz* to the Torah (see Section A) and served as a *Rosh Yeshivah* in the Yeshivah of Novardok.

Korban HaEdah. R. David ben Naphtali Frankel (1704–1762) of Prussia. To the Talmud Yerushalmi.

Kuntreisei Shiurim. R. Yisrael Ze'ev Gustman (1908–1991). Last *dayan* in Vilna before World War II and Rosh Yeshiva of *Netzach Yisrael* in Brooklyn and Jerusalem. Jerusalem, 1992.

Maginei Shlomo. R. Yehoshua Heshel ben Yosef (c. 1578–1648), defense of Rashi against the objections of the Tosafists. Also authored *Resp. P'nei Yehoshua.* Amsterdam, 1715.

Maharam Shik. R. Moshe Shik (see Sec. G.).

Maharash Cirilio. R. Shlomo Cirilio (16th century). To the Talmud Yerushalmi.

Maharsha, Chiddushei Aggadot, and *Chiddushei Halakhot.* R Shmuel Eidels (1555–1631).

Melekhet Shlomo. R. Shlomo Adani (1567–1624). To the *Mishnah.*

Meor Yisrael. R. Ovadiah Yosef (see *Yabbia Omer,* Sec. G.).

Minchat Asher. R. Asher Weiss. (see Sec. G).

Mishnah Achronah and *Mishnah Rishonah.* R. Ephraim Yitzchak (1761–1842) of Premislan. To the *Mishnah.*

Natan Piryo. R. Natan Gestetner. To several tractates, and sections of *Shulchan Arukh.* Bnei Brak, 1980 (see *L'Horot Natan,* Sec. G).

Nehor Shraga. R. Moshe Betzalel of Sochovalia. To *Massekhet Yevamot.* Vilna, 1872.

Nidrei Zeruzin. R. Shlomo Kluger. (see *HaElef L'kha Shlomo,* Sec. G).To *Massekhet Nedarim.* Zolkova, 1839.

P'nei Moshe. R. Moshe Margolies (c. 1710–1780). Commentary to the Talmud Yerushalmi.

P'nei Yehoshua. R. Ya'akov Yehoshua (1680–1756). Sudylkov, 1834. Subtitled *Apei Zuta* ("small face") to differentiate from the *Responsa P'nei Yehoshua* of his grandfather.

Rashash. R. Shmuel Strashoun (1794–1872) of Vilna. Printed in standard Vilna editions of the Talmud.

Sha'arei Chaim. R. Chaim Shmuelevitz (1902–1979), Rosh Yeshiva and Mashgiach of the Mir Yeshiva of Jerusalem, whose discourses are recorded in *Sichot Mussar.* Jerusalem, 1989.

Shenot Eliyahu. Gaon of Vilna (See *Biur HaGra,* Sec. F). To the *Mishnah.*

Shiurei R. Shmuel Rozovsky. R. Shmuel Rozovsky (1913–1979), student of R. Shimon Shkop and lecturer at the Ponevezh Yeshiva in Bnei Brak. To many *massekhtot,* in many collections and editions.

Siach Yitzchak. R. Yitzchak ben Zvi Hirsch Chayes (1538–1810). To *Massekhet Makkot.* Podgorze, 1900.

Tosafot Yom Tov. R. Yom Tov Lipmann Heller (1579–1654). Widely used commentary to the *Mishnah.*

Yachin (Tiferet Yisrael). R. Yisrael Lifshitz (1782–1860). Student of R. Akiva Eiger. Commentary to the *Mishnah* including sections entitled *Yachin* and *Boaz.*

Yam Shel Shlomo. R. Shlomo Luria (1510–1574) Prague, 1715. Known as *Maharshal,* he also authored the Talmudic commentary *Chokhmat Shlomo.*

E. THE RAMBAM'S MISHNEH TORAH AND COMMENTARIES

R. Moshe ben Maimon (1135–1204), known as the Rambam or as Maimonides, authored a codification of the laws in the Talmud, entitled *Mishneh Torah,* or *Yad HaChazakah.* The latter name is a reference to the organization of the work, which is arranged in fourteen volumes (the numerical value of the word *Yad* is fourteen). The following works are commentaries to the Rambam's code.

Avi Ezri. R. Eliezer Menachem Mann Shach (1899–2001), Rosh Yeshiva of the Ponevezh Yeshiva of Bnei Brak. Bnei Brak, 1995.

Chiddushei Rabbenu Chaim HaLevi al HaRambam. R. Chaim HaLevi Soloveitchik (1853–1918) of Brisk and the Volozhin Yeshiva. Originator of the method known as the Brisker Derekh. Jerusalem, 1997.

Derekh Emunah. R. Chaim Kanievsky (1928–2022). Bnei Brak, 1983.

Hagahot Maimoniyot. R. Meir HaKohen (thirteenth century), Rottenberg. Student of Maharam of Rottenberg.

Hasagot HaRa'avad. R. Avraham ben David (1120–1197) of Posquieres. Also authored commentaries to the *Rif* and the *Sifra,* and the *Ba'alei HaNefesh* to the laws of *Niddah.* In standard editions of the *Mishneh Torah.*

Kessef Mishneh. R. Yosef Karo (see *Shulchan Arukh,* Sec. F). In standard editions of the *Mishneh Torah.*

Lechem Mishneh. R. Avraham de Baton. Also authored *Responsa Lechem Rav* (see Sec. G). In standard editions.

Maggid Mishneh. R. Vidal Yom Tov (d. 1370) of Tolosa. In standard editions.

Ma'aseh Rokeach. R. Masud Rokeach (1690–1768).

Mishneh L'Melekh. R. Yehudah Rosannes (1657–1727). Conceptual commentary published in standard editions. Also authored *Parashat Derakhim* and *Derekh Mitzvotekha* on the *mitzvot.*

F. THE TUR AND SHULCHAN ARUKH AND COMMENTARIES

R Ya'akov ben Asher (ca. 1270–1340; son of the Rosh; see Section B) of Germany and Toledo, Spain, authored a codification of Jewish law entitled the *Arba'ah Turim* (the "four rows"; see *Shemot* 28:17), so named as it is divided into four sections: *Orach Chayim*, covering daily life, prayer, and festivals; *Even HaEzer*, on marital law; *Choshen Mishpat*, on civil law; and *Yoreh Deah*, covering the remaining areas of Jewish law, such as kashrut, *niddah*, mourning, vows, and other topics. Two centuries later, R. Yosef Karo (1488–1575), who authored the commentary *Beit Yosef* to the *Turim* (as well as *Kessef Mishneh* to *Mishneh Torah*), earned the title "the *Mechaber*" ("the Author") with his *Shulchan Arukh* ("set table"), which followed the organization of the *Turim* and took into account the rulings of the Rif, the Rosh, and the Rambam. However, the rulings are reflective primarily of the Sephardic background of their author, a fact rectified by R. Moshe Isserles (1520–1572), known as the Rama and author of *Darkhei Moshe* to the *Turim*, who wrote glosses, known as *Mappah* ("tablecloth"), to the *Shulchan Arukh*, representing Ashkenazic practice. Together with the Rama's glosses, the *Shulchan Arukh* has become accepted as the standard text of Jewish law, and the titles listed below are commentaries to that work (or the *Turim*, when indicated as such).

Arukh HaShulchan. R. Yechiel Michel Epstein (1829–1908), comprehensive code on all sections of the *Shulchan Arukh*, adding *Arukh HaShulchan HeAtid* to those areas not covered (ritual impurity, laws of agriculture relevant only in the land of Israel, sacrificial order, etc.). Rav of Novardok and father of *Torah Temimah* (see *Responsa B'nei Banim* 2:8, for a citation of the halakhic authority R. Yosef Eliyahu Henkin concerning the special qualities of this code). Warsaw, 1900–1912.

Avnei Miluim. R. Aryeh Leib Heller (see *Ketzot HaChoshen*, below). To *Even HaEzer*.

Bayit Chadash (*Bach*). R. Yoel Sirkes (1561–1640), Poland. Commentary to the *Tur*; also author of responsa (see later entries) and Talmudic emendations. Rav of Belz, Brest-Litovsk, and Krakow, and father-in-law of *Turei Zahav*.

Be'er Heitev. R. Yehudah ben Shimon Ashkenazi (eighteenth century). Amsterdam, 1742.

Be'er Heitev. R. Zechariah Mendel (d. 1706). Commentary digest of earlier authorities. Rav of Belz, Poland.

Biur HaGra. R. Eliyahu ben Shlomo Zalman (1720–1797). Towering scholar known as the *Gaon* of Vilna, or *Gra* (an acronym for *Gaon R. Eliyahu*). Author of more than eighty works.

Birkei Yosef. R. Chaim Yosef David Azulai (1724–1806), known as Chida. Author of many other works.

Chazon Ish. R. Avraham Yeshayah Karelitz (1878–1953), B'nei Brak, Israel. This seven-volume halakhic work actually combines the sections of the Talmud and the *Shulchan Arukh* and defies easy categorization. Bnei Brak, 1958. Also authored *Emunah UBitachon*.

Chelkat Mechokek. R. Moshe ben Yitzchak Yehudah Lima (c. 1615–c. 1670). To the beginning of *Even HaEzer*.

Chiddushei R. Akiva Eiger (see Sec. G). Compiled in several editions, printed in various editions of the *Shulchan Arukh*.

Chok Ya'akov. R. Yaakov Reischer (1661–1733) of Austria. To the laws of *Pesach*. Also authored *Resp. Shevut Ya'akov*.

Chokhmat Shlomo. R. Shlomo Kluger (see *HaElef L'kha Shlomo*, Sec. G).

Darkei Teshuvah. R. Tzvi Hirsch Schapiro (1850–1913), second rebbe of Munczatch. To *Yoreh Deah.*

Drishah and *Prishah.* R. Yehoshua Falk (1555–1614), of Lublin, Poland, and Lemberg, Germany. Commentaries to *Tur*. Also author of *Meirat Einayim* to *Shulchan Arukh.*

Eishel Avraham. R. Avraaham David Wahrman (1770–1840) of Butzchach.

Elyah Rabbah. R. Eliyahu Schapira (1660–1712).

Kaf HaChaim. R. Yaakov Chaim Sofer (1870–1939). Influential work of Sefardi *halakhah,* to *Orakh Chaim* and parts of *Yoreh Deah.*

Kerem Shlomo. R. Shlomo Haas. Jerusalem, 1974.

Kessef HaKodashim. R. Avraaham David Wahrman (see *Eishel Avraham*). To *Choshen Mishpat.*

Ketzot HaChoshen. R. Aryeh Leib Heller (1745–1812). Classic commentary to *Choshen Mishpat.* First published in Lviv, published both in standard editions of the *Shulchan Arukh* and stand-alone volumes as well as with super-commentaries. Frequent interlocutor with the *Netivot HaMishpat.*

Kitzur Shulchan Arukh. R. Shlomo Gantzfried (1802–1886). Warsaw, 1901.

Knesset HaGedolah. R. Chaim Beneviste (1603–1673). Jerusalem: *Keren l'Hotza'at Kol Sifrei Knesset HaG'dolah,* 1970.

Magen Avraham. R. Avraham Gumbiner (1637–1683) Poland. In standard editions.

> *Machatzit HaShekel.* R. Shmuel HaLevi of Kellin. In standard editions.

Magen Ha-Elef. R. Aryeh Leib Tzinz (c. 1768–1833) of Plotzk. To the laws of *Pesach.* Author of many works.

Mechokek Yehudah. R. Yehudah Leib Auerbach. To the laws of *Pesach.* Levov, 1791.

Mekor Chaim. R. Ya'akov Loerbaum (see *Netivot HaMishpat,* below). To laws of *Pesach.*

Mishnah Berurah. R. Yisrael Meir Kagan (1838–1933) of Radin. Commentary to the *Orach Chaim* section of the *Shulchan Arukh,* evaluating the positions of earlier authorities and arriving at conclusions. Includes the more in-depth *Biur Halakhah* and the *Sha'ar HaTziyyun,* listing sources. One of the preeminent moral authorities of the late eighteenth and early nineteenth centuries, he authored *Chafetz Chaim* (a name he came himself to be identified with) and *Ahavat Chesed* (see individual listings) as well as many other works, including *Likkutei Halakhot,* a three-part commentary to the Talmudical order *Kodoshim,* written in the style of *Mishnah Berurah.*

Netivot HaMishpat. R. Ya'akov Loerbaum (1770–1832) of Lisa. To *Choshen Mishpat.* Author of several works, including *Chavvot Da'at, Derekh Chaim, Beit Ya'akov, Torat Gittin, Emet l'Ya'akov, Mekor Chaim,* and others.

Nimmukei Orach Chaim. R. Chaim Elazar Schapiro (1871–1937), Munczaczer Rebbe. Jerusalem, 1998.

Orchot Chaim. R. Nachman Kahana (1861–1904) of Spinka. A compilation of the views of earlier authorities, with commentary, to *Orach Chaim.* Two volumes. Jerusalem: *Keter,* 1982.

Pitchei Teshuvah. R. Avraham Tzvi Hirsch ben Yaakov Eisenstadt (1812–1868) of Byalastok. Index of responsa arranged as commentary to the *Shulchan Arukh,* on *Yoreh Deah* (first pub. 1836), *Even HaEzer* (first pub. 1862) and *Choshen Mishpat* (first pub. posthumously 1876).

Pitchei Teshuvah to Orach Chaim. R. Yisrael Isser Isserlein (1827–1889) One of the rabbinical court judges in Vilna. To *Orach Chaim.*

Piskei HaMishpat. R. Simcha Yonah Klein. Summaries of responsa to *Choshen Mishpat.* Heichal HaMishpat: London, 2022.

Pri Chadash. R. Chezkiah da Silva (1659–1698). Printed in standard editions.

Pri Megadim. R. Yosef ben Meir Teomim (1727–1792), a supercommentary made up of commentaries to the *Taz (Mishbetzot Zahav),* the *Magen Avraham (Eshel Avraham),* and the *Shakh (Siftei Da'at).* In standard editions.

Sha'arei Teshuvah. R. Chaim Mordechai Margoliot (d. 1818) of Poland. To *Orach Chaim.* In standard editions.

Shulchan Arukh HaRav. R. Shneur Zalman of Liadi (1745–3813). First Rebbe of Lubavitch (Chabad) and author of the *Tania.*

Shvilei David. R. David Yehudah Zilberstein (d. 1884). Jerusalem, 1865.

Torat Chaim. R. Yaakov Shalom Sofer. To *Orach Chaim.* Paks, 1897.

Turei Zahav (Taz). R. David ben Shmuel HaLevi (1586–1667) of Krakow, Poland. Also authored a commentary to the Torah.

Urim V'Tumim. R. Yonatan Eibshutz (1690–1764) . To *Choshen Mishpat.* Jerusalem, 1968.

Yeshuot Ya'akov. R. Yaakov Meshulam Orenstein (1775–1839) of Levov. Also authored responsa. Zolkova, 1828.

Yosef Da'at. R. Yosef Shaul Nathanson (see *Shoel U'Meishiv,* Sec. G.).

Zayit Ra'anan. R. Moshe Yehudah Leib Zilberberg, Warsaw, 1869.

G. COLLECTIONS OF RESPONSA AND HALAKHIC AND TALMUDIC ESSAYS

The following works are either responsa, written to answer halakhic inquiries, or collections of essays on topics of halakhic and Talmudic analysis The titles of the works of responsa are generally preceded by the term *She'alot U'Teshuvot* ("Questions and Answers"), translated in the text as Responsa (or Resp.) and omitted in this listing.

Achiezer. R. Chaim Ozer Grodzenski (1863–1940). Three volumes. Vol. 1, Vilna, 1922; vol. 3, New York, 1946. Chief Rabbi of Vilna and leading halakhic authority of the pre-World War II era.

Agudat Ezov. R. Moshe Ze'ev Margolios (1767–1829). Vilna, 1885.

Afarkasta D'Anya. R. David Shperber (1877–1962) of Brashov. Jerusalem, 1991.

R. Akiva Eiger. R. Akiva Eiger (1761–1837) of Eisenstadt, Austria, and Posen, Poland. Two volumes of responsa. New York, 1945. One of the leading halakhic authorities of his time, he also authored glosses to *Shulchan Arukh,* as well as the Talmudic works *Chiddushim, Drush V'Chiddush,* and *Gilyon HaShas.*

Am Mordechai. R. Mordechai Willig (b. 1947) Rosh Yeshiva and Rosh Kollel at Yeshiva University and Rabbi of Young Israel of Riverdale, NY. Halakhic Essays in multiple volumes.

Arugat HaBosem. R. Moshe Greenwald (1853–1910) of Hungary, Chuster Rav. Svavalva, 1912.

Ashrei HaIsh. Rulings of R. Yosef Shalom Elyashiv, edited by R. Yechezkel Feinhandler. Jerusalem, 2017.

Ateret Chakhamim. R. Boruch Frankel-Teumim (1760–1828). Jozefow, 1866.

Ateret Ya'akov. R. Dovid Gottleib. Moriah Offset, Brooklyn, 2003.

Avkat Rochel. R. Yosef Karo (Author of *Shulchan Arukh,* see Sec. F). Leiptzig, 1859.

Avnei Chefetz. R. Aharon Levine (1879–1941), known as the Reisha Rav, author of *HaDrash ViHaIyun* on the Torah and *Birkat Aharon* on *Massekhet Berakhot.* Munich, 1947.

Avnei Derekh. R. Elchanan Naftali Prince. Jerusalem, 2010.

Avnei Nezer. R. Avraham Bornstein (1838–1910) first Sochachover Rebbe and author of *Eglei Tal* to the laws of *Shabbat.* Pietrikow, 1912.

Avnei Tzedek. R. Yekutiel Yehudah Teitelbaum (1808–1883). Lvov, 1885.

Az Nidberu. R. Binyamin Yehoshua Zilber. Fourteen volumes. Bnei Brak, 1969. Also authored several volumes of *mussar,* some anonymously.

B'Dvar Melekh. R. Yitzchak Raitport, Brooklyn, NY. 2015.

Badei Moshe. R. Moshe Williger. Jerusalem, 2014.

Be'er Halakhah. R. Eldad Sebag. Nveh HaTorah: Kiryat Arba, 2020.

Be'er Yitzchak. R. Yitzchak Elchanan Spektor (1817–1896) of Kovna. Preeminent halakhic authority of the late 19th century. Konigsberg, 1859.

Beit Av. R. Avraham Yudeliwitz (1850–1930). New York, 1919.

Beit Avi. R. Yitzchak Leibes. Av Beit Din of *Igud HaRabbanim.* New York, 1971.

Beit Ephraim. R. Ephraim Zalman Margolios (1760–1828). Also authored *Matteh Ephraim* and other works, including *Makneh U'Kinyan,* in defense of the position of his grandfather, the *Bekhor Shor,* regarding *ha'aramot* and Torah law. Lvov, 1818.

Beit HaLevi. R. Yosef Dov Soloveitchik (1820–1892) of Brisk. Rosh Yeshiva of Volozhin. Vilna, 1863.

Beit Ridbaz. R. Yaakov David Wilovsky (1845–1913), *Jerusalem,* 1908.

Beit She'arim. R. Amram Blum. Jerusalem, 2001.

Beit Shlomo. R. Shlomo Drimmer (1800–1872). Also authored *Yashresh Ya'akov* to *Yevamot.* Lvov, 1891.

Beit Yitzchak. R. Yitzchak Shmelkes (1828–1905). Przemysl, 1875.

Bigdei Yesha. R. Shmuel ben Yosef HaLevi of Bialostock. Vilna, 1844.

Bigdei Yom Tov. R. Yom Tov Krispin (17th Century). Izmir, 1874.

B'ikvei HaTzon. R. Hershel Schachter (b. 1941) Rosh Yeshiva and Rosh Kollel at Yeshiva University. New York, 1997.

Binyan Av. R. Eliyahu Bakshi-Doron. Six volumes. Haifa, Israel, 1983. Former Sefardic Chief Rabbi of Israel.

Binyan Olam. R. Yitzchak Eizek Chaver (1789–1852). Author of works in *Halakhah* and Kaballah, Warsaw, 1851.

Binyan Tziyon. R. Yaakov Etlinger (1798–1871) of Altona. Also authored *Arukh LaNer* to several tractates, and *Minchat Ani.* Altona, 1868.

Birkhat Retzeh. R. Zvi Hirsch Orenshtein. Lvov, 1889.

> *Milchamot Aryeh.* R. Aryeh Leib Broide. Glosses printed with the above.

Birkat Yosef. R. Yosef Landa. Lvov, 1869.

B'Netivot HaHalakhah. R. J. David Bleich (b. 1936). Rosh Kollel of the Yadin Yadin Kollel of Yeshiva University. Also authored *Contemporary Halakhic Problems* and many other works. Four volumes. Yeshiva University Press: New York, NY.

B'Ohalah Shel Torah. R. Ya'akov Ariel (contemporary.) Machon haTorah V'HaAretz, 1997.

B'Tzel HaChokhmah. R. Betzalel Stern (d. 1989) of Vienna, Melbourne, Australia, and Jerusalem. Six volumes. Jerusalem, 1967.

Chatam Sofer. R. Moshe Sofer (1763–1830). Responsa to the four sections of *Shulchan Arukh* and additional volumes. Vienna, 1855. Rav of Pressburg and one of the leading halakhic authorities of his time, he became the son-in-law of R. Akiva Eiger and ancestor to a long line of rabbinic scholars, beginning with his son *K'tav Sofer.* Also authored *chiddushim* to the Talmud and *Shulchan Arukh,* and *Torat Moshe* to the Torah.

> *Likutei Hearot.* R. Yissachar Dov Goldstein1988–1915)). Jerusalem, 1980.

Chavalim B'Ne'imim. R. Yehudah Leib Graubart (1861–1937) of Toronto. Pietrikow, 1901.

Chavatzelet HaSharon. R. David Menachem Manish Babad (1865–1937). Bilgoraj, 1931.

Chavvot Yair. R. Yair Chaim Bachrach (1639–1702) of Moravia. Lemberg, 1894.

Chayei Aryeh. R. Chaim Aryeh Leibush Horowitz. Krakow, 1890.

Cheker Halakhah. R. Naftali Hertz Landau. Lemberg, 1888.

Cheker Halakhah. R. Yitzchak Mandel. Machon Cheker Halakhah, Monroe, NY, 1999.

Chelkat Yaakov. R. Mordechai Yaakov Breisch (1896–1976) of Zurich, Switzerland. Tel Aviv, 1992.

Chelkat Yoav. R. Yoav Yehoshua Weingarten (1847–1922) of Kinsk. Responsa, including the *Kava D'Kashyata,* a collection of 103 Talmudic questions that has on its own inspired several books responding to its challenges. Edited, footnoted, and indexed by R. David Avraham Mandelbaum. Jerusalem: *Makhon L'Hantzachat Moreshet Chakhmei Polin,* 1997.

Chemdat Shlomo. R. Shlomo Zalman Lifshitz (1765–1839) (See Sec. D). Warsaw, 1836.

Chesed L'Avraham. R. Avraham Teomim (1814–1868). Lvov, 1898.

Cheshev HaEphod. R. Chanoch Padwa2000–1908)) of London. Jerusalem, 1963.

Chidushei R. Zelig Reuven Bengis. R. Zelig Reuven Bengis (1864–1953) Chief Rabbi of Jerusalem for the Edah Chareidis, author of *Leflagot Reuven.* Jerusalem, 1984.

Chikrei Halakhah V'Shut. R. Shmuel Mohilever (1824–1898), one of the pioneers of religious Zionism. Jerusalem 1944.

Chinnukh Beit Yehudah. R. Yaakov Tzvi Yalis (1778–1826). Warsaw, 1869.

Chut HaMeshulash. Collection of the responsa of R. Chaim of Volozhin (1749–1821), together with those of his son-in-law R. Hillel of Horodna and his grandson R. Eliezer Yitzchak of Volozhin. Vilna, 1882.

Derekh Yesharah. R. Yitzchak Yedidyah Frankel. Tel Aviv, 1981.

Divrei Chaim. R. Chaim Halberstam (1793–1876), first Sanzer Rebbe. Zholkva, 1864.

Divrei David. R. David Taharani. Beitar Ilit, 2015.

Divrei Malkiel. R. Malkiel Zvi Tanenbaum of Lomza, Poland. Seven volumes. Vilna, 1901.

Divrei Nechemiah. R. Nechemiah Ginsberg. Vilna, 1866.

Divrei Rinanah. R. Natan Note Kahane. New York, 1984.

Divrei Shlomo. R. Shlomo Shneider. (d. 1995) of Monticello, NY. Six volumes. Brooklyn, NY, 2000.

Divrei Ta'am. R. Aryeh Leib Houpt. Warsaw, 1904.

Divrei Yatziv. R. Yekutiel Yehudah Halberstam, Sanz-Klausenberger Rebbe. Netanya: Machon Shefa Chaim, 1996.

Divrei Yoel. R. Yoel Teitelbaum (1887–1979), first Satmar Rebbe. New York, 1947.

Dovev Meisharim. R. Dov Berish Weidenfeld (1881–1965), Rabbi of Tshebin. Jerusalem, 2011.

D'var Yehoshua. R. Yehoshua Menachem Ehrenberg (1904–1976) of Tel Aviv. Jerusalem, 1970.

Edut L'Ya'akov. R. Ya'akov DiBoton.

R. Eliezer V'Chidushav. R. Eliezer Gordon (1841–1910), rabbi and Rosh Yeshiva of Telz. Pietrokov, 1913.

Emek Halakhah. R. Tuviah Goldstein. Rosh Yeshiva of Emek Halakhah. 2008.

Emek Shealah. R. Mordechai Dov Twerski. Pietrikow, 1906.

Erekh Shai. R. Shlomo Yehudah Tabak. Sighet, 1909.

Eretz HaTzvi. R. Hershel Schachter (see *B'Ikvei HaTzon,* above) Yeshiva University Press: New York, 1992.

Eretz Tzvi. R. Tzvi Hirsch Frimer, Kozhaglover Rav. Student of the *Avnei Nezer* and Rosh Yeshiva of Yeshivat Chachmei Lublin. Lublin, 1939.

Even Pinah. R. Ben Tzion Nesher. Tel Aviv, 1994.

Even Shitiyah. R. Eliezer ben Shabtai Don Yichiya. Vilna, 1893.

Even Yikarah. R. Binyamin Aryeh HaKohen Weiss. Lemberg, 1894.

R. Ezriel. R. Ezriel Hildesheimer (1820–1899) . Tel Aviv, 1969.

Gan Shoshanim. R. Menachem Genack (Jerusalem, 1992),

Ginat Veradim. R. Avraham HaLevi (c.1650–1712) of Egypt. Jerusalem, 2008.

HaBari V'HaShema. R. Yekutiel Zeev Graus. Brooklyn, NY, 2019.

HaElef Likha Shlomo. R. Shlomo Kluger (1785–1869) Rabbi of Brody, Galicia, and other cities and author of many other works. Bnei Brak, 2016.

HaGry"I Herzog. R. Yitzchak Isaac HaLevi Herzog (1888–1959), Chief Rabbi of Israel from 1948–1959. Author of many works of responsa and *halakhah* addressing issues of the modern State of Israel.

Halakhot Ketanot. R. Yisrael Ya'akov Chagiz (1620–1674). Venice, 1704.

Har HaKarmel. R. Eliyahu ben Yechezkel of Belgore. Frankfurt on the Oder, 1782.

Har Tzvi. R. Zvi Pesach Frank (1873–1960), Chief Rabbi of Jerusalem from 1936–1960. Jerusalem 2009.

Harei Besamim. R. Aryeh Leib Horowitz. Lvov, 1883.

HaSaba Kadisha. R. Shlomo Eliezer Alipandri. Jerusalem, 1973,

Heikhal Hora'ah. R. Moshe Bransdorfer. Jerusalem, 2014.

Heikhal Yitzchak. R. Yitzchak Isaac HaLevi Herzog (see above). Jerusalem, 1960.

Hekhalei Shein. R. Shalom Dov Ber Grinzon. Warsaw, 1869.

Hitorerut Teshuvah. R. Shimon (Eiger) Sofer (1850–1944). Four volumes, accompanied by the commentary *Ikvei Sofer* of the author's grandson R. Akiva Menachem Sofer. Jerusalem: *Makhon Cha*tam Sofer, 1990. Grandson of *Chatam Sofer* and son of *Ketav Sofer.*

> *Ikvei Sofer.* R. Akiva Menachem Sofer. Glosses to the above by the grandson of the author, printed on the bottom of the page.

Hosif Moshe. R. Moshe Friedman. Brooklyn, 2006.

Iggerot Moshe. R. Moshe Feinstein (1895–1986) of Luban, Poland, and New York, NY. Eight volumes of responsa, beginning in 1961, New York. Considered one of the leading authorities of the late twentieth century, he was *Rosh Yeshivah* of Mesivta Tiferet Yerushalayim in the Lower East Side of Manhattan and also authored *Dibrot Moshe* to several volumes of the Talmud.

Igra Ramah. R. Meshulam Igra (1752–1802). Lemberg, 1873.

Imrei Avraham. R. Avraham Englard. Jerusalem, 1997.

Imrei Noam. R. Meir Horowitz (1877–1819) of Zikiv. Przemysl, 1878.

Imrei Shefer. R. Eliyahu Kalatzkin (see *Even Pinah*). Warsaw, 1896.

Imrei Yosher. R. Meir Arik (1855–1925). Munczacz. 1913.

Kanfei Yonah. R. Yona Reiss, Av Beit Din of the Chicago Rabbinical Council. RIETS Press: New York.

Kapei Aharon. R. Aharon Azriel (1819–1879). Jerusalem, 1874.

Keren L'David. R. Eliezer David Greenwald (1867–1927). Satu Mare, 1929.

K'tav Sofer. R. Avraham Shmuel Binyamin Sofer (1815–1871). Pressburg, 1873. Son of the *Chatam Sofer,* he also authored *chiddushim* to the Torah and to the tractate *Chullin.*

Kinyan Torah BaHalakhah. R. Avraham David Horowitz of Strasskurg, France, and later a rabbinical court judge in Jerusalem. Eight volumes.

Kol Mevaser. R. Meshulam Roth (1875–1962). Jerusalem, 1962.

Kovetz Teshuvot. R. Yosef Shalom Elyashiv (1910–2012), preeminent halakhic authority of that era. Jerusalem, 2003.

Kol Kitvei HaRav Henkin. R. Yosef Eliyahu Henkin (1881–1973). Collection of the halakhic writings of one of the most prominent authorities in America in the early 20th century.

Lachmei Todah. R. Yeshayahu Bassan. Venice, 1741.

Lev Aryeh. R. Aryeh Leib Grosnas of the London Beth Din. London, 1958.

Levushei Mordechai. R. Mordechai Leib Winkler (1844–1932). Budapest, 1913.

L'Horot Natan. R. Natan Gestetner (contemporary) of Bnei Brak, Israel. Seventeen volumes of responsa. Bnei Brak, 1973. Also authored many other works, such as commentaries of the same name to the Torah and *Pirkei Avot* and the festivals, and *Natan Piryo* to tractates of the Talmud and sections of the *Shulchan Arukh* (see individual listings).

Mabbit. R. Moshe ben Yosef di Trani (1500–1580). Lvov, 1861.

Machaneh Chaim. R. Chaim ben Mordechai Ephraim Fishel Sofer. Bratislava, 1862.

Machzeh Avraham. R. Avraham Menachem Menachem Steinberg (1848–1928). New York, 1927.

Maharam bar Baruch. R. Meir Bar Baruch (c. 1215–1293) of Rotenberg. Budapest, 1896.

Maharam Brisk. R. Mordechai ben Yehoshua Brisk. Tasnad, 1939.

Maharam Galanti. R. Moshe Galanti. Jerusalem, 1988.

Maharam Mintz. R. Moshe Mintz (c. 1435–1485) of Poland and Germany. Krakow, 1637.

Maharam MiRotenberg. R. Meir ben Baruch HaLevi (1320–1390) of Rottenberg. Berlin, 1891. Rebbe of the Rosh and the Mordechai.

Maharam MiRotenberg HaAcharonim. R. Moshe Rotenburg. Lvov, 1857.

Maharam Shik. R. Moshe Shik (1807–1879) of Hungary. Prominent student of *Chatam Sofer.*

Maharash Engel. R. Shmuel Engel. Seven volumes. Bardiov, 1926.

Mahari HaKohen. R. Yisrael ben Avraham Abele Rappaport. Lemberg, 1869.

Mahari Veil. R. Yaakov ben Yehudah Veil (c. 1385–1460) of Germany. Venice, 1549.

Maharia HaLevi. R. Yitzchak Aharon HaLevi Etinga. Lvov, 1893.

Maharik. R. Yosef Kolon (1420–1480). New York: Y. Ze'ev, 1957

Maharil. R. Yaakov ben Moshe HaLevi Molin (b. 1427). Krakow, 1881.

Maharil Diskin. R. Moshe Yehoshua Yehudah Leib Diskin (1818–1898). Jerusalem: *Chedvat Yisrael,* 1911. Rav of Brisk.

Maharit. R. Yosef Trani (1568–1639) of Greece. Lvov, 1861.

Maharash. R. Alexander Shmuel Halperin. Lvov, 1896.

Maharash Engel. R. Shmuel Engel (1853–1935). Berditchev, 1926.

Mahariaz Enzil.. R. Yekutiel Asher Zalman Enzil Zausmer (d. 1858). Lvov, 1882.

Maharshag. R. Shimon Greenfield (1881–1930). Vernov, 1931.

Maharsham. R. Shalom Mordechai Shwadron (see *Da'at Torah,* Sec. F).

Maharashdam. R. Shmuel Di Medina (1506–1589). Rav of Salonica, Greece, and cities in Turkey.

Mareh Yechezkel. R. Yechezkel Paneth (1783–1845). Sighet, 1875.

Mas'at Binyamin. R. Binyamin Aharon Solnick (1530–1620). Vilna, 1894.

Matat Yado. R. Matityahu Madanitzsky. Vilna, 1882.

Mayim Chaim. R. Chaim David HaLevi. Tel Aviv, 1991.

Mayim Chaim. R. Chaim Rappaport. Zitomir, 1919.

Mayim Chaim. R. Yosef Mashash (1892–1974). Fes, 1934.

Mei Be'er. R. Yitzchak Eizek Shor. Lvov, 1891.

Meishiv B'Halakhah. R. Yechiel Tauber, et al. Machon L'Hora'ah: Monsey, NY 1982.

Meshiv Davar. R. Naftali Tzvi Yehudah Berlin. Warsaw, 1849 (see *Ha'amek Davar,* Section A).

Meishiv Mishpat R. Ovadiah Yosef Toledano. Grandson of R. Ovadiah Yosef. 3 Volumes. Machon Et Yosef, 2018.

Meishiv Shalom. R. Shalom Yosef Feigenbaum. Bilgorag, 1931.

Rabbenu Meshulam Igra. R. Meshulam Igra1802–1752)). Warsaw, 1885.

Mekor Baruch. R. Baruch Kelai (d. 1597). Izmir, 1659.

Minchat Asher. R. Asher Weiss (b. 1953). Prominent contemporary authority and author of volumes in all areas of Torah under this title. Jerusalem: Machon Minchat Asher, 2012.

Minchat Avraham. R. Avraham Elkana Schapira (c. 1910–2007), Ashkenazi Chief Rabbi of Israel from 1983–1993 and Rosh Yeshiva of Mercaz HaRav. Jerusalem, 1990.

Minchat Aviv. R. Aharon Lichtenstein (1933–2015), Rosh Yeshiva of Yeshivat Har Etzion. Collected Halakhic Essays. Edited by Elyakim Krumbein, Maggid Books, 2014.

Minchat Chen. R. Noach Isaac Oelbaum. Jerusalem, 2022.

Minchat David. R. David Rozenberg of Monroe, NY. Four volumes. Brooklyn, 1979.

Minchat Elazar. R. Chaim Elazar Schapiro (1871–1937). Munczaczer Rebbe. Jerusalem, 1996.

Minchat Machvat. R. Mordechai Babad. Jerusalem, 1989.

Minchat Shai. R. Shmuel Yitzchak Shor (1842–1902). Lvov, 1891.

Minchat Shlomo. R. Shlomo Zalman Auerbach (1910–1995), preeminent halakhic authority of his generation. Jerusalem, 1999.

Minchat Yitzchak. R. Yitzchak Weiss (1902–1989). Ten volumes of responsa. London, 1955. Rabbinical court judge in Manchester, England, and later Rav of *Edah HaChareidis* in Jerusalem.

Mishkan Shilo. R. Shilo Raphael (1940–1994). Rabbinical Court Judge. Collection of halakhic essays. Jerusalem: Mossad HaRav Kook, 1996.

Mishkenot Ya'akov. R. Ya'akov Bruchin (1780–1844) of Karlin. Jerusalem: *Keren Orah*, 1960.

Mishnah Sakhir. R. Yissochor Shlomo Teichtal (1885–1945). Author of *Eim HaBanim Shemeikhah.* Jerusalem, 1986.

Mishnah Shleimah. R. Shlomo Gross. Rabbinical court judge of Belzer Chasidim of Boro Park, Brooklyn, NY. Jerusalem, 1991.

Mishnat Nechemiah. R. Zalman Nechemiah Goldberg (1931–2020). Rabbinical Court Judge. Collected adapted lectures. Jerusalem, 2021.

Mishnat Shalom. R. Shalom Pollak. 2008.

Mishnat Yosef. R. Yosef Lieberman. Jerusalem; Machon Yerushalaim, 1979.

Mishneh Halakhot. R. Menashe Klein. Machon Mishneh Halakhot Gedolot, 2000

Mishpat Kohen. R. Avraham Yitzchak HaKohen Kook (1865–1935) first Ashkenazi Chief Rabbi of modern Israel. Jerusalem, 1966.

Mishpetei HaTorah. R. Tzvi Shpitz. Jerusalem, 1998.

Nachalat Yaakov. R. Ya'akov of Lisa (see *Netivot HaMishpat,* Section F) New York, 1961.

R. Nachum Tributsch. R. Nachum Tributsch. Jerusalem: Machon Yerushalayim, 1989.

Naharei Afarsimon. R. Jacob Tennenbaum (1832–1897). Paks, 1911.

Ne'ot Deshe. R. David Shlomo Eibshutz. Jerusalem, 1962.

Neta Sha'ashuim. R. Tzvi Hirsch ben Yaakov Karo. Zholkva, 1829.

Neta Sorek. R. Shraga Tzvi Tenneboim (1826–1897). Munkatch, 1899.

Netzach Yisrael. R. Yisrael Grossman. Jerusalem, 1986.

Nishal David. R. David Oppenheim (1664–1736). Jerusalem, 1982.

Nishmat Chaim. R. Chaim Berlin (1832–1912). Jerusalem, 2008.

Ohalei Ya'akov. R. Ya'akov Elyah Undsdorfer. Montreal, 2018.

Ohel Moshe. R. Moshe Tzweig (1909–163). Jerusalem, 1960.

Ohr LeTziyon. R. Abba Ben Tzion Shaul (1924–1998). Jerusalem, 1986.

Oneg Yom Tov. R. Yom Tov Lipman Heilpern (1816–1879). Vilna, 1889.

Ori V'Yishi. R. Uri Shraga Feivel Toibes. Lvov, 1886.

Osef Chiddushei Torah MiMaran HaGra Kotler. R. Aharon Kotler (1892–1962), founder of Beth Medrash Govoha of Lakewood, NJ. Collected essays. Jerusalem: Oraysoh, 1983.

Panim Me'irot. R. Meir Eisenstadt (1670–1744). Amsterdam, 1715.

P'nei Meivin. R. Netanel Fried (1857–1916). Munkatch, 1913.

P'nei Moshe. R. Moshe Benveneshti (1606–1677). Kusthe, 1674.

P'nei Yehoshua. R. Yehoshua of Krakow (1593–1648). Jerusalem, 1982.

Pri HaSadeh. R. Eliezer Chaim Deutsch of Bonyhad, Hungary. Paks, 1906.

Pri Tevuah. R. Yehudah Leib Margolios (1747–1811). Noviy Dvor, 1796.

Radbaz. R. David ben Zimra (1479–1573), Chief Rabbi of Egypt. Also authored commentary to *Mishneh Torah.* Warsaw, 1862.

Rabbenu Yosef M'Slutzk. R. Yosef ben Meir Feimer. Jerusalem: Machon Yerushalayim, 2000.

Ramatz. R. Meir Tzvi Vitmeir. Przemysl, 1872.

Rashba. R. Shlomo ben Adret (1235–1310, see Sec. B) Bnei Brak, 1958.

Rashbash. R. Shlomo ben Shimon Doron (1400–1467). Levoro, 1742.

Ratz KaTzvi. R. Zvi Ryzman (Contemporary). Los Angeles, 2005.

R. Eliyahu Mizrachi (R'em). R. Eliyahu Mizrachi (c. 1450–1526) Jerusalem, 1938.

Rav Poalim. R. Yosef Chaim ben Eliyah (1834–1909) of Baghdad. Jerusalem, 1901.

Reishit Bikkurim. R. Betzalel HaKohen (1820–1878). Vilna, 1869

Rivash. R. Yitzchak ben R. Sheshet (1326–1407) of Barcelona, Spain. Costantine, 1547.

Rosh. R. Ashen ben Yechiel (see Sec. B). Jerusalem: Machon Yerushalayim, 1994.

Rosh Eliyahu. R. Eliyahu Katz. Bnei Brak, 2008.

Sefer Yehoshua. R. Yehoshua Babad. Zolkoa, 1829.

Sha'agat Aryeh. R. Aryeh Leib ben Asher Gunzberg (1695–1785). Warsaw, 1869.

Sha'arei Deah. R. Chaim Yehudah Leib Levitan. Lvov, 1878.

Sha'arei Tzedek. R. Menachem Mendel Paneth. Munkach, 1884.

Sha'arei Tziyon. R. Ben Tziyon Shternfeld. Petrikow, 1903.

Shavei Tziyon. R. Ben Tziyon Nesher. Jerusalem, 1985.

She'alat David. R. David Friedman (1828–1915) of Karlin. Petrikow, 1913.

She'alat Shalom. R. Shalom Toibesh. Zholkva, 1869.

She'alat Yitzchak. R. Yitzchak ben Zev Moshe Elbaum (d. 1986). Galante, 1949.

She'ali Tziyon. R. Dov Eliezerov. Jerusalem, 1962.

She'erit Yosef. R. Shlomo Wahrman (1926–2013), Rosh Yeshiva of the Hebrew Academy of Nassau County (HANC). Talmudic Essays. Far Rockaway, NY, 1977.

She'erit Yosef. R. Yosef Yedidiah HaLevi (1866–1930). New York, 1977.

Shem Aryeh. R. Aryeh Leibish Balhubar. Vilna, 1873.

Shem Olam. R. Moshe Shalom Stahl. Riga, 1925.

Shem MiShmuel. R. Shmuel Heller (1803–1884) of Tzfat. Jerusalem, 1979.

Shemen HaMor. R. Mordechai Robbio, rabbi of Chevron in the 18th century. Levorno, 1793.

Shenot Chaim. R. Shlomo Kluger (see *HaElef Likha Shlomo,* above). Lvov, 1856.

Shevet HaKehati. R. Shammai Kehat Gross (contemporary), of *Khal Maclzikei HaDas* (Belz), Israel. Five volumes. Jerusalem: Orayta, 1987.

Shevet HaLevi. R. Shmuel HaLevi Wosner (1913–2015). Bnei Brak, 1969.

Shevivei Eish. R. Shmuel Eliezer Stern. Heichalei Torah, 2021.

Shivat Tziyon. R. Shmuel Landau. Warsaw, 1913.

Shvut Ya'akov. R. Yaakov Reischer (c1670–1733). Lvov, 1897. Rav of Prague and other cities.

Shoalin V'Dorshin. R. Eliyahu Shlesinger. Jerusalem, 1997.

Shoel B'Shlomo. R. Asher Bush. New York, 2005.

Sho'el U'Meishiv. R. Yosef Shaul Nathanson (1810–1875), of Lemberg. Brooklyn, NY: *Harrirei Kodesh,* 1994. Also authored *Yad Shaul* to *Shulchan Arukh* and *Divrei Shaul* to the Torah.

Shraga HaMeir. R. Shraga Feivel Shneebalg of Stamford Hill, London, England. Eight volumes. Bnei Brak: Friedman, 1972. Also authored *Beit Pinchas* to the Torah and other works.

Shulchan HaLevi. R. Yisrael Belsky (1938–2016) Rosh Yeshiva of Torah VoDaas and Posek for the Orthodox Union. Modi'in Ilit: Mekhon Simchat HaTorah, 2011.

Shulchan Menachem. Collected rulings of R. Menachem Mendel Schneerson (1902–1994), the Lubavicher Rebbe. Jerusalem: Heichal Menachem, 2013.

Simchah L'Ish. R. Yaakov Shaul Elyashir (1817–1906). Jerusalem, 1888.

Tashbetz. R. Shimon ben Tzemach Duran (1361–1444). Lvov, 1891.

Terumat HaDeshen. R. Yisrael Isserlein (1390–1460) of Germany. New York, 1958.

Teshurat Shai. R. Shlomo Yehudah Tabak (1832–1907). Sighet, 1905.

Teshuvah MeAhavah. R. Eliezer Flekels (1754–1826), a student of *Noda B'Yehudah*. Prague, 1815.

Teshuvot VeHanhagot. R. Moshe Sternbuch (contemporary) of Johannesberg, South Africa, and Har Nof, Jerusalem. Seven volumes. Jerusalem, *Netivot HaTorah V'HaChesed*, 1986. Author of several works, such as *Ta'am V'Da'at* to the Torah; *Mo'adim U'Z'mannim* (see Section H); *P'shat V'HaIyyun* to the Talmud; and other works.

Tiferet Tzvi/Maharatz. R. Zvi Hirsch Bishko. Yozifov, 1866.

Tirosh V'Yitzhar. R. Tzvi Yechezkel Michaelson (1863–1942). Bilgoraj, 1937.

Torat Michael. R. Michael Forshlager. Jerusalem, 1960.

Torat Rabbenu Shmuel Salant. R. Shmuel Salant (1816–1909), rabbi of Jerusalem. Tel Aviv, 1953.

Tuv Ta'am Ve-Da'at. R. Shlomo Kluger (see *HaElef Likha Shlomo,* above). Lvov, 1852.

Tzemach Tzedek. R. Menachem Mendel ben Shalom Shachna Schneerson (1789–1866), third Lubavitcher Rebbe. New York: Otzar Chasidim, 1994.

Tzemach Tzedek. R. Menachem Mendel Krochmal (c. 1600–1661) of Nikolsburg. Amsterdam, 1675.

Tzitz Eliezer. R. Eliezer Yehudah Waldenberg. Twenty-one volumes, beginning Jerusalem, 1944.

Tzur Ya'akov. R. Avraham Yaakov HaLevi Horowitz. Jerusalem, 1955.

Tzvi V'Chamid. R. Yaakov Tzvi Waldman. Brooklyn, NY: Talpiot, 2009.

VaYa'an David. R. Chaim Yosef David Weiss. Jerusalem, 1996.

VaYashev Moshe. R. Moshe Ze'ev Zorger. Jerusalem, 1986.

V'Shav V'Rapha. R. Raphael Evers (b. 1954) of the Netherlands and Germany. Jerusalem, 2008.

Yabbia Omer and *Yechaveh Da'at.* R. Ovadiah Yosef (1920–2013), Sefardi Chief Rabbi of Israel (1973–1983). Yechaveh Da'at is based on his radio lectures. Jerusalem, 1976.

Yachel Yisrael. R. Yisrael Meir Lau (b. 1937), Ashkenazi Chief Rabbi of Israel from 1993–2003. Jerusalem: Yeshivat Chayei Moshe, 1992.

Yad HaLevi. R. Yosef Dov Levine (1866–1946). New York, 1949.

Yad Ramah. R. Moshe Hirsch Fuchs. Oradea Mare, 1940.

Yalkut Shiurim. R. Shaul Alter (b. 1957), founder and leader of Kehilas Pnei Menachem. Israel, 2017.

Yashiv Yitzchak. R. Yitzchak Shmuel Schechter (contemporary) More than 50 volumes, Kiryat Sanz, Netanyah: Machon Yashiv Yitzchak, 1998.

Yedidyah Taiah Weill. Yedidyah Taiah Weill (1721–1805). Jersualem, 1983.

Yehudah Ya'aleh. R. Yehudah Assad (1797–1866). Rav of Rete and Semnitz. Pressburg, 1880, and Bnei Brak, 1985. Student of R. Mordechai Benet.

Yeshuot Malko. R. Yisrael Yehoshua Trunk (1820–1893) of Kutno. Petrikow, 1927.

Zayit Ra'anan. R. Moshe Yehudah Leib Zilberberg. Warsaw, 1869.

Zekan Aharon. R. Aharon Walkin (1864–1940). New York, 1958.

Zekher Menachem. R. Zechariah Gelley, rabbi of Khal Adath Jeshurun of Washington Heights, NY. Lakewood: Machon Be'er HaTorah, 2008.

Zekher Yehosef. R. Yosef Zechariah Stern. Warsaw, 1899.

Zikhron Yehudah. R. Yehudah Greenwald (1849–1920). Budapest, 1923.

Zivchei Shlomo. R. Shlomo Zalman Freidman. Bnei Brak, 1984.

H. WORKS OF *HALAKHAH*

Ahavat Chesed. R. Yisrael Meir Kagan. (see *Mishnah Berurah,* Section F). Rulings on the laws of lovingkindness. Pietrikow, 1907.

> *Orchot Chesed.* R. Yehudah Dov Rotner. Glosses to the above. Israel, 2016.

Artzot HaChaim. R. Meir Leibush Malbim (see Sec. A). To the beginning of *Orach Chaim.* Breslau, 1837.

Avnei Shoham. R. Yesahayu Slomowitz of Antwerp. Essays on topics of the festivals. Antwerp, 2018.

Batei Yosef. Halakhic Rulings from the Roshei Yeshiva of the Rabbi Isaac Elchanan Theological Seminary, in the tradition of R. Joseph B. Soloveitchik. New York: RIETS/Yeshiva University Press, 2022.

Beit Matityahu, ribbit. R. Mattityahu Hirschman. To the laws of prohibited interest. Jerusalem, 2001.

Ben Ish Chai. R. Yosef Chaim ben Eliyahu of Baghdad (1834–1909). Bagdhad, 1912.

Birkat Moshe. R. Moshe Druk. Essays on the Festivals. Jerusalem, 2012.

Birkat Mo'adekha: Pesach-Shavuot. R. Shlomo Zalman Shmayah. Jerusalem, 2001.

Birur Halakhah. R. Yechiel Avraham Zilber. Bnei Brak, 1984.

B'Itah Achishenah. R. Yaakov Yosef. To the laws of Prozbol. Beit Shemesh, 2022.

Brit Yehudah. R. Yaakov Yeshayahu Bloi (1929–2013). To the laws of prohibited interest. Jerusalem, 1976.

Chafetz Chaim. R. Yisrael Meir Kagan. (see *Mishnah Berurah,* Sec. F) Classic work to the laws prohibiting gossip (*lashon hara*). Warsaw, 1877.

Chayei Adam. R. Avraham Danzig (1748–1820) of Vilna. Zitomir, 1858.

Chazon Ovadiah. Prozbol. R. Ovadiah Yosef (See *Yabbia Omer,* Sec. G.) Jerusalem: Machon Meor Yisrael, 2007.

Chelkat Binyamin: Ribbit. R. Binyamin Cohen. To the laws of prohibited interest Brooklyn, 2007.

Choshen L'Ma'aseh. R. Yonatan Meir Shoshan. To monetary law. 2022.

Chukkat Mishpat. R. Elchanan Peretz. To issues of monetary law. Jerusalem: Beit Din Tzedek Chukkat Mishpat, 2022.

Darkei Shmuel: Halakhah U'Minhag. R. Chanoch Toibas. Essays on matters of laws and custom in the tradition of R. Shmuel Tobias. Bnei Brak: Kloiz Darkei Shmuel, 2022.

Dat V'Halakhah. R. Moshe Shternbuch. On halakhic issues of the modern era. Jerusalem, 1970.

Derekh Chaim. R. Yaakov of Lisa (see *Netivot HaMishpat*). Vilna, 1839.

Divrei Soferim: Ribbit. R. Nachum Yavrov. Jerusalem, 1987.

Eilu Kofin L'Hotzi. R. Yosef Goldberg. Rulings regardings when and how it is permissible to compel a divorce. Jerusalem, 2013.

Eretz Chemdah. R. Shaul Yisraeli (1909–1995). Essays on the laws on the Land of Israel. Tel Aviv; Moreshet 1957.

Ezrat Nashim. R. Meir Meiri (1904–1968). Essays addressing questions of *agunot.* Frankfurt am Main, 1950.

Gesher HaChaim. R. Yechiel Michel Tukichinsky (1871–1955). To the laws of mourning,

Haggadah Shel Pesach Mo'adim U'Zmannim. R. Moshe Shternbuch (see *Teshuvot V'Hanhagot,* Sec. G). Jerusalem: Asher Ben Tziyon, 2019.

Haggadat Birkat Shir. R. Aryeh Leib Tzinz (See *Magen HaElef,* Sec. F). Warsaw, 1936.

Haggadah MiBeit Levi. From the luminaries of the tradition of Brisk. Jerusalem: Oraita, 1989.

Haggadat Minchat Asher. R. Asher Weiss (See Sec. G). Jerusalem: Minchat Asher: 2003.

Halikhot Shlomo. Rulings of R. Shlomo Zalman Auerbach,(1910–1995), pre-eminent halakhic authority and author of *Responsa Minchat Shlomo.* Edited by Yehudah Trager and Aharon Auerbach. Tel Aviv: Yeshivat Halikhot Shlomo, 1999.

Imrei Boruch: Tokef HaMinhag B'Halakhah. R. Boruch Simon, Rosh Yeshiva at Yeshiva University. Regarding matters of Jewish custom. Lakewood, NJ: Machon Be'er HaTorah, 2014.

Ka'Ayal Ta'arog. Comments and rulings collected from the rulings of R. Aharon Leib Shteinman on the Festivals. Jerusalem, 2018.

Kitzur Hilchos Bein HaMetzarim (A Summary of Halachos of the Three Weeks). Shimon D. Eider. Lakewood, NJ, 1978.

Likutei Beit Ephraim. R. Naftali Sofer. Includes citations from the teachings of the *Chatam Sofer.* Munkatch, 1892.

L'Ohr HaHalakha. R. Shlomo Yosef Zevin (1888–1978), founder of the Encyclopedia Talmudit and author of many other works. Essays on a broad range of topics. Jerusalem: Hotza'at Kol Mevaser, 2004.

Li'krat Shemittah Mamlakhtit be-Medinat Yisrael. R. Ze'ev Weitman, Alon Shevut: Mekhon Tzomet, 2000)

Ma'adanei Aretz. R. Shlomo Zalman Auerbach. Jerusalem: Bet Midrash Halakha Moriyah, 1972.

Ma'adanei Yom Tov. R. Yom Tov Zanger. Bnei Brak, 2006.

Ma'amar Mordechai. R. Mordechai Eliyahu (1929–2010), *Rishon L'Tziyon* from 1983–1993 . Jerusalem, 1973.

Ma'aseh Rav. Practices of the Vilna Gaon, as recorded by R. Yisachar Dov Ber ben Tanchum (1779–1855). Vilna, 1889.

Ma'avar Yabok. R. Aharon Brachya ben Moshe of Modena. Concerning the passage from this world to the next. Mantua, 1626.

Machaneh Ephraim. R. Ephraim Navon (1677–1735). Kushte, 1738.

Makneh U'Kinyan. R. Ephraim Zalman Margolios (see *Beit Ephraim,* Sec. F), in defense of the author's grandfather, the *Bekhor Shor,* and his position regarding *ha'aramot* and Torah law.

Marpei Lashon. R. Raphael Katz (Hamburger) (1722–1803). To the laws of *lashon hara* and related speech. Altuna, 1790.

Meishiv Nefesh. R. Eliav Silverman. Three volumes on matters of Jewish law.YU Press/Mossad HaRav Kook, 2021.

Mekadesh Yisrael. R. Yisrael David Harfenes. Volumes dedicated to laws regarding the festivals. Brooklyn, 2003.

MiDor L'Dor. R. Feivel Cohen. Concerning Halakhically acceptable ways to distribute property after death. Brooklyn, 2008.

Mikraei Kodesh. R. Zvi Pesach Frank (see *Har Tzvi,* Sec. G). To the Festivals. Jerusalem, 1992.

Minchat Aharon. R. Aharon Miasnik. To concepts of *Pesach.* Jerusalem: Machon Sha'ar HaMishpat, 1994.

Minchat Ani. R. Yosef David Zinsheim. Principles. Jerusalem: Machon Yerushalayim, 2020.

Minchat Emet and *Minchat HaAretz.* Anonymous treatises on the status of non-Jewish owned produce during the *Shemittah* year. Jerusalem, 1994.

Minchat Yerushalayim. Topics of *Shemittah.* Jerusalem: Minchat Yitzchak, 2000.

Mishpat HaGet. R. Nehorai Yosef Ochana. Regarding the laws of *gittin.* Jerusalem: Machon Deah, 2014.

Mishpat HaKinyan. R. Ovadiah Yosef Toledano (see *Resp. Meshiv Mishpat,* Sec. G.) Regarding the laws and concepts of transactions. Jerusalem: Et Yosef. 2008.

Mishpat HaTzava'ah. Regarding the laws of inheritance. R. Matityahu Schwartz. Jerusalem: Wagshal, 2000.

Mishpetei Aretz. R. Shaul Reichenberg. To the laws of *Shemittah.* Jerusalem: HaMachon L'Limudei Mitzvot HaTeluyot BaAretz ShAl Yedei Beit Midrash Gavohah L'Halakhah B'Hityashvut HaChaklait. 1993.

MiShulchan Rabbi Eliyahu Baruch: Moadim. R. Eliyahu Baruch Finkel (1947–2008) of Mir. Machon l'Hotza'at Kitvei R. Eliyahu Baruch, 2018.

Mo'adei Kodshekha. R. Eliyahu Shlesinger. Essays on laws and concepts of the Festivals. Jerusalem, 2012.

Mo'adei Yeshurun. A Compilation of Jewish Laws and Traditions with the Inclusion of Laws Arising from Modern Life Situations. R. Aaron Felder. New York, 1979.

Mo'adim L'Simchah. R. Tuvia Freund. Discussions of customs related to the festivals. Jerusalem: Otzar HaPoskim, 2004.

Mo'adim UZ'mannim. R. Moshe Sternbuch (see *Teshuvot V'Hanhagot,* Sec. G). Nine volumes. On the festivals. Jerusalem.

Nachalat Shivah. R. Shmuel ben David Moshe HaLevi (1625–1681). Collection of legal documents, with commentary. Bnei Brak: Machon Otzar HaPoskim, 2006.

> *Chelek L'Shivah.* R. Yosef Shaul Nathanson (See *Sho'el U'Meishiv,* Sec. F).

Tiferet L'Shivah. R. Yechezkel Aharon Schwartz. Glosses in the above edition.

Nachalat Tzvi. R. Gedalyah Felder (1921–1991) of Toronto. To the laws of adoption and conversion. Toronto, 1959.

Netinah L'Yitzchak. R. Levi Yitzchak Merkovsky. To monetary law.

Nit'ei Gavriel. R. Gavriel Zinner. To many subjects in many volumes. Jerusalem, 1997.

Orchot Rabbenu HaKehillot Yaakov. R. Avraham Horowitz. Practices of the Steipler, R. Yisrael Yaakov Kanievsky. Bnei Brak, 2014.

Otzar Machmadim. R. Natan Gottleib. Short discussions on a wide range of topics in many volumes. Jerusalem: Oz V'Hadar, 2018.

Otzerot Yosef: Shvi'it BaZman HaZeh. R. Yosef Engel (1858–1919). Topics related to *Shemittah,* in particular regarding the *hetter mekhirah*. Bnei Brak: Beit HaSefer, 1965.

Pe'at HaShulchan. R. Yisrael ben Shmuel of Shklov (1770–1839), student of the Vilna Gaon. To the laws of the land of Israel. Jerusalem, 1912.

Peirot Shevi'it. R. Zvi Cohen. Bnei Beraḳ, 2000.

Pesakim U'Ketavim. R. Yitzchak Isaac Halevi Herzog (see Sec. G). Jerusalem: Mosad ha-Rav Kook, 1989.

Pesakim V'Hanhagot. R. Zvi Pesach Frank (see *Har Tzvi,* Sec. G.).

Pitchei Choshen. R. Yaakov Yeshaya Bloi (see *Brit Yehudah,* above). To monetary law in multiple volumes. Jerusalem, 1986.

Sdei Chemed. R Chaim Chizkiyahu Medini (1832–1904) of Constantinople. Extensive ten-volume collection of halakhic essays, including citations of many contemporaries of the author.

Sefer HaChaim. R. Shlomo Kluger. (see *HaElef Likha Shlomo,* Sec. G.) Zholkva, 1825.

Sha'arei Halakhah U'Minhag. R. Menachem Mendel Schneerson. Jerusalem: Kehot, 1993.

Sha'arei Shvi'it. R. Moshe David Sharf. Jerusalem: Machon Ohr HaTzafun shel Chasdei Belz, 1986.

Shabbat HaAretz. R. Avraham Yitzchak HaKohen Kook. To the laws of *Shemittah.* Kefar Darom: HaMachon, 2000.

Shemittah. R. Yosef Tzvi Rimon Alon Shvut: Sulamot, 2021.

Shemittah K'Hilkhatah R. Moshe Shternbuch. Bnei Braḳ: Agudat Netivot ha-Torah ve-ha-Hesed, 1985.

Shemitat Kesafim K'Hilkhatah: Shevivei Eish. R. Shmuel Eliezer Stern. Machon Shevivei Eish, 2022.

Shenat Shabbaton. R. Akiva Yosef Shlesinger (1837–1922). Machon Lev HaIvri, 1986.

Shoshanat Yisrael. Rulings from R. Shlomo Miller of Toronto. Edited by R. Mordechai Yehudah Kanner. 2021.

Ta'am Ribbit. R. Moshe Shternbuch. To the laws of prohibited interest.

Ta'amei HaMinhagim. R. Avraham Yitzchak Shperling. Explanations, sources, and rulings regarding customs. Jerusalem, 1957.

Takanat Rabbim. R. Alter Azriel Meir Eiger. A proposal for the adoption of a standing, one-time general *hetter iska.* Warsaw, 1930.

Torat HaAdam. R. Moshe ben Nachman (Nachmamides, see Sec. A). To the laws of mourning and related topics. Venice, 1595.

Torat HaMoadim. R. Shlomo Goren (1917–1994), Ashkenazic Chief Rabbi of Israel from 1972–1983. Jerusalem: Hotsa'at ha-Idra Rabah u-mesorah la-Am, 1996.

Torat Zeraim. R. Aryeh Pomeranchik (1908–1942). To concepts of *Zeraim.* Tel Aviv, 1965.

Yesodei Yeshurun. R. Gedaliah Felder of Toronto. New York, 1977.

I. WORKS OF MUSSAR AND PHILOSOPHY

Derashot Shevet HaLevi. R. Shmuel HaLevi Wosner (see Sec. G). Bnei Brak, 1981.

Divrei Soferim. R. Tzadok HaKohen (1823–1900) of Lublin. Bnei Brak: Yahadut, 1967.

Machshivot Charutz. R. Tzadok HaKohen of Lublin. Jerusalem: Machon Har Berakhah, 2006.

Moreh Nevukhim. R. Moshe ben Maimon (Rambam, see Sec. E.). Classic work of philosophy, known as "Guide to the Perplexed" in English. Originally written in Judeo-Arabic and completed between 1186 and 1190, first translated into Hebrew by Shmuel ibn Tibbon in 1204.

Nefesh HaChaim. R. Chaim of Volozhin (1749–1821). Vilna, 1874.

Ner Mitzvah. R. Yehudah Loew ben Betzalel (Maharal) of Prague (1512–1609). Bnei Brak, 1972.

Pachad Yitzchak. R. Yitzchak Hutner (1905–1980). Philosophical essays arranged according to the festivals, with a volume of "letters and writings." Brooklyn: *Mossad Gur Aryeh,* 1960. *Rosh Yeshivah* of the Yeshivah Chaim Berlin in Brooklyn, New York, and the *Kollel Gur Aryeh.* In his youth, he authored *Torat HaNazir* to *Mishneh Torah, Hilkhot Nezirut.*

Poked Akarim. R. Tzadok HaKohen (1823–1900) of Lublin. Petrikow, 1922.

Resisei Lailah. R. Tzadok HaKohen (1823–1900) of Lublin Petrikow, 1926.

Sha'arei Teshuvah. Rabbenu Yonah ben Avraham Gerondi (1200–1263). Classic ethical work. Also authored a commentary to the *Rif.*

Sha'arei Osher: Shiurim B'Aggadot Chazal. Anonymous, 2022.

Yamim Echadim. R. Yosef Azoviv. Levorno, 1790.

Yisrael Kedoshim. R. Tzadok HaKohen (1823–1900) of Lublin. Bnei Brak: Yahadut, 1967.

J. JOURNALS, MEMORIAL AND JUBILEE VOLUMES.

Years provided for journals represent the first years of publication.

Beit Aharon VeYisrael. Torah journal of the students and faculty of the yeshivot and kollelim of the Karlin-Stolin institutuons of Israel and the diaspora. 1986.

Beit Yitzchak. Talmudical journal of Yeshivat Rabbenu Yitzchak Elchanan (Yeshiva University). 1952.

Divrei Mishpat. Journal devoted to matters related to *Even HaEzer* and *Choshen Mishpat.* Tel Aviv: Machon Divrei Mishpat, Mosdot Shirat Devorah. 1996.

Drushim. Published by the *Agudath HaRabbanim* of Poland.1923 .

Festschrift for Dr. Jakob Freimann. Cited in Hebrew as *Sefer Yovel L'Y Freiman.* Berlin, 1937.

HaTorah V'HaAretz. Neveh Dekalim, Chof Azah: Machon HaTorah V'HaAretz. 1991.

HaYashar VeHaTov. Journal devoted to practical issues of monetary law. 2006.

Mevakshei Torah. Jerusalem: Amutat Mevakshei Torah V'Chesed, 1992.

Moriah. Jerusalem: Moriah. 1969.

Noam. A Forum for the Clarification of Halakhic Problems. Jerusalem: Machon Torah Shelemah. 1958.

Ohalei Shem. Journal for the study of *Halakhah* and analysis of the writings of the Rebbes of Chabad. Kfar Chabad: Machon Ohalei Shem Lubavitch. 1989.

Orayta. Netanya: Kollel Avrekhim. 1992.

Techumin. Research Articles Concerning Torah, Society, and State/ Halakhic Monographs Concerning the Relationship of Torah to Modern society. Published by "Zomet" (*Tzva'atei Madda V'Torah*) Alon Shvut, Gush Etzion, Israel. 1980.

Tradition. A Journal of Orthodox Jewish Thought, published by the Rabbinical Council of America. 1958.

K. OTHER WORKS

Chikrei Zemanim. R. Alter Hilewitz. Analyses of Issues Related to the Jewish Calendar and Custom. Jerusalem: Mossad HaRav Kook, 1976.

Darkei Aharon. R. Aharon Weinstein. Six volumes. Jerusalem, 1947.

Darkei HaMachshavah HaHalakhatit shel HaRambam. Yaakov Levinger. An analysis of the Rambam's method in *Mishneh Torah.* Jerusalem: Magnes Press of Hebrew University, 1965.

Hadrat Ephraim. R. Katriel Ephraim Tchursch (1896–1979). Essays in honor of the completion of various Talmudic tractates. Jerusalem: HaVaad L'Hotzaat Sifrei HaRav K. P. Tscursch Shlita with Mossad HaRav Kook, 1970.

Iggerot Chazon Ish. Letters of R. Avraham Yeshayah Karelitz, the Chazon Ish (see Sec. F). Bnei Brak, 1954.

Iggerot Ra'ayah. Letters of R. Avraham Yitzchak HaKohen Kook (see *Mishpat Kohen,* Sec. G). Jerusalem: K.Y. Silman, 1923.

Ma'amar Shalosh Shavuot, R. Yoel Teitelbaum (see *Divrei Yoel.* Sec. G). Tract of the Satmar Rebbe against Zionism, taken from his *VaYoel Moshe.* Brooklyn, 1952.

Leaves of Faith Vol. II, R. Aharon Lichtenstein (see *Minchat Aviv,* Sec. G). Collected Essays. New Jersey: Ktav Pub. House, 2003.

Lekach Tov. R. Yosef Engel (1858–1919). Conceptual Talmudic essays. Bnei Brak, 2001.

Nefesh HaRav. R. Herschel Schachter, Rosh Yeshiva at RIETS. A halakhic biography of R. Joseph B Soloveitchik, including many of his positions on matters of Jewish law. Jerusalem: Reishit Yerusahalaim, 1994.

Ot Hi L'Olam. R. Rephael Pinchas Yehoshua Di Shigura. Izmir, 1856.

The Oxford Handbook of Judaism and Economics. R. Aaron Levine, ed. New York, Oxford University Press, 2010.

Sarei HaMeah. R. Yehudah Leib Maimon (1875–1962). Jerusalem: Mossad HaRav Kook, 1950.

Sefer HaIkkarim. R. Shlomo Eiger (1786–1852), also authored Responsa. Talmudic principles arranged alphabetically. Jerusalem: Mossad HaRav Kook, 1992.

Sefer Ohalim. R. Yehoshua Leib Diskin (see *Maharil Diskin,* Sec. G). Jerusalem: Midrash Rabi Rephael, 2011.

Sha'arei Yosher. R. Shimon Shkop (1860–1939), Rosh Yeshiva of Telshe and Grodna. Conceptual essays based on the structure of the *Shev Shmat'ta*. Warsaw, 1927.

She'erit Ya'akov. R. Yisrael Algaze (1680–1756). Kushtandina, 1751.

Shivat Tziyon. Avraham Yaakov Slutzky (1861–1918), ed. Collection of letters from rabbinic writers in praise of settling the Land of Israel. Warsaw, 1891.

Shnei Luchot HaBrit (Shlah). R. Yeshayahu Horowitz (1565–1630). Jerusalem: *Zikhron Yehudah,* 1993. Work of *halakhah* and Jewish thought.

Siach Sarfei Kodesh. Collection of citations from Chasidic masters such as R. Simcha Bunim of Presichcha, R. Menachem Mendel of Kotzk, R. Yitzchak Meir of Gur, and R. Chanoch Henoch HaKohen of Alexander. Lodz: Mesorah, 1928.

Siddur Beit Ya'akov. R. Ya'akov Emden (1698–1776), author of many other works. Zitomir, 1889.

Techukah L'Yisrael Al Pi HaTorah. R. Yitzchak Isaac HaLevi Herzog (see Sec. G). Three volumes of essays regarding the functioning of the modern Jewish State according to Jewish law and values. Jerusalem: Mossad HaRav Kook, 1989.

Tevuot B'Koach Shor. R. Yitzchak Eliezer Yakab. Regarding the position of the *Bekhor Shor* prohibiting the sale of animals over *Pesach* to allow the feeding of *chametz.* Jerusalem, 2003.

Values in Halakhah: Six Case Studies. R. Aharon Lichtenstein (see *Minchat Aviv,* Sec. G). Jerusalem: Maggid Modern Classics, 2023.

Source Index

TANAKH

Yoreh De'ah

Even Ha'ezer

Choshen Mishpat

Subject and Name Index

Maggid Books
The best of contemporary Jewish thought from
Koren Publishers Jerusalem Ltd.